Something Understood

Something Understood

essays and poetry for **HELEN VENDLER**

EDITED BY
STEPHEN BURT AND
NICK HALPERN

University of Virginia Press, *Charlottesville and London*

UNIVERSITY OF VIRGINIA PRESS
© 2009 by the Rector and Visitors of the University of Virginia
All rights reserved
Printed in the United States of America on acid-free paper

First published 2009

9 8 7 6 5 4 3 2 1

LIBRARY OF CONGRESS CATALOGING-IN-PUBLICATION DATA
Something understood: essays and poetry for Helen Vendler / edited by Stephen Burt and
Nick Halpern.
    p.   cm.
    Includes bibliographical references and index.
    ISBN 978-0-8139-2784-8 (alk. paper) — ISBN 978-0-8139-2785-5 (pbk. : alk. paper)
    1. Poetry—History and criticism—Theory, etc.   2. Vendler, Helen Hennessy—Criticism
and Interpretation.   3. Critics—United States—Literary collections.   I. Burt, Stephen.
II. Halpern, Nick.
    PN1031.S7276 2009
    809.1—dc22

                           2008046016

Contents

ACKNOWLEDGMENTS   ix

INTRODUCTION: *Helen Vendler's Aesthetic Criticism*   1
STEPHEN BURT

POEMS

Feverfew   19
JOHN ASHBERY

Little O   20
FRANK BIDART

In Owl Weather   22
LUCIE BROCK-BROIDO

A Wing   24
RITA DOVE

John Hall   26
MARK FORD

Shawl   27
ALBERT GOLDBARTH

"The People of the Book"   28
ALBERT GOLDBARTH

Later in Life   29
JORIE GRAHAM

Hermit Songs   32
SEAMUS HEANEY

Family Album   38
AUGUST KLEINZAHLER

The Life You Save   40
CARL PHILLIPS

central valley   41
D. A. POWELL

June Bug   42
DAVE SMITH

Heraclitean Backwash   43
CHARLES WRIGHT

CRITICISM

Tropes and Teams: *Teaching Poetry through Classroom Debate*   47
JAHAN RAMAZANI

"A sheapherdess thus sayd": *Immediacy and Distance in the Early Modern Lyric*   60
HEATHER DUBROW

The Bounds of the Incidental: Shakespeare's View of Accuracy   83
WILLIAM FLESCH

Reading Keats in Zambia   105
DEBORAH FORBES

Fine Suddenness: *Keats's Sense of a Beginning*   123
CHRISTOPHER R. MILLER

Foursquare: *The Romantic Quatrain and Its Descendants*   147
WILLARD SPIEGELMAN

Whitman, Tennyson, and the Poetry of Old Age   161
M. WYNN THOMAS

Incipience and Seriousness in Yeats's *A Vision*   183
NICK HALPERN

Lyric Poetry and the First-Person Plural: *"How Unlikely"*   193
BONNIE COSTELLO

Elizabeth Bishop's Cartographic Imagination Once More: *Rereading "The Map"* 207
ELEANOR COOK

Wallace Stevens, Ramon Fernandez, and "The Idea of Order at Key West" 227
GEORGE S. LENSING

Restlessness and Deformation: *Sylvia Plath's Feet* 239
DESALES HARRISON

Vendler's Ammons: The Snow Poems *and After* 265
ROGER GILBERT

Ashbery the Neoplatonist 291
LAURA QUINNEY

Called to Poetry: *Hardy, Heaney, Hennessy* 302
ELAINE SCARRY

NOTES ON CONTRIBUTORS 321

INDEX 327

Acknowledgments

Nick Halpern and Stephen Burt would like to thank Cathie Brettschneider, Angie Hogan, Ellen Satrom, and Jahan Ramazani for their help. Stephen Burt would like to express his love and thanks to Jessica Bennett, and to Nathan Bennett Burt. Nick Halpern would like to express his love and gratitude to Elizabeth Kunreuther, William Halpern, and Paula Halpern.

Something Understood

Introduction

Helen Vendler's Aesthetic Criticism

STEPHEN BURT

1

People who read poetry with a serious interest in how poems work now recognize the name of Helen Vendler, and the approach to poetry that her writings recommend. Her name can point to Wallace Stevens, to John Keats, to William Butler Yeats, to George Herbert (from whose sonnet "Prayer" our title comes), to William Shakespeare as a writer of sonnets, or to the recent poets whom Vendler champions: Ammons, Ashbery, Brock-Broido, Davie, Dove, Glück, Graham, Heaney, Kleinzahler, Merrill, and Rich, among others. We would not read them as we do without her writings about them, nor are they the only poets for whom such a claim could be made.

What else about Vendler and her criticism should we recognize? When we look at the great critics of the past, many of them appear as personalities: the curt moral insistences of a Samuel Johnson, the aggrieved friendly wit of a Randall Jarrell, the vatic insistences of a Harold Bloom. Vendler has not wanted to be such a critic: she has tried to show us, not herself, but her favorite poems.

One must, therefore, read quite a lot of her work at one sitting, or else reread it over the years, to get a sense of her as a writer in her own right. We used to hear—from Bloom and from Geoffrey Hartman, among others— that criticism was an art like poetry, with critics' "speculative instruments ... exercising their own textual powers" (Hartman 201). And yet criticism properly so-called, criticism as Vendler continues to practice it, remains an art in some ways more like architecture or the making of clothing: an applied art, with obvious instrumental purposes (to shelter residents, to describe prior texts), which nonetheless at its best reveals something of its makers, whether they are exuberantly idiosyncratic in their own styles or whether they strive instead, as Vendler has, for clarity and self-restraint in the service of already extant works.

Our sense of her as a writer might begin with her own definitions of her goals. Though "'Formalist,'" she writes, "is always, even now, a term used pejoratively"—she prefers the Paterian "aesthetic criticism"—any reader would note her attention to forms, without which poems, qua poems, cannot be discussed at all ("Life"). The goal of this aesthetic criticism "is to *describe* the art work in such a way that it cannot be confused with any other art work" (*Music* 2; emphasis in original). To do so with poems is to give sensitive enough accounts of the ways in which their language assumes the patterns it has. Most of her books demonstrate, in one way or another, the ways in which a change of form becomes, for a poet, a change of world: that is her explicit thesis in *The Breaking of Style,* and it is implicit in her discussion of Yeats (with his "march-like" trimeters, "nationalist" trimeter quatrains, "magical" repetitions, ottava rima, "disturbed" or amplified sonnets), of Shakespeare's felicitously and yet demandingly constructed sonnets, of the evolution of stanza shapes and juxtapositions in the sequence of Keats's odes (*Our Secret* 17, 182, 109, 181).

Yet to say only that Vendler attends to form is simply to say that she practices aesthetic criticism (or, perhaps, to say that she does it well). Other principles distinguish *her* aesthetic criticism from kinds practiced elsewhere. The most striking among such principles now might not even have seemed noteworthy at the outset of her career: Vendler holds that the art of lyric today, the art of poetry as Seamus Heaney or Louise Glück can practice it, remains close enough to the art of Sir Philip Sidney (if not indeed to the art of Catullus) that we can describe them with the same terms. Such a holding became controversial only in recent decades, as adherents of certain strands of modernism have claimed that those strands represented a wholly new art. By contrast, Vendler's practice must remind us, "one is unlikely to read contemporary poetry well without having read the poetry of the England from which it descends" (*Poems* xliv).

This historically continuous idea of lyric—by which each poem tries to be unlike all the rest, and yet participates in the same enterprise—also entails, for Vendler, ideas about generality and abstraction. When we read, admire, or judge a poem—Vendler's writings imply—we ought to see it in isolation from our own, accidental, lives and circumstances, since lyric (as against novel, drama, or epic) tries to present interior lives, what she calls "souls," apart from such circumstances. In reading a lyric poem critically and appreciatively, like may call to like, "the all-purpose pronouns 'I' and 'you'" take wing, as if historical, geographical, and social distance had never been (*Soul Says* 2). Lyric poems, indeed, invite us to try on the voices, the souls, of their (imagined or implicit) authors (however distant from us, or unlike us, the historical people who wrote the poems seem). "The lyric is a script written for performance by the reader—who, as soon as he enters the lyric, is . . . saying the words of the poem *in propria persona*" (*Given* xi). "The first thing a poem asks of you is to read it aloud as though you were saying it *as your own words*" (*Poems* 183; emphasis in original).

If poems, as we speak them, present inner lives, or "souls," the forms of poems are therefore like their bodies. The form of a poem, in a figure that Vendler invokes repeatedly, is like the body of a person, without which the ideas, emotions, spirit, or soul would have no manifestation in our shared (in the case of poems, our shared linguistic) world. Yeats's "forms . . . became the material body of his thoughts and emotions"; in Yeats's "prose sketches" for poems, "spirit has not yet found its appropriate body" (*Our Secret* xv, 3). This consistent set of analogies between lyric poetry and the soul, between the forms of lyric and the body, makes another one of the principles that Vendler's critical practice reveals.

One more principle follows from those analogies, a principle that stands against the impersonality often, and mistakenly, conflated with attention to form. The effort to understand how a form works as it does, why it moves us, why a poet chose to use it, is also an effort to imagine what that poet might have been thinking and feeling. The work of aesthetic criticism, in other words, must also include an effort of sympathy: "Criticism . . . ought to infer from the text the emotional motivation that . . . produced the originally unforeseeable contours of . . . the work of art" (*Poets Thinking* 5). The aesthetic critic must thus, at least some of the time, "put [herself] in the position of the writer of the poems" (in this case of Yeats) "attempting to track his hand and mind as he writes" (*Our Secret* xiv).

To see how a successful poem has solved its dilemmas of form, in fact, we must imagine ourselves all the way into a poet's inner life. "Poems of full complaint [such as] 'The Collar' . . . show the unhappiness of a person not, I think, naturally melancholy . . . [Herbert] was a person meant to be happy" (*Poetry of Herbert* 259). The Yeats who wrote "The Double Vision of Michael Robartes" "had been roused by passion and perplexity to such a pitch of folly in his daily life that he was ashamed" (*Our Secret* 369). The Yeats of "Sailing to Byzantium," rejecting the choir of the third stanza for the golden robotic avian of the fourth, "does not want his soul to live in a single-sex choral group, inhabiting eternity," since a "heart-less and body-less 'me' is not, and never can be, the authentic Yeatsian self" (*Our Secret* 33–34). Nor can a heart-less, body-less idea ever provide the core of a real poem.

We recognize Vendler's writing—we may learn to recognize it—not only by its recurrent principles but also by its recurrent devices, some of which (the comparison of lyric poems to dramas, e.g., in which the players are words) she inherits from the so-called New Critics, or else from her own teacher, I. A. Richards (*Art* 3). Other devices seem to belong to her, either because she invented them or because she has used them so often, in such exemplary ways. One such device is the deliberately inferior rewriting, in which she alters or rearranges lines to present avoided alternatives, or even "the conjectural . . . ur-form of the poem" (*Words* 50). "Would 'Nineteen Hundred and Nineteen' be a different poem if the order of its component parts were rearranged?" (*Our Secret* 77). Of course it would, and a worse one; so would "To a Friend Whose Work Has Come to Nothing," as her reshufflings of its rhymes prove (*Our Secret* 186). These demonstrative rearrangements in Vendler's own practice stem, perhaps, from the many "rewritings" and reductive adaptations of George Herbert by which lesser poets, hymn writers, and pastors, some seeking to use his words for collective worship, demonstrated by contrast the "depth of feeling, originality of invention and structural power" of Herbert's idiosyncratic poems (*Poetry of Herbert* 101).

Other devices come, not from comparing lesser or imagined poems to greater real ones, but from thinking about how we experience language, whether or not it comes to us in poems. She can assemble diagrams and charts in which a poem reveals a substructure analogous to the grammar of a complex sentence (*Coming of Age* 110–11). She puts together annotated multicolumn lists, with the phrases in a poem laid out separately like the parts of an engine (*Poets Thinking* 100; *Art* 218; *Our Secret* 179). She also compiles "recipes" or "patterns," sets of restrictions and rules by which a poet seems to have constructed a given poem. *The Poetry of George Herbert* includes a nine-part "recipe" for "Antiphon"—"a truly torturing set of conditions, as anyone can see by trying to write a poem on this pattern"—and then a seven-part "recipe" for "Grace": "The marvel of this poem is that with all its iron conditions, 'Grace' reads as a pure colloquial spontaneity" (*Poetry of Herbert* 211, 214). Such devices as rearrangements, diagrams, and enumerated "conditions" help Vendler reveal the arrangements within the poems she reads. To the reading of Shakespeare's sonnets alone—and of many other sonnets, including those yet to be written—she has contributed models that readers will reuse: the "couplet tie," the implicit prior speaker, the linked, repeated, root word (*Art* xv).

We also recognize her aphoristic one-sentence summaries of poets or poems. Sylvia Plath depicted "wild states of feeling which in the rest of us remain so inchoate that we quail under them, speechless"; Elizabeth Bishop contrived "a combination of somber matter with a manner net-like, mesh-like, airy, reticulated to let in light" (*Music* 283, 299). Shakespeare's Sonnet 57 with its key words "*do* and *think* and *no*," says (in her thumbnail version): "You do as you please; what should I do while you do that? Should I think no ill about you as you do it?" (*Art* 274).

Other memorable phrases reach beyond single poems, far into human life. Wallace Stevens, she writes, "has been too little read as a poet of human misery"; it may be that Vendler has been too little read for wisdom (*Words* 11). "Like most devotees, Stevens fears the god he worships" (in this case, the god of romantic love) (*Words* 56). "No pleasure is sweeter in the ear than something new done to the old" (*Music* 253). Seamus Heaney describes "the poverty of every child's restricted early life"; Stephen Spender's prose lacks "the personal inflexibility, moral deafness, and intellectual self-righteousness of most adults" (*Music* 151, 170). "The great effort of will required to convert grief into something that can legitimately be called not wailing or mourning or bleating but song is . . . the effort required to rise from childhood to adulthood" (*Odes* 263).

From such claims not just a body of poetry but a person emerges: one able to recognize and respond to other people's grief, alert to if not indeed used to misfortune, contemplative rather than volatile, more interested in defending the good than in any attempt to tear down the bad, attracted both to wintry spareness and to the well-ornamented, the imaginatively filled-out—a person who sounds, indeed, Stevensian. Wallace Stevens, Vendler has said more than once, "is the poet whose poems I would have written had I been the poet he was" (*Words* 3). When Stevens says "he" or "one," he can often mean "I," and we might ask occasionally whether, when she says "Stevens," she means "I": Stevens "is so chaste in self-revelation that his emotions are easily passed over" (*Words* 11, 27). No reader doubts Vendler's intellect. What uncareful readers may miss is precisely what unsympathetic readers do not see, what she has tried to show, in such intellective poets as Ashbery and Stevens: the emotional depth behind the conceptual surface, "conveying the poems as something other than a collection of ideas" (*Words* 4).

Vendler (so her writings suggest) finds herself drawn, as Stevens was also drawn, to the individual and independent more than to the communal; to the slowly unfolding, not to the quickly compact; to the reconsidered, the revised, or the palinodic more than to the merely or apparently spontaneous. She has often shown us how major poets revisit, rework, rewrite the same protopoem in the course of a few years (as with Keats's odes), within a single work (as in Whitman's "soul-reprise"), or over a career (as with Stevens, Yeats, Heaney): Heaney's "steady incorporation of his past into his present, and of first thoughts into second thoughts, makes . . . the finding of language more arduous with each decade" (*Poets Thinking* 57; *Seamus Heaney* 175).

She seems drawn as well to the poetry of autumn and winter more than to spring and summer; to tragedy over comedy; to the abstract, in a way that never rules out—but rather becomes a version of—the personal. Stevens's supreme fiction "must be abstract": in an "abstract" or "algebraic" poet, as Vendler has explained, the personal occasion that gave rise to the feeling in the form is not an occasion spelled out in the poem. "To read [abstract] poets without a personal calibration," without seeking "a point of origin in feeling," "is to read them emptily": our own personal investments, examples, values for x and y, from our lives, are what their words demand (*Words* 8, 12). The vocation of the aesthetic critic (who considers texts rather than contexts) thus resembles the abstract space of "soul" in lyric poetry generally, where "the human being becomes a set of warring passions . . . independent of time and space" (*Soul Says* 5).

Vendler's defense of algebraic or abstract reading and writing against those who want only "first-order," naive, or direct transcription also reminds us (if we require reminders) that intellectuals, people who find their home amid ideas, and aesthetic critics, who find their home amid works of art, have strong feelings too—feelings inseparable from what and from how they think. Jorie Graham's poetry thus attends as few others have to the emotions—to the exhilarations, even—of intellection: "Graham's lines mimic the fertile ruses of the mind—exploratory rush and decisive interruption" (*Soul Says* 237). The catena of nouns and noun phrases, each a figure for the titular noun, in George Herbert's "Prayer" ends, and can only end, by introducing "the hitherto neglected intellect"—that is what Herbert means by calling a prayer, as we have called this volume, "something understood" (*Poetry of Herbert* 39).

Not only do critics and poets drawn to abstraction have strong feelings, as Vendler's writings show; they also have ethics. For examples of strenuous ethical reflection on Vendler's own part (and on the part of her subject) one could do worse than read all her writings on Adrienne Rich, who "appears to manifest the reformer's faith that there is something that can be done against social evil": with this faith, with the poems it produces, Vendler will try to sympathize—though sometimes the poems are too simple, and she cannot (*Soul Says* 214). "Rich's great virtue is her struggle for authenticity . . . I have read, and not for political reasons, almost everything she has written" (*Music* 351, 374).

Readers who think Vendler so inward-turned, so library-bound as to be blind to one or another social or ethical problem, perhaps should know more about the "lesson of self-chosen vocation" in earlier parts of her life ("Unburied Life" 49). "When I went to have my program card signed on my first day at Harvard as a graduate student, the chairman said to me, 'We don't want you here, Miss Hennessy. We don't want any women here'" (Interview). Women at Harvard in those years, debarred from most sources of funding, lived "a relatively impoverished and isolated life. Most of the women left. But I was happy: I had Widener [Library]" ("Ups and Downs"). Things have changed. And yet, she insists, "We should not think ourselves better than our predecessors" (Interview).

Nor should we think that our one truth fits every case. Stevens's supreme fiction, like Keats's seasons, must change, its truths never resolved into one all-encompassing truth: for all the occasional asperity of her pronouncements, Vendler is temperamentally and by choice a pluralist, a nominalist, and an opponent of dogma. Ammons, Ashbery, and Merrill "have assumed the thankless cultural task of defining how an adult American mind not committed to any single ideological agenda might exist in a self-respecting and veracious way" (*Soul Says* 23). Vendler's sensibility remains abstracting (trying to explain, to find laws and patterns and rules) but also experimental, inductive, individualizing, as befits her early training in the sciences. The patterns she finds are patterns she encourages us to discover in poems, rather than patterns she will impose or invent: "the pleasure" in criticism "lies in discovering the laws of being of a work of literature" (*Music* 20).

"A work," not "works": each work has its own implicit laws, "no single description fits all lyrics," and each new work requires us to revise our hypotheses (if we have any) about how literature, in general, proceeds (*Given* xi). "Lyric poets show an inconsistency in their 'philosophy of life,'" she reminds teachers, "that is alarming to those who want poets to have an unchanging system of ideas" (*Poems,* "Instructors' Supplement" 4). The world is so various, holds so many patterns, that it seems false if not criminal to hold that all poems, all patterns, are instances of the same one: "Aesthetic inexhaustibility of the world and the emotions is Stevens' only principle of faith" (*Words* 59). Although insensitive readers have found in it only elaborations of Shaftesbury's philosophical system, Pope's *Essay on Man* in fact constitutes (once we have understood how its couplets work) his "admission of man's needs for the grids of system but at the same time his demonstration of the instability and insufficiency of all systems" (*Poets Thinking* 35).

Wary of ideological systems in general, Vendler is no friend to organized religion in particular. Albert Goldbarth's enthusiasm for Judaica is "the enviable preserve, perhaps, of those to whom the religion of their parents has done no damage" (*Soul Says* 80). "Any sentient adult," she asserts, "knows (whether admitting it or not) that life has no explanation; that truth and justice do not reign on earth; and that there is no one governing earthly events" ("Voice" 24). It is with some relish that she gives us Pope "energetically and usefully relegating theology to the realm of the impossible," and such relegations are for her one of the attractions of poetry (*Poets Thinking* 28–29). Among the arts, literature "appears as an element quintessentially profane," "diametrically opposed to the cultic, communal, ritualized impulses served by religion" (*Music* 48).

Vendler's stance against orthodoxies seems, as she tells it, to flow from the facts of her life. "Raised in an exaggeratedly observant Catholic household," she discovered that her parents (by order of the cardinal of Boston) would not let her attend any "godless, atheistic secular universities," only a Catholic college where "literature . . . was taught as a branch of faith and morals" ("Life"; "Ups and Downs"). She became a graduate student in English at Harvard by first choosing an undergraduate major in chemistry, winning a Fulbright Scholarship to Belgium in mathematics, switching to literary studies once in Belgium, and then spending a year at Boston University, where "my teachers led me from my literally medieval upbringing into the expansive precincts of secular thought" ("Life"). She had a son, David, in 1960, by the philosopher Zeno Vendler; they were later divorced.

Her professional trajectory perhaps informs her sense of literary history. The inheritances of forms and topoi (sonnet, pastoral, and so on), which for other critics indicate a univocal Great Tradition, or else a struggle over some notionally indivisible poetic inheritance, are for Vendler signs of individuality, independence, among the poets she would want to read: the couplet in general versus the couplet in Pope, the ballad stanza as Yeats or Davie received it versus the ballad stanzas that Yeats (who "gradually turns the form . . . Yeatsian") and Davie (who "wrests the form from ballad stanza to intellectual quatrain") actually wrote (*Our Secret* 145; *Music* 179). "If each poem is a new experiment, the ground on which it experiments is the past, both the past of the genre and the past of the oeuvre" (*Words* 4). "The speaker" in Shakespeare's sonnets "is a rebel against received ideas. He is well aware of the received topoi of his culture, but he subjects them to interrogation," as even the most tradition-minded poet, if he or she is a real poet, has to do (*Art* 20).

Vendler tries, as any good critic should try, to do justice to poets deeply and obviously unlike her—to comic, satirical poets such as Alexander Pope, to devout poets such as George Herbert and Czeslaw Milosz, to minimalist and undiscursive poets such as Emily Dickinson and Gary Snyder, to garrulous populist poets such as Allen Ginsberg, the "kibitzer and prophet" she has appreciated at some length (*Music* 265). There is no aspect, other than originality, which all the poets she admires share. And yet, as with any good critic, any good writer, she gives us not only strong arguments about her subjects but (however gradually) a personal universe—a sense not of how the world has looked to everyone but of how it has seemed, so far, to her.

Even in writing about the feeling, the inner life, in her prose, and about the rare traces of her own outward life in that prose, I have ended by explaining Vendler's ideas. This end should come as no surprise: ideas, feelings, and forms are for her inextricable in describing any art. Eliot's famous "dissociation of sensibility," with its segregation of ideas from emotions, certainly did not happen to her (though her early comments on his later career, with its "preciousness" and "religiosity," suggest that it eventually happened to him) (Eliot 64, Part 81). An insistence on ideas amid passions, on the arrangements and abstractions of art amid the mess and sensory detail of life, *and vice versa,* is one of the signatures of her criticism, and ensures her own writing its normally level tone—and so her readers must have been surprised, and moved, to come across, in recent years, flashes of personal, not particularly analytical, recollection. Stuck in France with her young son "cross, tired and near to tears," herself "near to tears from prolonged loneliness," she found that John "Berryman's despairing and exalted verses were a tonic to my mind, and I wrote about them with intense joy at their arrival in my bleak life" ("Reviewer's Beginnings" 401).

Many critics and scholars show their influence by what we have learned (from Thomas Kuhn and others) to call a research program, a set of generalizable claims or predictions that later researchers can test in further domains. Though they rely on axioms (it might be better to say on experience, both hers and ours) about reading poetry in general, Vendler's extended arguments usually have to do with poets and poems in particular. She has called herself "a critic incorrigibly unhappy without a text to dwell on"; in her work "each successful poem presents itself as a unique experiment in language" (*Music* 9; *Seamus Heaney* 7). What she says about Herbert is true of no other poet; what she says of Keats's odes and Shakespeare's sonnets does not fit other sonnets, other odes. She offers for other, future critics not a research program so much as an exemplary form of attention—and an example, of course, of attention to form.

Even more than with most good critics, it would be wrong to see Vendler's influence only in terms of what later writers of prose will do. Rather, she has shown us (including the very many among us who will not write lasting criticism of our own) how to read certain poets and certain poems, what to seek and what we might hear in them. Jarrell complained that modern critics had become "like conductors, [who] give you *their* 'Lear,' *their* 'Confidence Man,'" and so on (93). But critics have always been conductors in this sense, no more and no less so than friends who have read a good book before we have, and who might help us hear what they have heard. Vendler thus picks up the simile as an honorific: "the critic is an interpreter not as the exegete of a sacred text is an interpreter but, rather, as a pianist or conductor is an interpreter, holding up the work in a new and coherent manifestation [of] one of its many possibilities" (*Music* 48).

To Stevens, to Keats, to Yeats, to Robert Lowell, and to the whole generation of post-Stevens, post-Eliot poets who began writing after World War II, after *Transport to Summer,* but before (say) *A Wave, Made to Seem,* and the fall of the Berlin Wall, we have certainly had no better guide. And "guide" seems—more than "conductor"—to be the best word. Vendler is called to honor and to judge, but even more clearly called—as expert guides to forests and mountains, towns and museums, are called—to show and explain, to delineate features and structures, to show what a given poem does, and how its "permutations and combinations of shaped and musical language" work (*Our Secret* 376). "Almost every plane of the linguistic . . . appeals to" her, as it did, in her telling, to Merrill ("Ardor" 104). She explains what poems she finds successful and why, rather than saying (except where pressed) what poets seem greater or lesser than supposed rivals. So far from wishing to act as literary Rhadamanthus—and in notable opposition to other critics with similar authority—she has consistently omitted the most astringent, most unsatisfied among her essays and articles from the books in which she collects them.

"When you have seen the heart of the emotional drama" in Stevens's lyric poetry, Vendler advises, "you must repossess the poem as it exists on the page in all its originality and strangeness" (*Words* 44). Just so: when you have seen Vendler the essayist, the thinker, the individual writer, the careful listener, the tragic-minded pedagogue, the alert and patient guide, in her critical works, you must then go back and read her as she wishes to be read: as a critic and scholar subordinate to, in service to, the poets, helping us read them as they ought to be read.

2

This collection of poems and essays tries to present contemporary poetry as part of a continuing conversation, not only within itself, as styles and approaches play off against one another, but with the poetry of the recent and distant past. The collection also, we hope, demonstrates Vendler's achievement, and her continuing relevance, to the ways in which we read poetry (in particular, lyric poetry) now: it focuses on twentieth- and twentieth-first-century work, but it extends, as Vendler's work has extended, into that part of the past by which poets at work today are moved. All the poets are writers whom Vendler herself has admired, and all contribute verse we might link to some quality she has admired.

In writing on Ashbery, Vendler has insisted that we seek not just his stylistic inventions but the emotion that those inventions exist to convey, and so it is fitting that John Ashbery's "Feverfew" begins this collection: "the moon is unambiguous," he writes, and so is the eternal project in these lines, a project of representing nostalgia so oddly that we feel it as if it were new. Frank Bidart's "Little O," in contradistinction, is a poem of considered, even contentious statement, an *ars poetica* that—quoting Shakespeare and Stevens—makes a case for abstraction and for anti-naturalism, for a theater in which, as Vendler herself has put it, the actors are phrases and words. With Lucie Brock-Broido's "In Owl Weather" the poet speaks, in characteristically extravagant sentences, about the limits of imagination: she is at once a character in a book, or a "pamphlet," and a girl, or a woman, growing old in a Stevensian, northern rural cold, wondering (as Stevens also wondered) how far fictions can sustain her.

Rita Dove's figure for lyric poetry is not theater but song: her "A Wing" follows a classical vocal performance that both lifts the singer above, and ties the character she creates to, the body and the physical world. Mark Ford's sonnet-sized biography of the English Renaissance figure John Hall, best known for his verse satires, offers a mysterious (it might be better to say a deadpan) version of the claim that a poet's true body is in his poems: Hall's ineffective alchemical version of medicine can only lend pathos to his "sudden" demise. Albert Goldbarth's exuberant pair of poems remember the long life and high purposes Western culture has ascribed to books and reading, and the more definite, more personal purposes we ascribe to lyric poetry in particular, creating a site in which (as in Stevens's quiet house) "nothing else existed:/only him, and the book."

Jorie Graham's "Later in Life" pursues the "cry" of Stevens's "The Course of a Particular" and the exultancy from Stevens's "Transport to Summer"—though for Graham the cry is not vegetal but human after all, the introduction to a "great/desire for approval/and love," pursued through the extended, syntactically unpredictable sentences that Graham has made her own. Seamus Heaney's poem also meditates on reading and writing: it compares twentieth-century schoolboys to the monks and "anchorites" of medieval Ireland, conjuring (with a nod to Eliot) "a vision of the school the school/won't understand." Reminiscence of a different tenor occupies August Kleinzahler's "Family Album," in which temporal and spatial distance from home make counterclaims against nostalgia. Carl Phillips's contribution creates a double image—a lover's face, a seascape with beach and waves—familiar to earlier poets of Vendler's New England, to Walt Whitman, to Wallace Stevens, and to Robert Lowell. D. A. Powell's magnificent offering records—or does it refuse?—a change of season both Keatsian and Californian, a "terrible immanence of spring."

Two final poems, both a kind of *ars poetica*, give voice to what we might call opposing Vendlerian principles. Dave Smith's "June Bug" narrows a human gaze to the scope of an insect, and then sees in that insect the figure of *multum in parvo*, of many things in a tiny, well-organized, space, associated with lyric since antiquity. Charles Wright's "Heraclitean Backwash," with its glittering single lines, looks not to formal closure but to metaphysical openness, recognizing illimitably and undogmatically the vastness of visible and invisible worlds.

The critical essays exemplify, and extend, the aesthetic criticism Vendler has championed; some combine it with endeavors unlike her own. We begin with a topic too often overlooked but one that Vendler has always respected: the pedagogy of poetry. Her Harvard course "Poems, Poets, Poetry," and the textbook she developed from it, have shown thousands of students how to read lyric; Vendler's *Poets Thinking* also showed how apparently undiscursive poems could enfold all manner of argument. Extending both interests, and giving them fresh examples, Jahan Ramazani demonstrates how classroom argument, and organized classroom debates, can reveal the shapes and emotions in poems.

The criticism then proceeds in chronological order by poet and topic. Heather Dubrow considers ideas of the person made visible or audible in early modern lyric: what sort of "presence," and what sort of distance or absence, do sixteenth- and seventeenth-century forms create? William

Flesch considers the Shakespeare of the plays—as Vendler considered the Shakespeare of the sonnets—not only as a dramatic thinker but as a maker of architectonics. Self-quotations, many of them inexact, in Shakespeare's writing reflect the patterns established by meter and by memory, and speak to much larger questions of emotional development within the plays.

Two essays investigate the poetry of John Keats, a writer who—until Vendler's expositions—was too often, and wrongly, considered an uncomplicated aesthete. Juxtaposing her reading of Keats with her own experience in southern Africa, Deborah Forbes shows us what our lyric inheritance can and cannot do—and how her second thoughts about aesthetics and ethics came to overlap with Keats's own. Christopher Miller looks at Keatsian ideas of surprise, reacting both to external events and to changes of mood within the poet himself: his writings, here and elsewhere, extend (and place further in scholarship and history) the mode of analysis in Vendler's *The Odes of John Keats.*

Vendler's earliest (unpublished) writings on poetry concerned Gerard Manley Hopkins—her approaches have borne fruit for critics of much nineteenth-century verse. Willard Spiegelman investigates the quatrain and the inheritance of form generally in Romantic poetry: how did a generation known for innovation adapt the past for its own purposes? M. Wynn Thomas—perhaps the most convincing, and most original, scholar of Walt Whitman's poetry now at work—considers Whitman as a poet of old age, with and against Tennyson's lyric work on the same topic. Against oversimplified pictures of Whitman as sui generis, as a force that emerged out of nothing (or out of American popular culture), Thomas's scholarship gives us Whitman as craftsman, able to learn from work far quieter, and more apparently traditional, than his own.

The volume then moves into twentieth-century writings. Nick Halpern returns to *A Vision,* the subject of Vendler's first book, finding in Yeats's statement of mystical doctrine a sense of incipience, of vision evermore about to be. At the same time he explores the range of voices in that book. Essays on Stevens and Bishop combine aesthetic criticism with historical and archival research. Bonnie Costello takes up both poets' deployments of the personal pronouns "I" and "we," most of all in the generous "we" drawn from Bishop's "The Moose." George Lensing's consideration of "The Idea of Order at Key West" finds middle ground between the aesthetic of self-enclosed autonomy that has dominated some discussions of the poem and the historical response that governs others. Bishop's "The Map" might have figured in Vendler's *Coming of Age as a Poet,* since it is the first good poem Bishop wrote. In the hands of the Stevens scholar Eleanor Cook, "The Map" demonstrates not just Bishop's calling but also her careful ambivalence about her own background, and her ongoing attachment to the coasts and seas that link Bishop's Atlantic Canada to Bishop's and Vendler's New England.

Vendler as a reviewer and essayist has also examined, and championed, the poetry of A. R. Ammons and of Sylvia Plath. DeSales Harrison invites us to look at Sylvia Plath's feet—not only at her metrical feet but at the series of deformed or damaged boots, shoes, and feet in her poems. Harrison's claim seems likely to spark new considerations of Plath in the emerging field of disability studies, to which—he suggests—Plath also belongs.

Roger Gilbert's essay holds a unique place in our collection, since it shows not only how Vendler might help us to read a particular poet but how she seems to have helped Ammons write his poems. Gilbert uses the Ammons archive to show how this still underrated poet responded to his finest critics, Harold Bloom and Helen Vendler, and how, in effect, he created poems suited to both. After the Bloomian, prophetic *Sphere,* Ammons's *Snow Poems,* and his lyric "Easter Morning," reflect Vendler's interests in the secular, the empirical, the everyday. Laura Quinney's essay follows up Vendler's attention to Ashbery's subjects and to the "ruminative," roundabout ways in which those subjects emerge: in one of his recent collections, Quinney finds "desire for, and repulsion from, erotic contact" tracing itself back to Plato's *Symposium,* where "eros must remain unsatisfied."

We conclude with an ambitious critic who looks beyond single periods and single authors in order to capture truths about reading, and about the aesthetic, as matters of silence and speech. Elaine Scarry considers the idea of poetic calling, showing how poets call to later poets and to their readers, and how such callings appear in poets' work as speech and sound. Such callings remain evident, we hope, in the poems and essays collected here. As readers, and as writers, we are called at once to particular topics and arguments, to particular poets and poems, and to the larger enterprise of aesthetic criticism that Vendler exemplifies, for poetry past, and passing, and to come.

WORKS CITED

Eliot, T. S. *Selected Prose*. Ed. Frank Kermode. London: Faber and Faber, 1975.

"Feminism and Literature: An Exchange." *New York Review of Books* 16 Aug. 1990.

Hartman, Geoffrey. *Criticism in the Wilderness*. New Haven: Yale UP, 1980.

Jarrell, Randall. *Poetry and the Age*. Expanded ed. Gainesville: U of Florida P, 2001.

Stevens, Wallace. *Collected Poetry and Prose*. Ed. Frank Kermode and Joan Richardson. New York: Library of America, 1997.

Vendler, Helen. "Ardor and Artifice." *The New Yorker* 12 Mar. 2001: 100–104.

———. *The Art of Shakespeare's Sonnets*. Cambridge, MA: Harvard UP, 1997.

———. *The Breaking of Style*. Cambridge, MA: Harvard UP, 1995.

———. *Coming of Age as a Poet*. Cambridge, MA: Harvard UP, 2003.

———. *The Given and the Made*. Cambridge, MA: Harvard UP, 1995.

———. Interview with Bruce Cole, 2004. http://www.neh.gov/whoweare/vendler/interview.html (viewed 1 Oct. 2006).

———. "A Life of Learning." American Council of Learned Societies, 2001. http://www.acls.org/op50.htm (viewed 1 Oct. 2006).

———. *The Music of What Happens*. Cambridge, MA: Harvard UP, 1988.

———. *The Odes of John Keats*. Cambridge, MA: Harvard UP, 1983.

———. *Our Secret Discipline: Yeats and Lyric Form*. Cambridge, MA: Harvard UP, 2007.

———. *Poems, Poets, Poetry*. 2nd ed. New York: Bedford, 2002.

———. *The Poetry of George Herbert*. Cambridge, MA: Harvard UP, 1975.

———. *Poets Thinking*. Cambridge, MA: Harvard UP, 2004.

———. "A Reviewer's Beginnings." *Antaeus* 75/76 (1994): 400–405.

———. *Seamus Heaney*. Cambridge, MA: Harvard UP, 1998.

———. *Soul Says: On Recent Poetry*. Cambridge, MA: Harvard UP, 1995.

———. "The Unburied Life." *New Republic* 21 June 1999: 48–52.

———. "Ups and Downs with Harvard." *Harvard Magazine*, Nov.–Dec. 2001. http://harvardmagazine.com/2001/11/ups-and-downs-with-harva.html.

———. "The Voice at 3 A.M." *New York Review of Books* 10 June 1999: 24–27.

———. *Words Chosen Out of Desire*. 1984. Cambridge, MA: Harvard UP, 1986.

Poems

Feverfew

JOHN ASHBERY

It all happened long ago—
a murky, milky precipitate
of certain years then drawing to a close,
like a storm sewer upheaval. Road rage had burst its flanks;
all was uncertain on the Via Negativa
except the certainty of return, return
to the approximate.

Night and morning a horn sounded,
summoning the faithful to prayer, the unfaithful to pleasure.
In that unseemly alley I first exhaled
a jest to your comic, crumb-crusted lips:
What if we are all ignorant of all that has happened to us,
the song starting up at midnight,
the dream later, of lamb's lettuce and moss
near where Acheron used to flow?

But it's only me, now, I came because you cried and I had to.
Plaited bark muffles the knocker, but the doorbell
penetrates deep into the brain of one who lived here.
O brackish clouds and dangerous,
the moon is unambiguous.

Little O

FRANK BIDART

We are not belated: we stand in an original
relation to the problems of making

art, just as each artist before us did.

At the threshold
you can see the threshold:—

it is a precipice.

When I was young, I tried not to
generalize; I had seen little. At sixty-six,

you have done whatever you do

many times before. Disgust with mimesis,—
disgust with the banality of naturalistic

representation, words mere surface mirroring

a surface,—
is as necessary as mimesis: as the conventions

the world offers out of which to construct your

mirror fail, to see your face you
intricately, invisibly reinvent them. But

imagining that words must make the visible

a little hard to see,—
or speech that imitates for the ear speech

now is used up, the ground sealed off from us,—

is a sentimentality. Stevens was wrong. Genius
leading the disgusted over a cliff.

To see the topography of a dilemma

through the illusion that you are embodying
the soul of someone who has

lived there—

French theoreticians thought Shakespeare
a barbarian, because in their eyes he wrote as if

ignorant of decorum, remaking art to cut through.

In Owl Weather

LUCIE BROCK-BROIDO

In the pamphlet on page three you will find me

Clutching the yellow parasol, the one I used to get
Away with carrying. I loved once, in

The long-ago, nesting in the empty granary with
My barn boys, all of whom then wanted

Me. How many nights it was I did not marry
Them, preferring the company of animals

Who did not speak and slept curled to me and set
Me free thereafter to the feral dark, and then

   To overwintering. In owl weather I am

Apprentice to the common law of harm.
No harp, no rain, only

Overhearing in the next room
The surrealist's boot growing into

   The foot-soldier's missing hank

Of limb on the terrible concrete in the city
Of Teheran. It is a time when no living

Creature can lean its forehead into my hand.
The owl in the barn is so still

No one takes my word that he is real.
In the pamphlet on page seven you will find me

As a tiny odalisque on the endless blanket

Of the bower of my mother's bed, coquettish,
In a poplin nightgown and my small gold shoes,

With all my lionlikes about me—it is clear I am
Quite pleased with me. I wonder, can he

   Look up to the slip of moon late days

At the very moment I am looking too,
I wonder, is he warm, somewhere, in hay.

A Wing

RITA DOVE

for Helen Vendler

> *Die Zeit im Grund, Quinquin, die Zeit,*
> *die ändert doch nichts an den Sachen.*
> *Die Zeit ist ein sonderbar Ding.*
> *Wenn man so hinlebt, ist sie rein gar nichts.*
> *Aber dann auf einmal, da spürt man nichts als sie.*
> —MARSCHALLIN'S MONOLOGUE, *Der Rosenkavalier*

Her noble soprano swells the car radio,
tone escalating on tone, a wine goblet
filling, then pouring out:

as frightening a perfection as the Alps
glimpsed, unguarded,
at the free end of a cobbled alley

crisscrossed with Monday's laundry,
bed sheets and towels.
We've stopped to photograph Switzerland

en route to gentler climes. At this altitude
I'm lightheaded, though I've never felt
more brunette, here among the blondes

Schwarzkopf celebrated
(despite the irony of her name, a blemish
no native speaker hears). *Strange,*

the Marschallin trills, *but time*
changes nothing, actually.
Jolted, my chest stutters,

remembers to re-inflate—
glacial sun, iodine empyrean.
I lift the lens and snap. Even this deep

into summer, snow continues to pleat
those deadly crevasses—(*Hochsommer,*
the natives call it: high, deep, black,

white)—just as she continues
to thrill us with her icy passion, her
platinum Marschallin.

There's really no end to this
perfection: It stands there
ignoring you, until you notice—and then

there's nothing else.

John Hall

MARK FORD

Like Lord Cerimon he was familiar with the blest infusions
    That dwell in vegetives, metals, and stones:

He cured, he records, Michael Drayton of a tertian
    Fever with a spoonful of syrup of violets, and his own

Haemorrhoids with a pigeon he cut open alive, then
    Applied to his feet, to which it drew down

The vapours, while leeches set to work on his fundament.
    His beloved Susanna, Shakespeare's eldest, found

Relief from corruption of the gums and stinking breath, wind,
    Melancholy, and cardiac passion in his potent ointment

Of roses, capon grease, sweet almonds and mallow water. Accounts
    Of his triumphs were kept in condensed Latin;

None of the cases published in *Select Observations*
    On English Bodies mentions his father-in-law's afflictions

Or demise. He himself died fighting a sudden and virulent
    Outbreak of the plague: "Health is from the Lord." (Amen.)

Shawl

ALBERT GOLDBARTH

Eight hours by bus, and night
was on them. He could see himself now
in the window, see his head there with the country
running through it like a long thought made of steel and wheat.
Darkness outside; darkness in the bus—as if the sea
were dark and the belly of the whale were dark to match it.
He was twenty: of course his eyes returned, repeatedly,
to the knee of the woman two rows up: positioned so
occasional headlights struck it into life.
But more reliable was the book; he was discovering himself
to be among the tribe that reads. Now his, the only
overhead turned on. Now nothing else existed:
only him, and the book, and the light thrown over his shoulders
as luxuriously as a cashmere shawl.

"The People of the Book"

ALBERT GOLDBARTH

is a term originally wielded as an insult
to the Jews; then, in the way that these things often happen
(the Fauves, the Lost Generation, the Beats), adopted by them,
happily as an honorific. For me, although I'm born
a Jew, the term defines "my people" *across* the barriers
of religious and cultural claim: the man
on the plane whose open *Bleak House* is a portal
into extradimensional space; the woman who's fallen asleep
with *Daniel Deronda* as if with a lover; for them,
for all of them, whose reading goes under the words
and yet praises the words, ear and tongue and memory.
For them, I invoke the infant Moses
set upon the waters in a basket
of the Nile reeds that also gave us paper.

Later in Life

JORIE GRAHAM

Summer heat, the first early morning
                              of it. How it lowers the pitch of the
                              cry—human—cast up
as two words by the worker street-level
                              positioning the long beam on
the chain as he calls up to the one handling the pulley on
                              the seventh floor. One
                              call. They hear each other!
Perfectly! As the dry heat, the filled-out leaves, thicken the surround, the
warming
                              asphalt, & the lull in growth
                              occurs, & in it the single birdcries now and
                              again are placed, &
all makes a round from which sound is sturdied-up without dissipation
or dilation,
                              bamboo-crisp, &
                              up it goes up like a thing
                              tossed without warp of weight or evidence of
                              overcome
gravity, as if space were thinned by summer now to a non-interference.
Up it goes, the
                              cry, all the
                              way up, audible and unchanging, so the man
                              need
not even raise his voice to be heard,
                              the dry warm air free to let it pass without
                              loss of
                              any of itself along
                              its way . . .

I step out and suddenly notice this: summer arrives, has arrived, is
arriving. Birds grow
                          less than leaves although they cheep, dip,
                          arc. A call
across the tall fence from an invisible neighbor to his child is heard
                          right down to the secret mood in it the child
also hears. One hears in the silence that follows the great
                          desire for approval
                          and love
which summer holds aloft, all damp leached from it, like a thing floating
out on a frail but
                          perfect twig-end. Light seeming to darken in
                          it yet
                          glow. *Please* it says. But not with the eager
                          need of
Spring! Come what may says summer. Smack in the middle I will stand
and breathe. The
                          future is a superfluity I do not
                          taste, no, there is no numbering
here, it is a gorgeous swelling, no emotion, as in this love is no emotion,
no, also no
                          memory—we have it all, now, & all
                          there ever was is
us, now, that man holding the beam by the right end and saying *go* on his
                          ground from
                          which the word and the
                          cantilevered metal
rise, there is no mistake, the right minute falls harmlessly, intimate,
overcrowded,
                          without pro-
                          venance—perhaps bursting with
                          nostalgia but
ripening so fast without growing at
                          all & what
is the structure of freedom but this, & grace, & the politics of time—look
south, look
                          north—yes—east west compile hope
                          synthesize

exceed look look again hold fast attach speculate drift drift recognize
forget—terrible
> gush—gash—of
> form of
outwardness, & and it is your right to be so entertained, & and if you are
starting to
> feel it is hunger this
> gorgeousness, feel the heat fluctuate & say
> my
> name is day, of day, in day, I want
> nothing to
come back, not ever, & these words are mine, there is no angel to
> wrestle, there is no inter-
> mediary, there is something I must
tell you, you do not need existence, these words praise be they can for
now be
> said. That is summer. Hear them.

Hermit Songs

SEAMUS HEANEY

for Helen Vendler

> *Pent under high tree canopy*
> *A blackbird—listen—sings for me.*
> *Above the ruled quires of my book*
> *I hear the wild birds jubilant.*
> *—Ninth century*

i

With cut-offs of black calico,
remnants of old blackout blinds
ironed, tacked with criss-cross threads,
we jacketed the issued books.

Less durable if more desired,
the mealy textured wallpaper:
its brede of bosomed roses pressed
and flattened under smoothing irons.

Brown parcel paper, if need be.
Newsprint even. Anything
to make a covert for the newness,
learn you were a keeper only.

ii

Open, settle, smell, begin.
A spelling out, a finger trace:
one with Fursa, Colmcille,
the riddle-solving anchorites—

MacOige of Lismore, for instance,
who, when asked which attribute
of character was best, replied
'Steadiness, for it is best

when a man has set his hand to tasks
to persevere. I have never heard
fault found with that.' Tongue-tried words
finger-traced, retraced, lipread.

iii

Bread and pencils. Musty satchel.
The age of lessons to be learnt.
Reader, these were 'reading books'
and we were 'scholars,' our good luck

to get such schooling in the first place
for all its second and third handings.
The herdsman by the roadside told you.
The sibyls of the chimney corner.

The age of wonders too, such as:
rubbings out with balls of bread-pith,
birds and butterflies in 'transfers'
like stamps from Eden on a flyleaf.

iv

The master's store an otherwhere:
penshafts sheathed in black tin—was it?—
a metal wrap, at any rate,
a tight nib-holding cuticle—

and nibs in packets by the gross,
powdered ink, bunched cedar pencils,
jotters, exercise books, rulers
stacked like grave goods on the shelves.

The privilege of being sent
to fetch a box of pristine chalk
or perfect copperplate examples
of headline script for copying out.

v

'There are three right ways to spell *tu*.
Can you tell me how you write that down?'
the herdsman asks. And when we can't,
'Ask the master if *he* can.'

Neque, Caesar says, *fas esse
estimant ea litteris
mandare.* 'Nor do they think it right
to commit the things they know to writing.'

Not, that is, until there comes
the age of *cumhdach,* the 'book-shrine,'
its primary senses variously
cover, stronghold, thatch, protection.

vi

The psalms in Latin first—*The Battler*—
so called because borne three times
around a fielded army, sunwise,
it guaranteed a victory.

Then vellum from the hide of Odhar,
Ciaran's dun cow, made the leaves
for Ciaran's *Book of the Dun Cow.*
On one page, this faint inscription:

'A trial of pen by Mael Muire.'
In 1106 Mael Muire dies
'during raid on Clonmacnoise
by Vikings or an Irish war king.'

vii

'To every cow its calf, to every
book its copy.' Colmcille
rejects the judgement, goes to battle
to win the world's first copyright

and on Iona will atone,
his penance to convert as many
souls for Christ as bodies fell
when he joined battle at Cooldrevna.

Who at the end sets down his quill
one day in June 597
and leaves it to the novice Baithín
to carry on with his transcription.

viii

Sparks the Ulster warriors struck
off wielded swords made Bricriu's hall
blaze like the sun, according to
the Dun Cow scribe; and then Cuchulain

entertained the embroidery women
by flinging needles in the air
so as they fell the point of one
danced in through the eye of the next

to form a glittering circular chain—
as in my dream a gross of nibs
spills off the shelf, airlifts and loops
into a reeling gilt corona.

ix

Keepers of *The Book of Durrow,*
lament the stripping of the shrine
down to the 'plain rough leathern cover'
noted by Archbishop Marsh.

Also note a late re-binding:
50 yards of linen thread,
50,000 stitches, patches
peeled from holes rubbed in the vellum.

One hole, eye-hole, bored through leaves
top right, verifies tradition:
book was suspended thus in water
as part of cure for cattle sickness.

x

A vision of the school the school
won't understand, nor I, not quite:
my hand in a cold running stream
suspended, a glass beaker dipped

and filling in the flow. I'm sent,
the favoured, to fetch water
to mix with ink powder. I'm out
in splendid wideness, land and sky

and playground silent, a singing class
I've been excused from going on
behind the wall and steel-framed windows,
yet still and all a world away.

xi

'Well' in 'inkwell' now as far
as 'horn' from its first sense in 'inkhorn'
stuck point down in the floor
near the scribe's foot. Hence Colmcille's

extempore when a loudmouth lands
on Iona: *This harbour shouter,*
(it roughly goes), *his staff in hand,*
he will approach, he will come

inclined to kiss the kiss of peace,
he will blunder in,
his toe will catch and overturn
my little inkhorn, spill my ink.

xii

One put faith in riveters
who struck for pay, one in meaning
that runs through space like a word
screaming and protesting, one

in memories of love and words
of women: mine for now I put
in steady-handedness maintained
against its vanishing in books.

Of Lismore. Durrow. Kells. Armagh.
Of Lecan, its great Yellow Book.
The small, enshrined, atoned-for *Battler.*
The cured hides. The much tried pens.

Family Album

AUGUST KLEINZAHLER

Loneliness—huge, suddenly menacing
and no one is left here who knows me anymore:
the Little League coach,
his TV repair truck and stinking cigars
and Saul the Butcherman
and the broken arm that fell out of the apple tree,
dead,
dead or gone south to die warm.

The little boy with mittens and dog
posing on the stoop—
he isn't me;
and the young couple in polo shirts, ready to pop
with your firstborn
four pages on in shortshorts and beatnik top
showing her figure off at 16 . . .
1955 is in an attic bookcase
spine cracked and pages falling out.

Willow and plum tree
green pods from maple whirling down to the sidewalk . . .
Only the guy at the hot dog stand since when
maybe remembers me,
or at least looks twice.

But the smushfaced bus from New York, dropping
them off at night along

these avenues of brick, somber as the dead child
and crimes of old mayors
lets off no one I know, or want to.

Warm grass and dragonflies—
O, my heart.

The Life You Save

CARL PHILLIPS

So much felt simpler. We could look,
unmoved, upon the kingdom we'd made—that we'd
soon take leave of—and, even in the most ruined places,
still find a loveliness: vengeance
making pretty with the wild wisteria, the jackdaws
in all their ragged black shinery—part

Watch me, part *Close your eyes*—hunger
ravishingly more bronze
in the face meanwhile, one hand lifting the softer curls
gently away from it, the other covering, as if
for modesty, the mouth's gash—wet, lonely . . .

And always, the sea in front of us—to swear on, to be
undone by, to have meant never to suffer
defeat beside, at rest, and
in restlessness, always the sea:

                    Not harm, not rescue,
proof of nothing but yourself, you've been
nobody's fixable point of reference: you,
the blow-smitten thrall
of mutability—and you the master, coming back
for more,

            it seemed to say, its waves
cresting, breaking, like an idea about moral freedom,
or a memory of it, that dims until no longer
trustworthy. The stuff of legend. A lie I sing to myself, against
regretting. It begins "How long we slept, how easy, those last few nights."

central valley

D. A. POWELL

he said that he liked your book very much. and that he hoped it wasn't true.
—HELEN VENDLER

earlier the curtain of smoke hung as dark spots on pecked fruit
plumes still rising over paddies where the rice straw smoldered

kids like me blowing black snot into sleeves and checked bandannas
the farmers—almost extinct—wheezing along the earthen dikes
and the sky a mass of black lung: spittle settling upon the nutsedge

terrible immanence of spring: among the tules, marsh wrens trilled
& bitterns stalled vertically against the edge of irrigation ponds
where crawdads haggled a mouse, its carcass scavenged into bits

unstoppable noise from the slough: suckwhistle and croak of kites
the honk of canada geese not unlike the child's complaint of croup

couldn't describe the smell of almond wood, I know: couldn't describe
that marriage between bitter sod and brief light of joss paper burning

here I inhaled first plum blossoms and took the yellowjacket stings
saying "sticks, I live in the sticks, don't drive me home I'll sleep instead
on your rug, be your boy, just ask me to spread my legs, I'll spread"

my mind's a dingy billow of slashed stalk combusting in the slade
it opens like a gopher hole inopportune. opens its sorry leafage
against the buttes, against the blooms, against each new season

and a crazy man who ignited his shed and home: his laugh
a kind of coughing laugh: or the cry of a common hawk

June Bug

DAVE SMITH

for Helen Vendler

The carapace—is it that?—shrugging forward
like a Roman war-wagon, dark gleam
from sloped shoulders and the lowered head,
itself helmeted, swaying from side to side
as if the great weight, with one slip
of purchase, might haul everything backward,
the massive thighs and horn-embraced
legs that dig ponderously, the tip-toe
forenails that grip surfaces, least or best,
and those already wounded, so they seem,
trailing appendages, brogans worn, dragging.
To this, under the fore-armpits,
I tie my string, sun about us, an egg's center,
and wait.
      No sound. At first, no movement. Wait.
Then the big head, slippage until some crack
invisibly appears in the earth, and slant rays
of light leveraging it forward, grass blades
bent, twigs gone over like thin bodies,
small combatants scurrying aside, now and then
a pause, the heavy hold on air I think
may be death until, at last, it rises
up. Shrugs on. Soon it will be dusk, dinner.
The earth is darker, a coolness swells out.
Already this story breathes me. So I wait
as the string plays into darkness, until all is
tug and touch, imagined, the big thing breaking off.

Heraclitean Backwash

CHARLES WRIGHT

for H.V., fixed point in the flux

Wherever I am,
               I always wonder what I am doing back there,
Strange flesh in a stranger land.
As though the world were a window and I a faint reflection
Returning my gaze
Wherever I looked, and whatever I looked upon.

Absence of sunlight, white water among the tall trees . . .
Nothing whispers its secret.
Silence, for some, is a kind of healing, it's said,
                      for others the end of a dark road
That begins the zone of a greater light.
Fish talk to the dead in the shallow water below the hill.

Or so the Egyptian thought,
               who knew a thing or two about such things.
Strange flesh in a stranger land.
The clouds take their toll.
Like moist souls, they litter the sky on their way to where they're not.
Dandelions scatter across the earth,
                   fire points, small sunsqualls.

Criticism

Tropes and Teams

Teaching Poetry through Classroom Debate

JAHAN RAMAZANI

How can we teach poetry most effectively? How can poetry criticism be made to serve the classroom experience, and teaching be made to serve poetry criticism? What are the analytical tools students need for understanding the special capacities and intricacies of poetry? To address such questions, the poetry critic must be willing to step out of the highly polished shoes of critical and theoretical reflection into the more humble, rugged boots of pedagogy and deploy a nuts-and-bolts "how-to" rhetoric more common in education schools and teaching centers than in English departments. The poetry critic also needs to be willing to expose often unarticulated, bedrock assumptions about poetry. "My remarks in this manual about practice in the classroom," observes Helen Vendler of her teaching guide to *Poems, Poets, Poetry: An Introduction and Anthology,* "are based, of course, on my own convictions about the art of poetry and how to do it justice" (*Resources* 7). A critic of supreme interpretive powers, Vendler has not let her luminous gifts as exegete and writer, editor and thinker, deter her from offering practical guidance on how to stimulate thinking about poetry in the classroom. Among the convictions that animate her teaching: "Poets are above all the most gifted of linguistic practitioners . . . not philosophers" with "original ideas," nor "essayists, concerned to pursue a logical argument" (*Resources* 7). Another "purpose" of her teaching "is to convince students that many responses are usually present in a poem, that a poem can't be reduced . . . to a single 'meaning'" (*Resources* 28). Sharing these assumptions about the linguistic exuberance and dialogic complexity of poetry, I have attempted, like Vendler, to develop appropriate teaching strategies in my classes on poetry. In this essay I describe one such strategy—classroom debate—thus paying tribute to Vendler's synthesis of criticism and pedagogy, to the far-reaching impact of her teaching and her thinking about teaching on generations of students and colleagues who love poetry.

Poetry and debate may well be in some sense antithetical, the inward hum of meditative thought as against the outward din of rhetorical collision. W. B. Yeats encapsulates this difference in his famous dictum, "We make out of the quarrel with others, rhetoric, but of the quarrel with ourselves, poetry" (*Mythologies* 331). Folding multiple positions within its dense verbal texture, poetry makes audible the intellectual and affective nuances elided by the rhetorical wars in newspapers and talk shows. If we listen carefully enough, we might even be able to hear in it something close to the hum of emergent thinking—rambling, unshackled, turning in new and often contradictory directions. Debate proceeds not through private rumination but through gladiatorial combat between intellectual antagonists, its aim not the synthesis of ideas and emotions but the rigorous testing of arguments against each other. The dichotomizing rhetoric of debate may thus seem inconsistent with poetry's polysemic complexity. Yet, in spite of this discursive difference, or indeed perhaps because of it, debate can be an effective tool for teaching poetry. Through debate, students are encouraged to engage poems and classmates with energy and precision—no longer passive consumers but active producers of critical argument. Contending over such issues as whether Robert Frost's "The Road Not Taken" nostalgically endorses or ironically questions the difference made by taking the road less traveled by, whether Yeats's "Easter, 1916" is more nationalist or antinationalist, whether Sylvia Plath's "Daddy" is better described as a love poem or a hate poem, whether Derek Walcott's "A Far Cry from Africa" sympathizes more with the British empire or with anticolonial resistance, my students have helped me to understand the potential of debate as a means for bringing poetry to life in the classroom.

In the pedagogical literature on poetry, debate is seldom recommended (see, e.g., Showalter; Gedalof 50–51). Anxious about the ability of our students to grasp even the basics of the genre, we are often reluctant to devolve interpretive authority in the classroom; and so lecture, the Socratic method, and memorization and recitation remain more common strategies for teaching poetry. Surely, each of these techniques can play a valuable role in teaching poetry. The lecture format enables us to sketch historical contexts, explain poetic forms, and exemplify close responsiveness to poetry in hopes that students will adopt a similar practice in their reading and writing. Through the Socratic method, we direct student attention to fundamentals and subtleties of a poem, and we "model" diligent questioning of the text, of facile assumptions, and of one another's readings. Recitation of a memorized poem forces students to perform and take account of its sounds and resonances, its rhythmic and tonal modulations.

But debate can usefully supplement these strategies, I hope to show, by making poetry memorable and meaningful for students through what Paul Ricoeur calls "the conflict of interpretations." In the pedagogical literature on debate, the terms "structured," "cooperative," or "constructive controversy" are often preferred because "debate" may seem to be about winning, not about understanding the question (Johnson, Johnson, and Smith; Bredehoft). Yet despite debate's etymological linkage to "battle" and "beat" (*battuere*), I persist in using the word because it suggests reasoned argument between proponents of divergent views, based on each side's careful assessment of the evidence in relation to a thesis, whereas "controversy" describes less a process of inquiry, deliberation, and persuasion than a state of contentious disagreement.

While the psychologist easily sees the benefits of asking students to debate the pros and cons of day care, the historian of staging a debate on the causes of the American Civil War, and the political scientist of encouraging debate on U.S. foreign policy in the Middle East, the benefits of classroom debate may be less self-evident for the teacher of poetry, devoted to the painstaking, synthetic, affective, measured procedures of the genre. But however responsive our interpretive language and layered our readings, we don't typically speak or write in verse when analyzing poetry, notwithstanding the *ars poetica* tradition. Whether our critical analysis is informed by New Criticism or poststructuralism, formalism or historicism, psychoanalysis or feminism, it stands apart from the poetry itself and can be accepted, doubted, or denied on the basis of its logic, coherence, and use of evidence. Hence, the demand that students argue for their positions can help disabuse them of the common misperception in the humanities classroom that either knowledge is clear-cut, true or false, right or wrong, or it is purely subjective and anything goes (Kurfiss 1–3, 76). Having to develop a position in the face of the other side's skepticism, students learn that interpretive arguments are neither ironclad nor arbitrary, that they are more or less plausible and persuasive depending on the quality of the reasoning, analysis, and marshaling of detail. Further, the Big Questions typically used to generate classroom debate need not dwarf the minute particulars of the poetry. As any poetry critic knows, the desire to discover, assess, and present evidence for a credible interpretation can result in scrupulous attention to the nuances of individual words, the force of specific images, and the semantic effects of enjambment.

If poetry is no less susceptible to reasoned debate than are the issues of public life that are the usual grist for the deliberative mill—abortion, euthanasia, race, war, and so forth—then the gap between poetry's subtlety and unpredictability, on the one hand, and the ham-fisted sloganeering and clichés in public debate, on the other, may itself be productive. The disjunction could be seen as an opportunity for poetry to put pressure on public discourse, since the mind that has repeatedly tracked the minute shifts in tone, rhythm, diction, and imagery in lyric poetry may be less easily satisfied with one-dimensional platitudes and pronouncements. "The habit of attentiveness and accuracy, once gained in a particular field," as Vendler observes, "tends to make one attentive and accurate elsewhere" (*Resources* 20).

When should a poetry class make use of debate? Obviously, it is ill suited to historical coverage or the introduction of poets and literary movements, of stanza forms and scansion, and so it cannot possibly be the mainstay of one's teaching. Yet employed from time to time, it can dramatically enliven a poetry class and deepen its critical inquiry. I have used debate in three ways: as a culminating exercise requiring extensive out-of-class preparation in lieu of a final exam, as an in-class exercise addressing a general question about a range of poems, and as an in-class tool for exploring the complexities of a single poem. These first two uses of debate can be described briefly, because they more nearly conform to a standard pedagogical model in which students are asked to work in teams on a wide body of material and to address large, contentious issues of the field. In class meetings leading up to end-of-semester debates, I work with students to elicit their sense of what the recurrent and significant issues have been throughout the course. I then write these up and distribute them to the students. In one seminar on contemporary poetry, for example, the debate topics included questions of whether contemporary poets successfully fuse formal achievement and political commitment, whether the ethnic and transnational diversification of the contemporary poetic canon has enhanced or diluted its quality, and whether postconfessional lyricism or avant-garde experimentalism represents a greater achievement in contemporary poetry.

In my syllabus I had explained debate as one of the course requirements: "The purposes of this assignment are to offer you the chance to synthesize some of the material we have covered in class, in the absence of a final exam; to enable us to dramatize and analyze collectively significant critical issues of contemporary poetry; to help develop your skills of oral articulation and critical listening; and to offer an occasion for you to work collaboratively with classmates, extending our intellectual community beyond the classroom." Having outlined the why of debate, the syllabus continued by prescribing the how, setting forth questions to guide team

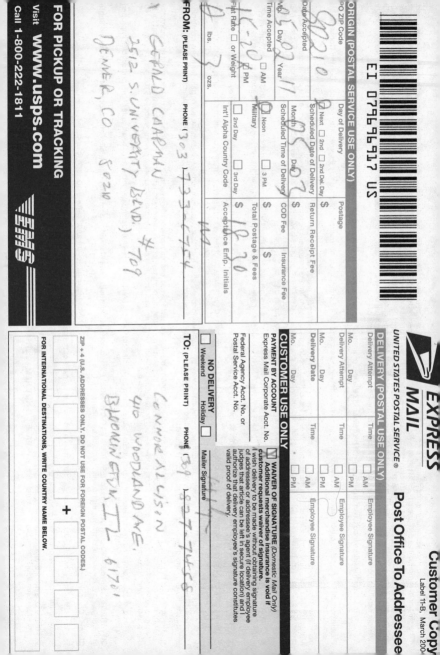

Service Guarantee: *Express Mail international mailings are not covered by this service agreement. Military shipments delayed due to customs inspections are also excluded.* If the shipment is mailed at a designated USPS Express Mail facility on or before the specified deposit time for overnight or second delivery day delivery to the addressee, delivery to the addressee or agent will be attempted before the applicable guaranteed time. Signature of the addressee's agent, or delivery employee is required upon delivery. If a delivery attempt is not made by the guaranteed time and the mailer files a claim for a refund, the USPS will refund the postage, unless the ZIP code was caused by: proper detention for law enforcement purposes; strike or work stoppage; late deposit of shipment, forwarding, return, incorrect address, or incorrect ZIP code; delay or cancellation of flights; governmental action beyond the control of the Postal Service or air carriers; war, insurrection, or civil disturbance; breakdowns of a substantial portion of the USPS transportation network resulting from events or factors outside the control of the Postal Service or acts of God.

A notice is left for the addressee when an item cannot be delivered on a first attempt. If the item cannot be delivered by the addressee on the second attempt and is not claimed by the addressee within five days of the second attempt, it will be returned to sender at no additional postage.

Please consult your local Express Mail directory for noon and 3 p.m. delivery areas and for information on international and military Express Mail services. See the Domestic Mail Manual for details.

Insurance Coverage: Insurance is provided only in accordance with postal regulations in the *Domestic Mail Manual* (DMM) and, for international shipments, the *International Mail Manual* (IMM). The DMM and IMM set forth the specific types of losses that are covered, the limitations on coverage, terms of insurance, conditions of payment, and adjudication procedures. Copies of the DMM and IMM are available for inspection at any post office and online at pe.usps.gov. If copies are not available and information on Express Mail insurance is requested, please contact postmaster prior to mailing. The DMM and IMM consist of federal regulations, and USPS personnel are NOT authorized to change or waive these regulations or grant exceptions. Limitations prescribed in the DMM and IMM provide, in part, that:

- The contents of Express Mail shipments defined by postal regulations as merchandise are insured against loss, damage, or rifling. Coverage up to $100 per shipment is included at no additional charge. Additional merchandise insurance up to $5,000 per shipment may be purchased for an additional fee; however, additional insurance is void if waiver of the addressee's signature is requested.

- Coverage extends to the actual value of the contents at the time of mailing or the cost of repairs, not to exceed the limit fixed for the insurance coverage obtained.

- Items defined by postal regulations as "negotiable items" (items that can be converted to cash without resort to forgery), currency, or bullion are insured up to a maximum of $15 per shipment.

- For international Express Mail shipments, insurance coverage may vary by country and may not be available to some countries. Indemnity is not paid for items containing coins, banknotes, currency notes (paper money); securities of any kind payable to the bearer; traveler's checks; platinum, gold, and silver (manufactured or not); precious stones, jewelry, and other valuable or prohibited articles.

- Items defined by postal indemnity regulations as "nonnegotiable documents" are insured against loss, damage, or rifling up to $100 per shipment for document reconstruction subject to additional limitations for multiple pieces lost or damaged in a single catastrophic occurrence. Document reconstruction insurance provides reimbursement for the reasonable costs incurred in reconstructing duplicates of nonnegotiable documents mailed. Document reconstruction insurance coverage above $100 per shipment is NOT available, and attempts to purchase additional document insurance are void.

- No coverage is provided for consequential losses due to loss, damage, or delay of Express Mail, or for concealed damage, spoilage of perishable items, and articles improperly packaged or too fragile to withstand normal handling in the mail.

COVERAGE, TERMS AND LIMITATIONS ARE SUBJECT TO CHANGE. Please consult Domestic Mail Manual and International Mail Manual, both of which are available at pe.usps.gov, for additional limitations and terms of coverage.

Claims: Original customer receipt of the Express mail label must be presented when filing an indemnity claim and /or for a postage refund.

1. All claims for delay, loss, damage, or rifling must be made within 90 days of the date of mailing; for international, call 1-800-222-1811.

2. Claim forms may be obtained and filed at any post office.

3. To file a claim for damage, the article, container, and packaging must be presented to the USPS for inspection. To file a claim for loss of contents, the container and packaging must be presented to the USPS for inspection. **PLEASE DO NOT REMAIL. THANK YOU FOR CHOOSING EXPRESS MAIL.**

deliberations outside class: "What are the best three to five major points of argument for our position? For each of these points, what are strong pieces of evidence we can provide, drawing from specifics of the poetry? In what order should we present these points? What are the weaknesses in our position? How should we address these weaknesses, in order to shore up our general lines of argument?" Finally, I stated that "debate teams should be ready to make a cogent, five-minute-per-person presentation of their argument and evidence. They should hand in a detailed outline of their argument on the day of the presentation. All members of the team should be responsible for some portion of the presentation. Attending to the other team's arguments, they should be ready to take extensive notes and to rebut or qualify the other team's views." For a syllabus, these instructions may well seem too elaborate, the structure nearly procrustean, but in my experience, because debate places so much responsibility in the hands of the students, the more detailed the instructions and the more tightly organized the debate, the better the chances that the event itself will be animated and instructive.

Indeed, I have been astonished by how well my students, working in teams of three to four, have performed in the synoptic debates scheduled for the semester's last two meetings. The format I follow is unsurprising: initial five-minute-per-person statements on one side are followed by initial statements by the other side, with seven-minute rebuttals, ten minutes of free exchange, and five minutes for each side's closing arguments. Some promoters of debate suggest that the greatest learning occurs when students are asked to switch sides at the end of the debate, and then, finally, to write up a collective report on the pros and cons of either side (Johnson, Johnson, and Smith, "Constructive Controversy"). Although I don't always allow time for such position swapping, I make sure to allot time for a final debriefing of fifteen minutes or so, in which the rest of the class gets involved in the discussion, and in which we review what we've witnessed and evaluate it together, asking participants in the debate to step out of their admittedly limiting positions of advocacy and engage in an open discussion of their views.

An abbreviated version of the same debate structure can also be focused on a question of more limited scope, requiring no out-of-class preparation by teams, which are instead cobbled together on the spot: Is Ezra Pound's early poetry antagonistic toward or collusive with modernity? Does Mina Loy's autobiographical poetry reinforce or subvert anti-Semitic and other ethnic stereotypes? Does Gwendolyn Brooks's formal verse extend or undermine New Critical principles? Is Plath's use of the Holocaust apt and powerful or recklessly exploitative? Is Charles Wright's poetry animated by religious longings or postreligious skepticism? Debate works especially well as an approach to substantive and unsettled questions to which the teacher believes that there are at least two viable, contrasting answers, not a single "right" one.

If such wide-ranging debates can be useful procedures for helping students grapple with broad, sometimes hotly contended issues, I have nevertheless found the most revealing and rewarding debates—and those truest to the verbal, intellectual, and affective complexities of poetry—to be those that are more sharply focused, namely, on a single poem. The selected poem or section of a poem must admit of at least two opposing readings. Thus, in my class on modern poetry, I ask students whether the last section of *The Waste Land*, "What the Thunder Said," envisions restoration and ekes out hope for the rejuvenation of the wasteland by religious, cultural, or poetic means, or whether it imagines continued sterility, little more than a series of ongoing fragmentations, scatterings, deaths, acts of futile mourning, and impersonation and ventriloquism. Similarly, to get at the vexed alienation and affinity between speaker and bluesman in Langston Hughes's "The Weary Blues"—a poem formally melding the blues and Euro-American lyric—I divide a class of fifty to seventy students in two, bidding them explore how the speaker's poetic forms and language affiliate or distinguish him from the bluesman whose performance he describes (Ramazani, *Poetry of Mourning* 144–47). Debating whether Frost's "Mending Wall" provides more support for its repeated aphorism "Something there is that doesn't love a wall" or for its seemingly contrary, also repeated, aphorism "Good fences make good neighbors," my students are asked to scour the poem's imagery, figurative language, verbal registers, use of embedded dialogue, and such formal properties as meter, line breaks, and punctuation for what these suggest about ideas of walls, limits, boundaries. As the students contend over such issues, they become intimately aware of how Frost adduces wise sayings while slyly contextualizing and complicating them, how Hughes's speaker both identifies with his alter ego and registers his social and formal difference, how the ending of *The Waste Land* enmeshes hope and despair in an inextricable medley. For the sake of dramatic tension, I find I must be willing to pose a question that is admittedly binary and general, yet that produces close attention to detail and awareness of poetic ambiguity.

One of the first times I staged a debate about a poem, I asked my students whether Philip Larkin's poem "Church Going" was more religious and nostalgic or skeptical and irreverent. They were to uncover all the evidence they could for Larkin the disenchanted secularist on one side and on the other side Larkin the pining, would-be believer. I told them that we all knew the poem to be more complex than either stance, and that their job in performing a position was thus to make visible one strand of meaning and feeling in the poem. With about fifty students, I divided the class down the middle aisle into eight teams of five to seven, starting with those in the front of the classroom (Frederick 48). The first pair of teams was responsible for finding evidence for their position in the first two stanzas, the following pair in the next two stanzas, and so on, until the last pair had only the final stanza. Each team chose a spokesperson, who was responsible, when the debate began, for stating briefly and cogently the team's thesis, its main two or three supporting arguments, and all the evidence of particular words, images, metaphors, enjambments, tonality, and so forth, that supported its position. After twenty minutes of brainstorming, each team stood in turn and faced the paired group across the aisle, with each spokesperson presenting the team's findings. The groups also had time to rebut the views of their opposition, having been encouraged to take notes and come up with specific responses to salient points. In their divergent readings of the title alone—whether it signals a nostalgic going to the church to find something wondrous and endangered, or a pessimistic recognition that the church is going to ruin and inevitable decline—the students dramatized the tension between the poem's disenchanted secularism and its spiritual longings. They enacted the question of whether, as the secularists felt, the speaker wants to make sure he avoids any religious or ritual event ("there's nothing going on") or, as the religionists argued, that he is mysteriously drawn to the church ("Yet stop I did: in fact I often do"). Is the interior space seen as boring ("Another church") and stale (flowers "brownish now," the air "tense, musty")? Or is it safe ("door thud shut") and alluring ("run my hand around the font"), even inspiring some "reverence" (the removal of his bicycle clips)? Does his diction suggest alienation ("some brass and stuff / Up at the holy end," the roof "Cleaned, or restored? Someone would know; I don't") or familiarity and closeness to the church as part of his life and heritage ("parchment, plate, and pyx")? Does he distinguish his own verse, with its witty, understated manner, from the grand religious rhetoric in big letters ("Hectoring large-scale verses" read too "loudly"), or is his rhetoric infected by the prophetic temptation to claim an apocalyptic ending—now of the church itself ("Here endeth")?

In this fashion, we went through the ensuing stanzas, the room brimming with excitement, my students passionately wrangling over the meaning of individual words and the entire poem. I was surprised by how well the students mediated—just as we hope they will in their papers—between the nitty-gritty of specific images or words or technical details and broad thematic concerns. Occasionally I intervened to make sure one team responded to the other, or to solicit the views of the rest of the class on the credibility of a point of argument, but I had never seen such intellectual fire in my classroom, nor such meticulous attention to connotation. By the end of the class, my students understood that what made the poem worth rereading was precisely that it blended the two perspectives they had so ably disentangled, that the poem was more complex in tone, rhetoric, and imagery than either of the views they had performed. Yes, the speaker is irreverent and unorthodox, sees the institution as irreversibly doomed, asserts that "superstition, like belief, must die," and feels "Bored, uninformed" in a church whose "purpose" is "obscure"; at the same time, he is drawn to a space that, unlike the "suburb scrub," evokes a mode of reflection that "never can be obsolete"—contemplation of great events in life, such as birth, marriage, and death—and that thus resembles poetry as a "ground" or "house" affording profound rumination, if only because, in both the literary and religious sites, "so many dead lie around."

In setting up teams, I sometimes assign students arbitrarily, asking them to assume a stance for heuristic purposes, but sometimes I assign them on the basis of positions they already hold, as indicated either by a show of hands or by e-mail responses before class. My role is to establish the teams, structure the debate around a meaty question, enumerate the kinds of evidence that should be examined (title, imagery, syntax, diction, enjambment, etc.), moderate the debate as it unfolds, and, finally, help the whole class arrive at a synthetic vision. Since, as Vendler notes, "the teacher both knows more and is more experienced than the students," the teacher's enumeration of specific aspects of the poems to examine crucially shapes the disciplined attention that students bring to bear on the poems (*Resources* 12).

One literary critic who has promoted intellectual debate—though not necessarily actual debate among students—is Gerald Graff, who has famously advocated "teaching the conflicts," by which he means the conflicts between different literary schools: canonizers and anticanonizers, feminists and the rear guard, left and right. Graff usefully suggests that interpretive conflicts vivify literature, help to form community through dispute, and reconnect the literary classroom to the extraliterary debates in society at large. But given Graff's unsympathetic attitudes toward poetry, perhaps it is unsurprising that the questions of value he favors—for example, whether "Dover Beach" is a good poem and should remain in the canon—are unpromising as an approach to teaching poetry (Graff; see also Cain). When students start out with the ultimate question of judgment, intellectually lively engagement with the nuances of the text is often blocked or forestalled.

I find that the questions I ask must be hermeneutically rich if they are to intensify my students' attention to significant particulars in the poetry—an awareness of complex detail and semantic undecidability that is less likely if the sides are debating whether the poem is good or bad, whether it should be in the canon or not. Answering the nationalist team's argument that Yeats sees the Easter Rising as an event of great "beauty" in "Easter, 1916," the antinationalist team focuses on the adjective "terrible," and in the end both understand the bidirectional force of Yeats's famous oxymoron. As Vendler asks of Yeats's vexed reactions to the executed rebels, "Can he celebrate them or not? His ambivalence suffuses the poem" (*Resources* 69; see also her *Our Secret Discipline* 16–26; Ramazani, *Yeats* 59–66). Similarly, the antithetical possibilities embedded in the word "ice-cream" emerge with stark clarity when students wrangle over whether Wallace Stevens's "The Emperor of Ice-Cream" lays its emphasis on living sensuality ("The only emperor is the emperor of ice-cream") or dumb death ("The only emperor is the emperor of ice-cream") (see Vendler, *Wallace Stevens* 50–53; Ramazani, *Poetry of Mourning* 90–93). In arguing over whether Seamus Heaney's "Punishment" presents the perspective of victim or victimizer, debaters dramatize the ambiguity in the poem's opening lines—whether the speaker identifies with the victim being led to execution, as if feeling the halter around his own neck, or with the executioner, as if holding the halter and tugging at it: "I can feel the tug / of the halter at the nape / of her neck." In such cases, the capacity of multivalent phrases, words, lines, and images to embrace conflicting positions becomes vivid in the classroom because students enact divergent readings. Indeed, despite the binary structure of debate, my ultimate goal in deploying it is the dramatization of the both/and of poetry, its capacity for mediating seemingly irreconcilable views. For me, this aim is more important than Graff's of teaching students about various critical schools; after all, the best poetry criticism, like the best poetry, is typically pluralist and synthetic, not easily reduced to one doctrine or another.

A last example may help show how the to-and-fro of debate can put into action the both/and of poetry. In my classes on poetry and on postcolonial literatures, the question of the ultimate sympathies of Walcott's "A Far Cry from Africa" (1956) has sparked heated debates. Prodded to scrutinize the poem's title, my students often begin by debating whether it means that the poet sympathetically listens to the distant cry of African revolt or whether he feels alienated from a revolutionary, bloody-minded Africa that is "a far cry from" the continent he has loved. One team notes the personification of Africa as beast in the word "pelt," suggesting the poet's identification with the colonizer's vision of the continent: "A wind is ruffling the tawny pelt/Of Africa. Kikuyu, quick as flies,/Batten upon the bloodstreams of the veldt." But the opposing group sees in the word an Africa slaughtered like a beast by the colonizers, as against the hopeful "wind" of anticolonial revolution now sweeping the continent. The pro-British team seizes on the seemingly racist comparison of the Mau Mau rebels to "flies," but the pro-African team emphasizes the agility of these "quick" insects, though seen as puny and worthless by the colonizers. The Mau Mau rebels, retort the Europeanists, feed off the repulsive "bloodstreams" of their anticolonial terrorism. No, say the Africanists, these "bloodstreams" are the aftermath of colonial violence and oppression, from which the anticolonial freedom fighters now draw their revolutionary strength. But the poet's very language shows his British allegiances, according to one team, which emphasizes the high literary diction in words like "Batten" and the use even of the Afrikaans term "veldt." The other team sees the poet as ironically twisting and emptying out these words and others like "paradise," echoing but inverting the colonial perversion of such terms: "Corpses are scattered through a paradise./Only the worm, colonel of carrion, cries:/'Waste no compassion on these separate dead!'" For one team, the "dead" for whom the poet conjures compassion are the white victims of the Mau Mau rebellion, such as the explicitly named "white child hacked in bed": "Statistics justify and scholars seize/The salients of colonial policy./What is that to the white child hacked in bed?/To savages, expendable as Jews?" For the other team, these "dead" are the victims of the colonial policy that Walcott mocks for distorting reality. They are treated as "savages," their slaughter compared to that of the Holocaust—the most extreme example of systematic and mechanized genocide in human history. And that's just the first stanza! As the debaters proceed through the rest of the poem, they increasingly incorporate the claims of the opposite side to strengthen their own position. In the final twists and turns of the poem, the speaker explicitly figures himself as "divided to the vein," famously balancing his "love" of the "English tongue" against his abhorrence of "The drunken officer of British rule," his blood ties to Africa against his revulsion toward the Mau Mau rebels' "slaughter" of innocents. By staging the conflicting impulses embedded in the fabric of the poem, my students make graphic and unforgettable Walcott's articulation of the inner divisions of postcolonial experience.

Although such debate consumes class time and detracts from "coverage," it has a number of advantages. It heightens motivation: students who have to rely on their own wits and on one another to argue a particular position in front of their peers seize on the poetry with astonishing energy. Debate can sharpen communication and critical thinking skills, with students gaining a keener understanding of what counts as evidence and argument in literary interpretation. It also makes poetry more memorable: if you have to stand and defend a particular reading of a particular phrase before your classmates, that phrase will more likely be emblazoned in your mind than if you merely jot down a professor's gloss. For me as a teacher, debate turns the classroom into a more dramatic and interactive space, and when I'm surprised and schooled by my students' independent critical thinking, I become a more engaged participant in the class. As I've tried to show, perhaps the greatest advantage of teaching poetry through debate is that it augments students' appreciation for poetry's capacity to embody conflicting visions of reality in its verbal intricacies. Through the interchange among students about Yeats's "Easter, 1916," Frost's "The Road Not Taken," Eliot's *The Waste Land,* Stevens's "The Emperor of Ice-Cream," Loy's "Anglo-Mongrels and the Rose," Hughes's "The Weary Blues," W. H. Auden's "In Memory of W. B. Yeats," Larkin's "Church Going," Plath's "Daddy," Heaney's "Punishment," and Walcott's "A Far Cry from Africa," the double vision of these poems—poems affectively, formally, and linguistically turned in opposite directions—comes to life in a way that neither lecture nor Socratic questioning nor recitation is likely to accomplish.

Applying Blake's maxim, I think we can say of teaching, "Without Contraries is no progression" (34); debate spins out the intellectual antitheses and tensions embedded within poetry. But the insistently binary structure of debate—seemingly the form's greatest liability—can become a tool for undoing binarism, since debate can be used to reveal how poems, unlike many other forms of discourse, mediate or elude, complicate or override logical oppositions—a space, to recur to Larkin's poem, "In whose blent air all our compulsions meet." And it is a grasp of poetry's multivoicedness, of its endless quarrel within, that is key to our students' continuing enjoyment of poems through a lifetime of reading. Twinning tropes and teams can be one of the many ways by which "those of us living a life of learning in what Stevens called 'the radiant and productive atmosphere' of poetry," in Vendler's words, "transmit as far as we can, in books and in the classroom, the beautiful, subversive, sustaining, bracing, and demanding legacy of the poets" ("Life of Learning").

WORKS CITED

Blake, William. *The Marriage of Heaven and Hell*. In *The Complete Poetry and Prose of William Blake*. Ed. David V. Erdman. Rev. ed. New York: Anchor Books, 1982.

Bredehoft, David J. "Cooperative Controversies in the Classroom." *College Teaching* 39.3 (1991): 122–25.

Cain, William E., ed. *Teaching the Conflicts: Gerald Graff, Curricular Reform, and the Culture Wars*. New York: Garland, 1994.

Frederick, Peter J. "The Lively Lecture—8 Variations." *College Teaching* 34.2 (1986): 43–50.

Frost, Robert. *Robert Frost: Poetry and Prose*. Ed. Edward Connery Lathem and Lawrance Thompson. New York: Holt, Rinehart and Winston, 1972. 16–17.

Gedalof, Allan J. *Teaching Poetry*. New York: Norton, 2005.

Graff, Gerald. *Beyond the Culture Wars: How Teaching the Conflicts Can Revitalize American Education*. New York: Norton, 1992.

Heaney, Seamus. "Punishment." *Opened Ground: Selected Poems, 1966–1996*. New York: Farrar, Straus and Giroux, 1998. 112–13.

Johnson, David W., Roger T. Johnson, and Karl A. Smith. "Constructive Controversy." *Change* Jan./Feb. 2000: 29–37.

———. *Creative Controversy: Intellectual Challenge in the Classroom*. Edina, MN: Interaction, 1992.

Kurfiss, Joanne G. *Critical Thinking*. College Station, TX: Association for the Study of Higher Education, 1988.

Larkin, Philip. "Church Going." *Collected Poems*. Ed. Anthony Thwaite. New York: Farrar, Straus and Giroux, 1989. 97–98.

Ramazani, Jahan. *Poetry of Mourning: The Modern Elegy from Hardy to Heaney*. Chicago: U of Chicago P, 1994.

———. *Yeats and the Poetry of Death: Elegy, Self-Elegy, and the Sublime*. New Haven: Yale UP, 1990.

Ricoeur, Paul. *The Conflict of Interpretations*. Ed. Don Ihde. Trans. Willis Domingo et al. Evanston: Northwestern UP, 1974.

Showalter, Elaine. "Teaching Poetry." *Teaching Literature*. Oxford: Blackwell, 2003. 62–78.

Stevens, Wallace. "The Emperor of Ice-Cream." *The Palm at the End of the Mind: Selected Poems and a Play*. Ed. Holly Stevens. New York: Vintage, 1972. 79–80.

Vendler, Helen. "A Life of Learning." The 2001 Charles Homer Haskins Lecture, 2002. ACLS Occasional Paper no. 50 (2002). http://www.acls.org/Publications/OP/Haskins/2001_HelenVendler.pdf.

———. *Our Secret Discipline: Yeats and Lyric Form.* Cambridge, MA: Belknap, 2007.

———. *Resources for Teaching "Poems, Poets, Poetry": An Introduction and Anthology.* Boston: Bedford, 1997.

———. *Wallace Stevens: Words Chosen Out of Desire.* Cambridge, MA: Harvard UP, 1986.

Walcott, Derek. "A Far Cry from Africa." *Collected Poems, 1948–1984.* New York: Farrar, Straus and Giroux, 1986. 17–18.

Yeats, W. B. "Easter, 1916." *The Poems.* Ed. Richard J. Finneran. Rev. ed. New York: Macmillan, 1989. 180–82.

———. *Mythologies.* New York: Macmillan, 1959.

"A sheapherdess thus sayd"

Immediacy and Distance in the Early Modern Lyric

HEATHER DUBROW

1

Poetry, Celan declares, is a handshake.[1] Or, following William Waters's acute and suggestively revisionist translation of a poet who so often resists translation, the passage in question describes poetry as a "pressing of hands," an expression that, as Waters demonstrates, deploys the double meanings of the German *Handwerk* to suggest both craft and the actions of literal human hands.[2] The more common rendition gestures toward the honesty and immediacy so commonly attributed to lyric. And, evoking that immediacy from other perspectives, Waters's translation in turn implies several additional sources and symptoms of it: a lack of intermediaries (no third hand intervenes in the pressing), an expression of what is directly apprehended (in this case tactilely experienced), an emphasis on the temporally present and on presence (what better instance of the sense of touch so often associated with lyric than the meeting of hands).[3]

Yet if one turns to a lyric that might at first appear to be a textbook example of everything toward which Celan's evocative observation gestures, whichever way it is translated, one encounters a sleight—and a slighting—of hand. Indebted to the so-called ugly beauty tradition, the libertine defiance of the opening stanza of Donne's "Indifferent" is immediate in many respects:

> I can love both faire and browne,
> Her whom abundance melts, and her whom want betraies,
> Her who loves lonenesse best, and her who maskes and plaies,
> Her whom the country form'd, and whom the town,
> Her who believes, and her who tries,
> Her who still weepes with spungie eyes,
> And her who is dry corke, and never cries;

> I can love her, and her, and you and you,
> I can love any, so she be not true.
> ("The Indifferent" [1–9])[4]

Not only does Donne's characteristic creation of a distinctive voice call up a sense of the speaker's presence, that figure also eschews temporal shifts by addressing us in the present about attitudes that appear unchanging. And the presence of an audience is established as clearly as that of the speaker: the deixis that, as many readers of lyric have acknowledged, so often encourages immediacy is here literalized inasmuch as "her, and her, and you and you" (8) achieves signification through an act of gesturing or pointing. A poem that glorifies in emotional distance insists in another sense on an immediate relationship with its readers, both the internal audience and other women and men as well.

The second stanza continues these types of immediacy. But Donne is the master of endings that turn the poem and in so doing often turn on and against the addressee.[5] In the third strophe he engineers a different but related type of reversal:

> *Venus* heard me sigh this song,
> And by Love's sweetest Part, Variety, she swore,
> She heard not this till now; and't should be so no more.
> She went, examin'd, and return'd ere long,
> And said, alas, Some two or three
> Poore Heretiques in love there bee,
> Which thinke to stablish dangerous constancie.
> But I have told them, since you will be true,
> You shall be true to them, who'are false to you.
> (19–27)

Pace commonplaces about Donne, the stanza reminds us that he does not always neglect mythology; here, however, the introduction of Venus is characteristic both in the fact that it startles us and in its insistence that Venus, rather than occupying a more elevated realm, shares the world and the values of the speaker. Indeed, whereas he seems to cede authority to her, she in fact serves his purposes. But if it sustains the amoral values introduced earlier, the conclusion, eschewing any aesthetic temptation of its own toward "dangerous constancie" (25), involves a number of abrupt shifts in the immediacy the text had so firmly established. We are pulled from the present tense commonly associated with lyric to not one but two alternative time sequences. That is, the poem removes the observations in the first two stanzas from the lyric present, establishing them instead as a song performed on a particular occasion; moreover, the third stanza contrasts the sequential events about Venus being narrated, what narratologists call story time, and the discourse time in which they are being told. Venus's own words, though enlivened by direct discourse, also lack the immediacy we encountered, or thought we were encountering, in the first eighteen lines of the poem: they are reported as occurring on a specific occasion in the past, and they themselves incorporate the reportage of indirect discourse, thus mirroring the changed status of the opening two stanzas. John Carey acutely asserts that Donne typically writes of "unique instances," and one might add that this poem supports his point precisely by rejecting the alternative temporality on which it opens.[6] To be sure, the deictic in "sigh this song" (19) re-creates some of the immediacy at the beginning of the poem—Donne is not constant even in his literary inconstancy—and arguably the intensity associated with singing contributes to that recovery as well. Yet the primary effect of those three words is to distance the opening stanzas by removing them from their apparent status of speech to that of an aesthetic performance in several senses of that noun.[7] Conversely, Venus's location in the world of myth emphasizes fictiveness at the same time that her presence is paradoxically associated with the apparent move from the fictiveness of the previous song to a more quotidian world. Moreover, that apparent move is itself called into question if we acknowledge the possibility that "this song" (19) refers to the third stanza as well as its predecessors.

In these and so many other ways, then, Donne's poem demonstrates the central argument of this essay: often what is most characteristic of lyric in the early modern period is not the sense of immediacy its proximal deictics, like a number of other devices, evoke but rather the coexistence of techniques suggesting that immediacy and those creating forms of distance. Numerous critics continue to posit immediacy as normative, the default position for early modern lyric and indeed its counterparts in other periods, with distancing devices seen as secondary or even aberrant; others, especially poststructuralists, assume that presence is the illusion that the text tries to maintain, while representation is the dirty secret that it tries to conceal, the aesthetic principle that dare not speak its name. However powerful demonstrations of lyric immediacy have been, they have typically unbalanced our reading of the mode by neglecting the interaction in question; however persuasive theorized denials of presence in certain senses have been, they have too often dismissed as a mere ploy its survival as a poetic effect.

My essay attempts to calibrate the balances by instead looking more closely at the too often neglected ways early modern lyric creates the impression of various forms of distance—and by tracing their relationship with the creation of forms of immediacy or apparent immediacy. Thus this essay directs its attention primarily to strategies for creating those impressions rather than to the extensive philosophical debates about presence (to what sources should its effect be traced? how viable is it? and so on), though in so doing it necessarily alludes to those debates and touches on possibilities for future contributions to them. And I focus primarily on poetry written between about 1500 and 1660, the period variously and contentiously labeled the English Renaissance and early modern England, though I gesture toward future work on texts of other eras.

2

Exploring immediacy and distance in early modern lyric poses a number of problems involving methodology and definition; many of them demand a lengthier discussion than this article can afford, but even a brief overview crystallizes the relevant complexities.[8] For these apparent polar opposites assume a wide range of forms, including some that blur the line between them, while in other instances the same technique, such as a refrain, may generate both members of the pair.

To begin with, immediacy may be evoked in lyric through several effects—in particular, the sort of tactility suggested by Celan's statement, types of vividness that may or may not involve the other four senses, voice in the senses emphasized by critics of twentieth-century poetry, and the type of rhetorical positioning accomplished by linguistic devices, notably deictics.[9] John Keats's poem, or possibly fragment, beginning "This living hand, now warm and capable" demonstrates how such techniques often unite in creating the sense that the poem is speaking directly to the reader. Indeed, it cries out to be included even in this essay primarily based on early modern lyric, not only because Helen Vendler has done illuminating work on its author, but also because it is arguably the best single example and examination in the language of the interplay of strategies that suggest immediacy:

This living hand, now warm and capable
Of earnest grasping, would, if it were cold

And in the icy silence of the tomb,
So haunt thy days and chill thy dreaming nights
That thou wouldst wish thine own heart dry of blood,
So in my veins red life might stream again,
And thou be conscience-calm'd. See, here it is—
I hold it towards you.[10]

A poem that thematizes touching, this extraordinary lyric enacts—or attempts to enact—analogues to tactility in many other ways as well, thus creating a sense of presence. The physical cold and warmth to which it refers mirror the subtle shifts between their emotional analogues (the poem moves between implicit threats and reassurances), and this intensity helps to create voice in the sense of realized subjectivity and hence one version of presence. And the deictics "This" (1) and "here" (7) build yet another version of it. These effects may well be intensified semantically, for, as Lawrence Lipking points out, if readers are the addressees and if they imagine the poet's living hand reaching toward them, "most . . . will strain toward Keats in sympathetic grasping."[11]

At the same time, all these assertions of the immediate are complicated by the unresolved paradoxes and ambiguities of the conclusion. A number of distinguished critics have commented acutely but not decisively on whether the living hand is extended as a peace offering or the dead one as a threat; the question of in what senses if at all the hand is present is further troubled by the issue of whether the addressee is in fact the reader after all, or a character in a play, or, as critics formerly assumed, Fanny Brawne.[12] However one resolves these dilemmas and disagreements, a corpse's hand is certainly vividly invoked in the course of the lyric, and it thus, as it were, gestures toward further complications in discussing and defining presence. For it reminds the reader that presence in the sense of a vividly realized image may be a sign of absence and loss in other senses: the corpse's hand can be here precisely when and because the living hand cannot, much as the poststructuralists have repeatedly emphasized that words, like other surrogates, testify to the lack of what they introduce.[13]

If, then, as the lyric by Donne on which this essay opened and Keats's poem both demonstrate, putative presence may assume a range of unstable forms, so too can its opposite number. I am defining mediatory elements for the purposes of this essay as textual strategies that delimit or distance the immediacy of a lyric, typically through a type of intervention or standing between—encasing that pressing hand in a glove, as it were. But versions of mediation vary in their structure from a headnote to the introduction of another voice, and in their effects from evading anticipated judgments of the text to showcasing such evaluations.[14] Certain methods of mediation, however effectively they distance the text in some instances, can heighten an impression of immediacy under different circumstances or even increase and diminish it simultaneously within the same passage of a poem—thus further complicating definitions of immediacy and its opposite number. Metapoetic allusions to holding the poem as a physical object, for instance, can both intensify and qualify the presentness of lyric. If we pursue Helen Vendler's argument that Shakespearean sonnets like 35 incorporate previous remarks by the self and respond to those made on a prior occasion by the addressee, that sequence exemplifies how the overlapping of temporalities can evoke both distance and immediacy.[15] Above all, reminders of representation often qualify immediacy in certain respects while intensifying it in others. Mediating, we may recall, implies bringing about or conveying, and sometimes part of what it effects is a different version of immediacy.

A brief and necessarily selective survey of some recent discussions of presence and its discontents can further clarify the definitions and approaches informing this essay. The putative presence of lyric has been anatomized—and celebrated—from a range of perspectives. Discussions of *Erlebnis,* still powerful despite the many attacks on them, stress the speaker's consciousness and voice more than its rhetorical impact on the reader; and in the sense of a realized subjectivity, the latter remains a crucial concept, especially in analyses of modern poetry.[16] Committed to emphasizing the figural elements in lyric, especially prosopopoeia and related figures, many other critics attribute presence—or apparent presence—to their handwork. Thus in an influential analysis of apostrophe, Jonathan Culler focuses on its role in producing "a detemporalized space with forms and forces which have pasts and futures but which are addressed as potential presences"—in other words, many of the characteristics of lyric immediacy.[17] Yet observe how "potential" hedges the bets and allies Culler's argument more closely with how Paul de Man and others approach the limitations and even bad faith of such figures. At the same time, the concern for tactile and other forms of vividness expressed by early modern commentators has not been neglected by their counterparts today. In particular, in organizing her brilliant analysis of poetry around the five senses, Susan Stewart draws attention to its sensual and sensory presence, though she also traces how that presence can be blocked.[18]

Other commentaries have, of course, suggested from a range of perspectives that lyric is distant from actual, lived experience (and in so doing, of course, often challenged that category itself). To begin with, treatises by poets also often complicate assertions or implications of immediacy presented elsewhere in the same document. If he praises the immediacy created by *energia,* in developing the Greek concept of the poet as maker, Sir Philip Sidney of course also turns to Platonic models; he draws attention to the element of artifice in art, an element redefined, defended, and celebrated when he famously compares the golden world of the poet to that of the First Maker: "[Nature's] world is brazen, the poets only deliver a golden" (100).[19] On very different grounds Wordsworth distances poetry from the here and now, famously defining it in terms of recollected emotion, while Shelley, for all his emphasis on the incarnational force of poetry, also stresses its role in representing something prior and separate from it: "Poetry . . . reproduces all that it represents. . . . Poetry is the record of the best and happiest moments of the happiest and best minds" ("A Defence of Poetry").[20]

Twentieth- and twenty-first-century criticism have witnessed numerous denials and rejections of the several types of immediacy traditionally associated with lyric, many of which are germane to early modern lyric. Most obviously and influentially, the deconstructionist attack on the concept of presence, famously spearheaded by the work of Paul de Man, has often included labeling its apparent exemplification by the lyric illusory.[21] In both theory and practice the Language Poets have condemned the concept of voice in the sense of the realized subjectivity of the speaker. The more sophisticated studies of lyric time often at the very least complicate an unqualified association of that form with the present tense, and cognate complications are introduced by such practices as the one to which I will turn shortly, assigning a title.[22]

3

As the relative brevity with which I summarize those and related debates suggests, my primary goal in this essay is neither to produce an alternative theoretical position nor even to engage at length with previous ones: I aim to explore how and why effects of immediacy and, even more important for our purposes, distance are produced in a given historical period, rather than the transhistorical potentialities and betrayals of language. To begin with, then, the dialogue between immediacy and distance in early modern lyrics is shaped by—and in turn helps to shape—a range of sources, notably rhetorical treatises. Those roots are, however, somewhat tangled by the verbal and conceptual similarities between the concepts of *enar-*

gia, which can roughly be translated as a vividness that makes it possible to see in the mind's eye, and *energia,* which suggests activity or energy.

Describing the workings of *enargia,* Quintilian declares that "vivid illustration, or, as some prefer to call it, representation, is something more than mere clearness, since the latter merely lets itself be seen, whereas the former thrusts itself upon our notice."[23] In the same book he goes on at some length to discuss how these intense portrayals, created by specified rhetorical figures, move the listener and "[place] a thing vividly before the eye" (8.3.81). In book 3, chapter 3, of his *Arte of English Poesie,* George Puttenham seconds Quintilian's emphasis on vigor when he tries to distinguish *enargia,* which appeals only to the ear, from *energia,* which involves sense: to the latter he attributes "strong and vertuous operation . . . efficacie by sence."[24]

Both the focus on an energetic depiction and the concern with its rhetorical effect on the reader recur when Sidney famously observes, "But truly many of such writings as come under the banner of unresistible love, if I were a mistress, would never persuade me they were in love; so coldly they apply fiery speeches, as men that had rather read lovers' writings . . . than that in truth they feel those passions, which easily (as I think) may be betrayed by that same forcibleness or *energia* (as the Greeks call it) of the writer."[25] Whereas "betrayed" could simply signify "to reveal" in early modern English, it is tempting to wonder whether Sidney's preoccupation with the treacheries of love, of rhetoric, and of their interrelationship unwittingly impelled his choice of the term (and no less tempting to observe that when its more common sense is adduced here, Sidney anticipates the poststructuralist emphasis on how apparently effective language in fact undermines itself).[26]

In any event, all of these early modern passages explicate how their authors conceive immediacy: it is produced by vivid descriptions, in language that evokes stereotypically male characteristics, and it is analyzed in terms of its rhetorical agenda, that is, in terms of how it shapes the reader's responses. More to my purposes here, these discussions gesture toward some reasons for the seesaw between immediacy and distance posited by this essay. The efficacy of contrast, a commonplace of rhetorical theory, argues for playing vivid passages against less intense ones; the hints of aggressive control, or even manipulation, of the reader activate anxieties indisputably common in early modern England about the dangerously suasive power of rhetoric, and hence could impel the writer to disown or at least distance its effects (as Sidney arguably does through the double meaning of "betrayed").

In addition to the impact of rhetoricians, a number of practices distinctive of though not unique to early modern England encouraged the juxtaposition of effects of immediacy and of distance. Thus certain genres popular in the period lend themselves well to impressions of immediacy in several of the senses I have enumerated. Religious poetry often involves invoking or attempting to body forth a scriptural event, a point to which I will return shortly, while the agenda of songs in masques is often calling forth a presence, the aesthetic analogue to the machinery that literally brought forth nymphs and goddesses. Famously demonstrating the affective intensity of so much devotional poetry, Robert Southwell's "Burning Babe" gives presence to the vision through repeated tactile references to heat; among the clearest of many instances of both the instrumentality and immediacy masques associate with lyric is the moment in Thomas Campion's *Lord Hay's Masque* where we are explicitly told that trees move in response to it.

Less familiar but no less important are the period's distinctive approaches to mediating immediacy and to combining an impression and a denial of presence. To begin with, many early modern poets avoided one potential strategy for creating distance, attaching a title to their work: Ben Jonson was one of the earliest poets regularly to assign his own titles, and the practice was by no means universal in the seventeenth century.[27] Yet to say that authors often did not add titles to their works does not deny that printers and scribal copyists often did so, thus creating cognate effects of distance. No better example exists than the opening poem of the pastoral collection *Englands Helicon*: the addition of the title "The Sheepheard to his chosen Nimph" to a song from Sidney's *Astrophil and Stella,* not identified in that context as pastoral, positions the reader as observer, looking out onto—and down into—Arcadia.[28] And, indeed, recent materialist work encourages us to look more closely at the visual effects of a book and hence at the ways not only authors but also printers and publishers contributed to impressions of immediacy and distance. In the 1595 edition, the heavy borders surrounding the sonnets of Spenser's *Amoretti* as well as the individual stanzas of his "Epithalamion" set them off and help to establish them as artifacts. Not only title pages but also so-called half-titles, the pages within a book that introduce individual texts, could have similar effects.

Moreover, despite—and precisely because of—many authors' difficulty in attaching a title, the period saw certain cognate practices that filled some of the same functions. Headnotes and other paratextual materials similarly may instruct the reader on how to approach the text, in so doing distancing her from it.[29] An introductory poem, such as the opening sonnet in Spenser's *Amoretti,* may situate the reader and complicate or qualify the immediacy of what ensues; in this instance, the sequence is turned into an object that the lady holds, making it immediate by literally creating that pressing of hands but distant by emphasizing that it is a material object. This type of framing is analogous to the introduction of a second speaker; witness, famously, the opening of Marvell's "Damon the Mower" and the conclusion of Milton's "Lycidas."

Similarly, many metapoetic devices create an effect of distance by drawing attention to the text's status as a text, sometimes by referring to the act of singing or writing, sometimes by embedding a lyric within another one. The poem-within-a-poem in Spenser's "Prothalamion" is a case in point, one example from so many. Refrains vary among themselves in many ways; in particular, they sometimes refuse but, more to our purposes here, often assume a mediatory function.[30] They may, for example, draw attention to their own status as a frame. And if, as I have demonstrated, other types of mediatory elements may contest the presentness of lyric by introducing different time sequences, refrains trope temporality, representing as they do a form of repetition that also looks backward to previous occasions and forward to future ones.

Moreover, certain texts and traditions that were exceptionally popular in the period both encouraged and modeled mediatory strategies. Psalms 1 and 2 arguably represent a type of headnote or frame for the ensuing poems; Dante's *Vita nuova* provided an influential precedent for an authorial decision to situate a lyric in relation to some sort of explanatory prose; many sixteenth-century editions of Petrarch's *Rime sparse* demonstrated editorial glosses; and the emblem tradition exemplified the interaction among different types of representation that gloss and extend each other.[31] Especially significant was the widespread familiarity with the Geneva Bible, which went through nearly 150 editions between 1560 and 1644; the commentaries with which it framed lyrics anticipated paratextual headnotes, while in this, like other editions of the Bible, the metapoetic references to singing and to the status of the current text as a poem throughout the psalms also anticipated widespread practices in both spiritual and secular lyric.[32]

Theological traditions also influenced more indirectly the early modern dialogue between techniques evoking immediacy and those suggesting distance. Often debated not only in this but in earlier eras was a broad and multifaceted problem: the extent and ways scriptural events could be immanent in the mind of the believer, alive in her or his culture, or both.

Liturgical events were seen as happening in the present even though they were associated with a distant historical moment and with recurrent previous celebrations of it.[33] The artistic practice, common in both the Middle Ages and the Renaissance, of portraying historically specific biblical stories in a contemporary setting implies the presentness of the Christian past; in a painting by Duccio in the Frick Museum, for example, the devil tempts Christ in a locale with recognizable Sienese buildings, while in Rogier van der Weyden's famous canvas *St. Luke Drawing the Virgin,* that disciple has the artist's features, and the people outside the window look like his, not Mary's, contemporaries. Even devotional works that do not explicitly evoke their own culture often do so implicitly, in that the type of frame used in altarpieces typically incorporates architectural elements, implying that the figure within it is, as it were, alive and well in that very church at that very moment.[34]

Indeed, a number of theological treatises and traditions devote themselves to ways our ability to re-create and represent scriptural events can be heightened within the parameters of its inevitable limitations. In particular, both Catholic and Reformed meditative traditions often emphasize strategies for creating a mental image of a scriptural event or character. One stage in the Ignatian meditation is the *compositio loci,* in which one pictures the place being contemplated, attempting to create physical immediacy.[35] Also highly influential in early modern England, as Barbara K. Lewalski insists in her corrective to an exclusive focus on Catholic writings, were the extensive Protestant writings on meditation.[36] The significance of these issues in early modern England was intensified by their connection to two distinct but related theological cruxes especially germane to the relationship between effects of immediacy and distance: the eucharistic debates about Real Presence and the millennial controversies.[37] Arguably, the tensions generated by these debates are present as a significant though subterranean undertow when even secular early modern lyrics attempt to negotiate the relationship between presentness, representation, and distance.

4

The workings of each of the poetic strategies and practices through which early modern texts create our dialogue between versions of immediacy and of distance might fruitfully be the subject of an essay in its own right. But as Helen Vendler has taught us by both precept and example, often one of the best arenas for studying questions about poetic technique is the complexity of a given text. Both the motivations for producing the intertwined effects in question and the strategies available for doing so are exemplified by the first song in Lady Mary Wroth's *Pamphilia to Amphilanthus*.

In this lyric a shepherdess laments the betrayal and inconstancy of her lover. But the ontological status of that lament is changed in the concluding stanza. Here, anticipating her own death, she concludes with the lines that she hopes will appear on her tombstone:

> And thes lines I will leave
> > If some such lover come
> Who may them right conseave,
> > And place them on my tombe:
> She who still constant lov'd
> > Now dead with cruell care
> > Kil'd with unkind dispaire,
> And change, her end heere prov'd.
> > (41–48)[38]

Thus the poem demonstrates that it is through the very interaction of immediacy and distancing that certain issues central to lyric are expressed. In this instance, the text stages in that way a problem of interest to many critics today, the relationship between the immediacy of voice, emphasized by the recurrence in close conjunction of the word "sayd" (17, 21), and the permanence, or apparent permanence, of writing.[39] The issue of stability in love mirrors that of the stability of texts recording love; the poet who ended the 1621 version of this sequence with a tribute to constancy here evokes a speaker who wants to create a tribute to her own constancy in a medium that will itself have the immutability, or apparent immutability, of inscription. But the feasibility of that project is no more certain than the survival of true love: even if a lover does come, she or he may not "conseave" (43) the lines rightly, and that in turn raises the question of how readers will "conseave" the lines. Moreover, the verb suggests not only comprehension but impregnation; the lover would be a kind of second maker, thus beginning the process of distancing the lines from the shepherdess that will culminate in the inscription.

These concerns are part of a larger semiotic preoccupation throughout the poem, the issue of what type of signs offer representation that is reliable in its message and lasting in its effects. We start with a reversal of the pathetic fallacy, so nature clearly does not always read the emotions of those within it accurately, nor can it necessarily be read as a register of those emotions; and the shepherdess proceeds to look for other signs she can deploy, announcing, for example, that the willow branches she will wear "shall my wittnes bee / My hopes in love ar dead" (27–28).

Juxtaposing this poem with others involving epitaphs reveals just how distinctive Wroth's approach to both the putative immortality of her poem and the related issues of representation, immediacy, and distance is. As William Waters has shown in his acute analysis of such lyrics, the inscription must depend on "a voice that it also, ceaselessly, hopes to ambush."[40] Or, to put it another way, the epitaph, like Keats's hand, attempts to reach out and touch someone in several senses of the latter verb. In many instances, ranging from Horace's ode 3.30 to its heir in Shakespeare's Sonnet 55 to some of the Rilke sonnets Waters analyzes, the dead person is closely associated with, if not necessarily completely identified with, the stone. But in weakening that linkage by simply expressing the hope that someone may someday carve her words on her tombstone, Wroth replicates and complicates the process of waylaying, establishing the need of two ambushes, which trope each other. She must waylay both the person who will find and inscribe the poem and that of subsequent readers—or, to put it another way, the process of representation becomes a virtual *mise en abîme,* since the shepherdess's words, already a representation, will be represented by the putative finder on the tomb, which will then represent them to onlookers in the hope that one of them will perform a version of the same process in voicing them. Observe too the way this sequence of events is further undermined: by the two conditionals in "*If* some such lover come / Who *may* them right conseave" (42–43; emphasis added), the first arguably emphasized through a spondaic or trochaic foot. In addition to the more general issues about language and immortality raised by Wroth's interpretation of the conventions surrounding epitaphs, might not these hesitations also encode Wroth's anxieties about whether her own work will be interpreted "right" (43) and about whether, for all the hermetic privacy Jeffrey Masten has found in her work, it will be widely read?[41] The related issue of exactly who is currently being addressed thus also recalls Keats's "This living hand."

These and many other questions are enacted formally through mediating devices; thus the semantic core of the poem is embodied in the techniques that variously create immediacy and distance. Most obviously, the poem is full of references to representation in its many guises, thus reminding us that what we are reading is a text and encouraging us to think how our reactions to it are a sample of the problematical relationship between speech and writing—on one level we are reading speech that is available to us precisely because it has been inscribed, and yet on another a recurrent concern of that inscription, as we have seen, is its own potential unreliability. The relationship between the immediacy of voice and writing is further complicated by our inability to determine which we are encountering at several points. That is, are we reading what is written on the bark or hearing her talk about the fact she will write on it? And in the final stanza, are we on some level reading the inscription, which is immediate in the sense of addressing us even though it is in the most literal sense inscribed, or hearing her recite what it will say, or hearing her read from a paper on which it is written?

If these alternatives evidently raise theoretical questions that recall the deconstructionist debates of the twentieth century, they also gesture toward questions about the relationships between oral delivery, scribal culture, and print culture that must have been of interest to Wroth and her readers, poised as they were at a moment when texts were transmitted in all these ways. In particular, the appeal to the person who may find the poem and reproduce it on a tombstone registers authors' dependence on those who circulated manuscripts and those who published them. One may recall in this context the conditionals cited in the previous paragraph.

Furthermore, the whole issue of immediacy is itself made immediate, pressing, by the way this lyric (much like the third song and ninth pastoral by Wroth's father, Robert Sidney) tricks the reader at least on an initial reading. That is, we are plunged into the poem by hearing a voice that delivers a transhistorical and transcultural lament: it is by no means clear that the speaker is a shepherdess or that a second figure is observing her. Then suddenly we read, "A sheapherdess thus sayd" (17), and another function of the repetition of that verb in line 21 is to intensify the abrupt distancing. A specific speaker defined by a profession shared by few if any of the readers is named; the poem is further distanced by being located in a pastoral landscape, adumbrated but not clearly established by the opening lines. In short, then, the poem creates an intense impression of the presence of the shepherdess, only to distance her and her speech through doubts about exactly what one is hearing or reading. Thus it stages in its workings its semantic core: issues about loss, betrayal, and representation, which call into question not only the promises of lovers but also the authority of the shepherdess and the reliability and permanence of her words.

5

Referring to distinctive though not unique cultural pressures such as debates about the Eucharist and distinctive though not unique poetic devices such as headnotes, this essay has examined the interplay of immediacy and distance in the early modern lyric. There, we have seen, it may enact problems central to the meanings of the text and draw on a range of poetic strategies. How, then, are the issues that Helen Vendler associates with lyric in her brilliant analyses of it—"how successful poems are put together, ideationally, structurally, and linguistically"—inflected by that interplay in the poems of other periods?[42] Two twentieth-century texts, chosen in part because, like Wroth's poem, they both thematize and enact the dialogue between immediacy and distance, can usefully introduce issues for future approaches to that large question.

As noted above, Anne Ferry traces the ways assigning a title to a poem asserts ownership and often distances both the reader and the author from the text in question.[43] The role of mediating devices like titles in negotiating the dynamic between presentness and its opposite, as well as in determining entitlement and its relationship to the sales pitch that is seduction, is nowhere more intriguing than in an analogue to early modern instances, not cited by Ferry, William Carlos Williams's "To a Young Housewife." In it the speaker watches himself watching a woman—

> Then again she comes to the curb
> to call the ice-man, fish-man, and stands
> shy, uncorseted, tucking in
> stray ends of hair, and I compare her
> to a fallen leaf.
>
> (5–9)[44]

—a process that involves implicit fantasies of seduction and the resulting guilt. Notice how the words "To a Young Housewife" fulfill many functions we have been exploring. The act of entitling of course distances the poet from the events and suggests his authority over them, thus anticipating the act of writing that is foregrounded throughout the ensuing text and in so doing introducing the appropriation of the eponymous character through poesy, an agenda trenchantly denounced by Rachel Blau DuPlessis.[45] But her argument underestimates the ways Williams's characteristic juxtaposition of different takes or images ("Then again" [5]) builds in its own critique of each of them. Similarly, the recognition that

Williams changed the title that initially appears on the lyric, "The Young Housewife," also suggests that one needs to qualify though not reject Du-Plessis's emphasis on male domination. In the revised version, the woman is established as a kind of side participant in the sense established by linguists, spoken to rather than just spoken about. If she is addressed, the agendas of the poem become more ambiguous: they encompass on the one hand a *carpe florem* injunction ("a fallen leaf" [9]) that demonstrates the connection between literary appropriation and attempted sexual appropriation and on the other a confession of the poet's dubious behavior that implicitly discourages a successful seduction. Similarly, the change in the title itself enacts those divided agendas, for the "To" draws closer to the woman, as it were reaches to press her hand, in a way that can be either a gesture of disinterested sympathy or a preliminary gambit in what is called "the olde daunce" by that energetic dancer the Wife of Bath.[46]

"I compare her" (8), like cognate metapoetic phrases in early modern poems we have examined, draws attention to the fact that we are reading a poem, that hothouse for figures of comparison. In so doing, those three words distance us from the action, much as the speaker is distancing himself by referring to rather than just demonstrating the act of comparison. But of course the phrase may refer as well to the mental act of making parallels, performed by people who are not poets, and this ambiguity is part of the point: through it Williams invites his readers themselves to compare the ways and the reasons a man may turn a woman into an image and how and why a poet does.

A similar self-consciousness about textuality in its many guises, literary and visual, shapes a lyric by a namesake of the modernist writer we just examined. "Last Things," a compelling poem in the contemporary poet C. K. Williams's recent collection *Repair,* thus offers an intriguing coda to the patterns exemplified by Donne, Wroth, and the other early modern poets whose forms of mediation are studied above. Its speaker reports that in a friend's darkroom, within a container of "dried fixative" (1), he discovered a picture of the friend's son Alex, taken by the friend the moment after Alex died. In the next stanza we learn that the existence of that photograph calls into question the bereaved father's publication of a commemorative book containing another, earlier, picture with a caption reading, "This is the last photo of Alex" (6). Acknowledging that his friend does not realize that he has seen what was in fact the later photo, the actual last picture, the poet then gestures toward connections between the potential transgressiveness of his own poem and that of the pictures; he will need to get the photographing father's permission to move, so to speak, that final photograph from what is in more senses than one a dark-room to the lit arena of the poem describing it: "Before I show this to any-one else, I'll have to ask his permission" (9). The text concludes,

> If you're reading it, you'll know my friend pardoned me,
> that he found whatever small truth his story might embody
> was worth the anguish of remembering that reflexive moment
>
> when after fifty years of bringing reality into himself through a lens,
> his camera doubtlessly came to his eye as though by itself,
> and his finger, surely also of its own accord, convulsed the shutter.[47]
>
> (10–15)

Through comparisons between and among the original photograph, the book, and the poem itself, this lyric explores contradictory interpreta-tions of aesthetic processes and achievements, all issues one encounters as well in relation to early modern lyric in particular. Art illuminates and "commemorate[s]" (4), but it violates when the photographer takes the final picture and when the poet writes about the unacknowledged one (notice the force of "pardoned me" [10]). It tells the truth or at least some "small truth" (11), but it lies through statements like "This is the last photo of Alex" (6). And more to my purposes in this essay, it is immediate ("the instant after his death" [2]) and artless ("his finger, surely also of its own accord" [15]), but it is also an object made from those immediate moments and preserved through "dried fixative" (1), an object whose representa-tions may be further distanced and distorted by a representation like that of the deceptive caption.

Taken from a collection published in 1999, the poem introduces an is-sue specific to its century and the succeeding one, the apparent truth-fulness of photography. (Of course, much as I have traced significant changes in attitudes to immediacy in the course of the early modern era, so one might fruitfully look at how that always problematical claim about photographs is further complicated as digital techniques advance.) Here, however, Williams explores the putative reliability of photography through forms of mediation common in the early modern period as well, the movement among temporalities, the imposition of a title by some-one claiming authority, and the concomitant establishment of frames that distance and often judge previous events. Temporally the poem moves rapidly among several events, including some that appear to occur in a lyric present. The temporal changes that thus occur throughout the text are part of an elaborate series of frames—or lenses—that, as that terminology suggests, deepen the connections between the crafts of poetry and photography, in so doing crystallizing questions about immediacy. On the one hand, through these frames Williams implies that art is a static material artifact, present in more senses than one, contained and containable; on the other hand, both the photographs and the lyric about them shimmer and slip because they are repeatedly evoked as representations. The text opens, after all, on a description of an object, the actual final photograph, encased within another object, the container, and associated with what is tellingly described as "fixative" (1); it moves to describing another photograph, contained within a book. Similarly, the poem begins on the incident of finding the photograph in the darkroom, an event rendered through specific, immediate details. The subsequent stanza, however, frames those impressions much as the photo itself will be fixed in the book; it records the way art itself may record and thus be a kind of fixative itself, commemorating, labeling, attaching a titlelike caption. Notice, too, the way "Before I show this" (9) functions paradoxically, recalling several metapoetic passages previously encountered: on the one hand, the proximal deictic intensifies the presentness established in so many other ways, and yet on the other, semantically the word reminds us that we are reading a representation—indeed a representation about a representation of a representation. Thus the word also establishes the senses in which the poem itself is an object that we may find, thus very similar to the original photograph and analogous to the book of photographs prepared by the father. The final word of the title, "Things," is telling.

A similar puzzle is that "ask his permission" (9) is followed not by what we might expect, "you'll know my friend gave it to me" but rather "you'll know my friend pardoned me" (10). Does this suggest that the poem was shown before or instead of the granting of permission? In that case, the line "Before I show this to anyone else, I'll have to ask his permission" (9) represents a thought on which the speaker did not act, though the reader is likely to assume he did; the immediacy of the switch to the present tense and the present moment hence involves a type of deception again comparable to the ethical questions raised about the photograph and its framing caption. And the reader, who has in effect been shown a photograph whose owner did not grant timely permission, is in a sense complicitious. Or is it implied that even that permission cannot erase what remains a violation in the poem we are reading? In short, these unanswered questions direct our attention back to the ways art may deceive, or at least not tell the whole story—a question explored throughout the lyric by its movements between apparent presence and allusions to representation.

The conclusion is in effect a commentary on and distancing of the meditations in the third strophe. The peculiar conditional "If you're reading it" (10) involves several types of distance. First of all, given that a particular "you" is reading the poem, the phrase ambiguously complicates the positionality of both speaker and audience. Does the phrase establish the possibility that the rest of the poem is also meditative, with only the possibility of a reader as an eavesdropper or bystander? Or does it pretend to honest internalized reflection in contrast to potentially rhetoricized address, thus offering another small deception in a poem about so many of them? Does it gesture toward an unspecified addressee different from the literal reader of the poem? Thus the lyric presents an analogue to the type of second-person address acutely traced by William Waters in which the poet stresses his failure to communicate: this text is halfway there, ambivalent and guarded in its relation to that model as in so much else.[48] A poem about how art attempts to communicate, it juxtaposes the apparently confident address of "This is the last photo of Alex" (6)—a reminder that deixis not only points to an object but points it out to someone, thus inviting that pressing of hands—with the uncertainties about whether the lyric does communicate to a potential reader.

Many issues and textual strategies, then, connect the two modern texts on which I am concluding to the Donne poem on which I opened and other early modern texts. Above all, we have seen that in both eras immediacy in its many senses is not the norm, not the default position from which lyric texts sometimes swerve, and not a mere ruse, but a potentiality that is variously invoked, thematized, challenged, and rejected. And in both periods many similar devices, such as recursivity and changes in verb tenses, enact the interplay between immediacy and distance so central to lyric. Continuing attention to the relationship of those two potentialities would enrich our readings of poems from many eras.

Yet obvious differences in how their interplay works in early modern as opposed to later poems also invite future study. It would be valuable, for instance, to analyze how the "patter" with which poets introduce their work at readings today fills functions analogous to those associated with headnotes in the early modern period. I have indicated the impact of early modern printing practices. How does the appearance—in both senses of the word—of a poem in an online journal contribute to effects of immediacy and distance? For if, as my opening reference to William Waters's commentary on Celan suggests, translating the word *Handwerk* from German to English is both perilous and rewarding, so too is translating the poetic strategies that variously achieve and undermine that pressing of hands when we turn from early modern poetry to its heirs and assigns in other eras.

NOTES

Portions of this essay appeared, in a different form, in my work *The Challenges of Orpheus: Lyric Poetry and Early Modern England,* copyright 2007 The Johns Hopkins University Press. That material has been reprinted with permission of The Johns Hopkins University Press.

1. Paul Celan, *Collected Prose,* trans. Rosemarie Waldrop (Riverdale-on-Hudson, NY: Sheep Meadow, 1986), 25–26.

2. William Waters, *Poetry's Touch: On Lyric Address* (Ithaca: Cornell UP, 2003), 159–61.

3. On touch in lyric, see esp. Susan Stewart, *Poetry and the Fate of the Senses* (Chicago: U of Chicago P, 2002), chap. 4 (144–95).

4. Throughout this essay I cite John Donne, *The Elegies and The Songs and Sonnets,* ed. Helen Gardner (Oxford: Clarendon, 1965).

5. In *The English Lyric from Wyatt to Donne: A History of the Plain and Eloquent Styles,* 2nd ed. (1967; rpt. East Lansing: Colleagues P, 1990), 301, Douglas L. Peterson cites the poem as an instance of its author's practice of presenting, then undercutting, fashionable attitudes; his approach is a valuable corrective to the still widespread practice of adducing biographical explanations for changes and contradictions in Donne's stance toward love.

6. John Carey, *John Donne: Life, Mind and Art* (London: Faber and Faber, 1981), 180.

7. Also telling is the way "sigh" (19) relocates what had seemed to be anti-Petrarchism on the borders of Petrarchism, demonstrating the contiguity of those movements.

8. For a more thorough discussion of these problems, see my *The Challenges of Orpheus: Lyric Poetry and Early Modern England* (Baltimore: Johns Hopkins UP, 2008).

9. As that brief summary suggests, I do not propose an equation between presence and realism, a term no less slippery and in most of its senses far less relevant to the early modern lyric.

10. *The Poems of John Keats,* ed. Jack Stillinger (Cambridge, MA: Harvard UP, 1978).

11. Lawrence Lipking, *The Life of the Poet: Beginning and Ending Poetic Careers* (Chicago: U of Chicago P, 1981), 181.

12. For fine readings of the poem that include these and other debates, see Timothy Bahti, *Ends of the Lyric: Direction and Consequence in Western*

Poetry (Baltimore: Johns Hopkins UP, 1996), 89–94; Jonathan Culler, *The Pursuit of Signs: Semiotics, Literature, Deconstruction* (Ithaca: Cornell UP, 1981), 153–54; Lipking, *Life of the Poet* 180–84.

13. Compare Culler's observation that "This living hand, now warm and capable" acknowledges the fictiveness of its own claims; his use of the term "mystification" for its workings is, however, revealing (*Pursuit* 154).

14. Paratexts such as title pages constitute another type of distancing device. On their workings, see Gérard Genette, *Paratexts: Thresholds of Interpretation,* trans. Jane E. Lewin (Cambridge: Cambridge UP, 1997).

15. Helen Vendler develops this argument at numerous points; see, e.g., *The Art of Shakespeare's Sonnets* (Cambridge, MA: Harvard UP, 1997), 185.

16. See, e.g., Emil Staiger, *Basic Concepts of Poetics,* trans. Janette C. Hudson and Luanne T. Frank, ed. Marianne Burkhard and Luanne T. Frank (University Park: Pennsylvania State UP, 1991), esp. 68. In apparent reaction against models of *Erlebnis,* Käte Hamburger insists on the immediacy of this form—but attributes it to her contention that lyric, unlike the other two modes, is experienced as a direct statement made by a real subject, not as fictive. See *The Logic of Literature,* rev. ed., trans. Marilynn J. Rose (Bloomington: U of Indiana P, 1973), 271.

17. Culler, *Pursuit* 149.

18. On deixis, see Stewart, *Poetry,* esp. 154–56, 221–22; Roland Greene, *Post-Petrarchism: Origins and Innovations of the Western Lyric Sequence* (Princeton: Princeton UP, 1991), esp. chap. 1 (22–62).

19. Sir Philip Sidney, *An Apology for Poetry,* ed. Geoffrey Shepherd (London: Nelson, 1965), 100.

20. I cite *The Complete Works of Percy Bysshe Shelley,* ed. Roger Ingpen and Walter E. Peck, vol. 7 (New York: Gordian, 1965), 117, 136.

21. For one of the most influential statements of this position, see Paul de Man, "Lyrical Voice in Contemporary Theory: Riffaterre and Jauss," *Lyric Poetry: Beyond New Criticism,* ed. Chaviva Hošek and Patricia Parker (Ithaca: Cornell UP, 1985), 55–72. Also compare Karen Mills-Courts's deconstructionist analysis of the interplay between incarnation and representation in poetry, in *Poetry as Epitaph: Representation and Poetic Language* (Baton Rouge: Louisiana State UP, 1990).

22. See, e.g., Sharon Cameron, *Lyric Time: Dickinson and the Limits of Genre* (Baltimore: Johns Hopkins UP, 1979); Anne Ferry, *The Title to the Poem* (Stanford: Stanford UP, 1996).

23. I cite Quintilian, *Institutio Oratoria,* trans. H. E. Butler, 4 vols. (Cambridge, MA: Harvard UP, 1921–22), 8.3.61–62 (future references appear in the text). For a useful overview of the concept of *energia* and Sidney's use of it, see Neil L. Rudenstine, *Sidney's Poetic Development* (Cambridge, MA: Harvard UP, 1967), chap. 10.

24. George Puttenham, *The Arte of English Poesie,* ed. Baxter Hathaway (Kent, OH: Kent State UP, 1970), 155.

25. Sidney, *Apology* 137.

26. *OED,* s.v. "betray."

27. The ways assigning a title to a text asserts ownership and may also on occasion distance both poet and reader are acutely traced throughout Ferry, *Title;* also compare John Hollander's related but different point that emblem books prefigure titles, in *Vision and Resonance: Two Senses of Poetic Form,* 2nd ed. (New Haven: Yale UP, 1975), 221–22. On Jonson's titles, see Ferry, *Title,* esp. 11–19.

28. I cite *Englands Helicon* (London, 1600).

29. On these issues, see esp. William W. E. Slights, *Managing Readers: Printed Marginalia in English Renaissance Books* (Ann Arbor: U of Michigan P, 2001); Evelyn B. Tribble, *Margins and Marginality: The Printed Page in Early Modern England* (Charlottesville: UP of Virginia, 1993).

30. On the many functions of refrains, see esp. John Hollander's important studies of refrains in chaps. 6 and 8 of *Melodious Guile: Fictive Pattern in Poetic Language* (New Haven: Yale UP, 1988).

31. For this reading of the opening psalms, see James Limburg, "Psalms," *The Anchor Bible Dictionary,* ed. David Noel Freedman et al., 6 vols. (New York: Doubleday, 1992), 524.

32. On the reflexiveness of the psalms, see Harold Fisch, *Poetry with a Purpose: Biblical Poetics and Interpretation* (Bloomington: Indiana UP, 1988), 118–20.

33. For a useful discussion of this and related beliefs, see A. B. Chambers, "'Goodfriday, 1613. Riding Westward': Looking Back," *John Donne Journal* 6 (1987): 193–94.

34. On changing practices of framing pictures, see Rayna Kalas, *Frame, Glass, Verse: The Technology of Poetic Invention in the English Renaissance* (Ithaca: Cornell UP, 2007); and her essay "The Language of Framing," *Shakespeare Studies* 28 (2000): 240–47.

35. See Louis Martz's influential study of the Ignatian meditative tradition, *The Poetry of Meditation: A Study in English Religious Literature of the Seventeenth Century,* rev. ed. (New Haven: Yale UP, 1962). Also see A. D. Cousins, *The Catholic Religious Poets from Southwell to Crashaw: A Critical History* (London: Sheed and Ward, 1991); the issue of immediacy is discussed on 32.

36. Barbara Kiefer Lewalski, *Protestant Poetics and the Seventeenth-Century Religious Lyric* (Princeton: Princeton UP, 1979), chap. 5 (147–78).

37. Debora Kuller Shuger, *Habits of Thought in the English Renaissance: Religion, Politics, and the Dominant Culture* (1990; rpt. Toronto: University of Toronto Press, 1997), esp. 37–41.

38. I cite *The Poems of Lady Mary Wroth,* ed. Josephine A. Roberts (Baton Rouge: Louisiana State UP, 1983).

39. Christina Luckyj has acutely traced the positive valences within the paradoxical treatment of silence in Wroth's poetry, demonstrating its association with female agency. Although these associations are not immediately present in the text at hand, their presence elsewhere in the sequence further complicates the

categories of speech and writing. See *'A moving Rhetoricke': Gender and Silence in Early Modern England* (Manchester: Manchester UP, 2002), 140–46.

40. Waters, *Poetry's Touch* 112.

41. Jeffrey Masten, "'Shall I turne blabb?': Circulation, Gender, and Subjectivity in Mary Wroth's Sonnets," *Reading Mary Wroth: Representing Alternatives in Early Modern England,* ed. Naomi J. Miller and Gary Waller (Knoxville: U of Tennessee P, 1991), 67–87.

42. Vendler, *Art* 12.

43. Ferry, *Title,* esp. chaps. 1–2.

44. *The Collected Poems of William Carlos Williams,* ed. A. Walton Litz and Christopher MacGowan, 2 vols. (New York: New Directions, 1986–88).

45. Rachel Blau DuPlessis, "'Corpses of Poesy': Some Modern Poets and Some Gender Ideologies of Lyric," *Feminist Measures: Soundings in Poetry and Theory,* ed. Lynn Keller and Cristanne Miller (Ann Arbor: U of Michigan P, 1994), 72.

46. *The Riverside Chaucer,* ed. Larry D. Benson and F. N. Robinson, 3rd ed. (Boston: Houghton Mifflin, 1987), 476.

47. C. K. Williams, *Repair* (New York: Farrar, Straus and Giroux, 1999).

48. On this type of poem, see Waters, *Poetry's Touch* 38–49.

The Bounds of the Incidental

Shakespeare's View of Accuracy

WILLIAM FLESCH

In her writing about poetry, Helen Vendler does something very rare in literary criticism, though it is as common as light in great poetry: she combines an exquisite sense of the texture of language with an unflagging attention to the depth and subtlety of the poem's thought.[1] It seems to be a remarkable and wonderful near coincidence that poets who have extraordinary command of their own poetic idiolect are also nearly always persuasive on a descriptive or conceptual level in their treatment of the world or the mind. This is not a true coincidence, however: thought is conveyed through language, and the more complete and worked out the expression of thought, the more total the resources of language, even those we wrongly regard as merely formal, it will call upon. Poetry is lost in translation because thought is lost in translation. Very little worth thinking is conveyed in wooden translations of poetry, which is why they seem wooden. Perhaps thought is a calibration of emphasis: the subtler the calibration, the subtler the thought.

Vendler's example makes the anti-Platonic point that poetic intelligence is a powerful synecdoche or proxy for intelligence in general. You can see this by contrasting great poetry with accomplished *vers de société*. It has often been said of light verse that it has to be perfect, whereas serious poetry doesn't. But I don't think this is quite the right formulation of the contrast. Light verse has to be perfect in a received form because the surprise and delight it offers is that of bringing out the perfection in the form. But the form is one we know already, and we won't feel any necessary connection between light verse and great intelligence. Praed and Calvary are wonderful but not deep, and there's no reason they should be. But it's hard to think of any skillful poetry as genuinely serious unless it manifests some serious thinking. Or perhaps it would be better to say that it's very rare to think of any serious poetry as genuinely *skillful* unless it manifests serious thinking. We could say that Swinburne and Hardy are exceptions who more or less prove the rule: Swinburne is skillful without quite sounding the depths that almost always go with such skill; and Hardy is deep without the skill that almost always seems to go with such depth.

Although Milton's note on the verse of *Paradise Lost* complains about the way rhyme hobbles communication, more significant is the converse example meter and enjambment offer. Varying the way sense is drawn out from verse to verse contributes to the expression of thought. There is some mystery to this, one which perhaps shows the relationship of thought to language—a mystery that risks vulgarization in deconstructive accounts of that relation. Perhaps one should just say here that certain moments in great poetry show that what poetry thinks about is language, but that in thinking about language it is thinking about human communication and human relation in general, and therefore about all that matters for human beings. Why else care about serious poetry or about poetry's being serious?

Vendler does care, and her interpretive practice is one in which extreme attention to the texture of language provides a way into a consideration of the thought behind and within that texture. She thinks about poetic language just as poets do; she thinks about poetic meaning just as poets do. Perhaps the most surprising application of this approach is in her book on the art of Shakespeare's sonnets, since the surprising truth she demonstrates there (and indeed everywhere) is that critics of Shakespeare's poetry have tended to scant both the formal qualities of his poetry and the thinking that it expresses, too often imagining the sonnets as clotted and unlovely bursts of emotional expression.

Since Ben Jonson, the subtlety of Shakespeare's use of poetic form has been undervalued, which means that much else in Shakespeare has been silently undervalued. Vendler counters that underestimation by showing how conscious of his own language Shakespeare is in the sonnets. His self-consciousness doesn't prevent our thinking of him as dazzlingly and inexhaustibly spontaneous, but it ought to prevent us from thinking of him as thoughtlessly spontaneous. He thought very hard about what he was saying and how he was saying it, in ways that some contemporary skeptics have denied could even have been part of his conceptual universe. Vendler demonstrates this in the sonnets. I would like to suggest ways of demonstrating and delineating this intense and minute verbal self-consciousness in the plays as well.

Such self-consciousness will be particularly visible in allusion and quotation, practices motivated by a writer's loyalty to some inextricable combination of thought and form in what he or she has read. Quotation isn't sharply discriminable from allusion since verbal echoes and conceptual echoes go together. It's for this reason too that quotation has proved fertile ground for both philosophy and literature. Literary modes of quotation, and their history, offer much interesting evidence to philosophical treatments of the subject, while those philosophical treatments can contribute to the theory of literary quotation.

Quotation always entails some issue of accuracy, and this essay originated in an attempt to come up with internal criteria for what should count as accuracy when editing Shakespeare. I'd been reading Shannon and Weaver's classic book on communication, and in particular on the relationship of signal to noise.[2] There can be no signal without noise, but this hardly undercuts the possibility of receiving a signal, and of correcting errors in the signal. One way we do this is by a process of narrowing and winnowing, a process attentive to restrictions on what the signal could be. There are two directions from which you can arrive at an approximation of the original signal: you can build up from the particular and you can descend from the general.

From the particular you can, for example, rely on redundancy as well as establish the probabilities of various ways a different sequence of signs or letters or words might continue: these are called Markov chains, and given a partial sequence you can fill in the gaps with a proportional degree of confidence. If we couldn't, we couldn't talk to each other.

From the direction of the more general, we can have a holistic sense of what a line means, say, and peg the words or the meanings of the words to make the line mean what it does. This may sound dodgy, but again it's something that we do all the time, and we couldn't learn language if we didn't do this. Quine sees words as placeholders in sentences: our understanding of sentences is prior to our understanding of words, he says (and I think he's right); words mean whatever they have to mean to make the sentences mean what they do. For the sake of brevity I won't say much more except to note that the word "sake" (which I've just used) is a canonical Quinean example of a word that we can't define individually although we know the meaning of sentences in which it appears.

Both these approaches—from the minutely particular and from the general and holistic—are already treated in Johnson's Preface to Shakespeare, where he considers what sorts of evidence make it possible to rectify the text. In the end the value of that evidence is judged by its conformity with Shakespeare's overwhelming expressiveness: "his language, not being designed for the reader's desk, was all that he desired it to be, if it conveyed his meaning to the audience." That it does convey his meaning Johnson does not doubt; in conformity with the sense of linguistic irreducibility that he observes too in the Preface to the *Dictionary*, Johnson allows for communication not term by term but line by line or sentence by sentence or speech by speech or dialogue by dialogue. It's for this reason that Johnson can lament, with justice, that "it is not very grateful to consider how little the succession of editors has added to this author's power of pleasing. He was read, admired, studied, and imitated, while he was yet deformed with all the improprieties which ignorance and neglect could accumulate upon him; while the reading was yet not rectified, nor his allusions understood."[3]

I cite Johnson (and by occasion Stanley Cavell, who makes a very similar argument from a Wittgensteinian point of view)[4] against the programmatic skepticism of recent theories of editing Shakespeare, because those theories seem to me philosophically naive. That naïveté takes the form of imagining *any* uncertainty in establishing a text as undermining all certainty in the text; that is, *any* noise vitiates the possibility of receiving the signal at all. The most radical form that such a claim takes is Jonathan Goldberg's provocative assertion that any inconsistency ruins the possibility of authorial intention; Margreta de Grazia's more plausible view, which I will take issue with below, asserts rather that the idea of intention or textual accuracy is anachronistic and therefore is misapplied to Shakespeare's work.[5]

The more radical view has already done a lot of damage to the way Shakespeare is edited, especially in the methods of Gary Taylor. In the Oxford Shakespeare's versions of the Quarto and Folio text of *King Lear* (source of the *Norton Shakespeare*), Taylor edits the Quarto "independently" of the Folio—that is to say, as though the Folio didn't exist. His justification for this odd procedure is this: because the Quarto is a separate and earlier version of the play (a position I think is obviously true), consistency demands that it be edited in just the same way as any other play text of the time. This means that Taylor is throwing out a tremendous repository of redundancy, since (let me stipulate) you can expect Quarto and Folio to be about 98 percent identical in lines that appear in both. What Taylor does is to conjecture emendations to lines in the Quarto as though there were no further evidence. But why do this? The Folio is there to clarify the vast majority of conundrums in the Quarto (and vice versa, which is actually important).

It is, in fact, disingenuous for Taylor to claim that he edited the Quarto independently of the Folio, since it appears he used the Folio apotropaically: that is, any solution the Folio offers is a solution that Taylor will try to reject if he can find another one instead. To take one example, the Quarto text has

DUKE. You know not why we came to visit you?
REGAN. Thus out of season, threatning darke eide night, . . .

But they're not threatening the night (not even Lear will do that). The Folio corrects this to the more reasonable and more beautiful

COR. You know not why we came to visit you?
REG. Thus out of season, thredding darke ey'd night . . .

Rather than emending the Quarto by referring to the Folio, Taylor offers his own correction *instead of* the Folio's, changing not the erroneous "threatning," but the correct "thus," so that Regan's line comes out as "*This* out-of-season threat'ning dark-eyed night." The line is nearly incoherent; though plausible, it is clearly a bad conjecture when compared to the Folio's correction. True: few editors would conjecture the emendation of threatning to thredding without some textual support, but here they have textual support, support that Taylor (consistently) spurns.

To argue as I do that there's a right way to revise the Quarto, and that the right way to do it is to refer to the Folio, is to argue for a robustness of signal or meaning or accuracy which the skeptics deny. One reason for that denial, as I've indicated, is their contention that the very idea of such robustness is anachronistic, and that Shakespeare would not have recognized it. It seems peculiar to think that he revised carefully without caring for accuracy—at best that argument cuts both ways—but I think we can go further by considering how Shakespeare treats the relation between original and reproduction within his own works. What I claim we'll find is a fairly subtle idea of meaning as a robustly distributed global feature of lines or sentences, rather than the vulgar-deconstructive atomistic idea that any change, no matter how incidental, has radical results. For editing Shakespeare, my principle would suggest that when it's easy to make two versions of a line mean the same thing you should. Not perhaps an exciting principle, nor should it be, but a conclusion that allows for an idea that is ultimately *literary*: lines are not concatenations of individual characters but literary expressions, expressions of literary ideas.

Let's say that one criterion for the literary is that it's the quotable, that some intrinsic thing within it elicits a desire in its audience to quote it (and such things as epigraphy, emblem books, and florilegia, as well as Longinus's treatise *On the Sublime,* show that this is not an anachronistic idea). Then the question of quotation, where the nature of verbal accuracy and fidelity is also an issue, becomes relevant and its practice illuminating.

What counts as quotation? From one highly influential philosophical point of view, quotation is a rigid inscription or hieroglyph[6] (though in practice philosophers are far less rigid than editors of diplomatic editions). But the peace bought by this near-mechanical idea of quotation comes at the cost of anything that makes it interesting, in particular the fact that people quote because what they quote conveys a *meaning* in addition to referring to an object (the original). Outside of titles, quotations are almost never merely *mentioned* in well-formed sentences, except for very particularized reasons, as in Lady Capulet's line "Marry, that 'marry' is the very theme / I come to talk of," to which I'll return, or for comic effect. Quotations are not merely mentioned, they are used as well, in obvious and transparent ways, and we are therefore much more able to parse an ordinary sentence like this:

(1) Vendler says her aim is to "tether Stevens's poems to human feeling."[7]

than a monstrosity like this:

(2) "Tether Stevens's poems to human feeling" is a predicate Vendler appends to the subject of her aim.

I want to argue that one important way of understanding how we ordinarily quote is to see direct quotation as conceptually derived from indirect discourse, rather than the other way around. In that case (1) would be a kind of tightening up of this:

(3) Vendler says that her aim is to tether Stevens's poems to human feeling.

with (1) conveying the added information that those last six words are her very own.

To see quotation as a variety of indirect discourse is to raise again the question of what counts as quotation. How much of what counts as quotation is governed by meaning, and how much by reference?

The history of practices of direct quotation shows a general evolution toward more minute reproduction of the original, so that now anything in quotation marks claims to be a word-for-word and often letter-for-letter reproduction of the quoted original (with most or all accidentals—e.g., hyphens when words are broken at the end of prose lines—regarded as relatively insignificant). It took the relatively recent use of inverted commas to frame quotations for this convention to take hold, but even through the mid-nineteenth century direct quotation might change the pronouns *and the tenses* in a quotation (most familiar now probably in Austen and Thackeray; I'll return to the question of tense shortly). Before this use of inverted commas, quotations were often not so obviously separate from the language quoting them; while citations from *other* texts were often italicized, reported speech was marked by a speech tag contiguous with part of the speech. ('Vendler says' is the speech tag in this sentence: "Vendler says, 'the loop of co-creation between Ashbery and his readers is indispensable.'") This contiguity occurred at only one edge (so to speak), so that at its other edge a reported speech could easily merge with indirect discourse or indeed with its reporting context.

Before inverted commas, and even for a century after their use became widespread, the practice of verbatim quotation had not been definitively institutionalized. Verbatim quotation goes back furthest in biblical quotation and exegesis, where the text is sacred and, according to Saint Bonaventure, so saturated with meaning that every letter counts. Even so, themes and mottoes derived from the Bible could be rendered in abbreviated, lapidary form for sermons and emblems, and in paintings containing what John Sparrow calls "visible words." But the scrupulosity that scholarship began applying to the texts of antiquity was not felt to apply to modern works, whose meanings were local, vivid, and secular.

A historically flexible view of quotation in a work of literature would therefore include anything indicated by a marker of quotation, generally a speech tag. The changing use of the marker records the changing history of quotational norms. Markers indicate what those norms were, and how they changed. The accuracy of the quotations doesn't verify or falsify the markers; the markers conform to prevailing standards of accuracy, for which they are therefore evidence. Moreover, markers are of ontogenic and not only phylogenic interest: you can see, looking at individual writers, individuated canons of accuracy. These are sometimes conscious (as when Trollope quotes a modified version of an earlier speech or sentence as a kind of urbane abbreviation or elegant variation for purposes of narrative felicity),[8] sometimes not (as when Freud misquotes his own account of his dream of "Irma's injection," changing "some" to a more convenient "three"),[9] but liable to be of great interest in either case. (Proust is particularly good at varying the same remembered utterance as a kind of tone poem of the rememberer's varying attitude and mood.)[10]

Self-quotation certainly affects editorial decisions. A garbled line purporting to be a repetition of an earlier series of words can be corrected with reference to those words, a speech tag can help correct a speech prefix, and so on. More interesting are the cases where inconsistent self-quotation leads timorous editors to correct for consistency (a principle recently championed by Matthew Bruccoli). Take an example from Dante: In *Paradiso* 10.114, St. Thomas points Solomon out and, alluding to 1 Kings 3.11–12, says of him that in point of wisdom and insight, after him, *Non surse il secondo*, "A second never arose." The relevant portion of the Vulgate reads:

11 et dixit Deus Salomoni quia postulasti verbum hoc et non petisti tibi dies multos nec divitias aut animam inimicorum tuorum sed postulasti tibi sapientiam ad discernendum iudicium

12 ecce feci tibi secundum sermones tuos et dedi tibi cor sapiens et intellegens in tantum ut nullus ante te similis tui fuerit nec post te surrecturus sit

11 And God said unto him [Solomon], Because thou hast asked this thing, and hast not asked for thyself long life; neither hast asked riches for thyself, nor hast asked the life of thine enemies; but hast asked for thyself understanding to discern judgment;

12 behold, I have done according to thy word: lo, I have given thee a wise and an understanding heart; so that there was none like thee before thee, neither after thee shall any arise like unto thee.

At *Paradiso* 11.26 Thomas *explicitly* quotes himself here in order to explain his meaning, but he says he's said ("*dissi*"), *Non nacque il secondo*, "A second never was born." One copyist changed that *nacque* to the near-synonymous *surse*, which is what he'd actually said; but the change was almost certainly wrong, and *nacque* is what the majority of MSS have. Why would Dante have had Thomas alter the word, in a text about the perfection of Paradisal expressiveness? There are many possible explanations: he himself might have been quoting his own earlier passage from memory and therefore misquoted it; or he may have felt that *nacque* resonated better in the new context and was sufficiently close to *surse* that the distinction was a trivial one; or he may have allowed that expression in Paradise, rather than being dependent on external signifiers, is a matter of the telepathic transmission of intuitive meaning, as he has just explained, a nondiscursive meaning more fully covered by the pair of words than by either alone (this would be the telepathic analogue of memory in Proust). I think at least that he wished to preserve as much of the meaning of the Vulgate that he makes Thomas quote as was consistent with his own exposition, and such preservation includes a range of meaning better covered by both *surse* and *nacque*. *Surse* is closer in sound and etymology to the Vulgate's *surrectus,* but for just this reason *nacque* might provide a corrective to a somewhat false cognate when Thomas comes to explain himself. I don't have a particularly urgent argument to make here about why Dante changed the word; I wish only to show how such a change might get lost as quotational and scribal ideas of accuracy developed and changed in tandem. But I will note that Dante's instinct, like that of most adapters (Shakespeare foremost among them, as in the strange, new, but often trivial use he makes of elements in his sources not important to his plot), is to preserve lexical items even if he redistributes them, so that Dante's *secondo* (a second) preserves the Vulgate's *secundum:* by which God *seconds* Solomon's wish for wisdom.

I want to stress one remarkable aspect of the kind of self-quotation that Thomas engages in here: the artful authority with which he does it. Generally in literature when characters quote themselves, or quote other characters, whatever they quote has first occurred within the natural flow of exposition. Quotation *notices* something that has already occurred, and registers or records it. Tennyson notices what he's said when he sorrowed most: "'Tis better to have loved and lost / Than never to have loved at all," and in repeating it notices that he's said it and that he was right to say it: what he has held "true" is now the "truth."[11] The tense of the reporting verb changes: "I feel" to "I felt," but the maxim reported and quoted stays the same. (It rhymes differently, though, "all" comes to rhyme with the permanent fact of "pall" and not the more tentative experience of whatever will "befall.")

Dante's Thomas has a somewhat different kind of control over what he's saying: the phrases that he quotes already existed in a quotational state. It's a phrase that Thomas intends to return to, and that he lays down as a marker to which he'll return, although Dante (the pilgrim) can't recognize this. We can, perhaps, because we may recognize it as a quotation (from the Vulgate), and therefore as already a token and not simple expression. Thomas does change the tenses from the Vulgate's future to the past, but this is because he's confirming not what God has said but what God has done in fulfillment of what he has said, and it is this that Thomas confirms: in the event, none after Solomon has arisen like unto him. The quotational object, the token, that Thomas displays gives him authority over the conversation, since he has objective and complete knowledge of the topic of conversation: the citation from scripture. What he says comes from the Vulgate and therefore has a preestablished design and objectivity. His earlier utterance isn't conceptually prior to its quotation: they are equally tokens of something objective, tokens that Thomas *possesses* and can perspicuously point out when he chooses to. He doesn't express himself: he displays thoughts already made objects (a truth we learn about thought in *Paradiso*).

Of course all that I've said about Thomas here applies equally to Dante the poet. Self-quotation of this sort foregrounds the work as artifice, in a way that's intrinsically interesting, rather like addressing the reader. Here quotation works not as a sign of the death but of the agency of the author. Joyce does something oddly similar in *Ulysses* at the only moment where the text acknowledges itself as structured. The structure is palpable everywhere but declares itself directly almost nowhere. This is one of the hallmarks of modernism: the refusal of the text to take itself as an object in the world it describes. (The gamelike self-referentiality of postmodernism is in its way also such a refusal.) But in the "Sirens" chapter of *Ulysses,* we read:

> Leopold cut liverslices. As said before he ate with relish the inner organs, nutty gizzards, fried cods' roes while Richie Goulding, Collis, Ward ate steak and kidney, steak then kidney, bite by bite of pie he ate Bloom ate they ate. (269)[12]

This was "said before" at the beginning of the "Calypso" chapter:

> Mr Leopold Bloom ate with relish the inner organs of beasts and fowls. He liked thick giblet soup, nutty gizzards, a stuffed roast heart, liverslices fried with crustcrumbs, fried hencods' roes. Most of all he liked grilled mutton kidneys which gave to his palate a fine tang of faintly scented urine. (55–56)

"Sirens" repeats the "said before" formulation four times, and the interesting thing is we don't know (in this third-person narrative) whom to imagine noting the repetition. But whoever it is has *read* the relevant passages; whoever it is acknowledges, and perhaps (if it is Joyce) controls *Ulysses* as a book and not as the flow of its incidents. At moments like these in Dante and Joyce the practice of quotation and that of composition are equally authoritative; the authority of the originator is marked by the fact that he or she is producing a text *for* quotation, and that authority is established and confirmed at the moment of quotation. Dante and Joyce both mime the tacit and natural idea that texts are transcriptions of experience, but both will show that even that apparently passive or derivative practice of quotation which Barthes cited as proving the death of the author is in fact an assertion of the writer's design and authority.

Shakespeare's discrepant self-quotations, which I'll focus on for the rest of this essay, present a much more complex case than Dante's or Joyce's, not least because plays *are* in the form of transcripts of the events they present. I take delight in discovering them as a subject of analysis, and offer them just for the pleasures of the local and particular. Nevertheless, I'll end by making a more general polemical contention, but one of less importance, perhaps, than the peculiar idiosyncratic flares of insight that each one can spark.

Let's begin with an easy and obvious one, the Nurse in *Romeo and Juliet* tells the story of Juliet's first fall, dilating it through three wistful variations:[13]

> Yea, quoth he, dost thou fall upon thy face?
> Thou wilt fall backward when thou hast more wit,
> Wilt thou not, Jule?
> .   .   .   .
> Wilt thou not, Jule? quoth he;
> .   .   .   .
> Yea, quoth my husband, fall'st upon thy face?
> Thou wilt fall backward when thou comest to age;
> Wilt thou not, Jule?
>
> (1.3.41–43, 55–57)

The invariant—the wonderful core of her memory, is her husband's "Wilt thou not, Jule?" and the report of Juliet's reply (which she will pun on in her response as well): "It stinted and said Ay." A word about these variations.

Variations *within* the lines given to a single character cannot escape notice and question by the actor memorizing them, so they are certainly not accidental. There are at least two main reasons for their occurrence. They lend variety of expression to a single meaning, a desideratum both for the Nurse and for Shakespeare—for any storyteller. And they tend to make the performance of the speech easier on an actor, who won't get flummoxed and repeat or skip as he recites the lines, as he might well do if the formulation is exactly the same each time (the mobile placement of the speech tag "quoth he," "quoth my husband" helps with this as well).

On the other hand, difference in one character's quotation of what another one says can't be explained by the hypothesis of ease of memorization (quite the reverse, in fact), and other reasons must come into play. Thus, again in *Romeo and Juliet,* when the Nurse reports Tybalt's death, Juliet thinks Romeo has died too, and demands of the skies:

> JULIET: For who is living, if those two are gone?
> NURSE: Tybalt is gone, and Romeo banished.
> (3.2.68–69)

Juliet takes some time to assimilate the news, and hold it all in her mind. Forty lines later she recollects Romeo's banishment:

> Some word there was, worser than Tybalt's death,
> That murdered me. I would forget it fain,
> But O, it presses to my memory
> Like damned guilty deeds to sinners' minds!
> Tybalt is dead, and Romeo banished.
> (3.2.108–12)

Why the change from "gone" to "dead"? Its advantages are clear: Juliet's rhetorical question at line 68 falls flat formulated as "Who is living if those two are dead?" since the answer is too obviously "everyone else." The adjective "dead" is a common one and doesn't have the effect her actual line gives of a sense of the world as a place of universal *absence.* The Nurse picks up on her word "gone" in replying "Tybalt is gone," and that repetition shows how the dialogue between them is finally getting traction. They are actually responding to each other for the first time in the scene. But her repetition of the Nurse's "word" would make no sense couched as direct quotation—"Tybalt is gone and Romeo banished"—since it would sound simply as though both Tybalt and Romeo had left Verona, and the antithesis is harsher than that. Moreover, the context of the second in-stance of the line no longer suggests that being "gone" means being "dead" (as it did earlier); but in the more explicit antithesis the removal of redun-dant context makes possible, Romeo's *banishment* takes on all the force of absence that had applied to both of them in Juliet's first formulation. The point is that the change costs little. No audience member will notice the verbal tweaking. It's the dialogic equivalent of a "cheat-cut" in the movies. Its advantages outweigh any downside.

Examples of this sort may be multiplied. Malvolio quotes Maria's false letter accurately enough throughout *Twelfth Night* that it's clear that Shakespeare refers to the actual draft and is not quoting the earlier scene by memory. Nevertheless, Shakespeare allows changes that clearly have no significance but economy, and this gesture toward economy speaks to his sense of what counts as accuracy (and of course Malvolio is a preci-sian). Thus Malvolio quotes Olivia the letter and reminds her that (as he thinks) she told him that she "wish'd to see thee cross-garter'd" (3.4.50); but this leaves out the letter's word "ever" ("wish'd to see thee ever cross-garter'd" [2.5.154]): there is a difference of aspect here from state to par-ticular event within the course of the plot. Of course Olivia's putative let-ter wasn't asking for a *signal* from Malvolio; it sought a state and not an action. But when Malvolio presents himself to her cross-gartered he does signal compliance, and his *action* is an *action* in the plot, not a state of being. The truncation of the letter focuses our attention on a particular moment in the plot, rather than a long-term change of state (like Viola's). I cite this moment as an example of Shakespeare's dramatic expertise: he consciously adjusts and tweaks the language for clarity and economy in ways that are meant *not* to be noticed. To take one more example of his professional sense of economy, the letter threatens Malvolio with Olivia's deciding to "let me see thee a steward still, the fellow of servants" (156–57), which Malvolio telescopes in his quotation into "let me see thee a *servant* still."

The point is that Shakespeare, when quoting himself, sacrifices scru-pulous verbal accuracy to other—more Shakespearean—effects. Even the quotation of a legal document may vary, so that the bond between Shylock and Antonio has several variations.[14] I imagine that when Shylock stresses "the very words," his excitement might get the better of him, or Shake-speare may be inflecting quotation with excitement. But sometimes, in a more Sidneyean or metaphysical mode, Shakespeare will himself, micro-scopically, carefully, and consciously take a text as target of recapitulation, and he rates minute verbatim reproduction low on the scale of scrupulous attention. In a witty moment in *The Rape of Lucrece* he recounts Lucrece's reaction to the picture of the treacherous Sinon with which she is trying to distract herself:

> It cannot be (quoth she) that so much guile,
> (She would have said) can lurk in such a look:
> But Tarquins shape, came in her mind the while,
> And from her tongue, can lurk, from cannot, took:
> It cannot be, she in that sense forsook,
> And turn'd it thus, it cannot be I find,
> But such a face should bear a wicked mind.
>
> (1534–40)

What the poem reports her as actually saying is this: "It cannot be that so much guile—"; at which point she interrupts herself (the comma after "guile" and the parenthetical speech tags frame her speech). The poem *then* narrates her on-the-fly revision as occurring not after "guile" but after "It cannot be": "It cannot be, I find, / But such a face should bear a wicked mind." I like the way this moment gives us an example of Shakespeare's sense of a parabolic vector or *jet* of expression ("jet" in the lovely mathematical sense), within a perceptual present of thought: like Hamlet (whom I'll consider in a bit) or Polonius ("By the mass I was about to say something"), Lucrece begins talking with a sense that she knows how she'll go on (to paraphrase Wittgenstein); and then she forsakes that sense, changes her direction, midutterance. Shakespeare, whose writing is so often improvisatory, must be describing his own experience of changing where he's going as he writes, rather than blotting lines afterward. The relevance of this moment to a calibration of the accuracy with which words record the expressions they represent is this: what she changes, what *Shakespeare* changes, is first of all the meaning of the *sentence* or *sense* of what she says. She both has and hasn't uttered the words "that so much guile": she's uttered them less than "It cannot be" but more than "can lurk in such a look." (In fact her "I find" is a speech tag substituting both semantically and metrically for his own parenthetical "quoth she.") Shakespeare has a graded sense of verbal accuracy, a sense that variation represents the "pencil" or congeries of meanings in a quoted phrase better than literal fidelity.

The reason for reformulations can be purely metrical, or they can mark a slight change in style, as in Henry IV's reformulation of a moment in *Richard II* when Richard calls

Northumberland, thou ladder *wherewithall*
The *mounting* Bullingbrooke ascends my throne,
The time *shall not be* many hours of age
More than it is, ere foul sin gathering head
Shall break into corruption . . .

(5.1.55–59)

Henry IV quotes "these words, now prov'd a prophecy":

Northumberland, thou ladder *by the which*
My cousin Bolingbrooke ascends my throne,
(Though then (God knowes) I had no such intent,
But that necessity so bowed the state,
That I and greatness were compelled to kiss.)
The time *shall come,* thus did he follow it,
The time *wil come, that* foul sin gathering head,
Shall break into corruption:

(2 *Henry IV* 3.1.70–77)

Henry (the Bolingbrooke Richard refers to) elides a full ten syllables to telescope two lines into one (a kind of rhythmic modular arithmetic). Now, some of these changes may be intentional on his part, since it would be embarrassing to him to quote Richard's strictures accurately. He modifies the opprobrious phrase "The mounting Bullingbrooke" to stress his own propinquity in blood: "My cousin Bolingbrooke." But "wherewithall" to "by the which" is strictly Shakespeare, that is to say, a fine indifference to being letter-perfect in quotation as long as the quotation continues *meter-* and *meaning-*perfect; influenced perhaps by a hyperdeveloped sense of euphony, which in any case trumps minute accuracy. I think Shakespeare winced at the repeated "shalls" in *Richard II* and explicitly revised "shall" to "will" in Henry's anaphoristic quotation. He liked the grim prophecy of vindication in the grand phrase "the time shall come," variations of which reappear in Malvolio and Gloucester ("But I shall see the winged vengeance o'ertake such children"); and having had Henry begin the resumption of quotation, he also had to indicate that the quotation *had been* resumed after the parenthesis with the medial speech tag "thus did he follow it." By using a medial speech tag he can get the rhetorical repetition and thereby also make the meter more powerful, its emphasis shifted to the beginning of the line. Leave out the repetition and you get: "The time shall come that foul sin, gathering head, / Shall break into corruption," and the unstressed "sin" makes the line tend toward doggerel. But the interruption and repetition give the pause after "will come" much more weight, and "foul sin" then takes on far greater spondaic stress, as it had with the more prominent pause in *Richard II* with its shift in direction on "ere" after "More than it is." I don't want to keep splitting hairs (though Shakespeare does): the main point is that when Shakespeare's characters quote, they will frequently preserve meter even as they adjust vocabulary and tweak rhythm. Quotation itself derives from a word meaning "to count" (as in quota or stock quotation), and *what counts* in quotation is a metrical substrate affecting the range of meanings of the words that fill it up, and not scrupulous accuracy in those words themselves.

Let me give one more example of the influence of quoting context on the accuracy of quotation. The apparition of the bloody child has told Macbeth to:

> Be bloody, bold, and resolute. Laugh to scorn
> The power of man, for none of woman born
> Shall harm Macbeth.
>
> (4.1.89–91)

When Macbeth tells his followers that he has no fear of Malcolm, he misquotes this moment:

> The spirits that know
> All mortal consequences have pronounced me thus:
> Fear not, Macbeth. No man that's born of woman
> Shall e'er have power upon thee.
>
> (5.3.4–7)

The misquotation here is misleading, to both Macbeth and the audience. Where the bloody child has ended the line on "born," Macbeth subordinates that word to "woman," which is where the sleight of hand occurs. But the rest of the reformulation is purely a matter of accurate-enough quotation, appropriate to the new context. "No man" abbreviates "the power of man, for none," with the word "power" picked up in line 7; the apparition's direct object "Macbeth" becomes a vocative here, and so on. I suspect that Shakespeare didn't bother to compare the speeches, since he didn't need to, but the *fact* that he didn't need to is what I am contending for.

It's worth noting that Macbeth ascribes the quotation to a plural speaker—"The spirits that know"—not to the singular bloody child (whom he does badly to forget). The plurality of the utterers quoted suggests a *generality* in quotation, the generality that consists in treating a quotation not as a specific object but as an instantiation of a less highly articulated kind or type, and it is this more general form that I wish to bring out. Shakespeare, like almost all writers who quote themselves (Joyce being a notable exception, but an exception who represents an extremely modern view of quotation), is more intent on getting "th'effect" as Hamlet says when Horatio asks him to quote his letter, than the "as's" (or "assis") right.[15] Getting what someone says right, rather than verbatim, is the most important desideratum in moments of self-quotation.

Moreover, Shakespeare is explicitly conscious of this fact. Thus Hamlet, justly taken by Robert Weimann as the articulator of a great deal of theatrical doctrine that Shakespeare is interested in, asks the Player to speak a speech to him:

> One speech in't I chiefly loved—'twas Aeneas' tale to Dido—and
>   thereabout of it especially when he speaks of Priam's slaughter. If it
>   live in your memory, begin at this line—let me see, let me see:
>   The rugged Pyrrhus, like th' Hyrcanian beast—
>   'Tis not so, it begins with Pyrrhus:
>   The rugged Pyrrhus, he whose sable arms . . .
>
>   (2.2.445–52)

—and then Hamlet knows how to go on. The moral of this moment, for our purposes, is that Hamlet can remember and love a speech even without remembering its *content* (compare this with Wittgenstein's critiques of William James's idea of memorization and mental content in *Zettel* and in his writings on the philosophy of psychology: Wittgenstein is precisely interested in showing that "knowing how to go on" is something different from having a sort of textual representation of content spread out before the mind's eye); Hamlet thinks of speeches as prior to lines, and indeed as being made up of *lines* not words, where what counts as a line is first of all a *rhythm* (think of Winnie in Beckett's *Happy Days* or the characters in *All That Fall*: "What are those marvelous words? And something something laughing loud amid severest woe"); of course words themselves finally *matter*, as what will fill a line out properly and make its meaning and its purpose work. Quine says that sentences are prior to words, and we can say that in Shakespeare lines are prior to words. "Wherewithall" and "by the which" are interchangeable.

I should add that what Hamlet is forgetting Shakespeare almost certainly remembers from Marlowe's *Dido Queen of Carthage*—her speech to Aeneas in angry denunciation of his cruelty to her: "Tigers of Hyrcania gave thee suck," which is a direct translation from the scene in the *Aeneid* that Marlowe also quotes in Latin. The whole of the Player's speech is a pastiche of Marlowe and might be thought of as at the limits of what still looks like quotation of some sort.

These are limits Shakespeare treats within the internal quotation in his own works as well, where a more important determinant of accurate communication is the *situation* in which one character is speaking to another (as when Henry IV quotes Richard to Vernon). We are to take it that Hal is, or thinks he is, representing himself accurately when he tells his father of his address to the crown when he thought his father dead. We have heard him say:

> O polished perturbation, golden care,
> That keep'st the ports of slumber open wide
> To many a watchful night! . . .
>   O majesty,
> When thou dost pinch thy bearer, thou dost sit
> Like a rich armor worn in heat of day,
> That scald'st with safety. . . .
>   (4.5.23–25, 28–31)

Hal now accurately reports that he has addressed the crown, but in different words:

> The care on thee depending
> Hath fed upon the body of my father;
> Therefore thou best of gold art worst of gold.
> Other, less fine in carat, is more precious
> Preserving life in medicine potable;
> But thou, most fine, most honored, most renowned,
> Hast eat thy bearer up.
>   (4.5.158–64)

Hal has many reasons to rephrase his speech, and Shakespeare has two more: to avoid repetition as confusing to an actor (as I've mentioned), and as otiose to an audience. Nevertheless, we can take it that Hal is fulfilling a canon of accuracy here in reporting to his father what he had said. Another example—nondramatic this time, so it's not a question of sparing an actor a potential moment of confusion—may be found in *The Rape of Lucrece,* where her report quoting Tarquin's threat of death and shame paraphrases but in no way verbally reproduces the original. Tarquin's speech and Lucrece's quotation of Tarquin's speech end with the same word—"infamy"[16]—but they get there by different but isomorphic routes, as skaters (to use an image from both Henry James and John Ashbery) trace different arabesques to a common end.

I'll conclude by making my polemical point about the editing of Shakespeare. De Grazia, Stallybrass, Goldberg, and still more radical editors of Shakespeare like Gary Taylor and Andrew Murphy have a vulgar-deconstructionist idea that in demonstrating the intense modifications made by editors of a constitutively corrupt text they may strike a blow against the sanctification of a kind of "living Shakespeare," and against the editorial fantasy of the lawful magic that would permit such a resurrection or re-naissance. I can disagree most clearly by citing a passage from *Shakespeare Verbatim,* where de Grazia disparages the idea

> that Shakespeare will in the end be revealed in all his pristine and unmediated purity. For his texts have never appeared unattended, not even in the first quartos and First Folio, not even in editions featuring no apparatus whatsoever. Some mechanism, stated or unstated, will always prepare the way for their reading. . . . There can, then, be no desire to recover Shakespeare on his own terms, Shakespeare as he was before the late eighteenth-century intervention, Shakespeare before the emergence of the sovereign modern subject; for this desire belongs to the very apparatus that is under investigation; before it, or beyond the pale, it cannot even be contemplated, much less retrieved. (13)

"There can, then, be no desire to recover Shakespeare on his own terms," she writes, but I am a refutation of this claim. I do desire this. And I think my desire is coherent, since "his own terms" are not primarily words or lexemes, but rhythms, lines, speeches, ways of speaking, ways of thinking, and ways of quoting, including ways of quoting Shakespeare. The doctrine of "meaning holism" that Quine espouses and that is consonant with modern mathematical theories of communication (and thus of textual editing) doesn't and oughtn't to begin with the particular in order to rise to the general. We begin with the general, the indirect discourse that I began by invoking, and from it we derive the minute particulars that best consist with it.[17]

I make this statement in a polemical spirit, since in practice I think that *any* well-argued-for editorial choice contributes to a holistic or general sense of Shakespeare. My polemic is merely against the complacent nominalism that derives great metaphysical conclusions from jeering at the arbitrariness of minute editorial choices. Arbitrary they may be, but the very fact that they're arbitrary is an index of their relative triviality. Even so vivid an example as the one that De Grazia, Stallybrass, and Goldberg trumpet (not without special pleading), the questionable existence of the word "weird" in the epithet applied to the three witches, loses force when you consider that our modern "weird" is largely influenced by the Shakespearean background. It's not that the language makes Shakespeare: for any words that *count* in his work, any words that we are tempted to *quote,* he largely makes the language (otherwise the words wouldn't count).

NOTES

1. See, most recently, Vendler's *Our Secret Discipline: Yeats and Lyric Form* (Cambridge, MA: Harvard UP, 2007).

2. Claude Shannon and Warren Weaver, *The Mathematical Theory of Communication* (Urbana: U of Illinois P, 1949).

3. *The Complete Works of Shakespeare,* The Dr. Johnson Edition (Philadelphia: Gebbie, 1896), 2:cxxix, cxxxvii.

4. Stanley Cavell, "Skepticism as Iconoclasm: The Saturation of the Shakespearean Text," *Shakespeare and the Twentieth Century,* ed. Jonathan Bate, Jill Levenson, and Dieter Mehl (Newark: Delaware UP, 1998), 231–47.

5. See Jonathan Goldberg, "Textual Properties," *Shakespeare Quarterly* 37.2 (Summer 1986): 213–17; Margreta de Grazia, *Shakespeare Verbatim: The Reproduction of Authenticity and the 1790 Apparatus* (New York: Oxford University Press, 1991); and De Grazia and Peter Stallybrass, "The Materiality of the Shakespearean Text," *Shakespeare Quarterly* 44.3 (Autumn 1993): 255–83.

6. See John Sparrow's *Visible Words: A Study of Inscriptions in and as Books and Works of Art* (London: Cambridge UP, 1969).

7. I am quoting a whole sentence containing an embedded quotation, from Laura Quinney's *Poetics of Disappointment: Wordsworth to Ashbery* (Charlottesville: UP of Virginia, 1999), 96–97; the variations are parallel to some of those that François Recanati sets out (using a phrase from Quine) in "Open Quotation," *Mind* 110.439 (2001): 637–87.

8. From *Can You Forgive Her?* (New York: Oxford University Press, 1999):

'You are in trouble, *I fear, Mr. Fitzgerald,*' said Mr. Palliser, as soon as he was close at Burgo's feet.

Chapter LXXVII
The Landlord's Bill

'You are in trouble, *Mr. Fitzgerald, I fear,*' said Mr. Palliser standing over Burgo as he lay upon the ground. (3:369; emphasis added)

9. Compare pp. 139 and 150 of *Interpretation of Dreams,* trans. James Strachey (New York: Avon, 1968). I do not know that this has been noticed before.

10. See William Flesch, "The Shadow of a Magnitude: Quotation as Canonicity in Proust and Beckett," *Ordinary Language Criticism: Literary Thinking after Cavell after Wittgenstein,* ed. Kenneth Dauber and Walter Jost (Evanston: Northwestern UP, 2003), 49–70, on 53.

11. From *In Memoriam A.H.H.*:

I hold it true, whate'er befall;
    I feel it, when I sorrow most;
    'Tis better to have loved and lost
Than never to have loved at all.
                                (sec. 27)

This truth came borne with bier and pall,
    I felt it, when I sorrow'd most,
    'Tis better to have loved and lost,
Than never to have loved at all.
                                (sec. 85)

12. Quotations from James Joyce, *Ulysses* (New York: Random House, 1961).

13. All Shakespeare quotations from *The Riverside Shakespeare,* ed. G. Blakemore Evans (Boston: Houghton Mifflin, 1974). Here and elsewhere I have silently emended where it has seemed both correct and noncontroversial to emend. This essay is my attempt to justify such emendation.

14. From *Merchant of Venice*:

If you repay me not on such a day,
In such a place, such sum or sums as are
Express'd in the condition, let the forfeit
Be nominated for an equal pound
Of your fair flesh, to be cut off and taken
In what part of your body pleaseth me.
                                (1.3.146–51)

A pound of flesh . . .
Nearest *the merchant's* heart.
(4.1.232–33)

Nearest *his* heart, those are the very words.
(253)

15. From *Hamlet:*

HAMLET: Wilt thou know
Th'effect of what I wrote?
HORATIO: Ay, good my lord.
HAMLET: An earnest conjuration from the King,
As England was his faithful tributary,
As love between them like the palm might flourish,
As peace should still her wheaten garland wear
And stand a comma 'tween their amities,
And many such-like as's of great charge. . . .
(5.2.35–43)

The joke (on a loaded-down ass) is lost if you accept Q2-4's "As sir."

16. Compare *The Rape of Lucrece,* lines 512–39 to 1625–38.

17. Compare Wittgenstein's famous account of Moses in *Philosophical Investigations,* part 1, sec. 79:

> I shall perhaps say: By "Moses" I understand the man who did what the
> Bible relates of Moses, or at any rate a good deal of it. But how much? Have
> I decided how much must be proved false for me to give up my proposition
> as false? Has the name "Moses" got a fixed and unequivocal use for me in all
> possible cases?—Is it not the case that I have, so to speak, a whole series of
> props in readiness, and am ready to lean on one if another should be taken
> from under me and vice versa? . . . Where are the bounds of the incidental?

Trans. G. E. M. Anscombe (Oxford: Blackwell, 1997).

Reading Keats in Zambia

DEBORAH FORBES

On a first reading, Keats's "Ode on a Grecian Urn" has little to say to an American woman living in Africa in the early twenty-first century. Keats's urn is a complete and uncorrupted object. As a composite pieced together by his imagination, it has not suffered the "rude / Wasting of old time" that has disfigured the Elgin marbles.[1] The speaker of Keats's ode tells us that the urn is "leaf-fringed" and finely wrought, but we are not invited to imagine a single particle of dust settling in its crevices. Although the speaker's fervent questions help us believe there is a concrete object before him, the urn is not exactly material: not only has it been invented by Keats, but the figures that decorate its surface behave more like human beings caught in a spell of "slow time" than inanimate carvings; only in the final stanza are we reminded that they are made of marble. If the urn embodies a "beauty" that is also "truth," we could be forgiven for taking Keats to mean that both beauty and truth are defined by their opposition to the ordinary world, Platonic ideals set against the "breathing human passion" below.

The Greek ideal of beauty, with its clean lines and symmetry, is a world apart from Lusaka, Zambia, where I live. Lusaka is a place of bare patches and loose threads. The forests have been cut down to make charcoal; maize withers on the stalk; shelters are improvised from sacks that once held rations from the World Food Program. Few things hold their original form; the child who begs at my car window wears a shirt that has been mended so many times, I can hardly believe it was once whole cloth. In the dry season, dust blurs every outline. Dust from dirt roads is beaten up into the sky until the horizon disappears. Dust drifts continually into our colonial-era home through louvered windows that will not close because seasons of rain and dust have ruined the hinges. Even if I wash the dust from my skin, it still clings to the lining of my throat.

One purpose of an urn is to hold the ashes of the dead, but "Ode on a

Grecian Urn" makes no mention of this function, allowing us to wonder whether the poem means to argue that the purpose of art is to contain and conceal death, offering instead the distraction of decoration. In Zambia, where at least 16 percent of the adult population is HIV positive; the majority lack adequate nutrition, sanitation, and health care; and the average life expectancy is thirty-nine years, death cannot be ignored. It happens in friends' houses and on the street. The rituals of burial cannot keep up with the sheer number of dead, and there are no decorative vessels for what remains, only cheap plywood coffins sold by the side of the road. It is almost impossible—almost unbearable—to hold these facts next to the elegant self-reflection of Keats's poem.

And yet his book remains open on my table, and the page that gathers dust declares, "'Beauty is truth, truth beauty,'—that is all / Ye know on earth, and all ye need to know" (lines 49–50). I return to Keats's ode because what is most bewildering about my life in Lusaka is not the deprivation visible everywhere, but the impressions of beauty I continually receive. Although the dust that sifts down over Lusaka smells of burning garbage and calls to mind the ashes of sacrifices very different from the one imagined in Keats's poem, it is not ugly. I would not even call it unclean; it is too fine for that. In the late afternoon, when the sunlight deepens before disappearing, the dust gilds the trees; the air shimmers; the sky is pink and low enough to touch. I must ask, as Keats does in his ode: what does it mean to experience something as beautiful? Does this experience have any claim to a "truth" greater than itself?

This question is an urgent one, because "Beauty is truth, truth beauty" is as good a statement as any of my excuse for being in Zambia. There is my official alibi: my husband, who works for a humanitarian nonprofit, has been sent here to develop programs to combat HIV/AIDS. But my own reason for being here—the one not given but privately, haltingly discovered—is akin to what Mr. Fielding says in *A Passage to India:* "I'm delighted to be here [. . .] there's my only excuse. I can't tell you anything about fairness"; or what Francesca Marciano writes in her recent updating of *Out of Africa:* "We're like ghosts here; we can't contribute to anything, we don't really serve any purpose. We don't *believe* in this country. We are here only because of its beauty."[2] (The contrast between Fielding's and Marciano's tones suggests the mixed feelings of good fortune and self-disgust it is possible to have as an expatriate in a [post]colonial country.) What binds me to this place is the precariousness, surprise, and persistence of beauty in a country where most people live hand to mouth.

But "beauty" by itself is not a good enough excuse. Keats's ode may be the most explicit celebration of aesthetic contemplation for its own sake in the English language, but even Keats finds it necessary to introduce another value—"truth"—at the poem's end. Some readers—notably T. S. Eliot—have found the closing beauty-truth equation to be a fatal overreach that mars an otherwise admirable poem. But as more sympathetic commentators have pointed out, "beauty is truth" is as much a statement of doubt as of faith: if this is all we know on earth, it is because other metaphysical and moral certainties have deserted us.[3] Living as a white American in postcolonial Zambia, the absence of certainty is also painfully specific. I live in the same house and employ the same kinds of servants as my colonial predecessors, but I must guard against their assumption of entitlement. I cannot assume, however generous my intentions, that I can be of any use to the people I live among; I cannot assume my right to be here at all. Even my husband, with a clearer purpose, works to be invisible as he equips communities to build upon their own resilience; his job is to make himself obsolete.

In this absence of spiritual and moral certainty, I am tempted to claim that the concept of "beauty" can be expanded until it contains everything, even as I remain uncomfortably aware of its limits, as Keats does in his poem. Like many visitors to Africa, it is the natural beauty of Zambia that first disarms me. In my second month, I drive with a friend to the man-made lake that forms the southern boundary of the country. We sit on the hood of an idle motorboat, surrounded by the skeletons of drowned trees. In the stillness, the world melts down. The deep blue water turns gold until the lake and sky are seamless and all that is left are us and the stripped-down sentinel trees. Zambia possesses rich, fleeting beauty that would be at home in one of Keats's poems, such as the mahogany flowers that open only at night: one breath and their liquid scent fills you and is gone. Then there is the everyday beauty of subtropical abundance—for an expatriate in Lusaka, life is strolling through the fruit-and-vegetable markets with a basket balanced against your hip, marveling at the sweetness of the strawberries, the cheapness of the roses.

But these are a tourist's snapshots. Like Keats, I soon feel the limitations of scenery,[4] and my gaze turns to the people who live against its backdrop. I own a painting that reminds me of driving toward town from the outskirts of Lusaka in the early evening. Figures emerge from and recede into the dusk beneath an enormous, streaked sky. They are ordinary figures: a woman balancing a basket on her head, plastic shopping bags in both hands; a man looking back at a settlement of concrete two-room houses; a child squatting at the edge of the road in some private game. I could say that these figures are beautiful because, underneath that im-probable but accurate sky, they are emblematic of our smallness on this earth; I could say that they are beautiful because of the lived life each face implies. But the truth is at once more simple and more difficult to understand. To me, the figures are beautiful because of their mysterious self-sufficiency; they form a whole of which I am not a part but have the chance to see as whole.

They are beautiful because, like the figures on Keats's urn, I see them in tableau. The main concern of his poem is what this way of seeing feels like, and what it possibly may mean. This preoccupation first becomes clear in the second stanza, where the speaker meditates on the peculiarly limiting immortality of the carved figures:

> Fair youth, beneath the trees, thou canst not leave
> Thy song, nor ever can those trees be bare;
> Bold lover, never, never canst thou kiss,
> Though winning near the goal—yet, do not grieve;
> She cannot fade, though thou hast not thy bliss,
> Forever wilt thou love, and she be fair!
>
> (15–20)

The youth and his beloved transcend time not because the sculptor has made them exceptionally beautiful or pointedly emblematic, but because they are literally outside human time by virtue of being carvings. It is the observer's formal distance from the "fair youth" that makes the youth seem exceptional, and the urn as a material object matters only insofar as it provides a convenient way to meditate upon this distance.[5] Here we be-gin to understand that the "beauty" the poem means to endorse is not the Greek ideal of proportion and order; it is not something that inheres in an object at all. Keats makes no mention of the (fictional) sculptor's skill; beauty is a manifestation not of the gifts of the creator but of the receptiv-ity of the viewer. (This orientation explains Keats's curious choice to name the urn, not the sculptor, as a "friend to man" at the poem's conclusion.) To conceive of beauty as an experience rather than a set of identifiable and fixed qualities dramatically expands its parameters, but also brings its very existence and meaning into question.

If we take Keats's poem, rather than the urn, as the model of this new idea of beauty, we find that the experience of beauty can be dislocating, even painful. Keats's urn is whole, but his poem is broken. It shifts tone without explanation; it starts over; it repeats itself; it leaps ahead. By the end of the poem, neither "beauty" nor "truth" (nor even "intensity" or "imagination") is a generality that can contain the speaker's Protean experiences.[6] Similarly, my assertions that life in Africa is more "real" or "elemental" than life elsewhere—no matter how good the faith in which I make them—are too vague to account for what I experience when I look around me. If there is a kind of experience that unites—or appears to unite—beauty and truth, it must take place in terms that are more concrete. Keats's ode gives us an example of these terms, and its value is the faithfulness of its fragmented surface to the specificity and unpredictability of the experience of beauty.

But the usefulness of this example in Lusaka is challenged by an important limitation. When the speaker of the ode looks at the figures on the urn and when I look at ordinary Zambian life in tableau, we both perceive beauty in part because a distance has been imposed. Life depicted on the urn is beautiful because of its suspended animation; the scene of people returning home at the end of the day on the outskirts of Lusaka is beautiful because I observe it as an outsider. In the private museum of Keats's poem, the potential moral costs of this distance recede into the background, but in Lusaka they are as pressing as the impression of beauty itself.[7] In order to feel the beauty of the scene in the painting, I must not feel too sharply the long hours the woman has likely worked, the burden of worry and frustration that the man likely carries, the hunger of the child. Being able to gaze at these figures in a painting, or from the window of a car traveling from the private game reserve where we have spent the afternoon to the comfort of our home, is a function of my privileged status. In some sense, the beauty I see in the poverty of Lusaka is a product of my exemption from it. In blinding myself—even temporarily—to the hardships implied by what I see, am I denying these hardships and the humanity of the people who suffer them? Does my pleasure in contemplation serve as an excuse for not doing something more practical to ameliorate the suffering I witness? The urn cannot address these questions.

And yet, despite the artificiality of the poem's premise—its double remove, through the mediation of the urn and the mediation of the poet's presentation of the urn, from lived experience—the ode turns again and again to the problem of suffering.[8] Most explicitly, the meditation on the fair youth gives way to "[a] burning forehead, and a parching tongue" and the climactic stanza begins, "Who are these coming to the sacrifice?" (30 and 31). This gravitational pull is not inevitable; to some extent it works against the poem's rhetoric of praise. In Lusaka, this attention to suffering reminds me that Keats's life was in many respects closer to that of the average Zambian than my own. In fact, stories similar to his can be found in the fund-raising material my husband's organization distributes, describing the plight of children orphaned by AIDS in Africa. Keats's father died in an accident when he was eight; his mother died when he was fourteen, most likely from tuberculosis (a modern scourge in Zambia). Afterward Keats and his brothers came under the unscrupulous care of a guardian who may have been guilty of what would be called "property grabbing" in today's development jargon. Keats was forced to leave school.[9] As is well known, he lost his youngest brother before he himself died of tuberculosis at twenty-five. Remembering these things does not solve the problem of whether—or how—"Ode on a Grecian Urn" addresses the moral questions raised by seeing beauty in the poverty of Lusaka, but it does suggest that these concerns are not as foreign to Keats as first appears.

The poem suggests it is possible to experience beauty so intensely that it feels like truth, but this experience is defined by instability. Beauty is produced by a formal distance from ordinary life, but this distance is continually qualified and altered by an imaginative participation in what is seen. The remainder of this essay will examine Keats's poem as a map of the possibilities of distance and participation involved in the experience of beauty—a map that I will try to use to orient myself in my own life in Lusaka. As the poem works to invent a more precise language for an experience of beauty that is also like an experience of truth, it may help me chart the moral blindness or insight that permits me to feel Lusaka as beautiful. At least Keats's ode should help me learn, as the speaker does over the course of the poem, to ask better questions.

Keats's poem opens, "Thou still unravished bride of quietness, / Thou foster child of silence and slow time." To arrive in Zambia is also to enter a place of startling quietness and slowness. I arrive in perfect ignorance of the local languages and knowing little of the local customs. Stranger still, I have left the hyperliterate world of Cambridge, Massachusetts, for a country with almost no written literary tradition. The continual buzz of opinion and interpretation falls silent. Time slows down. Though I arrive in the capital city, its rhythms are as much agrarian as urban; people are accustomed to waiting. Even the weather cannot help me get my bearings. Here there are no four seasons to suggest birth, youth, maturity, and death. Leaves turn spring green before they fall; trees bloom while everything around them withers; heat no longer means fertility. To one accustomed to the northern hemisphere, the rules of nature seem as suspended as they are in the images on Keats's urn. What can happen in this silence, this absence of landmarks?

The opening lines of Keats's poem offer an initial answer: you might idealize what you don't understand. The speaker of the ode imagines that the urn's silence is a mark of its purity. I come to Africa imagining that I will find landscapes barely touched by human industry and people with cultures that align them to the cycles of the earth. I expect to find gentleness and wisdom that has been lost in the consumerist complacency of America. I do find these things—but they are not all I find. As several interpreters have pointed out,[10] Keats's image of the "still unravished bride" carries the seeds of possible violence: the bride's "ravishment" may be imminent, and, as the closing language of the stanza suggests, ravishment is as likely to involve "maidens loth" and a "struggle to escape" as it is to excite "wild ecstasy" (8–10).

In Lusaka, the image of the virgin bride brings to mind not only my tendency to idealize this new place but a billboard at the junction between the affluent neighborhood where I live and the compound of bleak concrete houses that supplies its domestic workers. This billboard pictures a young girl (she may be seven or eleven—because of chronic malnutrition, it is difficult to guess the ages of children here) under the words, "Sex with me doesn't cure AIDS." UNICEF has put up the billboard to dispel the belief that having sex with a virgin (or, as it is sometimes put into action, raping a child) can cure the ubiquitous disease. For me, this billboard represents the flip side of my impulse to idealize—the danger of a disillusionment just as extreme. It reminds me that the people I now live among can be as mistaken and selfish and do as much damage as the people I have left behind, and that there are circumstances in which sympathetic participation is intolerable. The billboard is something that, no matter how I look at it, I cannot make beautiful.

The trouble with idealization and disillusionment is that both attitudes impose a distance between myself and the people I observe without a compensatory opportunity for imaginative participation. The speaker of the ode quickly abandons his idealization of the urn's silence for a list of surprisingly concrete questions: "What men or gods are these? What maidens loth? / What mad pursuit? What struggle to escape? / What pipes or timbrels? What wild ecstasy?" (8–10). In Lusaka I too begin to gather as much information as I can. But the poem's questions also suggest skepticism about how useful a catalog of facts can be. This passage provides us with our first description of the urn, but because this description is delivered under question marks, it brings into question the authority of our guide, who at a minimum should be able to tell us what "mad pursuit" and what "struggle to escape" he is seeing. The list of questions is the first strategy the poem develops for combining participation and distance in the speaker's attitude toward the urn: the questions simultaneously urge us to look closer and keep us at bay by withholding definite answers. The implication is that literal information is limited in its usefulness; it is more important that we learn how to dwell in suggestive questions. The problem with applying this advice to my life in Lusaka is that it may encourage me to avoid information that threatens to commit me to action, leading me instead to walk far enough away that I can remain locked in aesthetic contemplation. This problem will deepen but not be resolved as the poem unfolds.

In the next stanza, the poem begins again:

> Heard melodies are sweet, but those unheard
>   Are sweeter; therefore, ye soft pipes, play on,
> Not to the sensual ear, but, more endear'd,
>   Pipe to the spirit ditties of no tone:
>
> (11–14)

This passage expresses the hope that distance is not required in order to experience a beauty that is like truth; perhaps, instead, distance must be overcome in order to establish a direct spiritual communion between observer and observed. Visual art inadequately expresses this ideal because it requires separation between the eye and what it sees, and so for a moment the poet turns to music. Sometimes as I sit reading in our house in Lusaka, singing drifts in through the window, grows in strength, and fades away. An open truck is passing by, filled with women in crisp, bright *chitenges* and headscarves, singing at the tops of their voices. The beauty of the music comes not from individual modulations but from how completely the voices are wound together; they have made a rope of sound so strong nothing can fray it. The harmony feels as if it is being invented at that moment, uninhibited and perfectly ordered. Sitting there, I can believe that the music is part of me and I am part of it. No difference in culture or class prevents me from understanding these women, or better—there is nothing to understand, only unbroken song.

This feeling, illusory or not, cannot last. Keats's ode tells us it cannot last not only by moving directly to the passage about the "fair youth" but by linking these two sections with a colon: the illustration of the direct spiritual communion imagined in the first four lines is one of the most double-edged passages in the poem. At first, it appears that the speaker has bridged the distance between himself and the urn by assuming the feelings of the fair youth depicted upon it:

> Fair youth, beneath the trees, thou canst not leave
> Thy song, nor ever can those trees be bare;
> Bold lover, never, never canst thou kiss,
> Though winning near the goal—
>
> (15–18)

But then we remember that the poem has framed the relationship between the speaker and urn as one of similarly frustrated courtship; he too is struggling to approach his "still unravished bride." From this perspective, the speaker is not entering into the desires of the fair youth but projecting his own frustration upon him, an interpretation supported by the tension between praise and lament in these lines. The difference between these perspectives is critical: the speaker has either acted with exemplary humility or self-blinding egotism. In Lusaka, the analogous difference would be between, on the one hand, setting aside self-interest and trying to understand the feelings and needs of those we live among and, on the other, letting self-interest dictate understanding—for example, making the colonialist mistake of judging the natives to be unintelligent when we find them unintelligible. The fact that the poem packs both possibilities into the same four lines serves as a warning against the danger of contaminating empathy with projection.[11] When the speaker's dream of direct spiritual communion with the urn gives way to a more complex mixture of imaginative participation with and distance from the "fair youth," the question of the speaker's own agenda and responsibilities comes back into play.

Similarly, I cannot for long imagine myself seamlessly melded with the music of the singing women. My initial questions, like those of the poem, are brought to a close by answers that alter the feeling of mystery without resolving it. As I begin to know the people of Lusaka, I discover that as likely as not these women are singing a hymn of praise to Jesus. Here is unexpected familiarity, but also a new feeling of alienation. As a child of the Bible Belt South, whose sense of self was shaped by adoring and arguing with a fundamentalist grandfather, I have a long-running quarrel with Christianity. I know its language intimately and have rejected this language time and again for explaining my experiences to myself. Discovering that many Zambian women share this language should help me enter into their feelings, but if I have rejected this language for under-standing myself, then how can I use it to imagine the self-understanding of others? When I did not know what words were being sung (as when the urn still conveyed a melody of "no tone"), I could imagine that the music included me as completely as it included the women; its perfect otherness released me from trying to determine whether I was projecting my own desires onto the music or losing myself in it. But once the music has been translated into familiar terms, the problem of this distinc-tion returns with redoubled force, now complicated by the way in which the rhetoric of Christianity (as, for the speaker of the ode, the rhetoric of courtship) both invites a new kind of imaginative participation with the women who sing and imposes a distressingly familiar—and thus much more formidable—distance.

The music of the women is still beautiful, but my experience of its beauty is now crossed by puzzlement. The speaker of the ode appears to be puzzled as well, for in the next stanza he abandons his partial identi-fication with the fair youth and returns to the language of idealization: "Ah, happy, happy boughs!" "More happy love! more happy, happy love!" (21 and 25). The dream of full participation in the urn's toneless music be-comes its opposite: a vision of the gulf between the urn's reality and that of the speaker. The pressure of idealization reaches its breaking point and gives way to the most graphic images of suffering in the poem; the happi-ness the urn depicts is above "[a]ll breathing human passion [. . .] / That leaves a heart high-sorrowful and cloy'd, / A burning forehead, and a parching tongue" (28–30). Again, the impulse to idealize conjures up an opposing disillusionment as the possible fate awaiting the unravished bride and fair youth is made clear.

When the ode points out that the consummation of sexual love can lead to disappointment and illness, this observation evokes the existential problem that human beings are often not made happy by obtaining what they desire. In the context of Lusaka, the resonance of this line remains stubbornly literal. It brings us back to the question raised by "Sex with me doesn't cure AIDS": what can be done with that which cannot be made beautiful? The existence of needless suffering challenges the possibility of an experience of beauty all-encompassing enough to make a claim to truth. Keats's ode implies two responses to this problem. The first—perhaps inevitable—response is to accept that there are kinds of suffering that beauty cannot ease. The poem indicates this response by allowing the image of the burning forehead and parching tongue to end the stanza without any word of consolation. (In contrast, the speaker comforts the

fair youth: "yet, do not grieve" [18].) The poem's second response is to begin again, seeking a language now stripped of both idealization and disillusionment, turning an eye attuned to beauty to the spectacle of sacrifice.

We leave the frenetic exclamation points of the third stanza and return
to the realm of questions, now unfolding in slower time:

> Who are these coming to the sacrifice?
>> To what green altar, O mysterious priest,
> Lead'st thou that heifer lowing at the skies,
>> And all her silken flanks with garlands drest?
>>> (31–34)

Ritual sacrifice is one way that pain and death can be incorporated into a
larger structure of meaning. Both ritual sacrifice and art displace suffering onto a created form, allowing human beings to feel they have a measure of control. If the truth of suffering cannot always be made beautiful
in life, at least it can be incorporated into the beautiful forms of art. This
is the easiest answer to the challenge suffering poses to beauty—and it is
one that the poem will reject. These lines anticipate the coming rejection
by maximizing the distance between the speaker and what he observes; he
no longer identifies with a particular participant in the scene he beholds.

The speaker's distance from the sacrificial procession he observes is
matched by the scene's distance from actual suffering. The bloodshed and
waste of death are replaced by a "green altar," "silken flanks," and "peaceful citadel." The only intimation of animal pain comes from the heifer's
"lowing at the skies"—not only does this sound fail to express the pain
the animal will feel, but it risks distorting the cost that the sacrifice will
exact. If we experience the suffering of another as an atmospheric "lowing," a soundtrack that gives poignancy to a lovely landscape, our sense of
beauty becomes complicit in that suffering. This is the darkest possibility
of my experience of beauty in Zambia: that its depth comes because of its
proximity to human pain and death, not in spite of these things. If the
intimation of suffering can become a stimulant to those who are callous
to the full meaning and impact of loss, the antidote is a more complete
extension of imaginative sympathy.

The remainder of the stanza undertakes this extension:

> What little town by river or sea shore,
>> Or mountain-built with peaceful citadel,
>>> Is emptied of this folk, this pious morn?

And, little town, thy streets for evermore
        Will silent be; and not a soul to tell
            Why thou art desolate, can e'er return.
                    (35–40)

The speaker rejects the possibility, represented by the ritual sacrifice of the heifer, of death without grieving. He finds a way to participate in the grief of the scene by stretching his sympathy as far as it will go: he will mourn for every town that is emptied, every street that is silenced by every loss inflicted by time. Formal distance and imaginative participation are no longer opposing attitudes—in this passage, it is the speaker's ability to imaginatively step back from the scene depicted on the urn that allows his feelings to encompass the little town. He finds a vision of death large enough to include himself, and the haunting plural of "Who are these coming to the sacrifice?" is answered: we all are. For this, we are refused the consolation of art: neither the ritual nor the urn can contain the full measure of loss, and the poet relinquishes his claim to immortalize it in verse: "not a soul" can tell of the scope of desolation hinted at here.

In this stanza, the self-consciousness that defines every other part of the poem lifts. The first three stanzas operate under implicit, restless questions: how shall I look at the urn? This way? This way? In this fourth stanza, the grammar of questioning returns, but the questions no longer deliver equivocal bursts of information. Our guide is now confident in what he sees; he can tell us exactly what the heifer looks like and what she is doing. With the literal surface of the urn established, the grammar of questioning now evokes the problems of meaning and significance. These are questions that must be left open-ended; they cannot be definitively answered. Most importantly, these questions no longer keep the urn at arm's length but implicate the speaker directly: like the empty town, he too has been rendered silent by the impact of our collective losses.

The nearest analogy between the fourth stanza of the ode and my life in Zambia comes at the end of a day spent visiting households being helped by the organization that employs my husband. We have been accompanying foreign visitors, trying to help them understand the scale of loss these communities have suffered—many of the productive adults dead or dying, the most vulnerable left to care for each other—and also what outsiders can do to help. The households we visit consist solely of children—the parents and adults in their extended family have been lost to disease. We enter each small, dark mud hut and, as guests of honor, are given handmade stools or woven mats to sit upon. The children stand or squat shyly on the dirt floor. They point out the chickens they have been able to buy and talk about the school they are able to attend because of the organization's assistance. The visitors ask questions, take photographs, distribute small gifts. For me, these visits have a slightly staged quality—I know from my husband that preparations have to be made in advance, and that there is a risk that these preparations will distract the local staff from more pressing duties of caregiving. Entering these homes makes me self-conscious: I feel guilty about the comparative comfort of my life, guilty that the help we offer is so little, guilty that my feelings of sympathy will fade after the twenty-minute visit—and at the same time I am aware that my guilt is of little use.

Eventually we reach our last hut, half-concealed by decaying maize crops. A clear-eyed fourteen-year-old girl stands outside the door and tells us about her life: the new route she takes when walking to school to avoid "dangerous men," the search for food to feed her younger sister and brother when she arrives home. Her voice is quiet and self-assured; it carries no trace of the deprivations she endures every day. Her face—I do not think I am imagining this—is radiant. As she speaks, more children emerge from nearby huts, eyeing our white faces curiously. In parts of Africa a white person is called an *mzungu,* a word that means something like "ghost." But for a moment, standing there in the waning light, I am no longer a ghost haunting the margins of this place. My self-consciousness, my feelings of sympathy and guilt, no longer matter. I am part of the beauty of the scene, and its hope, and its suffering. I can see it as whole and be part of the whole at the same time. The sensation is almost physical, like a laying-on of hands. You belong here. This land, this people, claim you.

If I had not undergone my initial, painful self-consciousness, I would not have experienced its lifting as near miraculous. Similarly, the fourth stanza of Keats's poem would make far less impact were it not preceded and followed by the relentless self-questioning of the other four stanzas of the poem. Inevitably, self-consciousness returns. The closing stanza opens with what appears to be a retraction of the speaker's expansive vision of the urn:

O Attic shape! Fair attitude! with brede
Of marble men and maidens overwrought,

. . . .

Cold Pastoral!

(41–42, 45)

The speaker has completed the trajectory from the fantasy of unmediated communion with the urn ("Pipe to the spirit ditties of no tone") to complete disengagement from it. In the fourth stanza, the speaker's ability to step back from the scene he observes permits a fuller embrace of the loss that scene implies, but now we are reminded to be skeptical of the perspective distance provides. As the spell of the fourth stanza is broken, we can see in retrospect its limitations.[12] If grief is expanded into a realization that everything will die, it loses much of its power, which comes from the terrible specificity of loss. From a far enough distance, all human tribulation is as one, and this perspective inoculates us not only against sharp feeling but against questions of responsibility as well. These questions must return—just as feeling myself part of the world of the fourteen-year-old girl caring for her brothers and sisters does not absolve me from inquiring about my obligations as a citizen of this world.

In this context of self-criticism, the urn offers its final gesture of friendliness:

> When old age shall this generation waste,
>   Thou shalt remain, in midst of other woe
> Than ours, a friend to man, to whom thou say'st,
>   "Beauty is truth, truth beauty,"—that is all
>   Ye know on earth, and all ye need to know.
>   (46–50)

The ode has returned to the language of consolation renounced in the previous stanza. The empathy extended to the town emptied by sacrifice has been replaced by a generic statement of friendship. The speaker's role as lover—with all the questions of implicit violence, identification, and projection it raised—has given way to the more placid role of friend; what his voice gains in confidence it loses in urgency. These lines count the costs as well as the gains of a claim of shared humanity that transcends time and place.[13] An assumption of shared humanity is necessary to any act of empathy, but this assumption can also blunt our sensitivity to difference, and—as the neutered voice of the speaker suggests—blind us to the ways our own interests and desires implicate us in the human drama we claim to observe from a more expansive perspective. To feel empathy for those I live among in Lusaka, I must believe that what unites humankind is greater than what divides it: though we do not all suffer in the same way or to the same degree, our experiences of disappointment, illness, the losses imposed by time, and the ultimate loss of death give us some understanding of the grief of others. But this belief must be the means, not the end. As Keats does most persuasively in the penultimate stanza of his ode, I must continually invent new ways to imagine the experiences of others, and to guard against taking my own neutrality for granted.

It should be clear by now that the poem's closing proposition cannot be taken as a transparent statement of Keats's own beliefs. "Beauty is truth, truth beauty" is a general statement in a stanza that demonstrates the costs of generalization. It is offered as a token of universal friendship, but its content evokes the irreducible individuality of experience, and our aloneness as we try to make sense of our world. Whatever "beauty" is, the poem tells us that our sense of it comes from our unpredictable intimacy and estrangement from what we see. If it is true that our experience of beauty—with its shifting perspectives of empathy and projection and alienation and fleeting wisdom, its possibilities of generosity and selfishness and of confusing the two—is all we know on earth, then this realization is more frightening than consoling. And yet the poem's final words are words of comfort. Beauty is the quality of perception that reassures us that, however contradictory and bewildering our idiosyncratic experiences may be, sometimes, simply in themselves, they are enough. In this sense, the consolation of beauty is not a luxury but a necessity; it allows us to pause long enough to gather strength for the work of interpreting, choosing, acting. At the end of Keats's ode, we are permitted to rest only briefly; as a circular statement in a poem that resists closed forms, "Beauty is truth, truth beauty" sends us back to the beginning. All the questions must come flooding back.

If "Beauty is truth" is to remain my excuse for living in Zambia, it must lose its glibness on my tongue, its tinge of hedonism. It must serve as a reminder that I am still a beginner. My initial, fact-seeking questions have given way to more searching ones, but I must guard against a negative capability that is artificially worked up, an elaborate excuse for refusing to see in a way that will commit me to act. I must permit mystery to give way to puzzlement. I must be ready to discover that what I thought was empathetic absorption in another is only the projection of my own ego. When I step back from what surrounds me, I should do so not to push an ugly truth out of focus but to find a new way to be implicated in what I see, and—if I am lucky—to discover a vision of wholeness that has been lost. When the pressure of my self-consciousness lifts, I understand that I am living not in a place of misery but a place where creation is made new every day. I know this understanding to be unverifiable and fleeting, but I suspect it will always return. To see someone as beautiful is not the same as to ease her suffering, but our sense of beauty, if it is kept open and flexible, can help us not turn away from suffering; its truth may not be absolute, but it is a truth we can choose to live by.

Like the "Ode on a Grecian Urn," this essay cannot have a conclusion—but it is easier to show this in poetry. One assertion can be made with some certainty: Keats's poem has remained a friend to man, or at least to this woman, on foreign soil, 187 years after it was written.

NOTES

1. "On Seeing the Elgin Marbles," 12–13. All quotations from Keats's poetry are from the *Complete Poems,* ed. Jack Stillinger (Cambridge, MA: Harvard UP, 1982).

2. E. M. Forster, *A Passage to India* (New York: Harcourt Brace, 1924), 121; *Rules of the Wild* (New York: Random House, 1998), 10, emphasis in original.

3. Ronald Sharp, e.g., writes, "Since metaphysical truth cannot be certainly known, this human truth, beauty, is really the only truth there is for man, and it must be an intensity of his own making." See *Keats, Skepticism, and the Religion of Beauty* (Athens: U of Georgia P, 1979), 33.

4. Keats writes to Benjamin Bailey, "Scenery is fine—but human nature is finer" (13 Mar. 1818), and over the short course of his career turns away from Wordsworthian absorption in landscape toward a more dramatic ideal of poetry. Quotations from *Letters of John Keats,* ed. Robert Gittings (Oxford: Oxford UP, 1970).

5. In a similar vein, Grant F. Scott writes that "the ode is as much about the speaker as the urn and involves a dramatization of the circumstances of aesthetic observation." See *The Sculpted Word: Keats, Ekphrasis, and the Visual Arts* (Hanover, NH: UP of New England, 1994), 134.

6. Several commentators have suggested that Keats's epigram is not so much concerned with "beauty" or "truth" as with some elusive third term, embodied by the poem, that appears—however momentarily—to unite the two. Two possibilities, supported by language in Keats's letters, are "intensity" and "imagination." Sharp suggests "intensity" as a possible third term in the quotation above. Keats writes of *King Lear* that "the excellence of every Art is its intensity, capable of making all disagreeables evaporate, from their being in close relationship with Beauty & Truth" (letter to George and Tom Keats, 21 Dec. 1817). On imagination, Keats writes: "What the imagination seizes as beauty must be truth" (letter to Benjamin Bailey, 22 Nov. 1817). Walter Jackson Bate elaborates, "In the active cooperation or full 'greeting' of the experiencing imagination and its object, the nature or 'identity' of the object is grasped so vividly that only those associations and qualities that are strictly relevant to the central conception remain. [. . .] Hence 'Truth' and 'Beauty' spring simultaneously into being, and also begin to

approximate each other." See *John Keats* (Cambridge, MA: Harvard UP, 1963), 241. E. Douka Kabitoglou writes of "Ode on a Grecian Urn" that "the central issue is neither beauty nor truth, but imagination." See "Adapting Philosophy to Literature: The Case of John Keats," *Studies in Philology* 89.1 (Winter 1992): 126.

7. This recognition of the limits of the ode's moral urgency calls to mind the New Historicist complaint that Romantic poetry substitutes the imaginary, the aesthetic, and the merely personal for a more genuine engagement with material reality and political commitment. I do not wish to repeat this complaint, for I do not believe that the poem's silence about the historical context and political implications of its ideas is structurally necessary to its argument. Instead, accepting from the start that Keats's concerns and my own cannot be identical, I wish to seek ways that the poem's meditation on beauty and truth might apply beyond itself. This essay is an experiment in finding another way to give context and moral urgency to a poem that appears to set itself apart from such concerns.

8. Assuming for a moment that Keats's ode means to make the case that "beauty is truth," it is striking how difficult he chooses to make the task by deciding to meditate upon an invented urn. In doing so, he cuts himself off from the far easier version of beauty-is-truth evoked by the earlier Romantics. For example, when Wordsworth looks out upon a landscape and finds its beauty suggestive of "something far more deeply interfused" ("Lines Composed a Few Miles above Tintern Abbey" [96]), it is easy to accept this union of beauty and meaning because the beauty is encountered in nature. In terms of both Enlightenment philosophy and Christian theology, nature already has a claim to unite beauty and truth. In comparison, the self-consciousness of Keats's premise leaves him no recourse to theological (or quasi-theological) authority, which—for me, at least—makes the poem's engagement with the world outside itself and its quest for meaning all the more moving.

9. For an overview of this period, see the first two chapters of Bate's *John Keats*.

10. Barbara Johnson, e.g., writes, "The word 'ravished' can mean either 'raped' or 'sent into ecstasy.' Both possibilities are readable in the scene depicted on the urn." The implication of the urn's idealized silence, according to Johnson, is that "it helps culture not to be able to tell the difference between [women's violation and pleasure]." See *The Feminist Difference* (Cambridge, MA: Harvard UP, 1998), 134, 137. See also Daniel P. Watkins's *Keats's Poetry and the Politics of Imagination* (London: Associated UP, 1989), 104–20.

11. Here I use "empathy" as it is commonly used today, for example in Webster's definition: "the action of understanding, being aware of, being sensitive to, and vicariously experiencing the feelings, thoughts, and experience of another." But, as Kabitoglou points out, when the term "empathy" was created, it meant something closer to ego projection. She goes on to explain, "The truth of imaginative insight for Keats seems to lie in a total abandonment of the categories of observer/observed, when the identity of the observer as thinker and discrimina-

tor is dissolved, and consequently the distance or barrier between subject/object is collapsed[. . .]. The quality of the imaginative identification, however, has been a matter of critical dispute, and the displacement of 'self' into 'other' may bear an ambivalent character" (127). The slipperiness of the term "empathy" suggests that it is difficult to determine exactly which parts of the self are extinguished and activated when encountering a foreign object, and to distinguish between egotism and self-abnegation. The second half of Keats's second stanza bears the marks of this tension.

12. To my mind, the fifth stanza does not so much provide a conclusion as describe what happens when the main vision of the poem is over, like the end of "Ode to a Nightingale": "Fled is that music:—Do I wake or sleep?"

13. Recent historically minded commentators have made similar points. Watkins writes that "Ode on a Grecian Urn" "expose[s] Keats's occasional tendency to flatten certain issues of human oppression and human struggle into a natural conflict between the desire for immortality and the fact of mortality" (106). Michael Sider writes of the poem's closing stanza: "A [democratic] republic of taste, according to Keats, is by nature eternal and apolitical, its capacity for social change severely impeded by its timelessness[. . .]. The artistic civilization exists only as an alternative to the political world. As Keats presents it, a truly democratic republic of taste enjoys its social freedom at the expense of its historical reality." According to Sider, Keats means not to endorse this apolitical republic but instead to criticize Haydon's vision of it. See Sider, *The Dialogic Keats: Time and History in the Major Poems* (Washington, D.C.: Catholic U of America P, 1998), 163.

Fine Suddenness

Keats's Sense of a Beginning

CHRISTOPHER R. MILLER

1

Over thirty years ago, Helen Vendler proposed to imagine the "experiential beginnings" of Keats's odes, which were to be found not in the actual beginning of each poem but in some "corner" of it.[1] Seen in this way, the "Ode on Melancholy" arises from the lover's quarrel mentioned in the second stanza. Similarly, "human passion," with its symptoms of "burning forehead" and "parching tongue," afflicts the poet as he enviously confronts the marmoreal coolness of the Grecian urn. And the fugitive fantasy of easeful death in the "Ode to a Nightingale" should really be heard as the "true voice of feeling" that calls the poem into being, not a thought accidentally arrived at. Though Vendler grounds these "beginnings" in well-known facts of Keats's life, she does not lean heavily on biographical evidence or psychoanalytic speculation.[2] Rather, sadness, loss, and longing are reasonably assumed as *données* of Keats's life, and the main direction of critical interest lies in the poet's imaginative conception of those existential facts.[3]

This reconstructive approach has been a remarkably powerful one in Vendler's career. The seeds of the essay on Keats would eventually become a book that offered "conjectural reconstruction of the odes as they are invented, imagined, put in sequence, and revised"; and the idea of "experiential beginnings" would be subsumed under the poet's ongoing aesthetic concern with the formal capacities of poetry in relation to other modes of art.[4] Vendler's inquiry rests only lightly on biographical or historical details, and in the case of other poets, it need not rely on them at all. Almost nothing is known for certain about the origins and referential worlds of Shakespeare's sonnets; nevertheless, Vendler has imaginatively proposed contexts and situations for them. After her reading of Sonnet 116, I will forever teach this poem not merely as an affirmative statement about love but as a "savagely clarifying" response to a cynic who *does* admit impediments to the "marriage of true minds."[5] In a similar vein, I once heard her describe, in a lecture on Blake, the nature of the event that precedes the child's utterance in "The Lamb." Vendler explained, as many of us do, that the poem must be understood as a play on the rhetorical structure of the catechism, in which the pupil learns religious doctrine by memorizing a series of questions and answers. But she went on to explain, in her own way, that Blake's speaker was akin to the child who has just been to the dentist and must now *play* dentist with her younger sibling—or, in the absence of siblings, a compliant pet. Blake's speaker, having learned a religious lesson, exchanges the powerlessness of the pupil for the authority of the teacher by "practicing on" a captive audience.

It would exceed the limits of this essay to say how my own critical practice has its experiential origins in my dissertation adviser's teaching and writing; and in the presence of Vendler's work, one cannot help feeling somewhat like Blake's catechist, albeit with a less meek and mild audience. I would like instead to revisit Vendler's argument about Keats and focus on a particular category of experience, the very essence of a "beginning": surprise. It is this emotion that is supposed to precipitate the "Ode to Psyche"—one of two odes that Vendler excludes from her essay ("Indolence" is the other) because its origin is a "self-induced" vision of two mythical creatures.[6] Among the odes, "Psyche" presents the most discrete and narratable anecdote, as opposed to a meditation on an ancient artifact or a walk in an autumnal landscape or a mood. And yet it is precisely the self-enclosed nature of the episode that makes it immune to speculation about origins; there is no other place in the poem that might plausibly be identified as the "beginning" or prehistory of that dream vision.

Nevertheless, the shock that animates the poem is a powerful template of experience in Keats's poetry; and "surprise," along with related words like "startle," "wonder," and "amaze," is a key term. In both its etymology and in Keats's usage, the word has both mental and physical components: from the Old French verb *surprendre,* it originally meant "to overtake or seize," as in a battle; but it soon came to denote a cognitive phenomenon. Milton plays on both senses in his trope of being surprised by Sin: this is to be both actor and victim, and to feel both physically overwhelmed by an allegorical foe and mentally aware, a moment too late, of what one has done. A notable grammatical feature of the word "surprise" is that it can indicate both a physical event and a cognitive or emotional reaction to that event.

In several of Keats's early poems, surprise is therapeutic, as in the sonnet "On the Sea." Those who find their "eyeballs vexed and tired" and "ears . . . dinned with uproar rude" (11) are urged to seek sensory solace at the ocean: "Sit ye near some old cavern's mouth and brood / Until ye start, as if the sea nymphs quired" (13–14).[7] The poem, which advocates a form of creative indolence, was itself a momentary vacation from the writing of *Endymion* on the Isle of Wight in 1816. Touristic visits are predicated on sights and experiences that others have enjoyed; within that frame of predictability, Keats urges the restorative properties of surprise. There is of course a paradox in this recommendation, for the poet is essentially giving a recipe for startlement. Indeed, as I will show, the paradoxical situation of being *prepared for a surprise* is important in Keats's later poetry. No particular external event startles the brooding figure of the sonnet; rather, it is the internal phenomenon of falling out of the tidally induced reverie. To "start" is to come awake in what is understood in cognitive science as a "hypnic jerk"—the nervous spasm of those drifting off to sleep. Though this poet of bodily experience knows this to be a mere corporeal tic, he proposes a quasi-mythical beginning: the "as if" supplies a fantasist's cause for the jolt, a siren song for an Odyssean poet who has strayed off course.

The emotion of surprise defines a before and after: it not only ramifies into some other affect such as fear or joy but retroactively colors what has come before. To *start* from this hypnotic state is suddenly to realize that one has fallen into it; and to feel that one has been away a long time. Into this gap in consciousness the fantasy of singing nymphs rushes in, the daydream of a split second. In effect, "brood until ye start" means "brood until you *stop* brooding"—and resume your life with freshened perception and purpose. Keats favored the verb "start" in his poetry to denote either an emotional surprise or a physical jump. The word (derived from Germanic forms for "overthrow," "precipitate," and "overturn") acquired the sense of "begin" or "commence" in the early nineteenth century, but Keats never uses it in this sense; nevertheless, physical and mental startle reflexes are bound up with the poet's sense of a beginning. The moment certainly left an impression on Keats's friend Richard Woodhouse, who quotes it in a letter he wrote to John Taylor after hearing the poet read "Lamia": "You may suppose all these Events have given K. scope for some beautiful poetry: which even in this cursory hearing of it, came every now & then upon me, & made me 'start, as tho' a Sea Nymph quired.'"[8] In the "Ode to Psyche," the metaphor of startlement by a supernatural nymph becomes, so to speak, literal: the poetic trope of "as if" is turned into an immediate vision.

In Keats's early letters, we see a preoccupation with two forms of surprise: the ethical (the actions of other people in relation to one's expectations of human behavior) and the aesthetic (the sensory and affective impact of experience). "Nothing startles me beyond the Moment," Keats boasted in an 1817 letter to his friend Benjamin Bailey.[9] Of course: the essence of being startled is that it lasts only a moment; the experience defines a particular *kind* of moment. Beyond this obvious tautology, Keats adopts the position that whatever does surprise him in "the Moment" is quickly assimilated. Indeed, he begins the letter by discussing a letter of Benjamin Haydon's that offended Bailey, and counsels his friend to adopt a stoic stance toward the ways of the world: "What occasions the greater part of the World's Quarrels? simply this, two Minds meet and do not understand each other time enough to p[r]aevent any shock or surprise at the conduct of either party." Similarly, to his friend J. H. Reynolds, he rhetorically asks, "Why dont you, as I do, look unconcerned at what may be called more particularly Heart-vexations? They never surprize me—lord!" (22 Nov. 1817). In this counsel, Keats marks a neat cleavage—perhaps too neat—between the Heart that is vexed and the self that regards those troubles as an independent observer. To "look unconcerned" is to *regard* the disturbance without personal concern, but the intransitive sense of the phrase is not far from Keats's meaning: to *appear* unconcerned, without a visible trace of dismay.

In the realm of eighteenth-century aesthetics, on the other hand, surprise was an experience to be cultivated and valued. As Joseph Addison insisted in his series of essays "The Pleasures of the Imagination," it was the emotion signally associated with novelty.[10] In this respect, Keats's well-known axiom about poetry represents a significant corollary: "Poetry should surprise by a fine excess and not by Singularity—it should strike the Reader as a wording of his own highest thoughts, and appear almost a Remembrance."[11] We might think of surprise as *synonymous* with Singularity, in that it is brief, unique, and not to be repeated in the same way again. Here, however, Keats associates it with a "fine excess," which is experienced cumulatively, in time; and Keats's notion of "Remembrance" emphasizes this temporal dimension. In this case, Keats's ideal "surprise" is more like a shock of recognition than a shock of the new.

It is the surprise of recognition that lies at the heart of Keats's famous account of the imagination. As he writes in a letter to Bailey, the imagination is akin to Adam's dream of Eve in *Paradise Lost;* but it is also analogous to a more familiar, postlapsarian experience, one involving ordinary repetition rather than mythical creation:

. . . the simple imaginative Mind may have its rewards in the repetition of its own silent Working coming continually on the spirit with a fine suddenness—to compare great things with small—have you never been surprised with an old Melody—in a delicious place—by a delicious voice, felt over again your very speculations and surmises at the time it first operated on your soul—do you not remember forming to yourself the singer's face more beautiful tha[n] it was possible yet with the elevation of the Moment you did not think so—even then you were mounted on the Wings of Imagination so high—that the Prototype must be here after—that delicious face you will see—What a time! (22 Nov. 1817)

In this proto-Proustian episode, the moment of recognition both recaptures lost time and anticipates a "here after." Surprise here has two components: it is to be struck and delighted by the music itself; and it is to be seized with the involuntary return of forgotten thoughts and feelings. The remembered experience of hearing the singer for the first time is an elevated "Moment" in which surprise gives way to surmise: the auditory ("delicious voice") intensifies the visual ("delicious face"), and the earthly singer hints at the ethereal. The act of looking back to the first hearing of the melody brings the hearer to a moment of looking forward, to an ambiguous "hereafter"—an orthodox heaven for Bailey (who was preparing for the Anglican ministry) and something else for the agnostic poet. For Keats, there is at least an *earthly* "hereafter," or rather a hear-after: another moment in which a melody can be recalled and savored.

The curious mixture of the singularity and repetition in Keatsian surprise is particularly striking in a letter the poet wrote to his brother and sister-in-law in which he recounts a chance meeting in London with an anonymous female acquaintance, later identified by Reynolds as Isabella Jones. Keats decides to join her on a walk to Islington, where she plans to call on a friend who runs a boarding school: "As we went along, some times through shabby, sometimes through decent Street[s] I had my guessing at work, not knowing what it would be and prepared to meet any surprise."[12] In his paradoxical phrase, Keats wittily captures his mingled feelings. In one sense, to be *prepared* for any surprise is not to be susceptible to surprise at all. In another sense, the word "surprise" denotes not the unexpected or the unknown but the specific delight of a romantic liaison—in the same deliberate way that a Spenserian hero goes in search of "adventure" (a word whose etymology denotes the experience of coming upon by accident). "Surprise" is a word for a particular feeling, but here it is a noun for a genre of experience—a sly euphemism for a stage of courtship. And yet it also allows for the alternate scenario that Jones *will* disappoint him. Both possibilities, in their own ways, would be startling yet expected.

Keats's conception of surprise, as I have noted, involves repetition and recognition; and here, the expectation is that since the poet has kissed Isabella once before, he will kiss her again:

> As I had warmed with her before and kissed her—I thought it would be living backwards not to do so again—she had better taste: she perceived how much a thing of course it was and shrunk from it—not in a prudish way but in as I say good taste—She contrived to disappoint me in a way which made me feel more pleasure than a simple kiss would do . . .

Not to repeat the previous kiss is to go back to a time before the two had shared some intimacy.[13] And yet "living backwards" also has the auxiliary sense of repeating the past; and an exact repetition is of course impossible. In aesthetic terms, to kiss again would fail to recover the delectable surprise of that first kiss; and in the semiotics of courtship, as Isabella well knows, the second kiss would mean something different from the first—a deepening of a flirtation and a promise of increasing sexual intimacy. It is reasonable to conclude that the poet would prefer a "fine excess" to a Singularity—more kisses rather than just one unrepeatable and irretrievable moment. In a letter preoccupied with the boundary between gentility and vulgarity, Keats wittily describes his paramour's chaste forbearance in terms of aesthetic discrimination—a matter of "good taste." The paradox of "taste," which Keats's use of the term ruefully amplifies, is that it denotes both gustatory enjoyment and rational discrimination, both consumption and exclusion. In ethical terms, the surprise of Jones's response might be bluntly called disappointment, but in aesthetic terms, the encounter can be redeemed as a lesson in the unrepeatability of experience, the powers of expectation, and the strange delights of the unpredictable.

2

Simply put, the dream episode recounted in the "Ode to Psyche" expresses a Keatsian fantasy of being surprised in a forest: a desire that animates both the early vocational statement "I Stood Tip-toe" (in which the poet waits for sudden inspiration that never quite arrives) and the later and more worldly-wise romance of "Lamia" (in which a Corinthian youth is startled on his homeward journey by a wandering voice). In the former poem, Keats imagines being the poet who first invented the stories of Cupid and Psyche, Pan and Syrinx, Narcissus and Echo—more precisely, what it would *feel* like to be that poet. That feeling, he thinks, would be akin to "[w]hat Psyche felt, and Love, when their full lips / First touch'd" (142–43); or it would feel like the reading of a tale that "[c]harms us at once away from all our troubles: / So that we feel uplifted from the world" (139–40). In these iterations of "feel," Keats joins reader, poet, and characters in one affective circuit, a current of surprise. It is especially the *first* time that intrigues him: the moment that one is charmed with a story, the moment of poetic inspiration, the moment of erotic discovery. By proleptically joining the one-time experience of writing a poem or creating a myth with the experience of reading it, Keats imagines the surprise as perpetually self-renewing.

Though Keats well knows that he cannot be the originary poet he imagines in "I Stood Tip-toe," he nevertheless indulges in the fantasy of being that person in the "Ode to Psyche":

Surely I dreamt to-day, or did I see
　The winged Psyche with awakened eyes?
I wander'd in a forest thoughtlessly,
　And, on the sudden, fainting with surprise,
Saw two figures, couched side by side
　In deepest grass . . .

(5–10)

To faint with surprise is to lose consciousness just in the moment that the mind has been shocked into a new state of attention. What causes this reaction is not entirely clear. It might be the sight of mythical figures come to life in an ordinary setting; the interruption of a state of reverie and inattention with the jolt of the extraordinary; the voyeuristic frisson of catching lovers in flagrante; the spectacle of Cupid in postcoital repose rather than in his customary archer's stance; or the glimpse of the elusive Psyche, like the finding of a rare butterfly in its natural habitat. The figure of Psyche is herself a surprise, a fluke: the "latest born" deity in "Olympus's faded hierarchy" (24–25), too late for shrines or "antique vows" (36), and certainly a less obvious choice for poetic devotion than Keats's erstwhile favorite, Apollo. In this respect, the poet's astonishment at coming upon Psyche prefigures the reader's reaction to an ode addressed to a lesser-known mythological deity, much less a cultic hymn in the fashion of the previous century's sublime odes. In their surprising emergences on the scene—as goddess, as bard—Psyche and her poet have something in common.

The surprise in the "Ode to Psyche" might also be described as the most potent form of a mental event to be found in most of the odes: recognition. Keats glimpses Autumn toiling in the landscape ("Who hath not seen thee oft amid thy store?" [12]); declares himself to be among the few who sees Melancholy through and through ("seen of none save him whose strenuous tongue / Can burst Joy's grape against his palate fine" [25–28]); and, after some puzzlement, identifies three allegorical figures revolved in a daydream ("How is it, shadows, that I knew ye not?" [11]). All of these are forms of epiphany—literally, the appearance of a god—and might be partly inspired by scenes in epic, such as Odysseus's encounter with his disguised guardian, Athena. For Keats, they are functions of clarification and mastery—the finding of some order in the otherwise undifferentiated flow of experience. The recognition of Autumn represents the lowest interpretive level in that everyone can easily see and name the season and its stages (it is the lulled bees who will be truly *surprised* by the change). But there is a deeper level of recognition in the poem: everyone can *see* Autumn, but not everyone can *hear* her (even the deity herself must be reminded that she has her own music). To stand in a denuded landscape and hear this is to be, in the language of Keats's letter to Bailey, "surprised with an old Melody." The ode in which recognition is severely thwarted is the one in which it is most strenuously pursued. In the "Ode on a Grecian Urn," the poet's questions about the identity of the depicted figures cannot be answered; in the frustration of this historical silence, Keats can recognize and name only the urn itself. His disenchanted exclamations "Attic shape!" and "Cold Pastoral!" say, in effect, "I know what you are"—a member of a class of artistic objects, a genre of fiction, a literally cold artifact.

Curiously, the "Ode to Psyche" rhetorically doubles the shock of recognition, as if savoring what can be experienced only once. Though Psyche has been apostrophized in the first line ("O Goddess!"), and directly named in the fifth ("the winged Psyche"), the poet must nevertheless rehearse the triumph of finding Psyche with her immortal lover: "The winged boy I knew; / But who wast thou, O happy, happy dove? / His Psyche true!" (21–23). Despite the previous identifications, this structure of question-and-answer enacts a *virtual* surprise, a grammatical recapitulation of the delight of recognition and novelty. Notably, only Psyche is recognized by name, never Cupid. By this omission, Keats recalls Cupid's own wish in the story not to be seen or recognized by Psyche—even as he observes the monotheistic decorum of hymns (only one deity per poem) and the awareness that the "winged boy" is a poetic cliché that goes without saying. Psyche's surprise was to see Cupid by accident as he came to her under cover of night, and Keats recapitulates that discovery with "awakened" eyes. The adjective here functions primarily as a qualifier to suggest that the poet has had his vision open-eyed and not in a dream; but as a participle of completed action, the word also implies the cumulative effect of the surprise—the residual emotion purported to be the origin of the poem itself. It means either "awake," or "startled into a new state of wakefulness."

The rhyming of "eyes" and "surprise" in this passage is apt in that the eyes take in visual stimuli that cause surprise *and* iconically register their effect, in the widening of the lids and the arching of the brows. This dyad appears a few other times in Keats's poetry. In the tale of the cure of the "languid sick" that Keats borrows from Lemprière's Dictionary in "I Stood Tip-toe" and expands upon in "Endymion," the surprise of the lovers' reunion is mutual and general:

> And springing up, they met the wond'ring sight
> Of their dear friends, nigh foolish with delight;
> Who feel their arms, and breasts, and kiss and stare,
> And on their placid foreheads part the hair.
> Young men, and maidens at each other gaz'd
> With hands held back, and motionless, amaz'd
> To see the brightness in each other's eyes;
> And so they stood, fill'd with a sweet surprise,
> Until their tongues were loos'd in poesy.
>
> (227–35)

There is a doubleness in that phrase "wond'ring sight," for each person's newly bright eyes are a source of wonder, even as they wonderingly look out at the other. Akin to the word "surprise," "sight" denotes both event and thing—both the looking and the looked at. In the suspension of the moment, instantaneous seeing dilates into rapt *gazing,* and the conjunction of perception and emotion is caught in two couplets—both "surprise/eyes" and "gaz'd/amaz'd." The eyes might be expected to brim with tears of joy, but that sensation is displaced by a thoroughly figurative, intangible filling with "sweet surprise"—a spontaneous overflow that channels itself into "poesy"—a Keatsian trope for both speech and the alternative speech of a kiss.[14]

In the progress of poetry described in the early "Ode to Apollo" (1815), Homer performs his verses in the "western halls of gold," with an effect described as surprise: "what creates the most intense surprize, / His soul looks out through renovated eyes" (11–12). If the poets immortalized in Apollo's heaven receive the celestial gear of "adamantine lyres, / Whose cords are solid rays, and twinkle radiant fires," then it is only fitting that their eyes, too, would be "renovated." More to Keats's historical point, the renovation also refers to the English versions of Homer (Chapman's and Pope's) that bring the epic to new audiences. The poem, in other words, is as much about translation as about *translatio studii*. In this sense, the unattributed "surprize" lies on both sides: in the bard's discovery that he is still being heard in a time and place far beyond the Achaean shores, and in the modern reader's delight in discovering the poem. Throughout this early ode, there is just such an overlap between the acts of poetic utterance and reading, between the verbal world of the poem and the subjectivity of its hearers.

The act of *looking out* through a new pair of eyes is related to the act of "looking into" Chapman's translation of Homer—the experience that Keats would record in his sonnet of the following year. Here again, the eyes are the locus of discovery. The thrill of reading Homer is akin to coming upon a new ocean; and in a variation of the eyes/surprise dyad, the "eagle eyes" of "stout Cortez" rhyme with the "wild surmise" of his men. "Surprise" is an absent but implicit key word of the sonnet, affectively rendered in the iconic gestures of Cortez's staring at the Pacific and the men's reciprocal glances of silent, mutual confirmation. In these subtle bifurcations—Cortez and his men, the one (master) *and* the many (followers), outward gaze and social look, surprise *and* surmise—Keats renders the intertwined experiences of writing and reading, discovery and rediscovery. For Chapman has led Keats to this spot; and while other readers have gone before him, none has had precisely the same thoughts and feelings about the poem. The private experience of looking into a book ramifies into a sensation of looking out to a vista; and the momentary surprise of discovery is extended, temporally and cognitively, into the surmise of imaginative thought.

3

Keats was particularly drawn to record the surprise of first experiences; but those experiences are typically grounded in expectation or givenness rather than sheer chance. Poems such as "On Seeing the Elgin Marbles," "On First Looking into Chapman's Homer," and "Lines on Seeing a Lock of Milton's Hair" concern the occasion of first viewing, reading, or visiting something; and in each case, the experience is a kind of gift to a poet of modest means and few possessions: a loan of Chapman's translation of Homer from Charles Cowden Clarke, a visit to the Parthenon marbles in the company of Benjamin Haydon, a viewing of a prized lock of hair in the collection of Leigh Hunt.[15] Each poem centers on visual perception, though with different nuances: seeing the Elgin Marbles means deliberately *going to see,* as a tourist would speak of seeing Mont Blanc; looking into Chapman's Homer means *pursuing an interest,* with the studied casualness of an antiquarian or connoisseur; and seeing a lock of Milton's hair means *seeing up close,* with the empirical verification of firsthand contact. Each of these experiences comes with expectations: the beholder is *prepared* for a surprise. Within a framework of the given, however, the poet articulates an impression peculiar to him. Each of these encounters can be repeated, of course, but they can be surprises only once; and the poems on these occasions reflect this fact.[16]

In both the Elgin Marbles sonnet and the poem on a lock of Milton's hair, an experiential beginning is both overtly stated and strangely occluded. In both cases, the title flatly states the occasion, but the poem takes a circuitous path to the event. In Vendler's terms, this indirection might be described as the effect of abstract thought supervening upon the actual; but it can also, I think, be seen as a specialized case of Keatsian surprise, with its mixture of the startling and the familiar. The Elgin Marbles sonnet does not directly acknowledge the Parthenon fragments until the eleventh line, in a delayed *volta,* and then only in an offhand way. The previous lines elaborate an opening statement of indolence, ennui, and creative anxiety ("My spirit is too weak"), and when Keats finally describes the marbles, he does so in analogy to his emotional state: just as the contemplation of poetic "glories" afflicts the heart with an "undescribable feud" (9–10), so do the sculptural "wonders" in front of him cause "a most dizzy pain." Ekphrasis, then, is turned inside out: rather than giving a verbal illustration of sculpture, the poet uses sculpture as a trope to illustrate his mood.[17]

Did the Parthenon friezes cause the emotional state articulated by the poem, or only confirm a mental struggle already in progress when the poet set foot in the museum? Was the "imagined pinnacle and steep / Of godlike hardship" inspired by the marbles, or by an ongoing preoccupation? The poem's structure makes such questions of origin and causality impossible to answer conclusively; the sonnet blurs its own experiential basis even as it contemplates the marbles' orphaned state, the "rude / Wasting of old time" that erodes their link to the past. Keats's first impression of the marbles, then, cannot be treated as a discrete aesthetic experience, or isolated as an anecdote of surprise; rather, it takes part in an ongoing meditation that precedes the visit to the gallery and stays with the poet after he has left. The poet has come to the museum ready to be astonished, and the pressure of that expectation is keenly registered in his second attempt at addressing the subject, "To Haydon with a Sonnet Written on Seeing the Elgin Marbles." This poem gives further insight into why Keats might have delayed describing the sculptures directly: "Forgive me, Haydon, that I cannot speak / Definitively on these mighty things" (1–2). Keats's feelings of inadequacy and frustration—of not being equal to the task of proper ekphrasis, of insufficiently meeting Haydon's expectations of sublimity, of failing to be suitably surprised in the hovering presence of an observer—is thus formally enacted in the structure of the earlier sonnet.

The expectations of a mentor figure are once again very much on Keats's mind in the "Lines on Seeing a Lock of Milton's Hair" (1818); this time, the mentor is Leigh Hunt. In a letter to Benjamin Bailey in which he enclosed the poem, Keats explained the circumstances of its composition: "I was at Hunt's the other day, and he surprised me with a real authenticated lock of *Milton's Hair* . . . This I did at Hunt's request—perhaps I should have done something better alone and at home" (23 Jan. 1818). Christopher Ricks has located the emotional core of the poem in a feeling of embarrassment, and he is right in two important ways: as the poet's epistolary disclaimer suggests, there was some awkwardness in being asked to perform under Hunt's gaze, and the invocation of Milton might bring back uneasy memories of the overweening ambition on display in *Endymion*.[18] And yet while the poem is tinged with social discomfort, I would argue that it is the related feeling of surprise that more accurately names the precipitating event and structuring principle of the poem, and surprise that defines the problem of writing about a lock of hair that is anonymous and then suddenly named.

It was a surprise that had been planned by Hunt, of course: he set the scene of Keats's astonishment and then commissioned an enshrinement of that moment in verse.[19] Hunt had been given the lock, along with specimens from Jonathan Swift and Samuel Johnson, by his friend Dr. William Batty, and he had already written his own poetry on his prized possession.[20] In the project of making a collection, as Susan Stewart has remarked, "the more objects are similar, the more imperative it is that we make gestures to distinguish them."[21] Hunt's request that Keats write a poem on the lock might spring from the sort of competitiveness in which members of the Hunt circle wrote sonnets on assigned topics, but it also reflects the motive of differentiation that Stewart describes: to gather *other* people's reactions to the literary relic and thus to generate a verbal collection out of a material one. The specimen is, after all, only a bit of hair; the surprise of discovering its original bearer can be felt only once, and the act of gazing on it does not offer the same rewards as looking at a painting, sculpture, or other artifact. The way to multiply the value of the object is to ask others to record *their* first impressions of it; and this is precisely what Hunt does.

Hunt himself had parlayed the thrill of receiving the gift of the lock into three sonnets, which he published in his 1818 collection, *Foliage*. The first of these dramatically extends the moment into two successive surprises—the marvel of seeing the hair and the further gratification of receiving it as a gift from Dr. Batty: "I felt my spirit leap, and look at thee / Through my changed colour with glad grateful stare" (1–2). The second sonnet, the most well known of the three, meditates on the fact of Hunt's new possession; it is a kind of soliloquy that follows the scene of donation. In its dramatic immediacy, the poem recalls Macbeth's apostrophe to a hallucinatory dagger and Hamlet's soliloquy on Yorick's skull:

> It lies before me there, and my own breath
>   Stirs its thin outer threads, as though beside
>   The living head I stood in honour'd pride,
> Talking of lovely things that conquer death.
> Perhaps he press'd it once, or underneath
>   Ran his fine fingers, when he leant, blank-eyed,
>   And saw, in fancy, Adam and his bride
> With their rich locks, or his own Delphic wreath.[22]

In the fantasy of standing over Milton's shoulder, close enough to breathe on the poet's hair, Hunt indulges in a reverie of experiential origins, of being present at the creation of *Paradise Lost*. To look upon this lock of hair is to see the literally tangible inspiration that a blind—"blank-eyed"—poet took when he described the "rich locks" of his characters. After dwelling on the materiality of the hair, Hunt's sonnet transmutes it, in the sestet, into an allegorical emblem. In its ability to survive the body, its tactile softness and tensile strength, the lock of hair seems to say that "Patience and Gentleness is Power" (12). Not a memorable aphorism, but it strikingly anticipates the syntax and abstraction of another utterance attributed to an inanimate object: a few years later, Keats would make his Grecian urn say, "Beauty is truth, truth beauty." The gnomic statements of both lock and urn seem to float free of their contexts—not entirely explaining nor explained by their poems.

Called upon to record his own first impression of the lock, Keats obligingly supplies a narrative of surprise—in effect, enacting Hunt's dramatic script. But it is in subtle resistance to this script that he defers the relation of the anecdote, beginning instead with a long overture, as if he simply intended to write a hymn to Milton, or a progress of poesy in the vein of Collins's "Ode on the Poetical Character":

> Chief of organic numbers!
>   Old scholar of the spheres!
> Thy spirit never slumbers,
>   But rolls about our ears
> For ever, and for ever:
> O, what a mad endeavour
>   Worketh he,
> Who, to thy sacred and ennobled hearse,
> Would offer a burnt sacrifice of verse
>   And melody.
>   (1–10)

In its jaggedly exclamatory enthusiasm, the poem gives us a glimpse of the kind of Pindaric ode that Keats would implicitly reject the following year when he came to write his springtime odes. Perhaps resentful of Hunt's on-the-spot request, he might be rebelling against his friend's expectations by adopting this irregular form rather than writing a sonnet, the prosodic lingua franca of the Hunt circle's poetic competitions. Though Keats represents himself as being genuinely startled by the lock of hair, we might well imagine that he surprised Hunt in return—by delaying and veiling the occasion, by writing an ode rather than a sonnet, and by suggesting that the moment merely punctuates an ongoing preoccupation with his own powers. Indeed, there might be a veiled critique of the idolatrous (thus anti-Miltonic) underpinnings of Hunt's enterprise: in his reference to the futility of offering a "burnt sacrifice of verse," Keats might well have been aware from his reading of Homer that pagan burnt offerings included tufts of hair from the sacrificial animal. The surprise of seeing the lock of hair is a similarly flaring and self-consuming thing; and it is not certain that the heat generated from it can sustain a whole poem.

It is only in the final strophe that Keats reveals the occasion of the poem, draining it of the social particulars of time, place, and donor. The lock becomes a ghostly apparition, the moment distilled to a sudden shock:

> For many years my offerings must be hush'd.
>   When I do speak, I'll think upon this hour,
> Because I feel my forehead hot and flush'd—
> Even at the simplest vassal of thy power;
>   A lock of bright hair—
>   Sudden it came,
> And I was startled, when I caught thy name
>   Coupled so unaware;
> Yet at the moment, temperate was my blood—
> Methought I had beheld it from the Flood.
>   (32–41)

In quick succession, the lock visually *comes upon* the poet, without cause or donor; then the name of its bearer is aurally *caught*, without a speaker. Described more as a phenomenon than as an inert thing, the lock is inseparable from its emotional impact. In this way, it reflects the dual senses of the word "surprise" as both a discrete event and a feeling. (Other affect words, such as "anger," "grief," or "envy," do not share this characteristic.)

The gap between seeing the lock and hearing the name indicates Hunt's strategic management of the surprise. The word "unaware" marks this lacuna, and in the ambiguity of its referent, it aptly describes both the hair and its beholder. As animate as it might seem, the hair is of course oblivious to its coupling with a famous name. Like the Grecian urn, the lock is a thing orphaned from its source and unaware of its origins; its only "legend," so to speak, is a scribbled name in an envelope, and Keats would not have recognized it otherwise. In this sense, Keats registers the fact that the holy relic is after all only inert matter; like pieces of the true cross, its authenticity must be taken on faith. (Indeed, the verbal overlap in Keats's phrase "real authenticated" in the letter to Bailey registers the pressure of verification.) The poet, meanwhile, is himself "unaware" in two ways: in the broadest temporal terms, he begins his day not knowing that it will end with a surprise from Hunt's cabinet of curiosities; and within a narrower band of time, he is at first unaware of the hair's significance. Keats well knows that the lock is a strand of hair like any other, and yet he feels a frisson of material connection to the past.

Keats's surprise at learning of the lock's source must be an ephemeral sensation, and yet the experience is, in effect, described twice—just as the subject of the "Ode to Psyche" is named twice in the first stanza. It is the "hour" in which Keats feels his forehead "hot and flushed," and it is the "moment" at which his blood is nevertheless "temperate." The forehead is an apt locus of emotion for a poem concerned with a lock of hair: just as Hunt imagines himself a breath away from Milton's head, Keats touches his own. Oddly, Keats describes his own forehead as both "flushed" and "temperate," and the seeming contradiction might be resolved either as a temporal succession of sensations, or as the complex feeling of a single moment. The lock is at once both mundane and astonishing, and Keats's antediluvian trope captures this duality: on the one hand, he insists on the utter familiarity of the lock, as if he had been looking at it forever; on the other hand, he sees it is a portal to the sublimity of biblical time. "Nothing," as Keats assured Bailey, "startles me beyond the Moment."

In many ways, the poem on Milton's hair is out of proportion to its occasion; in effect, the energies and ambitions it displays were in search of the odal forms and subjects that Keats would discover the following year. In its desire to raise a cultic hymn of devotion, the poem wants to be the "Ode to Psyche"; in its meditation on the power of an object, it tends toward the material sublime of the "Ode on a Grecian Urn"; and in its commemoration of a moment of sensory and affective attention, it looks ahead to the "Ode to a Nightingale." More immediately, it seems to have inspired the poem that Keats wrote the following day, the sonnet "On Sitting Down to Read *King Lear* Once Again." Here, Keats marks a deliberate aesthetic experience rather than an unbidden shock; and the feverish forehead and burnt sacrifice of the day before are translated into the controlled fires of voluntary rereading: "once again, the fierce dispute / Betwixt damnation and impassion'd clay / Must I burn through" (5–7).[23]

4

The surprise poems I have so far mentioned all concern some object or external event; but in two notable cases, Keats took internal shocks as his subject. The sonnet "Why Did I Laugh Tonight?" and the "Ode on Melancholy" both concern sudden bursts of feeling, one mirthful, the other sad. In the case of the sonnet, it is notable that Keats would write a poem about what Wordsworth called, in one section heading of his 1807 *Po-*

ems, "Moods of My Own Mind." This phrase, in fact, stuck in Keats's own mind, for in his verse letter to Reynolds, in which he contemplates his own mercurial feelings, he closes with an apostrophe that echoes Wordsworth: "Away ye horrid moods, / Moods of one's mind!" (105–6). Around the same time, in a letter to Bailey in May of 1818, in which he profusely describes his own feelings of leaden depression, Keats apologizes for his self-indulgence: "my intellect must be in a degen[er]ating state—it must be for when I should be writing about god knows what I am troubling you with Moods of my own Mind or rather body—for Mind there is none" (21, 25 May).

Whether the mysterious laugh of the sonnet springs from the mind or from the body, the attempt to trace its microhistory is distinctly Wordsworthian; more specifically, the effort of analyzing a sudden, unbidden emotion resembles Wordsworth's "Surprised by Joy," which first appeared in the 1815 *Poems.* It is impossible to know whether Keats had Wordsworth's poem in mind when he wrote his sonnet, but very few of Keats's poems might be described as "moods of my own mind" in the Wordsworthian way that "Why Did I Laugh" clearly can. "Joy" is too strong a word for the feeling that Keats captures here, but the poem could be aptly subtitled "Surprised by Mirth":

> Why did I laugh tonight? No voice will tell:
>> No god, no demon of severe response,
> Deigns to reply from heaven or from hell.
>> Then to my human heart I turn at once—
> Heart! thou and I are here sad and alone;
>> Say, wherefore did I laugh? O mortal pain!
> O darkness! darkness! ever must I moan,
>> To question heaven and hell and heart in vain!
> Why did I laugh? I know this being's lease—
>> My fancy to its utmost blisses spreads:
> Yet could I on this very midnight cease,
>> And the world's gaudy ensigns see in shreds.
> Verse, fame, and beauty are intense indeed,
>> But death is intenser—death is life's high meed.

Like the sudden feeling of joy in Wordsworth's sonnet, the burst of laughter is an ordinary happening; it is remarkable only for its paucity of motivations. In both poems, the surprise springs from a ground of constant, unspoken grief, and it occasions a bout of self-questioning: for

Wordsworth, an inquiry about the "power" that could allow him to forget, even for a moment, that his dead daughter Catherine is not around to share his joy; for Keats, a more generalized question about how he could laugh when he is "sad and alone." In the light of Wordsworth's sonnet, Keats's silence on the exact nature of his sorrow and isolation is especially notable. His brother Tom had died of tuberculosis in December of 1818, and this event might be called the poem's blind spot, the reason why laughter would be surprising in the first place. No answer is given to the poem's insistently repeated question, but the kind of *non*answer changes through the three quatrains. In the first case, the question is asked in an utter vacuum, with neither a response nor an explanation for why the question is asked. In the second case, a reason is given for why the speaker should *not* have laughed: he is sad and lonely. Finally, the question of why he *did* laugh is dissolved in the bluff assertion of why he *can* laugh. The progression might be summarized as "Why? Why? Why *not*?" Keats's existential bravado in the conclusion echoes the boast that he had made in his letter that nothing surprises him beyond the Moment; and it anticipates the emotional stance more fully worked out in the "Ode on Melancholy."

The "Ode on Melancholy" can be read as the affective mirror image of "Why Did I Laugh Tonight?": its occasion of "the melancholy fit" is the inverse of the sudden gaiety described in the sonnet. If Keats had been thinking mythologically about his laughter, he might have turned from *asking* god or demon about its motivation to *recognizing* an allegorical figure (perhaps the Mirth worshipped by Milton's Allegro) as its source—as he does when he installs Melancholy in her shrine, spatially and temporally located amid happiness. This invention explains not the cause of melancholy but rather its nature. A laugh is an event in time and place, and an index of an emotional state; but the melancholy described in the ode is not so much a single affective occasion as an all-pervading mood—a feeling that saturates one's perceptions of the world, an emotional weather condition.

But in its onset, melancholy is also, in Keats's conception, *sudden.* Here, I am stressing the "melancholy fit" described in the second stanza, rather than the love suffering implied by the mistress's anger a few lines later. Vendler has insisted on the latter as the true occasion of the poem, and she has particularly strong support for this idea in the canceled first stanza, which depicts a doomed romantic quest launched on a Petrarchan bark. My divergence from this reading is a matter of emphasis: I do not wish to deny the lovers' quarrel as a possible cause, but I would like to consider seriously the implications of canceling that first stanza and demoting the mistress to one item (albeit a mismatched one) in a catalog. In short, I would like to propose that the experiential beginning is as mysterious and unaccountable as the strange laughter that motivates "Why Did I Laugh Tonight?"

In a string of negative commands ("No, no, go not to Lethe . . ."), the first stanza suggests a voluntary component in human emotion—urging the listener to avoid both literal and figurative opiates and soporifics, to shun both killing poisons and poisonous thoughts of suicide. These are all recommendations about what not to do in response to a melancholy state; but in the binary tradition of Milton's "L'Allegro," they also hint at the possibility that this emotion might be chosen or avoided, as if the totemic yewberries and owl were ways of declaring one's commitment to dejection. But of course melancholy cannot be avoided, and the second stanza flatly acknowledges this fact. It insists on the involuntariness—the surprise—of melancholy moods:

> But when the melancholy fit shall fall
>   Sudden from heaven like a weeping cloud,
> That fosters the droop-headed flowers all,
>   And hides the green hill in an April shroud;
> Then glut thy sorrow on a morning rose,
>   Or on the rainbow of the salt sand-wave,
>   Or on the wealth of globed peonies;
> Or if thy mistress some rich anger shows,
>   Emprison her soft hand, and let her rave,
>   And feed deep, deep upon her peerless eyes.

Not "if" but "when" the fit befalls you—catches you "unaware," to borrow from Keats's vocabulary. In a densely chiastic simile, the melancholy fit falls from heaven just as rain falls from a "weeping" cloud; and while "heaven" suggests the sky in which the cloud gathers, the figurative "weeping" elaborates the human mood of melancholy. In this way, the weather is a metaphor for a sudden feeling, and vice versa. Unlike the sonneteer who suddenly laughs, however, the speaker of the ode does not weep; his melancholy thoughts lie too deep for tears. Weeping, rather, hangs in limbo between human affect and natural phenomena. The phrase "from heaven," meanwhile, crystallizes the poem's wavering stance between origin and mystery, causation and causelessness. Colloquially, it means "out of nowhere," but in the poem's mythological context, it points to Melancholy's "sovran shrine," with its pantheon of "cloudy trophies." In this latter sense, "from heaven" discloses something like providence or grace. As a putative origin, then, "heaven" must be read both ways, because the poem itself works to rewrite the precipitous drop into sadness as a fortunate fall.

Keats's ode is of two minds on how to conceive of melancholy. On the one hand, it is a momentary, narratable event, a "fit" that comes out of the blue and surprises its victim; on the other hand, it is an emotion simultaneous with perceptions of beauty. That simultaneity is spatially represented in the architecture of Melancholy's shrine, tucked as it is within the Temple of Delight. The "Ode on Melancholy" is Keats's shortest ode, but in that brevity it manages a tight network of association and suggestion. The "weeping cloud" is a purely metaphorical entity, but through a relative clause, it takes on a life of its own as a phenomenon to be appreciated. Keats does not explicitly assure the reader that the melancholy fit will pass away, or that it will somehow be compensated or balanced, but he does so imagistically: though the cloud weeps, it also "fosters" similarly downcast ("droop-headed") flowers; and though it is a funereal "shroud," it only temporarily hides what the poet knows to be a green hill behind. Through a localized metaphorical description of the surprising effect of the melancholy fit, the poet unfolds a series of correspondences between the human realm and natural world: the fit is not only sudden but also short-lived, salubrious, and even beautiful.

The highest value in the poem is, quite simply, consciousness, and the activity of noticing goes on even in the first stanza of negative commands. For the strict purposes of those commands, it matters not that wolf's-bane is "tight-rooted," that nightshade is a "ruby grape," or that the sad owl is also "downy"; but in the descriptive exuberance of these epithets, their fine excess, the poet enacts what he calls the soul's "wakeful anguish"— noticing beauty even in the midst of cataloging poisons and opiates and contemplating oblivion. Even before he recommends such aesthetic contemplation outright in the second stanza, he does so implicitly in the first.[24] In the simplest terms, the counsel to enjoy sand-waves and peonies might be translated into a proverbial reminder to stop and smell the roses, except that Keats's recommendation does not entail the act of stopping one thing to do another, but rather a subtler kind of simultaneity: perceiving beauty even in melancholy. Even amid strife, the mistress's anger is "rich," her hands "soft," her eyes "peerless"—a Renaissance blazon smuggled into a lovers' spat. In the catalogs of both the first and second stanzas, Keats essentially urges mindfulness, first implicitly, then outright.

What I have said here about intense mindfulness—Hazlitt might have recognized it as a form of "gusto" or "power"—will come as no surprise to readers of Keats. But I hope to have shown a new way to read the poem with attention to the nature of Keatsian surprise: the paradox of expectation and startlement, the mental gesture of recognition, the salutary influence of shocks, the ideal of "fine excess," the conception of emotion as both cognitive and corporeal, voluntary and involuntary. Though we can imagine the experiential beginnings of this ode, it is still more true to Keats's sense of experience to see the "sudden fit" of melancholy as unaccountable, puzzling, strange; to see this affective rupture as opening the question of before and after, of prior happiness and future recovery; and to see the impulsive grasp of the mistress's hands as the deliberate and pleasurable surprise of someone else, a righting of the karmic imbalance caused by the sudden fit. In my suggestion that love suffering is not necessarily the origin of melancholy, I am anticipated by Vendler herself, who allows that if Melancholy is actually "intrinsic to life," then the poet doesn't need the mistress's rage as precipitant ("Experiential Beginnings" 597). But to follow her narrative premise, I might propose this: what if the lovers' spat were caused by one person's incorrigibly gloomy mood, rather than the other way around?

In a letter to Reynolds in April 1817, Keats asks his friend to share his latest reading impressions, which must necessarily be always changing, always yielding up a fresh insight: "Whenever you write say a Word or two on some Passage in Shakespeare that may have come rather new to you: which must be continually happening, notwithstanding that we read the same Play forty times" (7, 8 Apr.). This request gives us another sense of what Keats means by the phrase "surprise[d] by a fine excess": part of Shakespeare's abundance is that different phrases or passages will strike the reader at different times; one can never step into the same play twice. It also illustrates what it means for the imagination to be "coming continually on the spirit with a fine suddenness." For Keats, the surprise of reading was predicated on *rereading*—and, I might add, on the pleasure of revisiting the work of our most cherished readers.

NOTES

1. Helen Vendler, "The Experiential Beginnings of Keats's Odes," *Studies in Romanticism* 12.30 (Summer 1973): 591–606.

2. "An ideal criticism," Vendler has said, "would bring speculative thought, life experience, and anterior texts equally to bear on the written work, but no critic's mind can move in these three directions at once." See "The Function of Criticism," *The Music of What Happens* (Cambridge, MA: Harvard UP, 1988), 19.

3. Vendler's appraisal of the odes takes both ethical and aesthetic forms: it frankly admires the "heroism" of shifting narrowly personal concerns to a loftier register, and it articulates the imaginative act of ordering and shaping experience. In cognitive terms, the abstracting tendency of thought—especially Keats's way of thinking—filters the particulars of feelings and sensation. As Vendler observes, "Keats is unlikely to begin with any narrative account of an experience in life which gave rise to his poetry; the thoughts themselves, before he begins to compose, take pre-eminence over the events which provoked them" ("Experiential Beginnings" 602).

4. See Vendler, *The Odes of John Keats* (Cambridge, MA: Harvard UP, 1983), 3.

5. Biographical context has melted away, but what Vendler takes to be the precipitating experience has not—the grammatical ghost of an argument implicit in the poet's chain of negatives: "The prevalence of negation suggests that this poem is not a definition but rather a rebuttal—and all rebuttals encapsulate the argument they refute." Indeed, she goes so far as to write the misanthropic sonnet to which Shakespeare's responds. See Vendler, *The Art of Shakespeare's Sonnets* (Cambridge, MA: Harvard UP, 1997), 488.

6. Vendler, "Experiential Beginnings" 592.

7. John Keats, *Complete Poems*, ed. Jack Stillinger (Cambridge, MA: Harvard UP, 1982), 164–65. All quotations of Keats's poetry refer to this edition.

8. Hyder Edward Rollins, *The Keats Circle: Letters and Papers, 1816–1878*, 2 vols. (Cambridge, MA: Harvard UP, 1948), 1:94.

9. Letter to Benjamin Bailey, 22 Nov. 1817, *Letters of John Keats*, ed. Robert Gittings (Oxford: Oxford UP, 1970). All quotations from the letters refer to this edition.

10. "Every thing that is *new* or *uncommon* raises a Pleasure in the Imagination," Addison says, "because it fills the Soul with an agreeable Surprise, gratifies its Curiosity, and gives it an Idea of which it was not before possest." We are so vulnerable to habit and boredom that this emotion "serves us for a Kind of Refreshment, and takes off from that Satiety we are apt to complain of in our usual Entertainments." See Addison, *The Spectator*, No. 412, 23 June 1712 ("The Pleasures of the Imagination"), *Selections from the Tatler and Spectator*, ed. Angus Ross (Harmondsworth: Penguin, 1982).

11. To John Taylor, 27 Feb. 1818.

12. To the George Keatses, 14–31 Oct. 1818.

13. Christopher Ricks has suggested that "the delicate humanity of the letter comes out of embarrassment," particularly the intersubjective awkwardness of the near kiss: "to meet [Jones] again and not kiss her would be to be living backward, and might after all embarrass her; but once Keats has made his mistake he is at once freed from all self-reproach about it by her unembarrassable and unembarrassing magnanimity." See *Keats and Embarrassment* (Oxford: Clarendon, 1974), 220.

14. A passage from "Isabella" describing an encounter between the title character and Lorenzo gives us a gloss on the figurative "poesy" that passes between lovers: " . . . his erewhile timid lips grew bold / And poesied with hers in dewy rhyme" (69–70).

15. The poems that Keats wrote on his northern walking tour in the summer of 1818 necessarily record first experiences (e.g., "On Visiting the Tomb of Burns"), but they reflect a certain growing disenchantment with touristic reportage—with the constant state of readiness to be surprised. The doggerel poem "There was a naughty boy," which Keats sent to his sister, comically registers this feeling.

16. The difference between a surprise poem and other poems of aesthetic engagement is the difference between the "Elgin Marbles" sonnet and the "Ode on a Grecian Urn," between the sonnet on reading Chapman's Homer and the sonnet "On Sitting Down to Read *King Lear* Once Again," or between the lines on Milton's hair and the fragment "This living hand," in which the speaker studies his own hand and startles someone else with it.

17. For a reading that places the poem formally within the ekphrastic tradition and culturally within the contemporary dialogue surrounding the Elgin Marbles, see Grant F. Scott, *The Sculpted Word: Keats, Ekphrasis, and the Visual Arts* (Hanover, NH: UP of New England, 1994). As Scott remarks, the poem "transforms the traditional ekphrastic impulse to narrate the artwork into a desire to narrate the self watching the artwork" (45). If ekphrasis is signally concerned with making a silent artistic form speak, and with what W. J. T. Mitchell calls the "paragonal" competition between the sister arts, then Keats's sonnet is only tangentially related to the genre; it is far more concerned with giving voice to the poet's own feelings, far more intent on transcribing passing impressions than on the timelessness of art. See Mitchell, *Iconology* (Chicago: U of Chicago P, 1986).

18. As Ricks puts it, "a creativity from the past comes suddenly to reassert itself as a newly possible creativity; but the shock of recognition is like a sharp moment of love (as when in Sappho the loved one's name is suddenly vibrant), and is alive with embarrassment at youthfulness and at emulation all but preposterous" (164).

19. For discussion of Keats's writing of the poem, see Walter Jackson Bate, *John Keats* (Cambridge, MA: Belknap, 1963). "Keats was neither so naively excited nor so paralyzed as a year before when he was expected to write a sonnet on receiving a laurel crown. He does not seem to have been overeager to take up the challenge. But Hunt, without second thought, thrust before him a notebook, in which he himself had been writing a poem of his own ('Hero and Leander'), opened to some blank pages" (285–86). Despite its compelled nature, this writing exercise, as Bate remarks, was salubrious, and Keats's later biographer Andrew Motion agrees: "Keats was loath to admit it, but his sense of recommitment had something to do with his recent visit to Hunt. However compromised their friendship had become, the meeting reminded him of common sympathies." See Motion, *Keats* (New York: Farrar, Straus and Giroux, 1997), 225.

20. For a discussion of Hunt's collection, see John L. Waltman, "'And Beauty Draws Us With a Single Hair': Leigh Hunt as Collector," *Keats-Shelley Memorial Association Bulletin [Keats-Shelley Review]* 31 (1980): 61–67. In addition to the samples from Milton, Swift, and Johnson (which formed the nucleus of the collection), Hunt acquired locks from Keats, Wordsworth, Coleridge, Percy and Mary Shelley, Lamb, Carlyle, Hazlitt, and the Brownings, as well as Napoleon and George Washington. Each specimen was mounted on a leaf opposite a print depicting the original bearer and kept in an envelope containing the name and details of acquisition.

21. Susan Stewart, *On Longing* (Durham: Duke UP, 1993), 155.

22. *The Selected Writings of Leigh Hunt*, vol. 5: *Poetical Works, 1801–21*, ed. John Strachan (London: Pickering and Chatto, 2003), 232. Hunt wrote three sonnets on the subject of Batty's gift of Milton's hair: "To — —, M. D., On his giving me a lock of Milton's hair," "To the Same on the Same Subject," and "To the Same on the Same Occasion," all first published in *Foliage*. The second in the series, quoted here, is the one that became known as "On a lock of Milton's hair" from 1832 onward.

23. Keats copied out the poem in a letter to his brothers along with a note: "Nothing is finer for the purposes of great productions, than a very gradual ripening of the intellectual powers—As an instance of this—observe—I sat down yesterday to read King Lear once again the thing appeared to demand the prologue of a Sonnet, I wrote it & began to read" (23, 24 Jan. 1818).

24. In this way, the ode exemplifies the aesthetic principle that David Bromwich has seen at work in Keats's poetry: "Sensations are not nursed up for their own sake, as Pater would say they must be: they are neither enjoyed nor suffered, but rather are absorbed for the sake of self-concentration or an intensification that changes their character." See Bromwich, "Keats and the Aesthetic Ideal," *The Persistence of Poetry: Bicentennial Essays on Keats,* ed. Robert M. Ryan and Ronald M. Sharp (Amherst: U of Massachusetts P, 1998), 185.

Foursquare

The Romantic Quatrain and Its Descendants

WILLARD SPIEGELMAN

The opening stanza in a famous poem poses an ontological question:

> Twinkle, twinkle, little star,
> How I wonder what you are!
> Up above the world so high,
> Like a diamond in the sky.

Thus, Jane Taylor in 1806, harnessing Wordsworth's trope of another heavenly guide (his Lucy as a fair star, "when only one is shining in the sky") to the jaunty catalectic trochaic tetrameter of Blake's "Tyger," inter alia. Taylor's famous apostrophe may prompt a twenty-first-century reader to a related but more formal question: Why is this poem written in quatrains? That it is intended for children, and that nursery rhyme verse had long favored quatrains, is a historically valid but a philosophically insufficient answer. Taking a different tack, we might acknowledge that British Romanticism offered fertile ground for poetic experimentation, as we have long known, but any anthologist gathering flowers would also acknowledge that the soil was hospitable to more ordinary specimens, the quatrain above all. The task of looking for quatrains is not an arduous one; they spring up like weeds in the landscape. Nor is the task of classifying them. In terms of rhyme scheme the possibilities are less than a handful: *aabb, abab, abcb,* and the very rare *aaax;* in terms of rhythm the possibilities are more various. The question—"Why the quatrain?"—has historical, theoretical, and, indeed, ontological ramifications.

Among today's senior scholars, Helen Vendler and John Hollander may enable us at least to begin to answer this simple question with dexterity and nuance. Both were weaned on what now is often derided as the antique New Criticism (although Vendler has always referred to herself as an "aesthetic" critic, and Hollander's encyclopedic knowledge moves beyond easily categorizable method). Throughout her critical work, and in her textbook *Poems, Poets, Poetry* (73–87), Vendler tells her reader to attend to poems' forms, although in her chapter entitled "Poems as Pleasure" she merely lists the various stanzaic forms without delving more deeply into their particular *kinds* of pleasure. (In her recent book on Yeats, however, she devoted an entire chapter to his trimeter quatrains; see 182–204.) Nevertheless, as a distinguished reader of the entire range of lyric poetry in English, Vendler has made it her overt practice as well as her tacit methodology to approve the principle that there is no poetic detail too small to warrant attention. Hollander has actually gestured toward an answer to my question about the quatrain in his seminal but incomplete discussion of the issue in "Romantic Verse Form and the Metrical Contract," although his interest in genre and meter excludes any consideration of stanzaic form as a constituent of a poem's meaning. Here is Hollander's unarguable thesis: "The metrical choice provides a basic schematic fabric of contingencies governing the range of expressive effect. But it also establishes a kind of frame around the work as a whole. Like a title, it indicates how it is to be taken, what sort of thing the poem is supposed to be" (189). Ontology has reentered the discussion.

Like meter, I would propose, stanzas are often an indication of genre and always of effect, and consequently of purpose, however unconscious. Although they are a part of a poem's nonsemantic machinery, they alert us specifically to what a poem should look like. The appearance of certain shapes on the printed page parallels Jeremy Bentham's accurate though tongue-in-cheek definition of poetry as that which lacks a justified right-hand margin. "Prose is when all the lines except the last go to the margin—poetry is when some of them fall short of it" (442). In many contemporary instances, some of which I mention below, the very fact of quatrains—even if unrhymed and unmetrical—tends to *mean* that we are being presented with a poem, rather than another kind of thing. "Form's what affirms," says the partly self-parodying James Merrill in his "One Thousand and Second Night." In the following pages I hope to suggest, via a minitaxonomy, a prolegomenon toward a deeper understanding of some of the stylistic choices made by Romantic poets and of the legacy of those choices to twentieth-century poetry. So another way of framing the question "Why the quatrain" is a Hollanderish one: At what point does scheme (or arrangement) become trope (or figure of speech)? Or, to recast the same question in Vendler's terms: how and why do quatrains provide pleasure to both writers and readers?

What Donne called the "pretty rooms" of a sonnet's stanzas ("The

Canonization") and what Amy Clampitt, using the same bilingual pun, refers to as Petrarch's "little rooms" ("Losing Track of Language") have provided many poets with a safe haven, comfort, and—if nothing else—with the modest appearance of poetic form even in the absence of rhyme or metric certainty. In any poet, especially a great conventional one (e.g., Robert Frost) who willingly accepts and works within the restraints imposed by tradition, literature vies with life as uncertain combatants, and the most successful poets stage this conflict on battlefields upon which we can find the traces of their stylistic, formal, and musical choices. The allusive power of shape distills scheme into trope, makes form part of the poem's signifying process, and (especially with regard to quatrains) makes a mnemonic device appear to be an item of nature.

When, and for what reasons, in the life of an artist or in literary history does inventiveness lose out to nostalgia? When did the quatrain become a default mode? Whereas some groups of four—I think especially of Alcaic and Sapphic stanzas—can seem serious, indeed menacing to both a poet and a reader, it has been the fate of the rhymed quatrain to resist and deflect such menace, or to hide and repress it, except, that is, to the aurally astute listener/reader. Paul Fussell's *Poetic Meter and Poetic Form,* a major work after four decades, provocatively and helpfully both addresses and begs my questions. Calling quatrains "'natural' strophic form," Fussell implies what more recent critics have also attempted to prove: "something in four-line stanzaic organization (or in the principle of alternate rhyming) . . . projects a deep and permanent appeal to human nature" (141). What he calls "the illusion of primitive sincerity and openness" extends, of course, through contemporary poems that—however free their rhythms—appear on the page in groups of four: they *look,* as I have said, like what a reading audience thinks a poem should be. The stanzas function almost as identifying labels, which alert the reader to a specific kind of reading experience and demand a different kind of visual and auditory acuity. "Watch out for the line itself," they seem to say, "and then for its place in a discrete unit of four." Whether such forms are "natural" is debatable; that they have become commonplace and therefore immediately graspable is not.

The prosodists do not provide much additional help. In a work of almost 400 pages the poet-critic Timothy Steele not too usefully defines "quatrain" in his glossary as "a stanza of four lines." Shira Wolosky discusses quatrains exclusively as parts of sonnets (41–67; see also Corn). Derek Attridge says that all speech has a "natural tendency [there's *natural* again] . . . to gravitate toward simple binary rhythms and hierarchies based on such rhythms" (80–96). In *Rhyme's Reason* Hollander specifies eight varieties of conventional quatrain: *abab* (his example is in trimeter); the *In Memoriam abba* tetrameter stanza; *abax* (a post–World War I innovation); the ballad stanza, *abcb*, alternating four- and three-beat lines; the hymn or common measure of *abab*, also with alternating line lengths; Dickinson's slanted *abcb*; the *abab* tetrameter "long" measure; and the *Rubaiyat aaba* stanza (16–17).

This grouping marks a beginning but is hardly exhaustive, as we shall see. Fussell adds the clerihew and, more seriously, the couplet quatrain and the heroic quatrain (pentameter *abab*) used first by Davenant (in *Gondibert*), then by Dryden ("Annus Mirabilis") and Gray ("Elegy Written in a Country Churchyard"), and significantly by Wordsworth in his antiballad "Hart-Leap Well" in order to take advantage of the weightier, more flexible metrical possibilities in a pentameter line. Fussell even discovers a precedent for *In Memoriam* in Ben Jonson's "An Elegie." Other forms follow, as I shall show.

Literary histories, such as Albert Friedman's major work on the ballad revival, offer direction; they point to pathways that we have not yet fully embarked on, let alone reached an end of. Whether imitating the voice or form of "the people" in a sophisticated updating of the ballad, or supplanting narrative objectivity with lyrical intensity and personal involvement (as, most notably, Wordsworth does in the Lucy poems and other quatrain experiments in *Lyrical Ballads*), poets of the nineteenth and twentieth centuries in both England and America embraced the quatrain, in ballad and other forms, whether as a mode of nostalgia, as it is in Housman, or as a mode of detachment, as it is in Auden and Jarrell (Friedman 336, 347). Mary Kinzie, citing Hollander on "Song" in the 1974 *Princeton Encyclopedia of Poetry and Poetics,* suggests ways in which the original ballad quatrain developed into something far different: "The true ballads, with all their devices designed to promote memorability, give way to quatrains ornamented with descriptive texture and striking but not easily memorized diction. . . . [Compared with early ballads] eighteenth-century poems in ballad or common measure . . . fatten the stanza with adjectives while exaggerating the regularity of stress-to-nonstress alternations" (Kinzie 269).

An equally interesting and significant fact is the way in which the quatrain continues to exert a hold today, even if merely for purposes of ornament, on poets of all sorts. At the very least, it provides a visual sense of formality (as does any kind of stanza) to the most laggardly free verse. In her important work on the history of poetic memorization in England and America, Catherine Robson has analyzed the mnemonic, often mimetic function of rhythm and its connection to cultural indoctrination and educational practice. Felicia Hemans's "Casabianca," "the most memorized, the most recited poem of all, allows us to historicize meter and the heart together, to think about our relationship to literature in the most corporeal of ways" (Robson 151). But meter is separate from stanzaic form, and although the former has vanished, the latter maintains a ghostly vestigial presence in much contemporary poetry. Like the appearance of disorder in a work where secret order reigns (e.g., the rhyme in Auden's "Musée des Beaux Arts," or virtually any kind of unhearable syllabic arrangement in Marianne Moore and others), a stanza can provide an illusion of visual order for the reading eye, even though the absence of regular rhyme or rhythm undoes that order when the poet reads his or her work aloud. A successful poem of a certain width and length looks "right" to poet and reader. This very familiarity may in turn become an aid to the poet in the act of composition. One contemporary poet has told me that breaking a poetic draft into stanzas early on may helpfully suggest how to organize ideas, images, and thoughts, or to generate new lines, as the poem proceeds. In other words, the quatrain provides scaffolding for the actual construction of a poetic structure, and then survives as not just a vestigial skeleton but the very edifice itself.

Leafing randomly through the pages of virtually any anthology of twentieth-century poetry, one comes upon the quatrain phenomenon, even in poets one associates with other forms of articulation. Such canonical poems as Robert Lowell's "For the Union Dead," Donald Justice's "Men at Forty," John Ashbery's "These Lacustrine Cities" (and everything in *Shadow Train*), as well as countless poems by Robert Creeley, Frank O'Hara, Ted Hughes, Mary Oliver, and Charles Simic, are composed in four-line stanzas without a discernible, audible sonic shape. The poem as mansion is constituted by the foursquare rooms of its quatrains. Joseph Parisi and Stephen Young's anthology of eighty years of verse from *Poetry* includes examples of the phenomenon from such younger contemporaries as Debora Greger, Elizabeth Alexander, Sue Owen, and Michael Ryan. The volume also suggests the ways in which canonical modernist poets (Williams, Stevens, Auden, and Moore) could not resist the quatrain even though they favored other forms as well. Nor could other poets withstand the quatrain's strong magnetic draw: Hart Crane especially, as well as Yvor Winters, Robert Penn Warren, Josephine Jacobson, James Agee, Ben Belitt, and Robert Hayden, felt comfortable with quatrains that offered both containment and flexibility.

Such, I would argue, is one formal legacy of Romanticism. Long ago

M. H. Abrams wrote a classic essay on the "greater Romantic lyric," a genre (whether in the blank verse of "Tintern Abbey" and "Frost at Midnight," or in rhymed patterns like the Intimations Ode) that he defined by shape and cognitive arrangements rather than by pattern. The action, thought, diction, or dramatic circumstances of the poem end where they began, spiraling back upon the speaker's reflections, sensations, and memories. The Romantic nature lyric in Abrams's definition tells only part of the story of the Romantic way of making or at least arranging poems. Both formally and thematically, the earlier generation of Romantic poets was obsessed with the quatrain. For whatever reasons, the later generation was less prone to it. Among the second generation, of the three major male poets, Keats gave us only (but significantly) "La Belle Dame sans Merci," and "Meg Merrilies." Among Byron's notable efforts we have the jaunty "After Swimming from Sestos to Abydos," and the couplet quatrains of "The Destruction of Sennacherib" and "There's not a joy the world can give." The always inventive Shelley downplayed the form, using it, inter alia, in the highly charged couplet quatrains of "Song to the Men of England," "The Mask of Anarchy," and the mythopoeic "Sensitive Plant," the last of which may prove a point proposed by another quatrain master, Sir Walter Scott, who prepared his reader for what lay ahead in his introduction to "The Lay of the Last Minstrel," a poem that vigorously employs the quatrain and just as vigorously turns away from it: "A long work in quatrains . . . has an effect upon the mind like that of the bed of Procrustes upon the human body; for as it must be both awkward and difficult to carry on a long sentence from one stanza to another, it follows that the meaning of each period must be comprehended within four lines, and equally so that it must be extended to fill that space" (181).

Blake's and Wordsworth's experiments with conventional quatrains must be accounted startling. Of Blake's *Songs* one notices, first of all, that the quatrain *is* the default mode. Thirteen of nineteen songs in *Innocence* and twenty-two of twenty-six in *Experience* employ it. Second, the conventional ballad stanza—*abcb*, in alternating four- and three-beat lines—is more prevalent in *Experience* than in *Innocence*. In *Innocence* it is most prominent in "The Little Boy Lost" and "The Little Boy Found," and appears with *abab* variations in "The Divine Image," and with metrical variations in "The Nurse's Song." Otherwise, we have *abab* quatrains, in alternating four- and three-stress lines, or anapests. Couplet quatrains appear: "The Laughing Song," in tetrameter with lots of extra unstressed syllables, and "Cradle Song" (with various syllables), "A Dream," "On Another's Sorrows," and "The Chimney Sweeper." One poem stands out in this group for stanzaic uniqueness: "Holy Thursday" uses heptameter lines, in order to suggest the flow of the charity children into St. Paul's on Ascension Thursday: "Now like a mighty wind they raise to heaven the voice of song,/Or like harmonious thunderings the seats of Heaven among./Beneath them sit the aged men, wise guardians of the poor;/Then cherish pity, lest you drive an angel from your door" (61). Blake's twelve long, end-stopped lines refuse enjambment. (As an aside: consider those songs, predominantly in forms other than quatrains, such as "The Blossom" or "Night," that dramatically employ enjambment, which Blake seldom does in the quatrain poems.) End stopping gives a somewhat halting gait to "Holy Thursday"'s continuous movement. This has a consequence for both the poem's rhythm, which imitates the stop-and-go traffic of the procession, and its tone, so that the full ironic wallop of the last line comes at you with a shock because after eleven lines you have probably been seduced into the lilt of both traffic and music.

Each of the songs, in other words, makes its own demands on our ear, and each is unique in its metrical and stanzaic arrangements. And the ordering of them is, I would propose, as significant as it is in a suite of music. For example, *Innocence* opens with the catalectic trochaic tetrameter of "Piping down the valleys wild," which is juxtaposed with the anapestic "How sweet is the shepherd's sweet lot,/From the morn to the evening he strays" (54, 55). Is the shift deliberate? Regardless, does it have an effect? Another, more crucial way of posing my question is an Aristotelian one: Can we distinguish between essential and accidental data in assessing the status and meaning of a poem? What importance do we ascribe to the fact that the only song written in pentameter is *Innocence*'s "Little Black Boy"? (Interestingly, "The Chimney Sweeper" [68–69] seems to begin the same way, "When my mother died I was very young,/And my father sold me while yet my tongue . . . " before subsiding into anapests.)

In *Songs of Experience* let me observe that although the number of *abcb* quatrains has increased, the poems are not necessarily strict ballads. "Nurse's Song" is, but the short-lined "The Fly" and "The Sick Rose" are not. "A Little Boy Lost," no longer a narrative ballad but an acerbic dialogue between priest and child, maintains a regular foursquare base: all the lines are tetrameter, albeit with an *abcb* rhyming pattern. The most spectacular local effect, a testimony to the delicacy of Blake's musical sense, comes at the end of the three-stanza "The Garden of Love," with its regular tetrameter quatrains, some lines containing an extra syllable. Arriving at the gated garden of negation, with "Thou shalt not" writ over the door, Blake's speaker is stunned with a deadly vision whose musical extensions—two hypersyllabic lines—imply the eternity of the grave and of established religion and its legislation of repression: "And I saw it was filled with graves, / And tomb-stones where flowers should be, / And priests in black gowns were walking their rounds, / And binding with bri-ars my joys & desires" (212).

Blake owed a debt, of course, as much to nursery rhyme and broad-side ballads as to "high" literary English forms. For his part, Wordsworth turns out—thanks to the exhaustive study of Brendan O'Donnell—to have been the most inventive as well as the most revolutionary of the Roman-tic poets. O'Donnell quotes Saintsbury, who gave the laurels to Blake and Coleridge, saying of Wordsworth that "in no great poet does prosody play so small a part" (O'Donnell 6). But with approximately ninety different verse forms in his *Collected Works,* Wordsworth shows, both in precept and in verse, a vast range of stylistic accommodations to metric and stan-zaic possibilities (O'Donnell 4). Throughout *Lyrical Ballads* he prefers the *abab* (4,3,4,3) quatrain (think of "We Are Seven" and "Lines Written in Early Spring," three of the Lucy poems, "The Two April Mornings," inter alia); and the *abab* quatrain with three beats to the fourth line (consider "Anecdote for Fathers," "To My Sister," "Lines Written in Early Spring"). There are a few anapestic experiments and some pentameter ones. Only a single poem in Wordsworth's oeuvre (I'm relying on O'Donnell's count) is written in the traditional ballad stanza: "The Force of Prayer," his 1807 poem "of Sentiment and Reflection" on Bolton Priory, published both in the 1815 *Poems* and with *The White Doe of Rylstone* five weeks later. Even this, however, takes liberties, with extra unstressed syllables and the occa-sional tetrameter even-numbered line.

A major example of Wordsworth's dramatic rendering of the possibil-ities for multeity in unity, variety within sameness, is the trio of Yarrow poems. (If one wanted to look more closely at Coleridge, one might in-clude the more obvious "Rhyme of the Ancient Mariner," in which the few interpolated ballad stanzas, like the occasional longer stanza, stand out in rough contrast to the largely *abab* form Coleridge favors.) Strictly speak-ing, the Yarrow poems are octaves, but each consists of two quatrains, in alternating tetrameter and trimeter lines. They *sound* like quatrains. This is the same form as "The Children in the Wood," cited for different reasons by both Dr. Johnson and Wordsworth. Let me extend my arith-metical statistics: "Yarrow Unvisited" has eight stanzas, "Yarrow Visited" eleven, and "Yarrow Revisited" fourteen; Wordsworth expands his delib-erations as he moves from disappointment to experience to repetition. Most interesting is the rhyme scheme: in "Yarrow Unvisited" half of the quatrains are *abcb,* while half are *abab.* The second poem begins with two quatrains of *abab,* and subsides into *abcb* for its remainder.

The third poem is composed entirely of *abcb* rhymes. Does this fact have meaning? Perhaps, especially if we consider that the first poem is an exchange of viewpoints—is Yarrow worth visiting or not?—while the second begins in uncertain wonder ("And is this Yarrow?—*This* the Stream / Of which my fancy cherished, / So faithfully, a waking dream? / An image that hath perished!") and then renders its account of pleasures and delights stored within for future restoration "to heighten joy, / And cheer my mind in sorrow" (421–23). As readers of Wordsworth know, the most intense pleasures spring out of repetition, so it is no wonder that the homogeneity of the quatrain rhyme in "Yarrow Revisited" attests to the integrating re-experience when "Past, present, future, all appeared / In harmony united." Yarrow meets the visitors "with unaltered face," though inconstant, in the same way that the human self is both the same and not the same as it was before: "though we were changed and changing." At the end, speaking to the absent Walter Scott (with whom he had visited the place for the second time, in the past), Wordsworth unveils his master trope, light, which has three manifestations. Like the experience of Yarrow, light is a triune experience, portrayed in a uniform rhyme scheme. He requests that the stream "flow on forever," sacred to poets, who will experience it in three different ways, all of them illuminating: "To dream-light dear while yet unseen, / Dear to the common sunshine, / And dearer still, as now I feel, / To memory's shadowy moonshine!" (434–36). Past, present, and future come together as cogently as they do in the tenth stanza of the Intimations Ode, when Wordsworth finds strength in what remains behind, in the primal sympathy that must ever be, and in the faith that looks through death.

My survey of quatrain forms ends with three modest but interestingly novel experiments by poets previously deemed minor. Felicia Hemans's "The Image in Lava" (423–24) seems like a precursor of Tennyson's "Crossing the Bar" in the way the third, unrhymed, line extends and opens the stanza before a retreat in line 4 to a normative trimeter base. There is a precedent for this form in Percy's *Reliques:* two of the ballads, "George Barnwell" and "The Boy and the Mantle," use the same form, but for no obvious reason (see Laws 15–16). In Hemans's poem, which describes the impression of a woman's form, with her baby at her breast, found during the uncovering of Herculaneum, the rhythm suggests the slow flow of lava that moves out and captures the living, before holding and annealing them in perpetual entombment:

Thou thing of years departed!
　　What ages have gone by,
Since here the mournful seal was set
　　By love and agony!
　　　· · · · · · ·
And childhood's fragile image
　　Thus fearfully enshrin'd,
Survives the proud memorials rear'd
　　By conquerors of mankind.
　　　　　　　　(stanzas 1 and 3)

The 3-3-4-3 quatrain also happens to be the form of "Frankie and Johnny" and other blues ballads; for an ironic modern example, see Auden's "Victor" with stanzas like this: "It was the middle of September, / Victor came to the office one day; / He was wearing a flower in his buttonhole; / He was late but he was gay."

Finally, two examples of the least popular quatrain form: *aaax*. In Thomas Campbell's "Hohenlinden" (150–51), the rather stilted, halting quatrains prepare us for the bloody battle with their impulsive rhythm and repetitive sounds. Not only do the stanzas rhyme *aaab* but also, as we see, the final words of all the quatrains constitute an extended rhyme or part rhyme:

On Linden, when the sun was low,
All bloodless lay the untrodden snow,
And dark as winter was the flow
Of Iser, rolling rapidly.

But Linden saw another sight,
When the drum beat, at dead of night,
Commanding fires of death to light
The darkness of her scenery.
　　　　　　　　(lines 1–8)

The extended rhyme continues until the last stanza, when the half or phantom rhyme in "sepulchre" seems to change the poem's entire musical base, its tonic note:

Few, few shall part where many meet!
The snow shall be their winding-sheet,

And every turf beneath their feet
Shall be a soldier's sepulchre.
(lines 29–32)

The previous fourth lines ended in "rapidly," "scenery," "revelry," "artil-
lery," "rapidly," "canopy," "chivalry." "Sepulchre" (a partial rhyme? perhaps an eye rhyme? no rhyme at all?) confirms the finality of the fight, of
death, and, indeed, of the poem.

More poignant is Anna Barbauld's "A Thought on Death" (168), in
which the final "die" of each quatrain is balanced by the alleviating pred-
icating adjectives and noun phrases that move speaker and audience from
despair to relief, triumph, and finally to blessing:

When life, as opening buds, is sweet,
And golden hopes the spirit greet,
And youth prepares his joys to meet,
 Alas! How hard it is to die!

When scarce is seiz'd some valu'd prize,
And duties press, and tender ties
Forbid the soul from earth to rise,
 How awful then it is to die!

. . . .
When trembling limbs refuse their weight,
And films, slow gathering, dim the sight,
And clouds obscure the mental light,
 'Tis nature's precious boon to die!
(lines 1–8, 17–20)

The lines that end each quatrain have remained the same, all ending with
a variation on the infinitive "to die," but they have progressed as well.
Sameness and difference in iteration keep the poem and its reader buoyed
as we move to several kinds of termination. From "hard," through "awful," and then (in the stanzas I have not quoted) "easy" and "'Tis joy, 'tis
triumph," and finally "precious boon," Barbauld has used the nonce line,
the odd man out, so to speak, as a means of beckoning us to our common
destiny. In oddness inheres universality. Death or its infinitive rhymes
only but inevitably with itself.

At the start of this essay I offered some historical suggestions for the
popularity of the quatrain during the late eighteenth century and the first

third of the nineteenth. These begin with, but are hardly limited to, the educational viability of quatrain form for schoolroom purposes. Ballads and nursery rhymes, as well as hymns (Watt, Cowper, et al.), reached the apogee of their popularity in the late eighteenth century. More enduring would be the popularity of Gray's "Elegy." Even though its heroic quatrains were not as often imitated as the ballad stanza, it nevertheless looms large over the entire British landscape. It is a telling fact about contemporary trends in criticism, I think, that two recent works on Gray pay scant attention to the poem's quatrain structure, preferring in one case a Marxist viewpoint (Kaul 111–65) and in another a homosocial one (Gleckner). They prefer tropes and ideology to forms and sounds, semantic details to musical ones. What Empson memorably referred to as the poem's "massive calm" has been much more a source of gratification than irritation to those—communists and apolitical people alike, according to Empson— who are struck by what he called the poem's "complacence" (5). "Complacence" is a typical Empsonian exaggeration, employed in part for its value to shock; the "Elegy Written in a Country Churchyard" does more than accept a status quo or relish its pastoral quietude. But such complacence that exists does so not only in the poem's formal stanzas, although it begins there. Gray knew what kind of effect his quatrains would have.

One could go on. T. S. Eliot called the ballad a species of verse, not poetry, thereby degrading most quatrains except the terse, brittle, witty ones that he and Pound had composed in their early years. On the other hand, his contemporary I. A. Richards said of meter what I am proposing about the quatrain and indeed all stanzaic forms: "Through its very appearance of artificiality [it] produces in the highest degree the 'frame' effect, isolating the poetic experience from the accidents and irrelevancies of everyday experience" (145). Such a claim flies a bit in the face of Richards's master, Coleridge, and his own famous pronouncement (in *Biographia Literaria*, chap. 18) about meter, which, he says, for poetic purposes resembles "yeast… worthless or disagreeable by itself, but giving vivacity and spirit to the liquor with which it is properly combined." Even today, when a new kind of colloquial conversation, what Wordsworth called "the real language of men," has become the koine for most poetry, both the makers and the readers of poems tend to isolate the poetic artifact through the means of one sort of frame or another. It is ironic, but perhaps also appropriate, that on the one hand poetry so often finds its subjects in, and treats of incidents from, what Richards calls the accidents of everyday experience, but that on the other hand, in order to render these accidents into something essential, it must isolate and heighten them. Richards was well aware of this

Aristotelian distinction. There is no clearer frame than a stanza, although whether the stanza itself is merely an arbitrary, and thereby accidental, or an organic, and thereby essential, part of the experience it represents can be determined only with respect to individual examples, an experiment I perform above with regard to Blake's *Songs*. Containment and flexibility, terms I also used earlier, are essential to any poet's choice of form. The fact that quatrains still exist does not necessarily mean that they are "natural" (Fussell's term) but that today's poets are still heirs to the British Romantics, whose own experiments in form as well as diction and subject matter have licensed those of their descendants. Instead, I would propose that quatrains have been "naturalized."

These critical issues and disagreements revive the ontological question with which I began. I propose that the study of Romantic poetry, indeed of all poetry in English, must return to the kind of formal questions—with regard to measure, sound, and all other nonsemantic aspects of literary discourse as energetically as to tropes and semantic aspects—that will enable us to specify the cause and effect of local choices and to answer the general classifying question: "Why is this thing the way it is rather than otherwise?"

WORKS CITED

Abrams, M. H. "Structure and Style in the Greater Romantic Lyric." *From Sensibility to Romanticism: Essays Presented to F. A. Pottle.* Ed. F. W. Hilles and Harold Bloom. New York: Oxford UP, 1965. 527–60.

American Poetry: The Twentieth Century. Vol. 2, *E. E. Cummings to May Swenson.* New York: Library of America, 2000.

Attridge, Derek. *The Rhythms of English Poetry.* London: Longman, 1982.

Barbauld, Anna Letitia. *The Poems of Anna Letitia Barbauld.* Ed. William McCarthy and Elizabeth Kraft. Athens: U of Georgia P, 1994.

Bentham, Jeremy. *Collected Works.* Ed. John Bowring. Vol. 10. London and Edinburgh, 1843.

Blake, William. *The Complete Poems.* Ed. W. H. Stevenson. 2nd ed. London: Longman, 1989.

Campbell, Thomas. *The Complete Works of Thomas Campbell.* Boston: Phillips, Sampson, 1851.

Corn, Alfred. *The Poem's Heartbeat: A Manual of Prosody.* Brownsville, OR: Story Line, 1997.

Empson, William. *Some Versions of Pastoral.* New York: New Directions, 1960.

Friedman, Albert. *The Ballad Revival: Studies in the Influence of Popular on Sophisticated Poetry.* Chicago: U of Chicago P, 1961.

Fussell, Paul, Jr. *Poetic Meter and Poetic Form.* New York: Random House, 1965.

Gleckner, Robert. *Gray Agonistes: Thomas Gray and Masculine Friendship*. Baltimore: Johns Hopkins UP, 1997.

Hemans, Felicia. *Felicia Hemans: Selected Poems, Letters, Reception Materials*. Ed. Susan J. Wolfson. Princeton: Princeton UP, 2000.

Hollander, John. *Rhyme's Reason*. New, enl. ed. New Haven: Yale UP, 1989.

———. "Romantic Verse Form and the Metrical Contract." *Vision and Resonance: Two Senses of Romantic Form*. New York: Oxford UP, 1975. 187–211.

Kaul, Suvir. "Contesting Value(s): Gray's 'Elegy in a Country Churchyard.'" Chap. 3 of *Thomas Gray and Literary Authority: A Study in Ideology and Poetics*. Stanford: Stanford UP, 1992. 111–65.

Kinzie, Mary. *A Poet's Guide to Poetry*. Chicago: U of Chicago P, 1999.

Laws, G. Malcolm. *The British Literary Ballad: A Study in Poetic Imitation*. Carbondale: Southern Illinois UP, 1972.

O'Donnell, Brendan. *The Passion of Meter: A Study of Wordsworth's Metrical Art*. Kent, OH: Kent State UP, 1995.

Parisi, Joseph, and Stephen Young, eds. *The Poetry Anthology, 1912–2002*. Chicago: Ivan R. Dee, 2002.

Richards, I. A. "Rhythm and Metre." *Principles of Literary Criticism*. New York: Harcourt, Brace, 1924.

Robson, Catherine. "Standing on the Burning Deck: Poetry, Performance, History." *PMLA* 120.1 (2005): 148–62.

Scott, Sir Walter. *The Poetical Works of Sir Walter Scott*. Boston: Phillips, Sampson, 1854.

Steele, Timothy. *All the Fun's in How You Say a Thing*. Athens: Ohio UP, 1999.

Vendler, Helen. *Our Secret Discipline: Yeats and Lyric Form*. Cambridge, MA: Belknap, 2007.

———. *Poems, Poets, Poetry: An Introduction and Anthology*. 2nd ed. New York: Bedford, 2002.

Wolosky, Shira. *The Art of Poetry: How to Read a Poem*. New York: Oxford UP, 2001.

Wordsworth, William. *Selected Poems and Prefaces*. Ed. Jack Stillinger. Boston: Houghton Mifflin, 1965.

Whitman, Tennyson, and the Poetry of Old Age

M. WYNN THOMAS

1

"Why should the agèd eagle stretch its wings?"[1] It was a question that troubled Whitman increasingly as he approached seventy. Why, when half-paralyzed, confined to a cramped room in a tiny Camden cottage, and no more capable of soaring than the cheeping pet canary on whose caged company he so doted, should he continue to scribble? Why, above all, should he continue to publish? The question, voiced and unvoiced, haunts the two annexes he attached to the final edition (1892) of *Leaves of Grass: Sands at Seventy* and *Good-Bye My Fancy*. And answers are multiplied, both in the numerous prose apologias in which Whitman explained his intentions and in the annexes themselves. There is, for instance, an arresting grimness, a taciturnity, about the end of "L. of G.'s Purport":

> I sing of life, yet mind me well of death:
> To-day shadowy Death dogs my steps, my seated shape, and has
>   for years—
> Draws sometimes close to me, as face to face.
>
> (653)[2]

There is no ringing conclusion. The poem does not even end. It simply stops: the rest is silence. The impression is of a man disconcerted by death, even perhaps a little unnerved by it. And this is confirmed in the splendid "After the Supper and Talk" (636). An old man's progress toward death is likened to a guest after supper, reluctant to leave the company for the dark:

> Shunning, postponing severance—seeking to ward off the last word
>   ever so little,
> E'en at the exit-door turning—charges superfluous calling back—e'en
>   as he descends the steps . . .

161

Soon to be lost for aye in the darkness—loth, O so loth to depart!
Garrulous to the very last.

(636)

A new, sobering use is here found for the participial form so favored by
Whitman in his prime for exultantly conveying the restless, ceaseless pro-
creant urge of the world. In this instance it functions as a psychological
ploy to evade the finality of "closure." In extreme old age (for so seventy
was for him) Whitman discovers a motive for continuing to write which
is different from those offered previously in his poems and prefaces. He
writes, it now poignantly emerges, because he is afraid of the final, dead
silence after his last full stop, and because his poems are the means of
clinging to the company (and the "communion" as the poem expressively
puts it) of the living. It is an account by Whitman of his relationship to his
poetry, and through it with his reader, which is all the more marked by
pathos for its contrast with the confident claiming of relationship that fills
the clamorous poetry of his prime.

But counterpointing and counterbalancing these motives for old-age
poetry there are others prominently advertised in the two annexes. These
texts elsewhere repeatedly insist that they were published primarily as
proof of "undiminished faith" (614) and intended as a "résumé," a "repetition" (614). Sparse leaves they might be, but "confirming all the rest"
(633) of *Leaves of Grass*. Puzzling over the reasons why "folks dwell so
fondly on the last words, advice, appearance, of the departing," pointing out that "those last words are not samples of the best, which involve
vitality at its full, and balance, and perfect control and scope," Whitman finally concluded that dying words "are valuable beyond measure
to confirm and endorse the varied train, facts, theories and faith of the
whole preceding life" (639).[3] Published as a footnote to the poetic text,
this statement forms part of that running argument with himself which
Whitman conducted throughout his last years over whether he should
continue to write and publish or not. Characteristically, he managed to
make fine public and literary capital out of these doubts themselves, ex-
ploiting their dramatic potential in both his poetry and his prefaces. One
of the bright cluster of qualities that had belonged to Whitman as a poet
in his prime remained with him in his declining years: the gift for fashioning in poetry and out of his life a compelling dramatic personality. The
result is not only a scatter of fine individual poems but a masterly, or old-
masterly performance, the gradual construction of a character of himself
in old age.

Whitman's ways of describing or addressing himself to his broken body greatly contribute to this achievement and are particularly worth remarking. There is his impatience at his own querulousness, and fear that his life may be dishonored by weakness at the last:

As I sit writing here, sick and grown old,
Not my least burden is that dulness of the years, querilities,
Ungracious glooms, aches, lethargy, constipation, whispering
    ennui,
May filter in my daily songs

                                                                (614)

As he wonders what his seventieth year will bring, he displays a pitilessly bleak self-knowledge:

                    Wilt stir the waters yet?
Or haply cut me short for good? Or leave me here as now,
Dull, parrot-like and old, with crack'd voice harping, screeching?

                                                                (615)

And there is his shockingly brutal recognition of the isolating nature of physical decline:

            a torpid pulse, a brain unnerv'd,
Old age land-lock'd within its winter bay—(cold, cold, O cold!)
These snowy hairs, my feeble arms, my frozen feet.

                                                                (623)

The cool detachment of such self-appraisal, the fastidious distaste he shows for his own grotesqueness, is reminiscent of the tone of Ben Jonson's "My Picture Left in Scotland":

Oh, but my conscious feares,
        That flie my thoughts betweene,
        Tell me that she hath seene
            My hundreds of gray haires,
            Told seven and fortie yeares.
        Read so much weast, as she cannot imbrace
        My mountaine belly, and my rockie face,
And all these through her eyes, have stopt her eares.[4]

Recognizing in Jonson's poem a rare and wry honesty of self-recognition, W. B. Yeats tried to emulate it in his late poetry. And Whitman, too, strove to attain a similarly naked, unaccommodated vision of his drastically reduced physical condition in some of the poems in his two late annexes.

A little masterpiece of this kind is "The Dismantled Ship":

In some unused lagoon, some nameless bay,
On sluggish, lonesome waters, anchor'd near the shore,
An old, dismasted, gray and batter'd ship, disabled, done,
After free voyages to all the seas of earth, haul'd up at last and
    hawser'd tight,
Lies rusing, mouldering

(634)

Its effectiveness, like that of the later Imagist poetry to which it bears a passing resemblance, lies in its apparent innocence of its own power of suggestion. That is what saves it from sentimentality, as Whitman resists the impulse to license certain feelings in himself about his condition. In his description of the ship, he concentrates, and is thus able to shed, all his feelings of physical helplessness, uselessness, worthlessness, and loneliness. At the same time he refuses to identify with those feelings outright by representing himself as a dismantled ship. Whitman resists the lure of such self-indulgent despair: "I know, divine deceitful ones, your glamour's seeming," as he puts it in "Fancies at Navesink" (619).

The continuing alertness of mind in Whitman to which "The Dismantled Ship" implicitly testifies is an indispensable source of the dramatic life and moral honesty of the best of the late poems. As an old man, he continues, as far as his flagging mental energy will permit, to be an explorer of his many-charactered old age. He can use a poem not only to confirm another but also to qualify, or even contradict, the impressions already made. "You Lingering Sparse Leaves of Me" (633) sensitively works out a comparison between his late poems and the "lingering sparse leaves . . . on winter-nearing boughs." "The faithfulest—hardiest—last": the pun there at the end contributes its quiet, unassertive strength to the conclusion. But the next poem deliberately, startlingly, works the same simile out to a very different purpose, partly in the spirit of a kind of rebuke to, or at least reaction against, his previous acceptance (half-melancholy, half-defiant) of his diminished self. The very first line of this poem (532) contains unemphasized within it the dynamics of vision of the whole poem: "Not meager, latent boughs alone, O songs! (scaly and bare, like eagles' talons)."

That simile within a simile is very interesting: the songs may be like winter boughs bare as eagles' talons—but then eagles' talons are themselves instinct with power. In other words, the second simile, while apparently obediently echoing and buttressing the first, has without registering the fact effected a radical shift of emphasis that completely subverts, and even inverts, the original meaning. It is a beautiful example of how a poem can remain secretly faithful and obedient to the deepest inclination of the poet's meaning rather than serve his conscious will. It is a kind of Freudian slip through which the inner self betrays its secret stubborn obsession with joy and proves itself to be incorrigibly defiant and irredeemably hopeful. And the rest of the poem proceeds, all unconscious of having been anticipated, to produce hope in its own more sober way out of the original image. Life is represented as latent in these meager poems, ready to blossom at the first touch of spring. It is one of Whitman's last and most touching images for the meeting between his poems and some future reader. It is now enough for him to believe that his "leaves" may become "verdant" again and rejuvenated—"the stalwart limbs of trees emerging": implicit in the whole description, and adding a generosity of tone to it, is Whitman's recognition that such spring and summer can never return for him.

There is, then, genuine affirmation to be found in some of these poems.

> Go birds of spring: let winter have his fee;
> Let a bleak paleness chalk the doore,
> So all within be livelier then before.[5]

Feelings about old age similar to George Herbert's in these marvelous and ringing lines give rise to two particularly fine poems in these collections. One is "Sounds of Winter" (646), where the senses quietly harvest the richly distinctive sounds and sights of winter and leave the mind to glean a meaning of its own at the end. "Where are the songs of Spring? . . . Think not of them, thou hast thy music too":[6] Keats's famous encouragement to another season is very much in the spirit of Whitman's tribute to winter, and both poets affectionately emphasize the kindliest aspects of their respective seasons.

But there is one remarkable poem in which Whitman, accepting all that the natural and human season can bring, uncompromisingly celebrates the very wintriness of winter. "Of that Blithe Throat of Thine" (623) is perhaps the old Whitman's greatest vindication of the philosophy of life which he had propounded so confidently in his youth: the whole-hearted commitment of oneself to physical existence in all its aspects and implications because it is God-given. The poem is a quiet triumph, all the more impressive for Whitman's refusal to celebrate it. Nothing better distinguishes him from other life worshippers such as Hemingway than his tough-spirited insistence on persisting in joy:

> Not summer's zones alone—not chants of youth, or south's warm
>   tides alone,
> But held by sluggish floes, pack'd in the northern ice, the cumulus
>   of years,
> These with gay heart I also sing.
>
>   (623)

In this one poem, at least, Whitman acquires what Wallace Stevens called "a mind of winter."[7]

These last poems are offered by Whitman, in impressive part, as final incontrovertible testimony that his seasoned central vision is apt for all seasons. They may therefore seem entirely dependent on *Leaves of Grass* for their meaning. But that is not the case. The two annexes may be regarded as the flying buttresses of the massive edifice of *Leaves of Grass,* humbly designed to take the potentially oppressive weight of the earth-ward thrusts of its soaring central affirmations. Many different elements have contributed toward the fashioning of these buttresses, and one of them, it seems to me, is the relationship between Whitman's democratic ideology of aging and the old-age writings of a giant rival figure who continued to trouble his dreams.

2

Five days before he died, Whitman startled his young friend and amanuensis Horace Traubel. Racked by pain, his voice often choked and reduced to a whisper, he was lying helpless on his bed.

> Suddenly, his voice rose, quite firm and easy again for a minute at the start, then lapsing into the disastrous struggle now becoming his norm. "Horace," he said—and his voice stirred me by a something mandatory in his tone, "Horace, if I wrote anything more, I would

compare Tennyson, Whittier and me, dwelling quite a bit on the three ways we each have treated the death subject: Tennyson in "Crossing the Bar," Whittier in "Driftwood"—both ecclesiastical and theoretical—and my "Good-Bye, My Fancy"—based, absorbed in, the natural. That that I've just said is quite a significant"—here he broke off from vain effort to say more.[8]

Obsessed with his great English contemporary to the very last, Whitman continued, in the unabated anxiety of his long jealous rivalry with Tennyson, to travesty the relation between them as poets. As Christopher Ricks has noted, far from being conventionally "ecclesiastical," the laureate's religious faith in old age "remained humane and disconcertingly unorthodox."[9] The old man was said to have remarked, "There's a something that watches over us; and our individuality; and our individuality endures; that's my faith, and that's all my faith" (Ricks 296). Thus phrased, it seems a faith as vague, as heterodox, and as un-"theoretical" as Whitman's own.

But Whitman's very faith in himself as poet had long been predicated on an initially violent, but later much more conciliatory, repudiation of everything Tennyson represented. The compelling complex narrative of this unreciprocated obsession has been succinctly summarized by the editor of Whitman's *Notebooks and Unpublished Prose Manuscripts* in a note on several scraps of prose about Tennyson from the 1860s and 1870s.[10] These fragments are themselves eloquent testimony to the stammering intensity of Whitman's Tennysonian obsession, since they are the debris of his repeated attempts to piece together a statement about the English poet sufficiently powerful to exorcise his ghost.[11]

Even more than Emerson, to whom he felt an uneasy filial tie, and Carlyle, who was a worthy but not dangerous opponent, Tennyson was the contemporary who troubled WW. At the beginning of his career he announced anonymously . . . that he was about to replace the kind of poetry Tennyson represented and kept saying the same thing for the next twenty years. By 1870, he seems not to have been so sure. Possibly his growing awareness that his country was not accepting him led to a number of mildly foolish efforts to promote himself. . . . For all these reasons he felt a deep need for Tennyson's approbation and in 1871 sent him books through a mutual acquaintance. . . . Tennyson was courageous and understood the *Leaves* well enough to pronounce that they had 'go' . . . WW was immensely and pathetically proud of this approbation from the Highest Source. (*Notebooks* 5:1760)

Indeed, to track Whitman's relations with Tennyson during the last two decades of his life through the *Correspondence* and the Traubel volumes is not infrequently to be embarrassed by the painful evidence of the American's repeated, and sometimes desperate, attempts to assure others, but primarily himself, of the high regard in which he was held by the Englishman.

It was, of course, Whitman himself who had made the first direct overtures by sending Tennyson a sample of his work in late 1870, and when he received a polite acknowledgment he could not stop boasting to his friends that the laureate had even gone so far as to invite him to visit. For the next five years, he took immense pride in the fact that he received regular, politely cordial letters from the Englishman; but then he did not hear for two and fretted so terribly that he sent Tennyson a pitiful, half-beseeching rebuke.[12] Having tried unsuccessfully in 1885 to persuade William Sloane Kennedy to write a "criticism on Tennyson and Walt Whitman" (*Correspondence* 3:391), he produced one himself less than two years later. Anxious, as ever, to make Tennyson immediately aware of what he'd written, he sent him a copy, exulting when he received a courteous acknowledgment: "Is not this the only instance known," he eagerly inquired, "of the English Laureate formally 'noticing a notice'?" (*Correspondence* 4:76). And when his determined disciple R. M. Bucke proposed paying a visit to the by then extremely frail, mentally confused, and mostly bedridden Tennyson, Whitman furnished him with a personal introduction. Learning from Bucke that the poet's family was under doctors' orders to exclude all visitors, Whitman held his breath to see whether his own name and recommendation would be sufficient to work a rare open sesame. Always harboring deep—and very well-founded—misgivings about whether or not Tennyson really did regard him as his poetic equal, Whitman clearly felt that this was the moment of conclusive proof. So when Bucke proudly reported that not only had he been granted the rare privilege of a brief audience but the poet's son, Hallam, had uttered bland commendations of Whitman, he was delighted. Yet he remained "cute" enough not to be wholly convinced. Bucke himself had conceded in his report that "none of the Tennysons I imagine . . . have read you as really to understand you or what you are after—but have read you enough to know in a more or less vague way that you are a great force in this modern world."[13]

Bucke's words were confirmation of a suspicion long held by Whitman and clearly voiced on 15 April 1888: "'I don't think [Tennyson] ever quite makes me out.' 'But,' he had then hopefully added, 'he thinks I belong: perhaps that is enough—all I ought to expect.'"[14] It was much more, alas, than was actually the case. It is just as well that he was never made privy to the kind of blunt remark Tennyson had made only three years previously in private conversation with George Walter Prothero: "Walt Whitman [is] no real poet."[15] Contrast such sentiments with Traubel's touching report: "I remember a letter from Tennyson, surrounded by its ribs of black, redolent with savor of wind and water, a strain of poetry in itself, which Whitman for a long time carried in his vest pocket." In the days after receiving Bucke's report, Whitman continued to worry about where he stood with Tennyson. A letter was forwarded to him, via Bucke, from someone trying to recall the exact words Tennyson had used many years before when talking about Whitman. "It certainly seems to me," said the correspondent, "that his expression was 'one of the greatest poets' or 'he surely is a great poet' or words to that effect. But I could not be sure of the words or the form of the statement." Clutching at the straw offered by Traubel—that the very vagueness of the report was proof of its honesty—Whitman asked for the letter to be left near him overnight, so that he could give it his concentrated attention in an effort to determine exactly what Tennyson had said. "Oh! yes," he concluded pitifully, "I guess there need be no doubt but Tennyson is very friendly towards me—has a genuine admiration, of a sort."[16]

These incidents are worth noting because they indicate the depth and extent of Whitman's concern with Tennyson during his final years. Whitman scholarship has hitherto concentrated almost exclusively on Tennyson's influence on the early Whitman, which even took the form, on occasion, of poetic response.[17] A great admirer of "Ulysses," Whitman seems in part to have modeled "Prayer of Columbus" on it, and to have taken from it the trochaic measure for "Pioneers"; and Ken Price has further suggested that "Picture" may have been a kind of reply to "The Palace of Art."[18] All such responses are governed, of course, by the model Whitman had early established and thereafter assiduously cultivated, of himself as the ideological opposite of Tennyson, playing democrat to his "aristocrat" and relegating him to the "feudal" European past. But then, Whitman knew full well that "nations or individuals, we surely learn deepest from our unlikeness, from a sincere opponent, from the light thrown even scornfully on dangerous spots and liabilities" (898).

It has already been well understood by scholars that Whitman in his prime drew considerable creative energy from his "unlikeness" to the likes of Carlyle and of Tennyson. But no attention has been paid to the possibility (to put it no more strongly) that Whitman continued to do so during his final years, when his always uncertain confidence in his poetry began to be seriously sapped by his deteriorating physical condition, the attendant mental stress, and the doubts expressed even by some of those to whom he was closest about his occasional effortful excursions into shockingly short-breathed poetry. "[William] O'Connor kicks against [*Sands at Seventy*]," he noted in 1888. He "is unfavorable—seems to regard the new poems as in some sense a contradiction of the old—alien to the earlier poems—as if I had gone back on myself in old age." That, Whitman insisted, was not the case,

> Am I, as some think, losing grip?—taking in my horns? No—no—no: I am sure that could not be. I still wish to be, am, the radical of my stronger days—to be the same uncompromising oracle of democracy—to maintain undimmed the lights of my deepest faith. I am sure I have not gone back on that—sure, sure. The Sands have to be taken as the utterances of an old man—a very old man. I desire that they may be interpreted as confirmations, not denials, of the work that has preceded. . . . I recognize, have always recognized, the importance of the lusty, strong-limbed, big-bodied American of the Leaves. I do not abate one atom of that belief now, today. But I hold to something more than that, too, and claim a full, not a partial, judgment upon my work.[19]

His old age was to be represented as the old age of an indomitably convinced democrat. And who better than Tennyson, the contemporary author of celebrated old-age poems, to sharpen awareness of what it meant to be, in one's declining years, "an uncompromising oracle of democracy?"

3

"Dear old man," Tennyson teasingly opened a letter to Whitman in January 1887 before gracefully proceeding to describe it as sent from an "elder old man" (*Correspondence* 4:63). The laureate was ten years older than his correspondent and had, in 1885, published a notable collection of "old age poems." These attracted the immediate attention of a Whitman who always kept anxiously abreast of Tennyson's poetry, and his response came in the form of the essay "A Word about Tennyson." First published in *The Critic* (Jan. 1887), it was incorporated in 1888 into *November Boughs*, where it kept company with "Sands at Seventy," as if inviting a comparison between "the old man at Farringford" (1164) and the old man at Camden.

In the consistency of point of view between "Locksley Hall" and the recently published "Locksley Hall Sixty Years After" Whitman found confirmation of his own consistent characterization of Tennyson as the splendidly eloquent, elegiac voice of a dying society. Both poems are "essentially morbid, heart-broken, finding fault with everything, especially the fact of money's being made (as it ever must be, and perhaps should be) the paramount matter in worldly affairs" (1161). The insouciance of such a statement was somewhat disingenuous, given the aging Whitman's own ragings against his dollar-driven America, but then Tennyson acted as a lightning rod for many of the unacknowledged anxieties and misgivings Whitman had about his country—hence the intensity and complexity of his concern with the "royal English laureate." Professing here to believe that "the course of progressive politics (democracy) is so certain and resistless . . . that we can well afford the warning calls, threats, checks, neutralizings, in imaginative literature" (1163), Whitman is able to pronounce that Tennyson, like Carlyle, is a valuable adversary: "As to his non-democracy, it fits him well, and I like him the better for it. I guess we all like to have (I am sure I do) some one who presents those sides of a thought, or possibility, different from our own" (1163). He then revealingly adds, "different and yet with a sort of home-likeness." This is a moment of honest self-knowledge on Whitman's part, before he concludes his essay by condescending to Tennyson, damning him with the faint praise that American readers "owe to him some of their most agreeable and harmless and healthy hours" (1165). That Whitman should have then sent a copy of this essay posthaste to Tennyson is surely indicative of how blind the anxiety of his obsession had made him to the impression that such a piece— ingratiatingly patronizing when it wasn't grandly dismissive—was very likely to make on its unfailingly polite recipient.

In "Locksley Hall Sixty Years After," the aged Tennyson's blistering commentary on what he regarded as his own bellicose, exploitative, materialistic, and degenerate age, the convulsive energy of dark nihilism ("Chaos, Cosmos! Cosmos, Chaos! once again the sickening game" [1364]) moderates into the outrage of social denunciation: "Is it well that while we range with Science, glorying in the Time, / City children soak and blacken soul and sense in city slime? / . . . There the smouldering fire of fever creeps across the rotted floor, / And the crowded couch of incest in the warrens of the poor" (1367–68).[20] Through the poem there echoes a "Poor old voice of eighty crying after voices that have fled! / All I loved are vanish'd voices, all my steps are on the dead" (1368). The bitter despair in the poetry provoked at least one British reviewer to protest against this "rhymed recapitulation of the bad-blooded objurgations of gout-stricken

Toryism."[21] And the poem's prediction that "Demos [would] end in working its own doom" (1363) most certainly would have provoked Whitman. Moreover, it is likely that he would have read the poem in the context of a collection in which gloom bleaks through much of the poetry. So in some ways it does through Whitman's, but his manner of expressing it, and of coping with it, is very different—"democratic" in character (in his terms) as opposed to what he regarded as Tennyson's aristocratic response. For instance, he firmly links his "ungracious glooms" to his decrepit physical condition with its "aches, lethargy, constipation, whimpering *ennui*." Thus, instead of donning the singular mantle of the doomed prophet, he appears as everyman, sometimes grumpy victim of those great levelers, the mundane infirmities of body and of mind. Just as, for old age's angry yearnings for lost youth—Tiresias's "I wish I were as in the years of old"—he substitutes the equanimity of a fondness for "the meditation of old times resumed—their loves, joys, persons, voyages," thus substituting a model of life as continuity for the model of life as violent rupture. For Whitman, the "word of the modern, the word En-Masse" meant a faith that "Nothing is ever really lost, or can be lost" (620). And his fussing over the exact form of the title of the second annex (*Good-Bye My Fancy* should not, he insisted, terminate with an exclamation mark, although the poem of the same title did) may be attributed to his wanting to emphasize the matter-of-factness of the salutation. This was because, as he pointedly noted, "Behind a Good-bye there lurks much of the salutation of another beginning—to me, Development, Continuity, Immortality, Transformation, are the chiefest life-meanings of Nature and Humanity" (639).

However, before further considering such contrasts, perhaps deliberately measured by Whitman, it is worth noticing points of unexpected convergence between his outlook and Tennyson's. The latter's poem "The Wreck" is a Victorian melodrama about a forced and loveless marriage, resulting in a tragically unloved baby, a passionate adultery, and, finally, overpowering guilt. It includes a significant characterization of the cold husband as follows:

> He would open the books that I prized, and toss them away with a
>   yawn,
> Repelled by the magnet of Art to the which my nature was drawn
> The word of the Poet by whom the deeps of the world are stirr'd.
> The music that robes it in language beneath and beyond the word!

My Shelley would fall from my hands when he cast a contemptuous
    glance
Even where he was poring over his Tables of Trade and Finance;

(1335–36)

Here, as elsewhere in this late collection, Tennyson the darling of his
country despairs at the impotence of his fame, frankly recognizing what
the older Whitman, too, knew: that poetry changed absolutely nothing
in society. This is a feeling most compellingly worked out by Tennyson
in the "Tiresias" sequence of poems.[22] It begins with a genial Horatian
epistle of friendship addressed to his old friend Edward FitzGerald, famous author of *Omar Khayyam*, quietly rejoicing that "we old friends are
still alive,/And I am nearing seventy-four,/While you have touched at
seventy-five" (1318). The main body of the sequence then follows in the
form of the poem "Tiresias," a product of Tennyson's youth he here resur-
rects and offers as a gift to FitzGerald. The theme of this poem is the ancient Tiresias's desperate attempt to convince Menoeceus to sacrifice his
own life in order to save Thebes from the dreadful fate that, the prophet
foresees, will otherwise certainly befall it. Tiresias's desperation derives,
of course, from the fact that Pallas Athene had inflicted on him a terrible
punishment when he was young for having accidentally glimpsed her radiant nakedness: "Henceforth be blind, for thou hast seen too much,/And
speak the truth that no man may believe" (570). Such had been his terrible
fate ever since—the accursed gift of barren prophecy, from which he could
not escape even when dwelling now in "oldest age in shadow from the
night." All his long life he had therefore been condemned to experience
"the faces of the Gods—the wise man's word,/Here trampled by the populace underfoot" (574). Repeating in his old age this story that he had first
rehearsed in his youth must, for Tennyson, have powerfully reinforced his
identification with the ancient disregarded Tiresias. And this is an experience underlined by the epilogue to the poem. There Tennyson reveals
that FitzGerald, the intended recipient, had died before the poem could be
completed and sent. What more poignantly conclusive evidence could be
adduced for the poem's core truth?—that the words of a prophet or a poet
are powerless in the face of life.[23]

    Reflections such as these also haunted Whitman in his old age, evi-
dence again that though his vision may have differed centrally from that
of Tennyson, there were also many "sort[s] of home-likeness" that complicated and enriched the picture. Reluctant to express in poems the racking

self-doubts he confessed to Traubel, since (as Tennyson's lines indicated) that would mean indicting his beloved democratic masses, he resorted to such indirect expression as "To Those Who've Failed," with its revealing mention of "many a lofty song and picture without recognition" (613), and "The Bravest Soldiers" who "press'd to the front and fell, unnamed, unknown" (638). Insisting that "this late-years palsied old shorn and shellfish condition of me [was] the indubitable outcome and growth" of "those hot, sad, wrenching times" of his war service in the Washington hospitals (638), he found repeated expression for his chronic fear that he (and his democratic vision) had been wholly ignored by his society in his old-age poems about unwelcome veterans of past wars who "amid the current songs of beauty, peace, decorum" interject the unwelcome false note of "a reminiscence—(likely 'twill offend you)" (631).[24]

Primarily, though, Whitman seems to me to have used Tennyson's old-age poems as a foil for his own. Take, for instance, the Englishman's fondness for seeing in the ocean an image of what he feared most (and therefore denounced most loudly), a vision of the brutal senseless power of a godless material universe. So, in "Despair," a married couple seek to drown in the sea their despair at a universe in which they see "No soul in the heaven above, no soul on the earth below, / A fiery scroll written over with lamentation and woe" (1300). To such would-be suicides, the Whitman of "Fancies at Navesink" gives short shrift:

> Some suicide's despairing cry, *Away to the boundless waste, and*
>   *never again return.*
>
> On to oblivion then!
> On, on, and do your part, ye burying, ebbing tide!
> On for your time, ye furious debouche!
>
> (619)

For a Tennyson whose spirit had always been darkly shadowed by the dread that "Doubt is the lord of this dunghill and crows to the sun and the moon," stability could be kept only by clinging to the belief in a remedying afterlife. Mortal existence, he repeatedly affirms, can only be justified (and then only doubtfully) by the promise of a world to come.[25] And it is here, perhaps, that Whitman was most fruitfully able to oppose his own vision in old age to that of his great rival, by expressing his unqualified commitment (however effortful at times) not to an afterlife but to ongoing life. This, too, he believed to be an expression of a devout democratic relish for every one of life's minute particulars. This might be supposed to have come naturally to the poet who, in his prime, had so unforgettably celebrated "fog in the air and beetles rolling balls of dung" (51). But there is a different, darker, richer timbre to his old-age affirmations; they radiate a humility in the face of the luster of "the commonplace." To ward off the prostration that threatened him after the death of his beloved mother, following as it did hard on the heels of his first paralytic stroke, Whitman had assiduously trained himself to live in the moment, to magnify its gifts. "The trick is, I find, to tone your wants and tastes low down enough, and to make much of negatives, and of mere daylight and the skies" (780).

Accompanying the course of physical rehabilitation he underwent at Timber Creek was a therapeutic course of mental and spiritual reeducation, a gradual teaching of each of his senses to appreciate how their powers of apprehending the world could be paradoxically enlarged by the reduction of physical mobility and the straitening of circumstance. He concentrated intensely on "distilling the present hour" (809). The result was a new kind of writing, which should be recognized as being as much of an achievement as, say, the new poetic style William Carlos Williams so arduously and remarkably produced in the aftermath of his own stroke. The bent form of Wordsworth's old Cumberland beggar, proceeding at snail's pace, sees not "hill and dale, / and the blue sky" but "some straw / Some scattered leaf, or marks which, in one track, / The nails of cart or chariot-wheel have left / Impressed on the white road."[26] Unconsidered trifles came to bulk similarly large in the stricken Whitman's experience, and they are registered, in *Specimen Days,* in the luminous spareness of a prose that is the real poetry of his postwar period:

> autumn leaves, the cool dry air, the faint aroma—crows cawing in the distance—two great buzzards wheeling gracefully and slowly far up there—the occasional murmur of the wind, sometimes quite gently, then threatening through the trees—a gang of farm-laborers loading corn-stalks in a field in sight, and the patient horses waiting. (794)

Not, however, until his late annexes, and little pieces of Adamic purity of wonder like "Out of May's Shows Selected," does he himself seem to have realized that such writing constituted the different poetry of his old age.[27]

Apple orchards, the trees all cover'd with blossoms:
Wheat fields carpeted far and near in vital emerald green:

The eternal, exhaustless freshness of each early morning;
The yellow, golden, transparent haze of the warm afternoon sun;
The aspiring lilac bushes with profuse purple or white flowers.

(617)

The self-contained, end-stopped lines—syntactically and experientially the very opposite of the early writing, with its hectic forward momentum—indicate the self-sufficiency, and sufficiency for the self, of each discrete sensation. "The simple shows, the delicate miracles of earth," says Whitman again in "Soon Shall the Winter's Foil Be Here," are returned so that "Thine eyes, ears—all thy best attributes—all that takes cognizance of natural beauty, / Shall wake and fill" (630). In old age, his senses are still the means, as they were in "Song of Myself," to fulfillment; the realizing of self through a coming alive to the sensory world.

No wonder, then, that in wishing his poems on "the death subject" to be contrasted with those of Tennyson, the dying Whitman stressed that his be recognized as "based, absorbed in, the natural." He had, no doubt, forgotten that he had himself already written the very essay he was urging Traubel to write. His "A Death-Bouquet" (1266–68) was a brief comparison of the ways death had been treated by several poets, including Whittier and Tennyson (he singled out the very recently published "Crossing the Bar"). Noting that they, and poets as ancient as Phrynichus of "old Athens," had become absorbed in contemplating the movement of tides and of ships as the most richly suggestive tropes for dying, he wryly asked, "Am I starting the sail-craft of poets in line?" (1267). Indeed he was, and very much, it seems, with a view to adding his own vessels to this stately textual procession. The piece concludes with his little poem "Now, land and life, finalé, and farewell!" (1268). And in the light of the train of thought followed in this brief essay, it seems reasonable to suggest that at least two of the poems in *Good-Bye My Fancy*, "Sail Out for Good, Eidólon Yacht!" and "Old Age's Ship & Crafty Death's," are exercises in extending this tradition he had so sympathetically identified. Moreover, published as they were in 1891, they seem specifically to involve conversations with "Crossing the Bar" (1888). For the fade-out of the poem in which Tennyson gently acquiesces in dying, Whitman, ever the ebullient indomitable democratic individualist, pointedly substituted a robust yo-ho! of "challenge and defiance—flags and flaunting pennants added, / As we take to the open—take to the deepest, freest waters" (642).

In a piece published in *Lippencott's Magazine* to coincide with the appearance of *Good-Bye My Fancy* he had boasted that "every page of my poetic or attempt at poetic utterance therefore smacks of the living physical identity" (1345). While this "new last cluster" is "a lot of tremolos about old age," and "the physical just lingers but almost vanishes," the book "is garrulous, irascible (like old Lear)." He was right so to characterize it, as he was also right to insist that, to the very last, his poems were deliberately composed "in style often offensive to the conventions" (1345). And as his late writing and recorded oral comments indicate, he associated the conventional approach to old age and dying with Tennyson. Indeed, one of the essays he included in *Good-Bye My Fancy* itself notes that Tennyson, "over eighty years old," had "sent out long since a fresh volume, which the English-speaking Old and New Worlds are yet reading." He then reiterated his view of the laureate's poetry, that it was "flowery" and the author "the poetic cream-skimmer of our age's melody, *ennui* and polish" (1255). In going on to associate Tennyson with Shakespeare he was paying him a backhanded compliment, at once advertising his greatness and drawing attention to his superannuation. The same strategy is followed even in the poems of *Sands at Seventy*, when, in "To Get the Final Lilt of Songs," he speaks of the kind of wisdom granted old age—"to know the mighty ones / Job, Homer, Eschylus, Dante, Shakspeare, Tennyson, Emerson" (624). Tennyson is pointedly included there among the dead, as he was in "Song of the Exposition": "Pass'd! pass'd! for me, forever pass'd, that once so mighty world, now void, inanimate, phantom world, . . . / Blazon'd with Shakspeare's purples page, / And dirged by Tennyson's sweet sad rhyme" (343).

4

Whitman was a consummate salesman and inveterate self-publicist to the last. In a late reprise of the kind of feyness he had most famously exhibited in *Calamus,* he enticingly offered *Good-Bye My Fancy* to his readers as a mystery wrapped up in a riddle: "It will have to be ciphered and ciphered out long—and is probably in some respects the most curious part of its author's baffling works" (1345). Perhaps. What this essay has at least suggested is that it might be worth considering the possibility that concealed in the two late annexes was Whitman's obsessive conversation with Tennyson, "the boss of us all" and the one great contemporary figure who contested with him the privilege of being the supreme poet of old age. And there is one possible final twist to their poetic relationship. The very last poem Whitman completed was "A Thought of Columbus," the piece he handed to Traubel just ten days before his death in which, aware of himself as "A flutter at the darkness' edge as if old Time's and Space's secret near revealing," Whitman reverses his lifelong practice of addressing the future and addresses instead this phantom from the past in a final paradoxically prophetic act of homage and of (self-)acclamation.

What is interesting for present purposes is that Whitman had long associated Columbus with Tennyson. As has been noted, his own "Prayer of Columbus" had been modeled on Tennyson's "Ulysses." A few years later Tennyson had himself, as Whitman could surely not have failed to notice, published his own "Columbus." And then, on 4 April 1891, Traubel records Whitman's warm approval of the following notice that had appeared in the *Illustrated American*:

> OUR POET LAUREATE—That was a very foolish thought of the managers of the World's Fair—to ask a poem from Lord Tennyson in honor of the occasion. Tennyson is a great man. But his day is over. His recent work—especially the last song, "To Sleep!"—has detracted from rather than added to his reputation. Better, far better, he should relapse into silence. Moreover, he is a foreigner—a member, too, of the nation which scorned Columbus and refused his proffer of a new world. A Spaniard, even an Italian, would be better. Among the exponents of the latter-day renaissance of song in either country, it might be possible to find one who could do justice to Columbus, to Chicago, to America.
>
> But best of all would be an American poet. The children of the New World, which Columbus revealed to the Old, are best fitted to celebrate the glories of the new dispensation.
>
> Walt Whitman would be the ideal choice. He is an American, a democrat in the largest and best sense of the word, a son of the soil. He could give us a splendid chant, full of virility and breadth and wisdom. But we have not yet reached the ideal stage where we can appreciate him or his true worth. Lowell is a choice that would better please the more finical and dainty and scholarly mind.[28]

The editors of the Comprehensive Reader's Edition of *Leaves of Grass* note that the Columbus poem Whitman handed to Traubel at the very end of his life consisted of several fragments, some of which dated back to 1891—the date of this notice.[29] One wonders, therefore, whether that last poem might not after all be Whitman's final act of engagement with—and triumph over—his great rival, Tennyson. Because in this poem, Whitman pointedly lays claim to the privilege, as American poet, of being Columbus's heir. In his long (one-sided) argument with Tennyson, Whitman may thus have ensured he had the very last word. And if his last spoken words are reputed to have been a request to be turned on his water bed—the simple, pitiful, "Shift, Warry"—then the last words he authorized for publication were words of tribute to the great "Discoverer" who had unknowingly called a new, modern, democratic world into being:

(An added word yet to my song, far Discoverer, as ne'er before sent
   back to son of earth—
If still thou hearest, hear me,
Voicing as now—lands, races, arts, bravas to thee,
O'er the long backward path to thee—one vast consensus, north,
   south, east, west,
Soul plaudits! acclamation! reverent echoes!
One manifold, huge memory to thee! oceans and lands!
The modern world to thee and thought of thee!)[30]

As Columbus's heir, Whitman laid claim himself to being a "Discoverer," as Tennyson was not. "For all these new and evolutionary facts," he wrote, surveying the dying nineteenth century in his late essay *A Backward Glance o'er Travel'd Roads,* and for all the new "meanings, purposes, new poetic messages, new forms, expressions are inevitable" (659). In his prime, Whitman had altered expression repeatedly, as epic, elegy, war poetry, love poetry, all assumed new, democratic forms in his work. And now, at life's end, he succeeded in working one final miracle of transformation, producing a democratic poetry of old age. It did not, however, take the form he had longed for. To him was denied that mellow serenity and wisdom in age that, he had so long dreamt, would be the finest expression of the democratic spirit. Lacking that, he instead turned his very condition—paralyzed, exhausted, but indomitable—into the physical sign of the as yet unfulfilled promise of American democratic society. His old-age poetry faithfully recorded this truth and, greatly reduced in power and scope though he full well knew it to be, it retained a shy hold on his affections. As he wistfully remarked to Traubel, "Howells, James and some other appear to think I rest my philosophy, my democracy, upon braggadocio, noise, rough assertion, such integers." It is a tendency that, despite the best efforts of Randall Jarrell and many others, has persisted to the present day. But, he added, "while I would not be afraid to assent to this as a part of the truth I still insist that I am on the whole to be thought of in other terms."[31] It is a telling remark, all the more compelling because it is uttered so quietly and modestly. No wonder that he therefore warmed to

Traubel's speaking of the "dignity" of *Sands at Seventy*. And, in the light of such comments, it is perhaps time that we, however belatedly, take the advice Traubel gave, in an appendix he published after Whitman's death, to read the old-age poems "as indicating how this giant man, sitting here in the freedom which no physical disorder can destroy, is establishing a very heaven of purposeful stars."[32]

NOTES

I am grateful to Larry Buell, Alan Trachtenberg, and Gerhard Joseph for their advice on an earlier version of this essay. The first section is based on material first published in "A Study of Whitman's Late Poetry," *Walt Whitman Review* 27.1 (March 1981): 3–14. It was part of the body of work that first brought me to Helen Vendler's attention.

1. "Ash Wednesday," *T. S. Eliot: Collected Poems, 1909–1962* (London: Faber and Faber, 1963), 95.

2. All quotations from Whitman, unless otherwise stated, are taken from Walt Whitman, *Complete Poetry and Collected Prose*, ed. Justin Kaplan (New York: Library of America, 1982).

3. Whitman's responses to dying and to death are subtly considered by Harold Aspiz in *So Long! Walt Whitman's Poetry of Death* (Tuscaloosa: U of Alabama P, 2004).

4. *Poems of Ben Jonson*, ed. George Burke Johnston (London: Routledge and Kegan Paul, The Muses Library, 1962), 128.

5. "The Forerunners," *The Works of George Herbert*, ed. F. E. Hutchinson (London: Oxford UP, 1971), 177.

6. "To Autumn," *The Poems of John Keats*, ed. H. W. Garrod (London: Oxford UP, 1966), 219.

7. "The Snow Man," *Collected Poems of Wallace Stevens* (London: Faber, 1969), 9.

8. Horace Traubel, *With Walt Whitman in Camden*, ed. Jeanne Chapman and Robert MacIsaac (Oregon House, CA: W. L. Bentley Books, 1996), vol. 9 (October 1, 1891–April 3, 1892), 576.

9. Christopher Ricks, *Tennyson* (London: Macmillan, 1972), 296.

10. Walt Whitman, *Notebooks and Unpublished Prose Manuscripts*, ed. Edward F. Grier (New York: New York UP, 1984), 5:1757–68. For the mixed reception the United States afforded to Tennyson's earlier poetry, see John Olin Eidson, *Tennyson in America: His Reputation and Influence from 1827 to 1858* (Athens: U of Georgia P, 1943). The relationship between Tennyson and Whitman is usefully outlined by Harold Blodgett in *Walt Whitman in England* (Ithaca: Cornell UP, 1934), 122–35. And while theirs was in many respects a complex rivalry, the earlier Whitman was nevertheless indebted to the Englishman, not least for a

poetry that had revealed to him the potentialities of soundscapes and of metric. See Laurence Buell's important essay "Walt Whitman as an Eminent Victorian" (to be published in a forthcoming volume from Nebraska UP). I am very grateful to Professor Buell for sharing the essay with me: it should be regarded as complementing my own.

11. It is interesting to note Ricks's opinion, "The best criticism of Tennyson is by Walt Whitman" (312).

12. Walt Whitman, *The Correspondence,* ed. Edwin Haviland Miller (New York: New York UP, 1961–), 3:52, 133; 2:125 (further citations are in the text). Whitman first heard from Tennyson in July 1871.

13. Traubel, *With Walt Whitman in Camden,* vol. 8 (February 11, 1891–September 30, 1891), 431.

14. Traubel, *With Walt Whitman in Camden,* vol. 1 (New York: Rowman and Littlefield, 1961), 36.

15. *The Letters of Alfred Lord Tennyson,* ed. Cecil Y. Lang and Edgar F. Shannon Jr. (Oxford: Clarendon, 1990), 3:332.

16. Traubel, *With Walt Whitman in Camden* 8:583, 441–42, 442.

17. For Tennyson's influence on Whitman, see Floyd Stovall, *The Foreground of* Leaves of Grass (Charlottesville: UP of Virginia, 1974); Kenneth M. Price, *Walt Whitman and Tradition: The Poet in His Century* (New Haven: Yale UP, 1990); and the entry in J. R. LeMaster and Donald D. Kummings, *Walt Whitman: An Encyclopaedia* (New York: Garland, 1998).

18. Price, *Walt Whitman* 30–34.

19. Traubel, *With Walt Whitman in Camden,* vol. 2 (July 16, 1888–October 31, 1888) (New York: Rowman and Littlefield, 1961), 9.

20. All quotations from Tennyson are from *The Poems of Tennyson,* ed. Christopher Ricks (Harlow: Longmans, 1969).

21. J. M. Robertson, "The Art of Tennyson" (1889), in *Tennyson: The Critical Heritage,* ed. John D. Jump (London: Routledge and Kegan Paul, 1967), 412.

22. It is noteworthy that Whitman scribbled some notes for Bucke on the verso of pages from the 1885 Tiresias (*Notebooks* 5:1536). It therefore seems reasonably safe to assume his familiarity with this text.

23. Another poem relevant to this theme is "The Dead Prophet," an astonishing attack on Froude for publishing a biography that revealed the clay feet of one of Tennyson's idols, Carlyle: "Dumb on the winter heath he lay,/ His friends had stript him bare,/ And rolled his nakedness everyway/ That all the crowd might stare" (1324).

24. Whitman also had another motive for thus accounting for his physical condition in old age: "'That which you told me the other day—that some, even of our fellows, question whether this paralysis came of the war, was not the result of the youthful'—he hesitated and laughed—'indiscretions, so to say—that was news to me. Yet it is not the worst that has done duty against me'" (*Correspondence* 8:79).

25. Tennyson's struggle with himself, even in old age, to overcome the temptations of a nihilistic atheism is powerfully expressed in "The Ancient Sage" (1349). As for his imaging of old age, in a private note to me the Tennyson scholar Gerhard Joseph shrewdly notes that Tennyson "adopted 'the mask of great age' (as W. D. Paden first called it in *Tennyson in Egypt: A Study of the Imagery* in his earlier works) as a juvenilian melancholic pose that he carried into his mature poetry, so that there's always something more or less theatrical to Tennyson's old age poems from, say, 'Ulysses' on down. Quite different from Whitman?"

26. "The Old Cumberland Beggar," *Wordsworth: Poetical Works*, ed. Thomas Hutchinson, rev. Ernest de Selincourt (Oxford: Oxford UP, 1969), 443.

27. The equivalently affirmative old-age piece by Tennyson is "Early Spring," a lovely lyric relishing the way "the Heavenly Power / Makes all things new, / And domes the red-plumed hills / With living blue" (1314). But this is a reworking of an early (1834) poem.

28. Traubel, *With Walt Whitman in Camden* 8:126.

29. Walt Whitman, *Leaves of Grass: Comprehensive Reader's Edition*, ed. Harold W. Blodgett and Sculley Bradley (New York: New York UP, 1965), 581.

30. Whitman, *Leaves of Grass* 582.

31. Traubel, *With Walt Whitman in Camden* 1:272.

32. Traubel, *With Walt Whitman in Camden* 8:586.

Incipience and Seriousness in Yeats's *A Vision*

NICK HALPERN

Prospective readers of Yeats's *A Vision* sometimes wonder if there will be a way to take the book seriously and, if not, whether there will still be a way to take pleasure from it. I want to suggest that there may be a way to do both. Insufficient attention has been paid, I think, to a peculiar aspect of Yeats's own pleasure in the production of *A Vision*. Again and again, in writing (and in writing about) *A Vision,* Yeats tells us that he feels himself filled with a conviction of *incipience.* The sense that something extraordinary is about to happen can seem more compelling to Yeats than anything that does subsequently happen or fail to happen. Helen Vendler wrote *Yeats's Vision and the Later Plays* partly in order to answer the Yeatsians who held that *A Vision* was unconnected to normal experience; she showed how Yeats's book offers, in fact, "intelligible statements" about "the poetic process, the poetic mind and the poetic product" (255). Sharing her confidence that *A Vision* is, even in its most eccentric moments, fundamentally about "normal experience" (255), I want to single out the feeling (both aesthetic and psychological) of incipience as one of those experiences. Attention to Yeats's dramatizations of incipience, rather than, say, to his obsession with gyres and cones, may make *A Vision* compelling to first-time readers. Those dramatizations are, I suspect, what draws many who keep returning to the book.

It might seem odd to call "compelling" a work initially so difficult to connect with. If we are to think of Yeats as like us, generations of readers have learned, we must think of him as, in Auden's words, "silly like us." It would be a terrible error, probably, to try to become serious like Yeats. Even as a thought experiment, in fact, it seems impossible to imagine Yeats the prophetic prose writer as serious. The phrase "serious like us" has a peculiar double power, either to shut off speculation or to set it going. What if Yeats, rather than, say, Wittgenstein, were the voice we summoned when we tried to evoke what seriousness sounded like in the first half of the twentieth century? To take Yeats as the model would mean already having somehow found a way to validate for oneself not just the prophetic but the occult voice. Among impossible projects this might seem to some readers a tempting one: it would mean a poet could sound serious without having to sound austere or astringent. A serious voice (rather than a crazy or playful one) could talk about endless abundance, and what to make of an augmented thing. Wallace Stevens called such a voice the "more than human voice" and, though he was tempted by it, understood that it was more productive of good poems if he talked about rather than adopted it (296). Most twentieth-century poets have felt the same way. Yeats felt differently. The "more than human voice" is precisely what is incipient. Prophetic speech, after long silence. And then it comes. The sense of incipience continues, but now it is even more intense. The voice is about to change our lives.

The drama of incipience is staged in many places in *A Vision*. It is there, first of all, in our experience of reading. Yeats makes us eager to hear the "marvellous things" he promises us. Then he delivers. Reading certain pages—"splendid pages," Vendler calls them (253)—we imagine what it would feel like to read a book that actually did what *A Vision* claims to do, and arrive at a passage of bracing clarity and shrewdness that makes us feel (knowing it's absurd) that *A Vision is* that never-to-be-written book. We turn the page and the sensation vanishes. The words on this page seem neither beautiful nor true, just silly, and not even "silly like us." Will the sense of expectation return? We press on, hoping for the return of that combination of exalted language and uncanny applicability and discover, many pages later, a lovely and accurate and serious passage. The lucid, keen, insightful voice, the undisappointing voice, has returned, and maybe for good this time. But the next page is—to use Yeats's own language—"arbitrary, harsh, difficult" (*Vision* 23). Yeats sometimes allegorizes this effect as his Frustrators: they frustrate him; he frustrates us, although a reader frustrated not just by vagueness and murk but also by the didactic and schematic might feel frustrated more often than Yeats does. What such a reader wants from *A Vision* is that serious, beautiful voice offering us true and absorbing insights. One reads on, sure of its imminent return. Incipience, it turns out, isn't the onetime experience it's said to be.

Readers may experience the excitement of *A Vision* as intermittent, and so does Yeats, probably, but for him (and potentially for his readers) that intermittence generates suspense. When will the true and beautiful material return? Yeats, like us, is along for the ride; he is, as he often reminds us, as much a reader as a writer. Like James Merrill in *The Changing Light at Sandover,* Yeats presents himself not just as a producer of prophetic speech but also as a passive consumer of it. Allen Grossman, another contemporary prophetic poet, is generally just the producer of prophetic speech, a choice that limits the effects available to him. Yeats, like Merrill, wants access to all the effects available to him.

Some of these effects—passivity, for example—he understands instinctively, professionally, how to dramatize. One way to dramatize passivity is to claim (sometimes really to feel) incomplete understanding. "Even when I wrote the first edition of this book," Yeats writes, "I thought the geometric symbolism so difficult, I understood it so little, that I put it off to a later section" (*Vision* 80). Did he really not understand it all? Barbara Croft writes, "There is ample evidence that Yeats himself did not fully master the raw material of *A Vision.*" She suggests that "the genius of the book is that Yeats consistently sees himself as caught within the system, as having only partial vision, and struggling to understand and express his perceptions" (9, 157). Croft is right, although the words "caught" and "struggling" don't quite capture the atmosphere of hopeful exuberance emanating from so many passages in *A Vision.* Yeats, enjoying the dramatic possibilities of partial understanding, exploits them both in his book and in his letters about the book. Referring to material dealing with "individual mind," Yeats writes to Ethel Mannin, "I have not published it because I only half understand it" (*Letters* 916). His tone is breezy. Partial vision is inherently dramatic: what is a man who looks through a glass darkly but a man about to see face to face? A reader might imagine Yeats, like Stevens, inventing criteria for a supreme fiction. Yeats's first condition might be: *It must be only half-understandable.*

For one later prophetic poet the way to read *A Vision* is to only half *try* to understand it. In *The Changing Light at Sandover,* Merrill writes: "For as it happened I had been half trying / To make sense of *A Vision*" (14). Half trying is a delaying tactic Yeats might appreciate; though, in fact, he affects not to care much what attitude his readers take. He is more concerned with the postures he himself can assume and the pleasures potentially afforded him by each posture. Delayed understanding, for example, might offer as one of its delights the sense that for once the future (rather than the past) holds all the cards. One is delaying something delightful in order to prolong the pleasure of anticipation. The discoveries will be (in anticipation, as they are in memory) continual. "I read," Yeats tells us, "with an excitement I had not known since I was a boy with all knowledge before me, and made continual discoveries . . . " (*Vision* 12). One anticipates, as if in a dream, what one will experience as if it too were a dream. *A Vision,* Croft writes, "is not definitive; it gives no answers and reaches no conclusions. If one is stringent about truth, it is not true. Instead, it is generative, it sets the mind dreaming, wandering in a vast, endless speculation that is, in itself, satisfying. We would have been surprised, even disappointed, to have had anything else from Yeats" (9). Yeats, meditating on the idea of satisfaction unachieved, uses the Stevensian word "suffice." At the end of "Meditations in Time of Civil War" he writes, "The half-read wisdom of daemonic images / Suffice the ageing man as once the growing boy" (*Collected Poems* 206). The half-read, half-understood suffices on bad days to distract one from the used-up past and the disappointing present. On good days the half-read and half-understood images generate an atmosphere of extraordinary suspense, the kind of suspense one feels as an intimate emotional and intellectual sensation and associates with the drama of a relationship. We are continually being given more to do, more to understand. Randall Jarrell, in "A Girl in a Library," tells us that "the soul has no assignments" (15). For Yeats, the soul has one assignment, whose due date his daimon keep extending.

In *The Changing Light of Sandover,* JM, talking about his own system, cries out, "Oh, let's complicate / It irretrievably!" (191). There is a similar love of complication in *A Vision,* when complication means delay. Reading the Vision Papers, we notice that the spirits sometimes won't tell Yeats what is prophecy and what isn't. One spirit tells him that the prophecy he is looking for is already there—somewhere—in the "ideas intuitions, impressions sentences" he is writing down (Harper 2:210). But there is no time to stop and look for them and, in any event, more keep coming: there is an endless supply of intuitions, impressions, and sentences for meditation to master, a reliable abundance of images to be grateful for. Should *A Vision* incorporate the letters of the Hebrew alphabet, Kabbalistic numerology, the zodiac, the pictorial cards of the tarot, the seven days of creation? Probably. The condition to be avoided is retrievable complication. When a spirit tells Yeats, "I am not nearly done" and "You must just go on noting & be content to wait for synthesis," the reader participates in the drama of a yearning gratified (Harper 2:19, 275). The speaker in Elizabeth Bishop's "The End of March" longs to "read boring books, / old, long, long books, and write down useless notes" (180). Most of all, perhaps, she would like to hear a supremely confident voice (inner or outer, it would hardly matter) giving her permission to "just go on noting." It does seem like a version of happiness. Yeats is fortunate and knows it; he is grateful to be permitted just to write down notes and wait for synthesis.

Prophecy is as dramatically interesting when it is incomplete as when it is complete—more interesting, because one can still participate in it. "Who does not distrust complete ideas?" Yeats asks in his autobiography (325). The complete idea has no more need of us.

"The poet," Yeats tell us in "Per Amica Silentia Lunae," "because he may not stand within the sacred house but lives amid the whirlwinds that beset its threshold, may find his pardon" (333). The threshold is where the drama is. One lives there, at least one feels most alive there. Readers may not immediately think of *A Vision* as Paterian, but it does at times seem to urge a way of living. The present tense—all that is the case—can, Yeats seems to suggest, be made bearable if one imagines every moment filled with the feeling of something about to start. As for the past, one can try to remember incipience there. One might even be able to experience *nostalgia* for incipience, a mental operation that might seem willed, pointlessly strenuous, inevitably ill-fated—Stephen Spender, trying it, came up with a poem called "One More New Botched Beginning"—but Yeats makes nostalgia for incipience seem natural and graceful. In his memoir he asks, "Is it true that our air is disturbed, as Mallarmé said, by 'the trembling of the veil of the temple' or that 'our whole age is seeking to bring forth a sacred book?' Some of us thought that book near towards the end of the last century, but the tide sank again" (210). True incipience can never be botched. The book is still near, still arriving.

Anticipation will always return, and Yeats will exploit it by methods both unsurprising and surprising. Where another writer might make as much use as possible of the traditional future tense of prophecy, Yeats is more liable to take the ordinary future tense and give it an unexpected charge. Even when some piece of conceptual work has already been completed, he will present it to his readers as something just about to be done. "I have now only," he tells us, "to set a row of numbers upon the sides to possess a classification, as I will show presently, of every possible movement of thought and of life [. . .]" (*Vision* 78). *I have now only to . . . I will show presently*: such phrases are fundamental to the way *A Vision* operates on us and to the pleasure Yeats seems to find in writing it. He finds occasions for incipience everywhere, along with examples of it. "Flaubert," he tells us "is the only writer known to me who has so used the double cone. He talked much of writing a story called 'La Spirale.' He died before he began it, but something of his talk about it has been collected and published" (*Vision* 70). If "All Soul's Night" (the poem which concludes *A Vision*) were in prose it would sound more like an opening paragraph than a closing one. "I have a marvellous thing to say," the poet tells us, reveling in the "surely some revelation is at hand" tone. Yeats's appetite for the experience of incipience may be what drew him back in his autobiography to tell the story of the poets of the nineties, with their promise yet to be fulfilled. Even when he seems to be laying everything out in charts and diagrams, there is still an atmosphere of delay, of suspense. "I am not yet ready to discuss" is a characteristic phrase. Stevens in his poem "The Pure Good of Theory" refers to "all the preludes to felicity" (320). Yeats wants to miss none of them.

If you think about your own vision dramatically, you are likely to think of other people's visions as dramatic as well. Theories, too, are likely to be seen as occasions for drama—if not the theorist's occasion, then your own. The pure good of theory for Yeats is, in part, its generation of a vocabulary to be exploited for dramatic excitement. I said that complete ideas seem less interesting to Yeats than incomplete ideas, but no idea is complete as long as one hasn't made up one's mind about it. A system that might seem static and monolithic to us becomes, in Yeats's imagination, a thing in flux. His relationship to systems—his own or another's—is never completely established. He dramatized even his complete rejection of certain theories as somehow still to take place, even when his position was settled for everyone who knew him. "How far can I accept socialistic or communistic prophecies?" he wonders in *A Vision* (301). Not very far, most of his readers might have said, but for Yeats the interest is in the provocation of the postponed answer, in the answer always just about to be given. Incipience can be played for comedy. On the penultimate page of *A Vision*, he writes, "I remember a Communist described by Captain White in his memoirs ploughing on the Cotswold Hills, nothing on his great hairy body but sandals and a pair of drawers, nothing in his head but Hegel's *Logic*. Then I draw myself up into the symbol and it seems as if I should know all if I could but banish such memories and find everything in the symbol" (301). Yeats can't resist the comic possibilities in the representation of a mind on the verge of knowing all, hindered at the last minute by a scruple.

R. P. Blackmur wrote that Yeats was "never able to retract his system, only to take up different attitudes towards it" (92). Yeats himself observed slyly that "all imaginable relations may arise between a man and his God" (*Vision* 240). One of the attitudes or relations Yeats seems to have found most seductive is what might be called amused vindication. He writes Ethel Mannin in 1936: "If you have my poems by you look up a poem called 'The Second Coming.' It was written some sixteen or seventeen years ago and foretold what is happening" (*Letters* 851). And Michael

Robartes will have visions of the future at the breakfast table as he awaits his early tea (*Vision* 50). Yeats also performs for his readers in a style that might be described as prophetic nonchalance. Mixing Dante and P. G. Wodehouse, he abbreviates Beatific Vision as "BV." There are rhetorical occasions of astonishing casualness in *A Vision,* moments that seem to bring with them an atmosphere of happiness not reminiscent of other prophetic works. These are sometimes the moments in which, without retracting his vision, Yeats manages to seem very far away from it. At such times, to borrow Stevens's words, the writer "bathes in the mist / Like a man without a doctrine" (204).

Generally, of course, Yeats prefers to be a man with a doctrine, ideally a man perpetually discovering one. In his memoir he writes about developing when he was young a new religion of poetry and tells us, "I wished for a world, where I could discover this religion perpetually" (77). Even more exciting, of course, is the sensation of not knowing exactly what he is about to discover. In a letter to Lady Gregory about *A Vision,* he writes, "I live with a strange sense of revelation and never know what the day will bring" (*Letters* 644). Always more revelations, and always new relations to them. Another attitude he adopts is that of the lover. Like Whitman and Merrill, he likes to introduce an erotic undersong to his grandest prophetic strains. The connection between the prophetic and the erotic had been made early for Yeats. Roy Foster writes, "From the early 1890s, he had been preoccupied by prophecy, partly as a way of anticipating his future with Maud Gonne, whom he apostrophized as an avatar of the coming era" (1:163). But even Maud Gonne can blur into a dream of incipience, a blissful sense of pure futurity. Ian Balfour quotes Yeats on William Blake: "There have been men who loved the future like a mistress, and the future mixed her breath into their breath and shook her hair about them" (128). In the future the prophetic writer may find love with his mistress, or he might love the future as if it were a mistress. That the two can seem to readers of Yeats like the same thing to him might make us wonder if Yeats loves anything (or anyone) more than incipience. Yeats would not be alone, of course, in loving people and ideas primarily for their ability to awaken that kind of excitement in him. We like to have something (God, a supreme fiction, another person) to anticipate a total comprehension of, and to perform "all imaginable relations" with.

Whatever we choose, the most important criterion, perhaps, is that it helps us to love the future. A reader of *A Vision* can easily feel that writing it helped Yeats to love the future, to feel somehow about to be filled by it, as if his whole experience of interiority were itself a drama of incipience.

"Full of the future" is a phrase that recurs in Yeats's writing. Here, again writing to Lady Gregory, he uses the phrase about his father: "He believes he is at last going to paint a masterpiece [. . .] & is as full of the future as when I was a child." Although Yeats studied to be as little like his father as possible—John Butler Yeats was the opposite he wanted never to embody—he did resemble his father while he was writing *A Vision*. Yeats's father worked on his "masterpiece" (a self-portrait) year after year, constantly starting over. After hearing of his father's death, Yeats wrote to his sister Lily: "He has died as the Antarctic explorers died, in the midst of his work & the middle of his thought, convinced that he was about to paint as never before" (Foster 2:211). *A Vision* too, although Yeats published two versions of it, was never quite completed. He wrote, "I could I daresay make the book richer, perhaps immeasurably so, if I were to keep it by me for another year, and I have not even dealt with the whole of my subject, not even begun with what is most important. . . . Doubtless, I must someday complete what I have begun" (Harper and Hood xii–xiii).

Three weeks before he died, Yeats wrote Lady Elizabeth Pelham, "In two or three weeks—I am now idle that I may rest after writing much verse—I will begin to write my most fundamental thoughts and the arrangement of thought which I am convinced will complete my studies. I am happy, and I think full of an energy, of an energy I had despaired of. It seems to me that I have found what I wanted" (*Letters* 922). What seems to bring him happiness is not that he is writing or beginning to write but that he is *about to begin* to write his "most fundamental thoughts." Had Yeats's father written this letter (it sounds like him), Yeats might have mocked him for the tone taken. Had Yeats's father been alive to read this letter, he might have made gentle jokes about his son producing a deathbed edition of *A Vision* and after that a séance edition. Yeats's love of the sensation of incipience was like his father's, even if he did finish *A Vision* and his father was never able to finish anything. Both son and father spoke of happiness and energy and the future up until the end.

What about Yeats's readers? Reading *A Vision*, one might become aware of a desire reactivated by the presence of prophetic tonalities and registers. Such a reader may remember a hope (activated initially maybe by a religious text in childhood), a yearning that somehow the prophetic voice with its extraordinary authority might begin to speak specifically and helpfully, that it will offer a sort of prepsychoanalytic talking cure in which the healer does all the talking. I described earlier the drama of intermittency and suspense. But what does the reader experience after he has finished the book? John Berryman represents one such reader. In one of his Dream Songs, he writes, "Yeats on Cemetery Ridge / would not have been scared, like you & me / . . . said disappointed & amazed Henry" (356). Berryman's words "disappointed & amazed" seem right as a way to describe the way many readers experience the work of twentieth-century prophetic poets. If Yeats himself felt real disappointment, he would only touch on it, rarely avow it. And when he did avow it, he did so slyly. At the end of the chapter of his autobiography called "Reveries over Childhood and Youth," he tells us that he is "sorrowful and disturbed" and adds, "It is not that I have accomplished too few of my plans, for I am not ambitious; but when I think of all the books I have read, and of the wise words I have heard spoken, and of the anxiety I have given to parents and grandparents, and of the hopes that I have had, all life weighed in the scales of my own life seems to me a preparation for something that never happens" (71). Not something that has never happened, or will never happen, just something that has not happened yet.

I began by saying that the power of Yeats's book comes from the skill with which he dramatizes incipience. I also said that he was serious *like us.*

"All imaginable relations"—to adopt Yeats's phrase—may come into play between a poet and his desire to express himself seriously. A reader is tempted to imagine some of those relations, taking Yeats out of his own system and putting him (temporarily) back in ours. There is, in *A Vision,* the voice of eighteenth-century sober-mindedness, its gravitas maintained amid a storm of occult enlightenment. There is the super-serious, last-Romantic voice and the prickly, remote high-Modernist voice. (With every voice, Yeats captures the sense of consequence and the note of suspense peculiar to that age.) He even seems to have, in *A Vision,* the voice of our own time: straight-faced, sly, postmodern. What will the next age be like? For that topic he has a hushed and weighty voice. We can imagine his relations to serious expression in the context of a human life. He has a child's mock seriousness: There's a game kids play where you look in your friend's eyes and say, *I have something very serious to tell you.* (In Yeats's version: "I have a marvellous thing to say.") Then you pause. Neither player may look away or laugh. The tension builds. He has an adult's urbane seriousness: "My dear Ezra, Do not be elected to the Senate of your country. I think myself, after six years, well out of that of mine" (*Vision* 26). He has an old man's voice, spooked and spooky: "I have mummy truths to tell" (305). Any of the voices in *A Vision* are as authentic as any other. We carry so many real tonalities inside us but imagine ourselves as having just the one real voice: earnest, sincere, a little sad. Reading *A Vision,* a reader might think: my life is full of incipience, and I have range and freedom just where I thought I was most limited.

WORKS CITED

Balfour, Ian. *The Rhetoric of Romantic Prophecy.* Stanford: Stanford UP, 2002.

Berryman, John. "#334." *The Dream Songs.* New York: Farrar, Straus and Giroux, 1969.

Bishop, Elizabeth. *The Complete Poems, 1927–1979.* New York: Farrar, Straus and Giroux, 1983.

Blackmur, R. P. *Language as Gesture: Essays in Poetry.* New York: Columbia UP, 1952.

Croft, Barbara. *Stylistic Arrangements: A Study of William Butler Yeats's* A Vision. Lewisburg: Bucknell UP, 1987.

Foster, R. F. *W. B. Yeats: A Life.* Vol. 1, *The Apprentice Mage.* Vol. 2, *The Arch-Poet.* Oxford: Oxford UP, 1997, 2003.

Harper, George Mills. *The Making of Yeats's* A Vision: *A Study of the Automatic Script.* 2 vols. Carbondale: Southern Illinois UP, 1987.

Harper, George Mills, and Walter Kelly Hood. *A Critical Edition of Yeats's* A Vision *(1925).* London: Macmillan, 1978.

Jarrell, Randall. "A Girl in a Library." *The Complete Poems.* New York: Farrar, Straus and Giroux, 1981.

Merrill, James. *The Changing Light at Sandover.* New York: Alfred A. Knopf, 1992.

Stevens, Wallace. *The Collected Poems.* New York: Vintage Books, 1982.

Vendler, Helen. *Yeats's Vision and the Later Plays.* Cambridge, MA: Harvard UP, 1963.

Yeats, William Butler. *The Autobiography of William Butler Yeats.* New York: Scribner, 1999.

———. *The Collected Poems of W. B. Yeats.* Ed. Richard Finneran. New York: Scribner, 1996.

———. *The Letters of W. B. Yeats.* Ed. Allen Wade. New York: Macmillan, 1955.

———. "Per Amica Silentia Lunae." *Mythologies.* New York: Macmillan, 1978.

———. *A Vision.* New York: Macmillan, 1965.

Lyric Poetry and the First-Person Plural

"How Unlikely"

Lyric poetry sanctions us to talk about ourselves, one by one. "My heart aches, and a drowsy numbness pains my sense," writes Keats, upon hearing a nightingale in a garden. Even when the "I" is not pronounced, poetic statements about the observable world tend to circle back to reflect the state of the observer. "A red fox stain covers Blue Hill," observes Robert Lowell of a Maine landscape after tourist season, and then reveals "my mind's not right." As Helen Vendler has argued, the "I" of lyric, unlike that of the novel, tends to abstraction. The social particulars are sometimes there to give the texture of experience, but they peel away and we are left with something at once more personal and more universal. And when we utter the poem, Vendler stresses, we become the individual whose emotions are expressed; we inhabit the "I" of lyric, and solitude becomes intimacy. Taking up this aspect of intimacy, contemporary theorists of lyric have shifted their attention from the speaker to the addressee. The "I" of lyric, they argue, so often depends upon a "you," a divinity, an art object, a fallen hero, a lover, a reader. Poems are not just idle musings, John Stuart Mill's "feeling confessing itself to itself in moments of solitude"; they are intimate communications. And the reader is in various ways involved in this experience of intimacy or transport, whether on the side of the speaker or the addressee. "This thou perceiveth, which makes thy love more strong." "Already with thee, tender is the night." "Closer now I approach you . . . I stop here waiting for you." John Ashbery's "Paradoxes and Oxymorons" brings the peculiar condition of lyric address to its logical extreme: "the poem / Has set me softly down beside you. The poem is you." Of course this readerly "you" of lyric cannot be fore-known. As Holocaust survivor Paul Celan observed, lyric "can be a message in a bottle, sent out in the— not always greatly hopeful—belief that somewhere and sometime it could wash up on land, on heartland perhaps. Poems in this sense . . . are under way: they are making toward something."

And what poems are "making toward" might be more than a fellow solitary, might be a union, a group, even a community. The shuttle between "I" and "you" in the structure of lyric address will sometimes produce or perform a "we." Yet criticism about the lyric has mostly overlooked poets' use of the first-person plural. The exception is W. Ralph Johnson, who long ago in *The Idea of Lyric* called for the renewal of classical "choral poetry." He takes Whitman as his model. Whitman's "I" is really a "we," since it speaks to a culture's aspirations. At the same time, I want to add, that public voice in Whitman is built up from and returns to the most intimate terms of address, and seems to emerge within the process of the poem: "We understand then, do we not? What I promised without mentioning it, have you not accepted?" The "we" in modern lyric has a range from intimacy to publicity, often within the same text, and sometimes even simultaneously, so that the term "choral poetry" seems inadequate. Classical choral poetry serves and enforces a shared cultural identity and consensus values. Modern poetry's "we" is more self-conscious, highly sensitive to political and historical change. (Yeats: "we make out of the quarrel with others, rhetoric, but of the quarrel with ourselves, poetry.") As we continue the critical project of historicizing lyric subjectivity we might well shift our attentions from the slippery singularities of personal identity, and even from the psychodynamics of personal address, to the fluent and problematic modes of connection registered in modern poetry's use of the plural pronoun. In what circumstances and in what terms might the poet speak of "we"?

Yeats approached the word with great caution in "Easter 1916," distancing himself from the partisan passions that led to bloody martyrdom. At the same time, he recognized the death of the Irish nationalists as a spur to collective feeling. The poem begins in social divisions, with "I" and "them" of the Dublin club scene; nationalist divisions that provoked the rebellion surface later. But the poem turns in the last stanza to ties of family and rituals of mourning that unite us as human: "our part / To murmur name upon name, / As a mother names her child." As so often in modern lyric, the public "we" must be built up from a more private, but common, experience. "We know their dream; enough / To know they dreamed and are dead." The poem acknowledges Ireland's political awakening, but it reaches beyond an "us" (the Irish) and a "them" (the English) who offended. Yeats posits a "we" brought together in an act of mourning, death being that antisocial force that paradoxically provokes a ritual of community. But another "we" stirs in the poem, one that is transhistorical and nonpartisan, a "we" of poetry, crossing into our own lives.

The thirties made the use of the plural first person almost obligatory, a mark of popular solidarity, a union song, often at the expense of lyric's allegiance to the individual. "We" did the work of particular ideologies. But in "The Idea of Order at Key West" Wallace Stevens found a way to reconcile these urges of personal expression and social engagement, to see them as continuous rather than competitive. He begins with a scene of Romantic solitude, a singer on a beach. But the poem, composed during the Great Depression, gradually turns toward a more collective vision: toward a shared experience of hearing. At the end of the poem we learn that Stevens was not alone as he listened to the singer on the beach, that Ramon Fernandez heard the song as well. But the first-person plural pronoun is introduced well before we meet "pale Ramon." We are prepared, then, for the turn from the private world of the singer to the social dimension of the town, and finally to an expansive humanist pursuit "of ourselves and of our origins" within the vast, impersonal cosmos. And while we must rely on the poet's testimony for access to the singer's song, the sonic reality of the poem brings that song into our ears so that the "we" of this last, enlarged humanity is not merely an abstraction but something in which readers participate.

W. H. Auden resisted becoming the mouthpiece of the left, and was uncomfortable with the slogan ending "September 1, 1939," "we must love one another or die," famously canceling the poem from his *Collected Poems*. Despite Auden's rejection of it, readers have continued to admire the poem, especially since 9/11, perhaps because it formulates a project for poetry: to voice shared feeling and even ideals of community, to discover a durable, ethical "we" against the violence of totalitarianism, or the blank indifference of capitalism. Perhaps poetry is "a way of happening," an invisible hand that can reach to us beyond the isolation of the self and even of the partisan group.

Attention to the "we" in poetry causes us to pose several questions: What conditions allow the poet to speak as if in accord with others? Can the poet construct a "we" that retains multiplicity within its choral force? When does the poem give assent to this claim of collective identity and when does it distance itself? Does the poem point to the "we" as an already established identity, or does it produce this "we" in performance? In great modern poetry the meaning of "we" is explored, renewed, discovered, or created. It does not settle on a complacent or a tribal identity, or mask a restricted as a universal interest. In "The Poet and the City" Auden made the distinction between "society," an organization of atomic entities, and "community," an organic unit charged by a shared purpose or feeling. His poetry often critiqued society while it sought community.

In his essay on the choral lyric, Johnson extols a classical form in which "the voice of the poem is the representative of the community singing for and to the community about the hopes and passion for order, survival, and continuity that they all share." But since classical times the dominant mode has been solo lyric, emerging from and speaking of alienation and fragmentation, not *wir und Welt* but *ich und Welt*. Johnson praises Whitman for creating a modern choral form, one that could accommodate the pace of change, the intervention of technology, and the freedom of democratic individualism. Whitman's choral lyric, Johnson argues, is not a reflection of the realities of America, but a vision of American possibility: "What choral poets do is not so much to state the fact of good community as to imagine the possibility of good community." For many modern poets that possibility has been obscured by a great struggle and resistance to failed social orders. Whitman may claim to speak for the unvoiced, but for much of literary tradition the male covered up the female voice in the name of a false universality. "I am he is we are the one who find our way back to this wreck . . . [back to] the book of myths in which our names do not appear," wrote Adrienne Rich in "Diving into the Wreck," one phase in her long struggle to bend language out of its habit of patriarchal exclusions. The poet must be vigilant in creating a voice "differentiated yet a part of the whole." Notably, despite his choral ambitions, Whitman seldom used the first-person plural, confident, perhaps, that his singular voice contained multitudes, or perhaps aware that the "we" can so often sound like imperial decree.

In thinking about the "we" of poetry the idea of language as performance may provide a model. The linguist J. L. Austin in *How to Do Things with Words* drew attention to the problem of thinking about language as description of reality. Some utterances, he observed, *establish* rather than represent prior realities—wedding vows, promises, threats, for example. These are social performances that can't be measured by the true/false distinction. Austin began to apply this notion of *performance* to language more generally. At the same time, he recognized that "performatives" often depended on prior social context, so that cause and effect, history and rhetoric, collapsed into each other. Literary critics saw that poetry in particular flaunts what Austin called "illocutionary" or rhetorical effects, *how* a thing is said rather than *what* is said, the excesses of sound or word choice or image that create affective power. It is a speech *act,* rather than a statement about reality. Poems do not have much social force in our own age; even the audience for whom poetry makes something happen is relatively small. On the other hand, poems often *portray* language as performance, presenting speakers in implicit social contexts, engaged in speech acts. Because poems are so hyperaware of rhetoric, they can also *expose* the social practices of language. William Carlos Williams's "This Is Just to Say," for instance, reminds us that language is a social transaction, not just the record of a prior action. The cheeky "just" of the note, left perhaps on the breakfast table or the icebox door, is part of this story of forbidden fruit, of transgression, of confession and plea for forgiveness. Poetry is performative in the sense that it is social—it posits, and hopes to realize, an audience; it arises out of and for social reality organized in verbal communication, and it has an impact on that social reality. But it also has the power to reveal the linguistic forces in that reality, to bear witness to language in action.

These ideas are helpful, I believe, in thinking about the first-person plural in poetry, especially in our own time, when the sense of community is so troubled. Poetry sometimes (1) wants to refer to or speak for a preexisting group, or (2) wants to expose or critique "we" as performance. But (3) it also often tries to bring into being a particular "we" that has been obstructed in history; hence the appeal of poetry in emerging cultures. Poetry's ultimate performance, though, is "abstract," as Vendler says; it calls up human feeling without confining it to historical particulars.

I would like to look at Elizabeth Bishop's distinctive treatment of the pronoun "we" because I think it is instructive for contemporary poetry. Her practice of the first-person plural constitutes a kind of journey, both geographical and conceptual, a journey about which she was increasingly reflective. Reading through Bishop's work we can form a taxonomy of uses of the first-person plural and of its problems for the modern poet, problems of empathy and of community and consensus. Bishop's "In the Waiting Room," the opening poem of her final book, presents the subject of the choral voice in crisis, and we can read back in her work for the sources of that awakening. The "we" of *Geography III* begins in a sudden "cry of pain," an "*oh!*" that has no single location, no finite referent, though it arises from very particular experience of hearing her foolish aunt's voice. Young Bishop, almost seven, sits in a dentist's waiting room in Worcester, Massachusetts, in February 1918. But she is surprised by the disorienting force of the voice, which seemed to come from her own mouth: "it was *me* . . . / I—we—were falling, falling." The poem pushes beyond this intense, interpersonal empathy, and beyond Worcester, Massachusetts, to something more global. The *National Geographic* the child is looking at may frame distant continents as "other," and far off, but the imagination defies such boundaries. The experience of identifying with her aunt's pain, coming after the terrifying images of Africans and volcanoes, leads to the young Bishop's awareness of social and linguistic contingency: "You are an I, / you are an Elizabeth, / you are one of them." And then: "What similarities . . . / held *us* all together / or made us all just *one*?"—"how '*unlikely*'" (emphasis added). Critics have focused on the shock of self-identity, of the "I" bounded by social and linguistic constrictions. But the real shock of the poem may be in the far more unlikely, even subversive unity of "us" not social, which has more to do with the body in pain than with any cultural foundation. "In the Waiting Room" is a poem of memory, looking back to a formative moment in the poet's consciousness, perhaps the moment that determined her vocation. But it's a late work, representing Bishop's remarkable ability, at the end of her career, to link the personal and the global, to imagine an unlikely "we." I will return to *Geography III*, but I'd like to look briefly at some earlier work where her use of the first-person plural takes several preliminary turns.

Bishop's first volume, *North & South*, rooted in Modernist poetics, often uses the first-person plural as a form of the impersonal. Like others of her generation, she had read "Tradition and the Individual Talent," and its "impersonal theory of poetry" seems to have retained its hold on her long after some of her contemporaries had reversed direction and moved toward a confessional mode. Sometimes the "we" in early Bishop is merely a polite marker of address, as in: "we must admire her perfect aim" ("The Colder Air"). Yet more often the pronoun seems highly indeterminate, a word suspended in a symbolic space; it evokes no community, real or imagined, but presents a faceless allegory: "We'd rather have the iceberg than the ship," begins "The Imaginary Iceberg." The "we" here seems to gesture at something that it hasn't fully identified. Even in the more descriptive poems of *A Cold Spring*, her next volume, the movement toward a choral voice arises only by turning from scene to symbol and from local observation to abstract aphorism: "our knowledge is historical, flowing and flown" is the famous aphoristic conclusion to "At the Fishhouses."

Not surprisingly, perhaps, the "we" is scarce in Bishop's urban poems, where she describes a life of solitude in crowds. The city is often a dehumanizing space, within which love is a brutal transaction or a desperate escape. Bishop's "Varick Street" certainly reflects this perception, "*And I shall sell you sell you / sell you of course, my dear, and you'll sell me.*" The last stanza of the poem offers an image of love as a frail retreat: "Our bed / shrinks from the soot / and hapless odors / hold us close." Such alienation, however biographical, was only part of a broader lyric antagonism toward the social order. In another poem Bishop calls playfully and warmly upon Marianne Moore to rescue her from the moral darkness of urban life: "we can sit down and weep; we can go shopping . . . or we can bravely deplore, but please / come flying." This "we" is more conspiratorial than choral; it forms an alliance against the world.

But a more engaged, social "we," influenced by W. H. Auden, is also cautiously present in Bishop's early work. We hear it in the sestina "A Miracle for Breakfast," 1934, her "social conscious poem . . . about hunger," as she called it. The poem is in some ways a sardonic updating of the biblical parable of the loaves and the fishes, now reduced to unnourishing crumbs and coffee (multiplied relentlessly in the sestina form). The Depression provoked many poems with a collective sense of man, but for Bishop this could not mean a simple subordination of private to public perception, partly because the public realm was fragmented. As Thomas Travisano has noted, "She is part of a needy community, a more scattered and lonely one than the crowd waiting for Jesus, because each sits isolated on a balcony" (48). In this parable Bishop is cautious about speaking for others. The poem begins with fact: "At 6 o'clock we were waiting for coffee / waiting for coffee and the charitable crumb." But common hunger does not lead to community. The capacity for faith or doubt eventually reorganizes the group into increasingly smaller units. "Some of us stood around waiting for a miracle." Bishop speaks against, not with, this group, as she gives individual witness: "I can tell what I saw next: it was not a miracle." For a moment the earth seems more paradise than paltry crumb. But imagination does not feed the multitude. The poem lurches back to the meager, mundane reality of isolation and hunger. It is only much later, in "The Moose," that she will imagine this vision of nature's plenitude as something shared and nourishing.

If "A Miracle for Breakfast" shows Bishop struggling with the social "we," "The Map" takes up the challenge of the "we" in global terms. There would seem to be no issue of personal pronouns where maps are concerned. They are objective, geographic charts. But in approaching the map imaginatively, Bishop reminds us that the relation between world and diagram is never so straightforward. "We can stroke these lovely bays" as if continents were like horses in a stall. But the "we" that enjoys the free play of the imagination over the map must ultimately perform in the world, and on the stage of history.

In the poems dealing with real places, Bishop seems most aware of the political complexity of the first-person plural. Poetry may evoke an impersonal or universal "we," may even invite intimacy, but the experience of location, both physical and cultural, marks us out in structures of otherness. "Roosters," also from *North & South* but later, presents that stage of history in order to awaken a slumbering, complacent populace to Guernica-like horrors. The "active displacements in perspective" collapse the sense of distance and otherness. The roosters "wake *us* here" (emphasis added); the pins on the map cry "this is where I live" and thus challenge the contemplative quiet of "The Map," which suspends location and subsumes populations into shapes and colors. The cries of those struggling under Fascist oppression wake us here, in the United States.

"Over 2,000 Illustrations and a Complete Concordance" perhaps best reveals Bishop's early struggle with a hegemonic "we." The poem never explicitly mentions the Bible, perhaps because the speaker is part of Christian culture. We are clued to the book's identity by the marketing boast in the poem's title, and later by the pictures of sacred scenes. This illustrated edition of The Book is a cultural object heavily weighted with cultural bias. The Great Code is "complete," it says, all reality resolved into pattern. But experience doesn't measure up. "Thus should have been *our* travels" (emphasis added) opens the poem, voicing a speaker, the representative of companions whose experience has not conformed to the "engraved" images. In this poem the first-person plural pronoun slips from one usage to another: it is sometimes interpersonal (fellow travelers), sometimes broadly cultural (Christians versus Moslems), other times impersonal, and these different "we's" exist in some tension. While the speaker clings to a dominant cultural "we" that the edition presumes, the poem's description distances the speaker from the book's design. The "invisible threads above the Site," "the toils of an initial letter," the "grim lunette," all declare the lifeless artifice of this totalizing representation. Yet the speaker remains tied to the book's cultural perspective so that irony is hard to locate. The "squatting Arab," is a threat, especially when he becomes part of a "group of Arabs," part of a different "we," "plotting, probably, / against *our* Christian empire" (emphasis added).

As the speaker's restless mind burns through the sacred page into travel memories, the cultural conflicts remain, but the cultural confidence of the speaker is less certain. Empire's Other looks back—"the fat old guide made eyes." "Khadour looked on amused" as they made the requisite tourist pilgrimage to the "holy grave." Not engravable truth but rather mortality surges under this current of secular memories. Perhaps people are not definitively divided into rulers and subversives; perhaps people are "only connected by 'and' and 'and.'" (The Bible's narrative style tells us so, in fact, so that some authority returns to the book.) Peering into the antisocial reality of death, the speaker becomes momentarily singular, the "we" becomes an "I" as she faces death, unprotected by her cultural superiority: "It was somewhere near there / I saw what frightened me most of all" (emphasis added)—a grave half filled with dust, "not even the dust of the poor prophet paynim who once lay there." The speaker quickly exchanges this dust for the pollinating "gilt" of the illuminated book, the dust / of eternity which promises to cancel sin and mortality. The Bible is not repudiated; it calls her back. But her orientation toward the book, and hence her evocation of the first-person plural, have changed. The book awakens less cultural hubris, more personal longing. The address works in stages. "Open the book," the speaker instructs her congregation of one. This is not the commanding voice of Christian Empire, or clerical authority. "Why couldn't we have seen / this old Nativity while we were at it?" The old Nativity itself seems presemiotic, the sight of an infant and also an "infant sight," for an eye not so culturally conditioned or world weary. The demotic "family with pets" suspends sectarian narratives and provokes a more universal chorus, of the human longing for connection, for innocence and for an escape from time and loss: "Why couldn't we have . . . looked and looked our infant sight away." The poem ends with a plea made on behalf of a "we" far more inclusive than its initial voicing, but continuous with it.

"Over 2,000 Illustrations" opens questions about location and identity that resound throughout the remainder of Bishop's poetry, linking the experiences of particular travelers (inevitably embedded in a culturally and historically distinct "we") to broader themes, and testing experience against presumptions. Indeed, culture shock is the central theme of her next book, *Questions of Travel*. "Should we have stayed at home and thought of here?" asks the speaker of the title poem. What begins as a story of travelers' discontent becomes a meditation on human desire and restlessness: "must we dream our dreams / and have them, too?" "Arrival at Santos" ranges through the pronouns in search of an appropriate stance, beginning with self-address: "Oh, tourist, . . . Finish your breakfast." A presumptuous "I" (registered in the line ending "I presume") emerges out of this imperative address, and also a third person, a she, a fellow traveler. But this "Miss Breen" is herself an eccentric figure, marking the "we" of North American tourists already a troubled category when the boat arrives: "*We* are settled. / The customs officials will speak English, *we* hope" (emphasis added). Such a "we" can never be settled, must always be interrogating itself: "We leave Santos at once;/we are driving to the interior." That last "we" seems to reach beyond the travel itinerary to a journey of both self-reflection and cultural immersion, and to invite the reader along.

In *Questions of Travel*, then, Bishop developed an excursive "we" of constantly adjusted perspective. While the volume's stories of encounter undermine a discourse of difference, they do not for the most part answer the longing for connection (the family with pets) that arises at the end of "Over 2,000 Illustrations." This unfinished project becomes central to *Geography III*. The volume can be read, I believe, as a series of meditations on the limits and possibilities of community, on the nature of the human "family voice," as she calls it. I will focus my remaining remarks on the most affirmative instance of this investigation, Bishop's poem "The Moose" (a public poem, or at least a poem read first on a public occasion, to celebrate a very exclusive group indeed, the Phi Beta Kappa initiates at Harvard). It tells a story of common people on a bus, on their way from Nova Scotia to Boston, but most of them very remote from the venerable gates of Harvard. She placed the poem strategically at the center of *Geography III*, eleven pages into this twenty-one-page book. Around it are poems that also involve human connection—its vertiginous discovery in "In the Waiting Room," its painful absence in "Crusoe in England," its realization through art in "Poem," its displacement by bureaucracy and media in "12 O'Clock News." In "The End of March," although the speaker recalls her desire to live alone in her "proto-crypto dream house," it's boarded up, and the poem's fears and joys are shared by companions. But "The Moose," understated as it is, represents the fullest and most optimistic performance of community. The poem recounts its story in present tense, so that the emotional wisdom and sense of connection emerge for the reader. The poem asks what we must relinquish in received or inherited connection in order to become open to connection on another level.

"The Moose" begins, however, in the departure from community and in much evidence of fragmentation. The village this poem leaves behind was once home, perhaps, but a sparse, provincial home, the "narrow provinces/of fish and bread and tea," without any Christian miracles to unite the community. The fragmentation is inscribed in the landscape itself: places called "the Economies—/Lower, Middle, Upper;/Five Islands, Five Houses." The family is breaking up; not even the herd dog can keep it together: "a lone traveler gives/kisses and embraces/to seven relatives/and a collie supervises." Behind this image of social fragmentation is a greater force against community, a force of nature that annihilates and darkens. This force is represented repeatedly in *Geography III* in the icon of the erupting, then blackening volcano. In "The Moose" this threat is subdued, figured only in the setting sun, but the "burning rivulets" reflected in the river (the bus is going west in the sunset) anticipate the threat of oblivion that emerges with the encroachment of night and woods. Out of this condition of fragmentation and oblivion a community will form, among strangers on a bus. Discourse is not the basis of this community; in fact speech seems hopelessly inadequate to the experience. The group gathers instead in a subcurrent of feeling, urged by a simple "yes, sir, yes" (Nova Scotia accent). Yet rudimentary language plays an important role in this human coalescence.

For much of the poem Bishop avoids locating the voice at all. We are back in the perspectiveless mode of description in *A Cold Spring,* without a personal pronoun claiming the voice, surveying the landscape in detachment. But as the poem witnesses a "lone traveler" saying good-bye to relatives, the perspective of the description narrows as if to share that traveler's view. The voice does not individuate itself, but perspective enters the bus, looks out, then in, then out again, and the voice of the poem seems more engaged. As the poem retreats into dream in the second half we might expect to enter the realm of the solo lyric, but this dream is collective even as it imagines a conversation "not concerning us." The dream enters a space not unlike that of the "family with pets" in "Over 2,000 Illustrations," universal in its appeal but far less remote and colorless than that of the old Nativity. In "The Moose," instead of an eternal infant *sight,* we *hear* "Grandparents' voices . . . talking, in Eternity." "Grandparents" is capitalized, as if a proper noun, so that they are at once generic and particular grandparents—Adam and Eve but *ours.* Everyone has grandparents, and the stories of fragmentation that they recount are themselves common— "She died in childbirth . . . the son lost . . . He took to drink . . . She went to the bad." (Here again we find "everything connected only by 'and' and 'and.'") The grandparents may speak of a particular community in decline, but the sense of loss and acceptance, that "peculiar affirmative," is translocal. These voices are "recognizable, somewhere, / back in the bus," a space of collective unconscious, perhaps, the repository of all travelers' memories.

While "The Moose" is taken up with visual description through its first two-thirds, in the last third, including the dream, quoted speech, the medium of social connection, dominates. The rudimentary quality of the quoted language may seem to highlight its inadequacy in describing experience. But at the same time, Bishop shows its rhetorical force. The archetypal grandparents first use the "we." "'Life's like that. / We know *it* (also death).'" While the poet is translating their barely audible, indrawn "yes," her use of quotation marks the words as *utterance*. The structure of the statement draws attention to itself. It does a certain work, making death an object of *knowledge* rather than fear, and putting death in a parenthesis, subordinating it to Life. This ancient knowledge of pain and loss would seem an unlikely basis for the formation of communal joy, but it is necessary to the epiphany that follows, as if to suggest, structurally at least, that a certain acceptance of pain is a prerequisite of joy. One is always surprised by Joy. Joy here comes from the relinquishment of narrow ideas of home, comes rather from knowledge and acceptance of death—of "*it*," and here, from a redescription of nature under a female sign of the Moose. ("'Look!—*It's a she*'" [emphasis added].) The language of description at least as it is produced by the passengers on the bus breaks down in the encounter with the moose. We are aware more of its sonic value ("our quiet driver,/ rolling his *r's*") and its affective power ("A man's voice assures us/ 'Perfectly harmless.... '") than its truth value. The accents mark out this group locally, but at the same time this "we" becomes abstract in just the way Vendler suggests the "I" of lyric often does, however particularized it may be. This "childish" language, more performance than description, to use J. L. Austin's terms, plays a part in producing the collective effect to which the poem bears witness:

> Why, why do we feel
> (we all feel) this sweet
> sensation of joy?

These lines border on sentimentality—why does Bishop, so reticent in other poems, risk such a bald statement of feeling here? The monosyllables mark the simplicity of the beholders, but the form of the sentence is complex, again suggesting something about the sentence's claim on us. This is an assertion inside a parenthesis inside a question, qualified, uncertain, but also protected. It distinguishes certainty of feeling and experience from certainty about the causes of feeling. This experience does not establish community, that is, on a basis of knowledge or revelation but rather on coincident sensation (the localization of feeling in and from the senses) and on rhetoric. The repetition of "why" (why, why) marks the speaker's astonishment—arising in the midst of darkness. Perhaps the asking of the question is itself an aspect in the formation of this community (as in Wallace Stevens's "The Idea of Order at Key West": "Whose spirit is this? we said, .../... and knew/ That we should ask this often as she sang"). Bishop's question is never answered; as with Stevens, a question of cause is displaced by an assertion of effect. We don't *know,* but we do *feel.* If "why" is repeated, "we" is also repeated, even intensified with "all," as if to counterbalance wonder with confidence, as if to suggest not only that the joy is communal but that the communal is at once the product and a further foundation of the joy. This "we" of the story is local and incidental, not even as long as a bus ride, but it seems to arise in the story's telling, in the poem itself, where it can be revived with each new reading, and can extend to the reader.

What allows Bishop to speak with such assurance for others? The passengers inside the bus are themselves in a kind of metaphoric parenthesis in the landscape. Community forms, that is, in the parenthesis within dispersed, undifferentiated being. Here we might consider not just the language of the passengers, but the poem's own language as performance, as a cautiously choral lyric presenting the possibility of community, creating community in the utterance of "we." Whatever its source or habitation may be, the moment of joy passes. With it Bishop relinquishes the first-person plural that marked the crest of the experience; the poem returns to the impersonal as a norm: "by craning backward / the moose can be seen / on the moonlit macadam." But perhaps the passive voice here, if it relinquishes communal identity, draws us as readers into the experience, allowing it to linger, allowing us in fact to share this "sweet sensation of joy."

I'm less interested in resolving such questions than in reading the poem as a parable about the formation of a communal moment, one that can only be transient, perhaps, one that depends more on the rhetorical than the descriptive power of language, but a moment that might inspire the building of a more enduring community. I have been exploring the connection in Bishop's poetry between the "we" established in lyric address and the "we" of dramatized communities. In this sense "The Moose" can represent poetry more generally. Readers of poetry are like passengers on a bus, stopped in a moment of epiphany. Poetry performs a "we" that, while it does not transcend history, seems at times to reach beyond its differences and distances. But compared to Whitman, Bishop is careful with her choral claims. The fragile "we" formed in art may be, as she says of art in "Poem," "the little that we get for free, / the little of our earthly trust." Not quite a foundation for a democratic order.

How will contemporary poets, in a world at once more proximate and more divided than ever, approach the imperatives of the first-person plural? Bishop, writing in a time of war (World War II, Vietnam), and remembering from her childhood an even earlier time of war (Feb. 1918), asked what similarities held us all together and made us all just one. At the moment, we certainly do seem to be under a big black wave, another and another. But perhaps it is precisely the task of poetry to imagine, out of such an abyss, some inclusive place of connection, whether formed in a cry of pain or a sweet sensation of joy.

SELECTED BIBLIOGRAPHY

Austin, J. L. *How to Do Things with Words*. 1955. Ed. J. O. Urmson. New York: Oxford UP, 1962.

Bishop, Elizabeth. *Complete Poems, 1927–1979*. New York: Farrar, Straus and Giroux, 1983.

Celan, Paul. *Collected Prose*. Ed. Rosemary Waldrop. New York: Routledge, 2003.

Johnson, W. R. *The Idea of Lyric*. Berkeley: U of California P, 1982.

Mill, John Stuart. "What Is Poetry?" 1833. *Mill's Essays on Literature and Society*. Ed. J. B. Schneewind. New York: Macmillan, 1965.

Travisano, Thomas J. *Elizabeth Bishop: Her Artistic Development*. Charlottesville: UP of Virginia, 1988.

Vendler, Helen. *Soul Says: On Recent Poetry*. Cambridge, MA: Harvard UP, 1995.

Elizabeth Bishop's Cartographic Imagination Once More
Rereading "The Map"

ELEANOR COOK

On the outside front cover of Elizabeth Bishop's first collection of poems, *North & South,* is a device called a compass rose. It is a navigational device, familiar from old maps or modern charts, and consists of four main petal-like extensions from a central point, indicating north at the top, south at the bottom, east to the right, and west to the left. In the spaces between the main petals are four shorter petals, marking the 45-degree angles of northeast, southeast, southwest, and northwest. In the form that Bishop chose, there are eight yet shorter petals indicating north northeast, and so on. She also chose straight-line petals in a diamond shape rather than curved ones. All the petals are shaded down one-half of their length, in such a way that adjacent half petals are always contrasted, making the directions easier to read. A circle encloses the entire compass rose, whose four large petals touch the perimeter. The device is repeated on Bishop's title page, and also on her frontispiece, but with a difference. Here, the letter *N* appears in large script at the center top above the compass rose, the letter *S* similarly at the center bottom, and an ampersand is centered on the right-hand side.

It is a pity that the device was not reprinted in Bishop's 1969 *Complete Poems* or her *Complete Poems, 1927–1979* (1983). A thrice-repeated device calls attention to itself, and this device suggests something more than a collection of northerly and southerly poems. It suggests voyaging, sailing, and above all navigating. All the more if we happen to know that Bishop came from a seafaring family on her mother's side and was an ardent sailor herself. She told friends about her great-grandfather, Captain Robert Hutchinson, who sailed the North and South American coasts in the nineteenth century, and who went down with his ship and all hands off Sable Island (or else off Cape Sable) in 1866.[1] In her teens, she went to a camp at Wellfleet, Massachusetts, for the summers of 1924 through 1929, where she excelled at swimming and sailing, and sea chanteys too (*One Art* xxiii). She was good enough to sail a fifteen-foot sailboat at the age of eighteen,

along with two young friends, from Plymouth to York Harbor in Maine—
arriving to the shock of one friend's parents (Fountain and Brazeau 30).
Bishop was a water person. All her life, she lived on or near the ocean, and
she loved to fish and to swim. "I love to go fishing, you know—any kind of
fishing," she wrote to her Aunt Grace in 1963 when she was planning a visit
to Nova Scotia (letter to Grace Bowers, 28 Oct. 1963, Vassar, Box 25, file 11).
Her 1932 Newfoundland travel diary mentions a sudden high dive into a
gorge "amid loud cries" when a schooner sailed into sight of a swimmer clad
as nature intended ("Travel Diary to Newfoundland," Vassar, TS and MS,
2 [TS]). A friend recalled "very clearly" from a student summer on Cape Cod
that Bishop said, "If anything ever happens to me, take me to the ocean."[2]

Even without this biographical knowledge, we might surmise an invitation to a voyage in a collection that opens with a poem called "The
Map." Bishop chose the same poem to open her 1967 *Selected Poems,* published in the United Kingdom by Chatto and Windus, and to open her
1969 *Complete Poems.* I want to look at this poem in itself, and then very
briefly as a way of entering Bishop's work, extending some of the critical
work already done on it.

"The Map" was written in early 1935, probably before Bishop's twenty-
fourth birthday on 8 February.[3] It is an astonishing poem for a twenty-
three-year-old. So much of Bishop's rich oblique method is at work here
that the poem anticipates some of her finest effects. Even here, she is mapping her worlds. She is also, I think, taking her bearings and preparing to
choose her course and navigate.[4]

The poem had its origin in an actual map, and the story is familiar. In
a 1978 interview, when asked about the "extensive imagery of maps and
geography" in her work, Bishop replied:

> Well, my mother's family wandered a lot and loved this strange world
> of travel. My first poem in my first book was inspired when I was
> sitting on the floor, on New Year's Eve in Greenwich Village, after I
> graduated from college. I was staring at a map. The poem wrote itself.
> People will say that it corresponded to some part of me which I was
> unaware of at the time. This may be true. (Interview with Alexandra
> Johnson, Monteiro 101)

The poem opens thus:

> Land lies in water; it is shadowed green.
> Shadows, or are they shallows, at its edges . . .

"Shadowed green" is a little puzzling until line 2 clarifies it. The map must be one of those with shaded edges along the coastlines in a narrow strip, while the large expanses of water are "simple blue." The effect, momentarily anyway, is to make the adjoining land look as if it casts a shadow. The map can look briefly as if it were almost two-dimensional, with the land standing a little above the water's edge. In line 2, the observer looks down with her mind's eye into those shadows. Lines 2 to 4 translate map colors and shading into actuality, the mapped shore into actual shore seen close up.

The question in line 2—shadows or shallows?—can sound entirely whimsical. It is not. In fact, there is one set of circumstances where it is a crucial question. If you are a sailor, you need to know whether you are seeing shadows or shallows on a coastline. Otherwise you are in danger of foundering. (Navigational charts often indicate the depth of the water along the shoreline.) If you are a writer, it is just as well to know about shallows too.

Incidentally, the matter of translating maps into actuality has elicited some surprising comments from critics. Sometimes the words "confuse" or "confusion" are used of the process, as if we were always confused when we translate the marks on a road map to what our eyes in the car are seeing, and vice versa. Sometimes, portentous remarks are made about maps and absolutes like capital-T Truth. All such remarks should be tested against actual sailing in an actual boat, following a navigational chart. Thoughts about absolutes may be helpful in some contexts, but for actual sailing you want an accurate map, giving up-to-date information about the matters that a cartographer commonly treats.

In lines 4 to 8, the perspective changes, and the shaded coastlines are seen differently. The sea now appears to be a garment or covering, with the land pulling it around itself. The shaded edges are no longer shadows. The next two questions seem to be separated from the terrain's actual behavior. Whether fanciful or touched with allegory or gesturing toward well-known metaphors of the sea (of which, more later), these lines do not appear descriptive like lines 1 to 4. In fact, I think they are, more obviously for a seacoast.

> Or does the land lean down to lift the sea from under,
> drawing it unperturbed around itself? . . . .

The question to ask is much the same as for line 2. Under what circumstances would these lines be accurate or significant? Surely, during the flowing of the tide—not the ebbing, not here anyway. Bishop's Nova Scotia home was Great Village, which lies close to the innermost point of the Bay of Fundy, famous for its phenomenal tides, the highest in the world:

> My aunt lives on an enormous (for that part of the country) farm about three miles from the Village. It is always described as the most beautiful farm on the Bay of Fundy, and I think it must be. You know about the Bay of Fundy and its tides, I imagine, that go out for a hundred miles or so and then come in with a rise of 80 feet. (to Marianne Moore, 29 Aug. 1946, *One Art* 139)

Just so, the land gives the effect of lifting or drawing or "tugging at the sea from under" (line 8) when the tide is flowing. It doesn't, of course. But on the Bay of Fundy, as on other long tidal stretches, things can look different. Bishop wants the verbs here for other reasons, I think, but reasons that emerge only gradually from the poem.

Even on some freshwater coasts, there is a similar effect. Not of course from tides, but rather from pressure. On the coastlines of any large body of water, rising pressure will cause the water to drop, while a low-pressure system will cause the water to rise, as in an old storm glass. Again, the land does not really lift or draw or tug the water; it is the atmosphere above that does so. But the effect can look that way.

The word "unperturbed" is a little surprising in itself, while being finely positioned so that it can modify subject or object, the land or the sea. If the land, then it calmly lifts and draws the sea around it or tugs at the sea from under, as if the sea were a garment, a trope that Bishop will return to at the end of her second stanza. If the sea, then the word works in two ways, first the usual general meaning, and second the meaning in a marine context. The word "unperturbed" is a benchmark for measuring the sea. Calculations are made on the basis of "the unperturbed sea level" or "the unperturbed sea depth" or floor, and so on. That is, measurements are taken "in the absence of tides, winds, currents and other factors," as the online *Proceedings of Estuarine and Coastal Modeling* puts it. The word "perturbed" also functions in a marine context. A geographer, for example, may speak of Labrador's "perturbed sea-ice border," say, for January. The land in Bishop's poem may well be unperturbed as it lifts or tugs at the sea, though a sea being so lifted and tugged is by definition a perturbed sea. Yet the adjective "unperturbed" is also associated grammatically with the sea, and the action being described resembles the everyday action of dressing. The ambiguous grammar suggests an ambiguous placing of two different kinds of writing, so that they quietly interweave: both ordinary descriptive writing and also a kind of fable where impossible things can happen in the most ordinary way.

"The Map" appears to have begun as a sonnet. The first version in Bishop's notebook shows a twelve-line poem with three quatrains rhymed *abba cddc effe*. It consists of the first stanza of "The Map" plus lines 1 to 4 of the third stanza. The rhyme scheme is demanding, for Bishop has chosen to use identical rhyme words for the *a*-rhymes, a type of rhyme particularly hard to make sound natural. She does it, quite unobtrusively. In the first draft, the poem lacked only a final two lines to make it into a sonnet variation on both main types of sonnet: the Italian *abba* octave extended into three quatrains each with its own rhyme scheme, and a final Shakespearean couplet added.

On the next page of her notebook, Bishop wrote what is now the second stanza of her poem, an eleven-line unrhymed stanza, beginning with the lines on Newfoundland and Labrador. Newfoundland's shadow "lies flat and still." The illusion of a map's coastline casting a shadow does not work for an island, where we see the shading all round the land. At least, I assume that is why the shadow lies flat and still, at least in the first instance. Bishop moves on from shoreline observation to add another color to green and blue and tan. She looks again at her map, observing the yellow color of Labrador and finding an appropriate reason for it. "Labrador's yellow, where the moony Eskimo / has oiled it."

"The Map" focuses on boundaries from the first lines onward, as critics have remarked: boundaries of sea and land, a boundary of glass over a map, boundaries of towns and cities whose names spill outward, boundaries of peninsulas and adjacent land, boundaries that divide countries. And a boundary between two degrees or kinds of emotion, a line beyond which "emotion too far exceeds its cause." I want to suggest one other way in which boundaries inform this poem, a way suggested by its place-names. The place-names define the map as one of (or including) the North Atlantic. Not surprisingly, Bishop has chosen two *N*-words for northern territories, Newfoundland on the North American side and Norway on the European side. Not surprisingly, Labrador follows immediately on Newfoundland, for they constitute one territory. (License plates on cars read "Newfoundland and Labrador.") This remains true, even though Newfoundland is an island and Labrador a sizable portion of the adjacent mainland, running as far north as a little over 60 degrees latitude, just above the southernmost part of Norway. Most critics have assumed that the map Bishop gazed at in 1934 included the Canadian Maritime

Provinces—a likely assumption, but not on the evidence of the place-names. The place-names of Newfoundland and Labrador have led them astray. Newfoundland and Labrador were not part of Canada when Bishop took her walking trip in Newfoundland in 1932 or when she published this poem in 1935 or when she collected it in 1946. Newfoundland and Labrador joined Canada only in 1949.[5] That is why Bishop's 1932 travel diary speaks of government help in the Depression as coming from the English government.[6] When Bishop wrote this poem, Newfoundland was still a British crown colony by choice, its constitution temporarily suspended by request in 1934 because of impending bankruptcy during the Great Depression. The huge tract of adjacent mainland, annexed to Newfoundland in 1774, was disputed territory from 1902 onward. It was finally given to Newfoundland in 1927 in "one of the most celebrated legal cases in British colonial history, the Labrador boundary dispute."[7] (Some Quebeckers do not accept it to this day.)

Why might this matter? A look at Norway provides a parallel. Norway's present boundaries were also established within living memory of Bishop's 1935 and 1946 readers. It separated from Sweden in 1905, a peaceful separation that is a model for conflict resolution. Bishop's two named northern territories, then, both come with a fairly recent history of boundary disputes. Even more important in the early 1930s, these were boundary disputes that were settled peacefully. Bishop's poem does not take place in a historical vacuum, even if it is not centered on historical events. The place-names of Newfoundland and Labrador, along with Norway, might remind the reader historically of Norsemen and a Norse empire. (The two areas, one on each side of the North Atlantic, are united by the prevailing spring winds, the easterlies that drove fishing ships from Norway to Greenland, and then beyond to Newfoundland and Labrador, long before Columbus came to the Americas.)[8] The place-names might remind the reader economically of the once-huge North Atlantic fisheries. They would more likely remind the reader of recent claims to shorelines like those described with care in stanza 1. (The Labrador boundary dispute rested on questions of watersheds and shorelines. Shorelines would of course be measured according to an "unperturbed sea level.") The recent histories of Newfoundland and Labrador and of Norway also reminded readers of other ways to decide such claims than by aggression or war.

The "moony Eskimo" has always suggested to me the typical Inuit round face, accentuated when a parka hood is pulled up. At the same time, it has suggested the extended acquaintance of the Inuit with the moon during long winter nights when the sun did indeed set on this corner of the British Empire. Why "oiled it" and oiled it "yellow"? Because oil, yellow oil—whale and fish and seal oil, not the modern kind—was vital for survival in the far north.[9] And because seal oil became a staple trading commodity.[10]

Yet the entire sentence is slightly odd, because of that word "where." Is all of Labrador colored yellow? The sentence should then read "for" or "as" rather than "where the moony Eskimo/has oiled it." Is this the kind of map with miniature regional illustrations, where a small round Inuit face might appear against a yellow ground in one spot? What about the areas not inhabited by the Eskimo? Prowse's *History of Newfoundland* speaks of the Eskimos in Labrador, but also of the Indians there (see chap. 19). Or does that yellow appear for some other cartographic reason? Adele Haft may have found a solution. She has identified a possible map, a "red map," as Bishop indicated: "'The Map' had to do with a red map. There was nothing particularly noteworthy about it, but I was attracted by the way names were running out from the land into the sea" (interview with J. Bernlef, Monteiro 66). In this map, "Cartography of the World 1921," areas are colored according to available surveys on a scale of one to five, from "accurate trigonometrical surveys" to "unmapped." A good deal of Labrador is colored yellow, indicating "unmapped."[11]

Two well-known and remarkable sentences end the second stanza, returning the poem's focus explicitly to boundaries while greatly extending its possible contexts. The first sentence reads:

> The names of seashore towns run out to sea,
> the names of cities cross the neighboring mountains
> —the printer here experiencing the same excitement
> as when emotion too far exceeds its cause.

The change in tone is palpable. So is the heightening of the affective vocabulary of the poem: "unperturbed," "lovely bays," and now "excitement"—a putative excitement playfully assigned to the printer, at least in the first instance. Helen Vendler first heard the allusion to T. S. Eliot:

> Eliot's famous criticism of *Hamlet*—that it did not work as an "objective correlative" of its author's presumed feelings because Shakespeare's emotions had been too intense for the invention constructed to contain them—hovers behind Bishop's remark here, as she defends the tendency of the work of art to run beyond its own outlines: why should not the names of cities run across the neighboring mountains,

if excitement makes them do so? Experiences far too large for human comprehension are rendered attainable by the map.[12]

To follow Eliot, the printer here has failed qua artist. In a work of art (or so Eliot argues), an emotion that exceeds its cause indicates the failure of the artist, even of a Shakespeare; Hamlet's emotion toward his mother is Eliot's case in point. Shakespeare has not found an objective correlative to correlate emotion and story, "a set of objects, a situation, a chain of events which shall be the formula for that *particular* emotion."[13] Bishop, on the other hand, has done so. A possible artistic failure in a printer provides an exact objective correlative for some "emotion that too far exceeds its cause," that is, some overreaction. Here is a trope that exactly indicates this condition, this excess, this odd state that most of us experience in greater or lesser degree at some point in our lives, as Eliot said: some perturbation, some excitement, some agitation beyond an obvious cause. What the particular emotion might be here, Bishop does not say. In the printer's world, there are conventions that allow for writing down such apparently excessive emotions, conventions that we all accept as we read maps where names of towns and cities sprawl far beyond their boundaries. Similarly with the conventions in writing poems, conventions that find ways of ordering excess emotion. A cartographic convention so troped may also stand as a warning to Bishop's young self about possible hazards in writing. The touch of humor (usually ignored) speaks to Eliot's occasional solemnity. Even more, it indicates Bishop's writerly confidence, young as she was and painfully shy as she was.

The next sentence, a crucial one that closes the second stanza, confirms this:

> These peninsulas take the water between thumb and finger
> like women feeling for the smoothness of yard-goods.

This is a sentence that suggests three different contexts, all related by one word. First, the women, and the craft of a seamstress, a home craft that women in charge of a household commonly possessed or knew where to find in Bishop's day. Here, the sense of boundaries is very different from what just precedes it. This is another example of correlation, finding the correlation between the look of a fabric and the feel of it. If the simile does suggest an emotion, it is in the first instance an everyday emotion, a measured, considered, experienced, perhaps pleasurable emotion in reading fabric. There may be very little of what we commonly call emotion when cloth is so felt. These are feelings involved in ordinary work, feelings we surmise in the look of the eye, the gestures, of a woman making decisions about cloth or food or any one of those elementary matters over which women traditionally presided, and which we so easily take for granted. These women are reading texture through their fingertips in order to make something. A good seamstress knows what fabric suits what garment or household article. A smooth fabric rather than rough suggests a lighter or finer or more delicate function.

As with the trope of the printer, so with the trope of the women. Both tropes are highly skilled in a number of ways. Here, it is as if these women can measure out the sea (an activity usually reserved for the Almighty, "who hath measured the waters in the hollow of his hand," the *deus artifex*)[14]—measure it out like yard goods. Bishop is once more turning all those tropes of the sea as a garment, some of them very familiar: the "sea-girt isles"; "and round it hath cast like a mantle the sea"; "The Sea of Faith / Was once, too, at the full, and round earth's shore / Lay like the folds of a bright girdle furled"; "then all collapsed, and the great shroud of the sea rolled on as it rolled five thousand years ago"; "The water . . . / Like a body wholly body, fluttering its empty sleeves"—this last from a poem published not long before Bishop wrote hers.[15]

These peninsulas take water between thumb and finger. To go back to my earlier question for Bishop's work: in what other context might these words work? Who else feels water for smoothness? Who else but sailors? Not by taking water between thumb and finger, but by feeling for the smoothness of the water through the skin and the eyes and the ears. Sailors read the water much as the women read cloth. Against the look of it, they test the feel and smell of the air above it, the sound of it ("the distant rote in the granite teeth"),[16] and more. As with the women, such judgment may be called intuitive, but only if we define the adjective as that combination of knowledge, experience, and instinct that mysteriously issues in an art or craft: sewing, sailing, sculpture, medicine. Bishop's simile of women and yard goods does not describe an amateur or beginning seamstress.

When the "peninsulas take the water between thumb and finger," it is as if they could also take a pen between thumb and finger, as if the peninsulas could write down themselves. The prefix "pen" before *insula*, Latin "island," means "almost" (from Latin *paene*). Our word "pen" as a writing implement derives from Latin *penna* or "feather," the original quill pen. A *paene insula* is like a thumb and finger, which can take between them *penna*. That is, these lines suggest a third occupation beyond the sailor's, an occupation already suggested in the preceding printer's sentence: that of a writer. All three occupations, sewing, sailing, writing, are linked by the one word "craft," which is also the word for the boat that the sailor sails. (*Steering the Craft* is Ursula Le Guin's happy title for a handbook on writing skills.) Both writer and reader may test a passage, feeling for smoothness, a term commonly used of words or of a style. Certain diction, said Dante, is smooth (*pexa*) rather than shaggy (*De eloquente vulgari*). Hamlet directs the players, "in the very torrent, tempest, and, as I may say, whirlwind of your passion, you must acquire and beget a temperance that may give it smoothness" (3.2.6–8).

"These peninsulas," says Bishop. What peninsulas? Any on that map, one supposes, starting with Labrador, the "great Arctic Peninsula" (e.g., Prowse 607 and passim). It is so huge that we seldom think of it as a peninsula, but so it is, with Hudson Bay and its straits on one side and the Atlantic with the Gulf of St. Lawrence on the other. Across from part of this enormous peninsula lie the Canadian Maritime Provinces. Norway is also half of a prominent peninsula. But I want to make a case shortly for another peninsula.

Bishop's third stanza moves back to a rhymed double quatrain, again repeating the initial rhyme words of an *abba cddc* scheme. "Mapped waters are more quiet than . . . ," and we expect something like "than the actual sea." What we hear is "more quiet than the land is," itself a quiet observation of maps, where mountains are marked by wavelike squiggles— the waters "lending the land their waves' own conformation." Land then begins to move like water, with Norway's north-south mountain range acting as the spine of some hare (an Arctic hare?) running south. Unspecified profiles of land "investigate the sea." Mapped waters are more quiet than the land is in another way. Most maps show expanses of land divided by colors that mark the boundaries of different countries. The restless, sometimes dangerous sea is often an expanse of "simple blue." Now the land is no longer unperturbed (if it ever was), but agitated.

If the questions in stanza 1 sound whimsical, the questions here sound even more so. Are colors on a map assigned or can countries pick? If a country is conquered and made part of someone's empire, its color is assigned, as red was for the British Empire on British maps. What color best suits a country's character or its "native waters"? Yet we already have an example of colors suiting native territory: "Labrador's yellow, where the moony Eskimo / has oiled it." British red, at least in the Union Jack, stood for courage. Or so Bishop's childhood *Primer* taught her.

The flag is red, white, and blue.
The red says: "Be brave!"[17]

And that word "native," read retrospectively against line 10, reminds us that Labrador has been inhabited for centuries by indigenous peoples, who also once inhabited the other two territories. What might they say about a map of an area that they know intimately? How might they extend the cartographer's knowledge? In 1934, how did their history resonate against North American or European twentieth-century history? And to read allegorically: how does one ascertain one's own native waters and their best color?

The following line on topography sounds odd: it "displays no favorites," so that "North's as near as West." A favorite is near to one's heart, so that a measurable outer distance and an unmeasurable inner one are both in play here. North is clearly Bishop's favorite, compared with West, but the notion sounds strange. Haft observes that the popular Mercator projection distorts the higher latitudes (46–47). At 60 degrees latitude, for example, points west appear much farther than in actuality. When you are sailing in these latitudes, you know well that "North's as near as West" for any given distance. The rhyme requires "West" but the logic would surely prefer—while not requiring—"West's as near as North." I wonder if Bishop is also reminding us of the difference between north and west considered simply as directions on a map. North and south gather to a point, while east and west do not. Or rather each gathers to two points, for there is not one north, but two, just as there is not one south, but two. There is the true north, the geographical north, and there is the magnetic north. The northern place-names take on another dimension when we recall this fact, a very familiar fact to sailors. Newfoundland lies considerably south of Norway by the standard measure of latitude, but they are on the same isomagnetic lines (of equal horizontal and of vertical force).

The compass rose reminds us of all this. It is an essential device on any navigational chart, whether for mariners, fliers, or others. When navigating, you plot your course from point A to point B. Then by means of parallel rulers you transfer it to the compass rose so that it passes through o degrees. After that, you must make two simple mathematical calculations because of the magnetic north. You must take into account the angle of deviation between the true north and the magnetic north. You must also take into account the variation of the magnetic north, because it moves around, changing over the years.[18] Local magnetic forces, such as the strong magnetic force at the northernmost tip of Labrador, may or may not be pertinent. Without these calculations, you will be following a "false north." In the first draft of Bishop's last published poem, "Sonnet," the phrase "the false north" is attached to lines about the compass needle:

Caught—

. . . .

and the compass needle
wobbling and wavering,
undecided.
(in Harrison 268)

I want now to turn to another series of names on this map. They are scattered. Possibly they belong to a narrative or several narratives. But the poem does not tell us, nor does it even gesture toward such readings. These names are made up of the affective words in this poem, which are unexpected, to a greater or lesser degree, but never disruptive: "unperturbed . . . lovely . . . excitement . . . quiet . . . agitation . . . delicate." The tone varies. As noted, "unperturbed" is a marine word for certain measurements as well as an affective word. The printer's excitement and the agitation of Norway's hare both come with a touch of humor. A set of contraries in signification divides four of these words, two by two: "unperturbed" and "quiet" as against "excitement" and "agitation." The word "lovely" stands alone in various ways. The word "stroke" takes a little of its color from these affective words. Only one remark addresses this vocabulary directly, and the tone is partly playful: "as when emotion too far exceeds its cause."

The word "delicate" is puzzling as part of a puzzling last line: "More delicate than the historians' are the map-makers' colors." The line elicits some astonishing remarks by literary critics about history and historians, as if they had never read any good history or given a moment's thought to the art and discipline of writing history. Or as if they had never observed that Bishop is talking here about "historians," not about "history" as the march of events. John Ashbery, as we might expect, has more sense:

How could the map-makers' colors be more delicate than the historians'? How could the infinity of nuances and tones which is finally transformed into history, a living mosaic of whatever has happened and is happening now, prove more delicate—and not in the sense of

softness or suavity but in the sense of a rigorously conceived mathematical instrument—than the commercial colors of maps in an atlas,
which are the product, after all, of the expediencies and limitations
of a mechanical process? Precisely because they are what is given us
to see, on a given day in a given book taken down from the bookshelf
from some practical motive. (8)

The practical motive here, I think, is Bishop's mapping of a voyage for herself as writer. No doubt, there was also a personal voyage to be mapped at
this time. But there is only one personal matter that the poem delicately
but unmistakably intimates.

It is New Year's Eve, a time for reckoning with public and personal history, especially of the year just passing and the year fast approaching. For
Bishop, the year 1934 was just ending and the year 1935 about to begin. In
the wide world, Japan's army had begun to move aggressively against its
mainland neighbors, and Hitler had begun to move aggressively toward
dictatorship within Germany. Her mother had died some seven months
earlier. Bishop had not seen her for eighteen years. She died mad and confined to an asylum, where she had lived since that scream Bishop remembered as a child. Not until 1953 could Bishop find a way to write about that
scream in her story "In the Village." In 1934, on that map, she could see
where her mother had died, and, across the peninsula, where she herself
had lived. (I am assuming that the Canadian Maritime Provinces were
included, as well as the Atlantic coast farther south.) She could see the
Bay of Fundy as well, just as she had seen it as a child, the bay where the
highest tides in the world sweep in and out. She could see the coastlines
where her great-grandfather had sailed and which a great-uncle knew too
("Large Bad Picture"). The sight of that map helped, I think, to focus her
eyes and mind as she stared at it. As David Kalstone saw, "Objects hold
radiant interest for her precisely because they help her absorb numbing or
threatening experiences" (220).

With the map or the writing of "The Map" came a memory of Eliot
writing on excessive emotion, on Hamlet and his disgust with his mother,
also called Gertrude like Bishop's own poor mother. Hamlet went mad
temporarily, or was he pretending? "Rest, rest, perturbed spirit," Hamlet's
blessing on his father's ghost, sounds even more appropriate as a filial response to Bishop's mother's ghost. Her mother had gone mad, overcome
by a grief that too far exceeded its cause, the early death of her husband.
Bishop remembered her being fitted for a dress, and the dressmaker
crawling on the floor with pins in her mouth to mark the bottom hem.

The dressmaker, she wrote years later, had reminded her of Nebuchadnez-zar crawling on the ground and eating grass because (she did not need to write) he had gone mad. Bishop associated her mother with yard goods. In her story, the dressmaker is moved to tears by the beauty of the fabric, and of course by more. An unfinished poem by Bishop is titled "A Mother Made of Dress-Goods" (*Edgar Allan Poe* 156–57). In the first draft of her well-known villanelle "One Art," she wrote: "I have lost one ~~long~~ pen-insula and one island . . . . " (ibid. 225). Most of mainland Nova Scotia is composed of a long peninsula. "These peninsulas" together with "yard-goods" in "The Map" cannot but evoke a mother who has just died. "These peninsulas" would speak to any reader of 1935 or 1946 who knew a little about Bishop's background. Only a few close friends might perhaps think of Bishop's mother living and dying there.

The draft of "The Map" takes only two pages, and there are very few changes. In effect, as Bishop said, "the poem wrote itself." On the verso side of the second page is the earliest draft of another poem, another poem about her mother that Bishop never finished, "Swan-Boat Ride":

> The white swan bit the finger of her glove
>
> . . . .
>
> White swan—destruction in the quiet park—
> She raised her veil over her nose to kiss me.[19]

The affective vocabulary in the poem can delicately evoke maternal thoughts.[20] No history of Bishop's personal life on New Year's Eve 1934 could be as delicate as the intimations of this map-maker's poem.

It is more usual among critics to associate this affective vocabulary with Bishop's homosexuality, though if her memory is accurate she was not fully aware of this at the time. "People will say that it corresponded to some part of me which I was unaware of at the time. This may be true." It is hard to see how she could have been aware, given the personal decisions on her mind at the time.

On that map, on New Year's Eve of 1934, Bishop could see the island where she had hiked two summers before, Newfoundland. She could also very likely see where Cuttyhunk Island is located off New Bedford, Mas-sachusetts. She had spent several weeks there during July of 1934, part of them on holiday with a young man who very much wanted to marry her, and whom she liked.[21] Did she love him? By all evidence, the person she now loved to the point of obsession was her roommate at Vassar, Marga-ret Miller. (See Frank Bidart in Fountain and Brazeau 70.) She was alone on New Year's Eve, having been sick with flu and asthma since Christmas Day; Miller had nursed her since then, until (Bishop said) she was exhausted; she had just left (1 Jan. 1935, *One Art* 29). Miller had nursed her like a mother, as we say, an action likely to stir memories of an actual mother as Bishop stared at that map.

> Name it "friendship" if you want to—like names of cities printed on maps, the word is much too big, it spreads out all over the place and tells nothing of the actual *place* it means to name.

Thus a journal entry written some time between 25 July 1934 and 22 August 1934.[22] If the occasion of New Year's Eve raised questions about 1934 and 1935, one of them must have been the question of marriage. And emotion that exceeded too far its cause? It is easy to speculate about all these things in hindsight, and in doing so to skew the poem. The poem's affective vocabulary is a challenge for the reader. Do we read this poem as if it were a seventeenth-century poem of correspondences, the land as the beloved's body, Donne's "my America, my Newfoundland"? Bishop had studied seventeenth-century poetry closely. If she had wanted a poem of allegorical correspondences, she would have written one.

It is possible to look back at Bishop's life in 1934, at least what we now know of it. It is possible to surmise circumstances that bear on the poem, and I have done so. But a warning about works of art is due, a warning that more than one critic has emphasized. Works of art are not dissolvable back into the circumstances that produced them. These help to make up what Aristotle called the efficient cause of a work of art, and only that. Lyric voice in a poem is not an autobiographical voice, but something other, though related. (See esp. Costello.)

If some personal voyage hovers in the background of "The Map," it is not the immediate business of this poem. This poem indicates a writer's voyage to be taken, a course to be followed. It intimates causes, subjects, knowledge, emotions that inform this voyage. Along the way, they may become more explicit. They are not so here. Instead, the poem tells us what an acutely observant eye can see. "Watch it closely": so Bishop ends her poem "The Monument":

> It is an artifact
> of wood . . .
> But roughly and adequately it can shelter
> what is within (which after all

cannot have been intended to be seen).
It is the beginning of a painting,
a piece of sculpture, or poem, or monument,
and all of wood. Watch it closely.

Bishop has already begun to chart her writing course in "The Map." To speak only of her technique: consider rhyme, consider how she doubles back on herself, consider grammatical person, consider how she rewrites a centuries-old trope, consider diction. In the first stanza, she demonstrates her command of rhyme, as already noted. The use of same-word endings became one mark of her style: "the characteristic use of repeated terminal words in adjacent lines, whether in a rhymed or unrhymed poem" (Hollander 246). In the second line ("Shadows or are they shallows"), Bishop doubles back on herself, looking again, and incorporating that second look into her poem. This device of including second thoughts is another hallmark of her style, one that she liked and made her own, using it throughout her work and developing its possibilities. "Our visions coincided—'visions'/is too serious a word" ("Poem"). "Nature repeats herself, or almost does" ("North Haven").

Similarly with the use of person, often quiet, as here: "We can stroke these lovely bays"—as if we were swimmers in the waters, as well as stroking skin or, faute de mieux, glass over a photograph. Who are these "we"? As if anticipating the question, Bishop throws down the gauntlet in the first line of the poem that follows in *North & South*: "We'd rather have the iceberg than the ship." Would we indeed? Not if we were on the *Titanic,* and there is Newfoundland in the first poem to remind us that the *Titanic* sank 400 miles off its shores in 1912. Of course, this is an "imaginary iceberg," but the line startles nonetheless, startling us into observing grammatical person in a poem more closely.

As for a fresh trope that evokes and adds to the long history of a given trope—here, on the sea as a garment—that is a skill that marks a major poet. Such a trope must be truly fresh, that is, surprising. Bishop, when asked what a poem's most essential quality is, replied, "Surprise"—Aristotle's sine qua non for good metaphor. Nor is it the trope alone, but the very lexis of the trope that is fresh. For this is apparently the first use of the word "yard-goods" recorded in writing. It predates by six years the earliest illustration given by the *Oxford English Dictionary.* How quiet it is, this introduction into the language by a twenty-three-year-old of an everyday working word, probably heard locally.

The craft is here. The sailor is taking her bearings and preparing to choose her course. By 1946 Bishop knew how to proceed and to plot a course through *North & South*. Of the five poems chosen by Marianne Moore in 1935, only "The Map" appeared good enough to Bishop to include in her first collection. More than include: it starts the voyage.

And us? For reading is a voyage too, and reading poetry is a pleasure trip as well as a voyage of knowledge. We too must test our skills, take our bearings, plot a course, find our true north and calculate the effects of a magnetic north. What voyage do we ourselves undertake when we read this poem? Sometimes, as Herbert Marks says, such voyaging can "entail no personal risk," unlike more engaged reading and unlike the poet's own voyaging. And all too often, such voyaging follows a quite different route from Bishop's, sailing away from the art to which she devoted her life. "Those hungry for this kind of immediacy have no use for poetry, which controls the pain that memory inflicts by holding it at a distance and interweaving it with a verbal memory of its own" (197). Or, to quote Helen Vendler, "What is missing . . . from many [biographies] concerning poets is a justification of its efforts. Who is Bishop that we should care about her? What is poetry that we should care about it?" ("Numinous Moose" 6). Look, says "The Map." What might we see? For all that, what might we see as we gaze on the map or other object that epitomizes our own location in the world?

NOTES

I am indebted to Vassar College Libraries, Special Collections, and in particular to Dean Rogers. The Senate Research Committee of Victoria College, University of Toronto, kindly provided financial assistance for the trip to Vassar. I am also indebted to Farrar, Straus and Giroux, and to Alice Helen Methfessel, as well as to the Vassar College Libraries, for permission to print excerpts from unpublished material written by Elizabeth Bishop and to reprint excerpts from "The Map." (For details, please see nn. 1, 6, 10, 21, 22 and below.)

Excerpt from "The Map" from *The Complete Poems, 1927–1979*, copyright © 1979, 1983 by Alice Helen Methfessel. Reprinted by permission of Farrar, Straus and Giroux, LLC. Excerpts from unpublished materials written by Elizabeth Bishop copyright © 2008 by Alice Helen Methfessel. Printed by permission of Farrar, Straus and Girous, LLC, on behalf of the Elizabeth Bishop Estate, and by permission of Special Collections, Vassar College Libraries.

1. In letters of 1946 and 1951, e.g., Bishop mentions Sable Island as the place where Hutchinson's ship sank; Sable Island lies in the Gulf of St. Lawrence and is known as "the graveyard of the Atlantic"; to Marianne Moore, 29 Aug. 1946 (*One Art* 139); also to Robert Lowell, 11 July 1951 (ibid. 221). Later, she corrected this to

Cape Sable, the southernmost tip of Nova Scotia. "My great-grandfather & his ship & all hands went down in a famous storm off Cape Sable—not the Island, the cape" (letter to Philip Booth, 5 Feb. 1973, Vassar, Box 25, file 1).

2. Fountain and Brazeau 44. Robert Fitzgerald is said to have remembered Bishop saying to him that she would have been a sailor if she had been born a boy (ibid. 1).

3. A letter to Marianne Moore on 25 Jan. 1935 comments on Moore's introduction to Bishop's poems in *Trial Balances* (*One Art* 29–30); presumably Moore had a copy of "The Map."

4. There is a compass rose inlaid in the ground floor of the main Vassar Library, the Frederick Ferris Thompson Library (1903), but it was covered by carpeting about 1998. It was a blue and grey mosaic, about four feet in diameter, and located at the foot of the stair off the central lobby. I owe the fact to a poem by Keith Ekiss, and the details to Dean Rogers's memory. To date, the Vassar historian does not know whether it was part of the original floor.

5. Adele Haft is the only exception I have found, in a footnote in her "The Poet as Map-Maker" (58n5); oddly, the text remains inaccurate.

6. "The Government Fisheries are here. Newfoundland pays half, and England pays half" ("Travel Diary to Newfoundland," Vassar, TS 3).

7. Labrador was transferred by statute to Québec in 1774, then reannexed to Newfoundland in 1809. The 1927 decision in favor of Newfoundland was made by the British Judicial Committee of the Privy Council (s.vv. "Labrador," "Labrador Boundary Dispute," *Canadian Encyclopedia*).

8. Norway stands in the same relation to the North Atlantic on the European side as Labrador does on the North American side. Their coastlines are very similar.

9. John Ashbery also says that "Labrador is yellow on the map not by chance but because the Eskimo has oiled it so as to make it into a window for an igloo" (10).

10. In his *History of Newfoundland,* D. W. Prowse provides records showing that trade in seal oil in 1813 brought in 50,161 British pounds (711); one hopes that some of this made its way back to native sealers. When in Newfoundland, Bishop was fascinated by Prowse's massive history and tried to obtain a copy ("Travel Diary to Newfoundland," Vassar, TS 2, 4).

11. It appeared in the large *Times Survey Atlas of the World* (1922), which Haft calls "a landmark atlas" (44).

12. Vendler, "Elizabeth Bishop" 298. Vendler was one of Bishop's earliest and most appreciative critics.

13. Eliot, "Hamlet" 145. The collection of essays was first published in 1932. Bishop's use of "Tradition and the Individual Talent" in a student essay demonstrates how clearly she read his criticism; see Costello 342. She would have known both essays from *The Sacred Wood* (1920), where "Hamlet" appears as "Hamlet and His Problems."

14. See Isaiah 40.12 and 15: "Who hath measured the waters in the hollow of his hand. . . . behold, he taketh up the isles as a very little thing." On the *deus artifex,* see Curtius 544–46.

15. The quotations are from Milton, *Comus,* line 21; the hymn "O worship the King," by Sir Robert Grant (1779–1838); Arnold, "Dover Beach"; Melville, *Moby-Dick,* the last sentence of the last chapter before the epilogue; Stevens, "The Idea of Order at Key West."

16. "The Dry Salvages," line 30, by another poet who was also a sailor, T. S. Eliot.

17. Lines 5–8 of the eleven lines beneath the Union Jack, and above the three flags that make up the Union Jack. See the *Primer,* reproduced by Sanger 17; see also "Primer Class," in Bishop's *Collected Prose* 5, 10.

18. See the standard handbook by Chapman; I am indebted for this information to the painter Tim Zuck, who is also a sailor.

19. *Edgar Allan Poe* 155, just before "A mother made of dress-goods . . . "; for the quotation and other drafts, see ibid., 346–47.

20. Ford hears in lines 4 to 8 of "The Map" a contrast, the "maternal land" leaning down and lifting a garment quite unperturbed (245). Jonathan Ellis notes the connection of "yard-goods" with memories of Bishop's mother (66).

21. ["Recorded Observations: begins with 'Cuttyhunk, July 1934.'"], Vassar, Box 72A, file 3. According to Robert Seaver's sister, who stresses her brother's deep attachment and her own expectation of an engagement, Bishop told him before leaving for Paris in July 1935 that she would never marry anyone (Fountain and Brazeau 44–47, 64, 67–68).

22. ["Recorded Observations: begins with 'Cuttyhunk, July 1934.'"], Vassar, Box 72A, file 3, 9.

WORKS CITED

Ashbery, John. "Second Presentation of Elizabeth Bishop." *World Literature Today* 51 (1977): 8–11.

Bishop, Elizabeth. *Collected Prose.* Ed. Robert Giroux. New York: Farrar, Straus and Giroux, 1984.

——. *Complete Poems, 1927–1979.* New York: Farrar, Straus and Giroux, 1983.

——. *Edgar Allan Poe & the Juke-Box: Uncollected Poems, Drafts, and Fragments.* Ed. Alice Quinn. New York: Farrar, Straus and Giroux, 2006.

——. *One Art: Letters.* Ed. Robert Giroux. New York: Farrar, Straus and Giroux, 1994.

——. Papers. Special Collections, Vassar College Libraries. (Cited as Vassar.)

Canadian Encyclopedia. Edmonton: Hurtig, 1985.

Chapman, Charles Frederic. *Piloting, Seamanship, and Small Boat Handling.* 64th ed., rev. Elbert S. Maloney. New York: Sterling, 2003.

Costello, Bonnie. "Elizabeth Bishop's Impersonal Personal." *American Literary History* 15 (2003): 334–66.

Curtius, Ernst. "God as Maker." *European Literature and the Latin Middle Ages.* Trans. Willard R. Trask. Princeton: Princeton UP, 1953. 544–46.

Eliot, T. S. "The Dry Salvages." *Four Quartets.* London: Faber and Faber, 1944. 25–33.

———. "Hamlet." *Selected Essays.* 3rd ed. London: Faber and Faber, 1951. 141–46.

Ellis, Jonathan. *Art and Memory in the Work of Elizabeth Bishop.* Aldershot: Ashgate, 2006.

Ford, Mark. "Elizabeth Bishop at the Water's Edge." *Essays in Criticism* 53 (2003): 235–61.

Fountain, Gary, and Peter Brazeau. *Remembering Elizabeth Bishop: An Oral Biography.* Amherst: U of Massachusetts P, 1994.

Haft, Adele. "The Poet as Map-Maker: The Cartographic Inspiration and Influence of Elizabeth Bishop's 'The Map.'" *Cartographic Perspectives* 38 (2001): 37–65.

Harrison, Victoria. "The Dailiness of Her Center: Elizabeth Bishop's Late Poetry." *Twentieth Century Literature* 37 (1991): 253–71.

Hollander, John. "Elizabeth Bishop's Mappings of Life." *Elizabeth Bishop and Her Art.* Ed. Lloyd Schwartz and Sybil P. Estes. Ann Arbor: U of Michigan P, 1983. 244–51.

Kalstone, David. *Becoming a Poet: Elizabeth Bishop with Marianne Moore and Robert Lowell.* New York: Farrar, Straus and Giroux, 1989.

Marks, Herbert. "Elizabeth Bishop's Art of Memory." *Literary Imagination* 7 (2005): 197–223.

Monteiro, George, ed. *Conversations with Elizabeth Bishop.* Jackson: UP of Mississippi, 1996.

Prowse, D. W. *A History of Newfoundland from the English, Colonial and Foreign Records.* 1895. Facsimile repr., Belleville, Ont.: Mika Studio, 1972.

Sanger, Peter. "That Primary Primer: Some Pages from Bishop's Childhood." *Newsletter* of the Elizabeth Bishop Society of Nova Scotia 6.1 (Spring 1999): 2–10.

Vendler, Helen. "Elizabeth Bishop." *The Music of What Happens: Poems, Poets, Critics.* Cambridge, MA: Harvard UP, 1988. 284–99.

———. "The Numinous Moose." *London Review of Books* 11 Mar. 1993: 6.

Wallace Stevens, Ramon Fernandez, and "The Idea of Order at Key West"

GEORGE S. LENSING

Wallace Stevens's "The Idea of Order at Key West" is a staged poem. A speaker sees and hears a woman who is walking along a seashore singing, perhaps in or near Key West, Florida, where Stevens journeyed from his home in Hartford, Connecticut, on business trips in the 1930s. (The poem first appeared in a magazine called *Alcestis* in 1935.) The speaker appears to witness the woman's song at some distance from her: she is presented "striding there alone." Between the "constant cry" of the ocean and the words of the woman's song (which remain unrecorded in the poem), he makes a series of discriminations that deny a "medleyed sound" between cry and song and, at the same time, concede the possibility that "It may be that in all her phrases stirred / The grinding water and the gasping wind," even as the word "gasping" itself suggests pathetic fallacy. In any case, with a tone of confident omniscience, he concludes that, for the woman herself, "when she sang, the sea, / Whatever self it had became the self / That was her song."[1]

In dramatic narrative, the speaker then turns from the seashore and singing woman to the calmer harbor, where fishing boats are anchored and illuminated by "glassy lights" as night falls. In the company of a figure named Ramon Fernandez, he then produces his own interaction with the sea, one visual rather than aural, although his description addressed to Fernandez is like the woman's song: both are verbal. This is his description of the lights from the boats reflecting upon the harbor waters as they

> Mastered the night and portioned out the sea,
> Fixing emblazoned zones and fiery poles,
> Arranging, deepening, enchanting night.

Then, as a kind of coda to the poem's dramatic enactments, the speaker summarizes a "Blessed rage for order" with which the poem concludes:

The maker's rage to order words of the sea,
Words of the fragrant portals, dimly-starred,
And of ourselves and of our origins
In ghostlier demarcations, keener sounds.

The question I wish to raise is whether the role of the woman's song as described by the speaker and the role of his own words capturing the reflection of the lights of the fishing boats are of equal "magnitude." (I am adopting the word used by Helen Vendler in discussing the poem and in her conclusion that "the greater magnitude of the human voice" dominates "the voice of the ocean" [68] in the first part of the poem.) It is my contention that the woman's song, at least as it is interpreted by the speaker, is inferior to that of the speaker's own words directly quoted in addressing Fernandez. Before examining such a conclusion, however, I want to return briefly to the dramatic quality of the poem, which I described in the first sentence as "staged."

As I have been suggesting, the whole of the poem is laid out as a dramatic performance to which we as readers are assigned the role of audience. The speaker, especially in the first part of the poem, is a kind of dramatic chorus, just as a voice of the sea itself becomes a "sunken coral [choral] water-walled." In the third and fourth lines of the poem, the water is described as costumed, "Like a body wholly body, fluttering / Its empty sleeves." The poem denies that either she or sea is mask, but thereby implies that each could be suspected of theatrically masking the other, even as the suggestion of "masque" is also hinted at. The sea is indeed masked as "ever-hooded" (recalling the fluttering sleeves of the sea earlier described and contradicting the denial of "mask") and "tragic-gestured." The ear of the speaker is allowing for the "voice" of sea, sky, cloud, sunken coral, and it hears the "speech" of air. He sees the larger vista of the scene as "Theatrical distances," as if this cosmic phenomenon were a kind of giant stage on which the voices and speech were enacted and sung on "high horizons." As the speaker then looks down upon the woman striding and singing, there is another extension of that vista for the benefit of himself and those accompanying him as audience: "Then we, / As we beheld her striding there alone. . . ." Finally, in the last stanza, with its recognition of the universal human "rage to order words," words themselves become "fragrant portals," or passageways, another extension of the poem's stage setting.[2]

As the poem introduces the diction and devices of dramatic performance, it is the role of listener or audience that seems especially significant. There are several listeners in the poem: the speaker, who hears the woman's song, and Ramon Fernandez, who hears the speaker's own words after line 33 and perhaps through the whole of the poem. The reader, like a witness to a theatrical performance of masks and tragic gesturings, makes up a third. Few other poems by Stevens are set up in such a layered fashion. Why, we may ask, has he chosen to establish such a pattern here? Part of the answer to this question consists of the way in which we recognize the role of Ramon Fernandez himself, the silent listener and the only named figure in the poem.

It is well known that Stevens himself, responding to queries about the name, first said that it was "arbitrary" and that "I used two every day names. As I might have expected, they turned out to be an actual name" (*Letters* 798). Six years later, he modified this disclaimer by adding, "I knew of Ramon Fernandez, the critic, and had read some of his criticisms but I did not have him in mind" (*Letters* 798). Then, a few months later, he reiterated, "I simply put together by chance two exceedingly common names in order to make one and I did not have in mind Ramon Fernandez. Afterwards, someone asked me whether I meant the man you have in mind. I had never even given him a conscious thought. The real Fernandez used to write feuilletons in one of the Paris weeklies and it is true that I used to read these. But I did not consciously have him in mind" (*Letters* 823). It is difficult to know how seriously to take the poet here, who seems to be saying, "Yes, I knew who he was and had read his work, but I pulled the names out of the air for the sake of the poem." The names, of course, are hardly "exceedingly common names," implying, as they do, a Spanish or Latin American persona. It is also difficult to believe that Stevens had, in fact, never given the critic "a conscious thought" in the act of selecting the names.

Ramon Fernandez was born in Paris in 1894 and died fifty years later in the same city. He was thus a Frenchman—his father was Mexican and his mother French. He wrote book-length studies on Gide, Proust, Barrès, Molière, and Balzac, and he was also a novelist. He was one of the principal pillars of the journal *Nouvelle Revue Française* (the Paris weekly referred to by Stevens and to which he subscribed), and he wrote book reviews for the French periodical *Marianne,* a source from which Stevens wrote out two quotations (not by Fernandez) in his commonplace book, *Sur Plusieurs Beaux Sujets.*

The personal politics of Fernandez shifted through the course of his life with notable zigzags. When an essay by him appeared in the *Partisan Review* in 1934, the editors identified him politically: "Ramon Fernandez is one of the foremost critics on the Continent. Until recently a humanist, his turn to the Left at the time of the February riots [1934] in France illustrates the rapid radicalization of French intellectuals" ("Contributors" 2). In his "Open Letter to Andre Gide," also in 1934, however, Fernandez put distance between himself and the Communists: "But the Communist Party, stocked with the catchwords and formulas of the past, proposed to me a dogmatism which offends in me the defenses I have so carefully erected against the assaults of prejudice" (273). After the German occupation of Paris in 1940 (and after the writing of Stevens's poem), Fernandez became a collaborator, identifying himself with a manifesto supporting Franco at the beginning of the Spanish Civil War and continuing his association with *Nouvelle Revue Français* after its editorial policy became pro-German. In 1941 he attended an International Congress of Writers in Weimar, Germany. Fernandez died in 1944, before the overthrow of the Nazis.[3]

Before his political collaboration, however, Fernandez was praised by T. S. Eliot, who published him regularly in the *Criterion* and translated at least two of his essays for that journal. Of him, Eliot once wrote that he was "incidentally, a critic as well qualified to pronounce upon English literature as any English critic living" (753).

As the poet of "The Idea of Order at Key West," Stevens speaks through an unnamed persona, an observer who is, in fact, a poetic singer himself. As we have seen, that speaker is also a listener who hears the song of the woman and interprets it. Thus he moves from being only an observer of and listener to the woman's verbal song to creating her identity and defining her significance through his *own* words and voice. His, of course, is the only voice that we hear in the poem, so that Stevens in one way or another must speak through him. The poem then goes on to employ another listener, Fernandez, and the speaker brings him forward with a command in the present tense ("tell me, if you know, / Why. . . . "). The command is related to an earlier event they witnessed together and is now cast in the past tense: the reflection of the lights of the fishing boats upon the waters of the harbor. Thus, for the poem to trace the movement from the external woman's song, to which the speaker is auditor, to his own fixing of "zones" and "poles," he chooses to introduce an external auditor as an agent of listening (Fernandez), who thereby assumes the role that the speaker himself had earlier performed as hearer of the woman's song.

Although unheard by us in the poem, the song of the woman is verbal song and the ensuing visual description ("glassy lights"), too, is rendered verbally, both makings gesturing toward the poem's conclusion and the apotheosis of "words" in the final stanza. In the absence of a listener, however, words are monologic, directed interiorly. In a sense, they are as silent as the woman's actual song (otherwise uttered, we are told, "word by word") and as silent as Fernandez's own unrecorded reply to the "tell me . . . / Why" command. But the speaker himself *does* hear the woman's song, just as Fernandez does hear the rhapsodic words of the speaker's own delineations of the lights of the fishing boats. Moreover, we, too, the readers, are also listeners and interpreters—so many Ramon Fernandezes who want to understand why. I believe that the writings of Fernandez are especially useful in helping us to understand why the woman's song as it is rendered in the poem is nonetheless inferior to the speaker's own verbal response to the sea-in-harbor.

The first point I wish to make about Ramon Fernandez, then, is that he is our own surrogate in the poem and that, as a listener, he is necessary to make it possible for the "rage to order words" to occur. The alternative is to be a "listener" who is "nothing himself" (8) because he has metamorphosed into a dehumanized snow man. Song without ear (in the words of the Key West poem) is "sound alone": "But it was more than that."

"The Idea of Order at Key West," as A. Walton Litz (193–94) and others have observed, progresses from an aesthetic that debates the song of the woman and the plunging of the sea in mutually mimetic representations ("Even if what she sang was what she heard") and moves on toward a more affective and romantic aesthetic (creating an "enchanting night" out of a "rage for order"). In this fashion, the poem moves from song as mirror to song as lamp. The song of the woman becomes for her the creation of her own world, what must be called a solipsistic invention imputed to her by the speaker. But the tension between imitating the world and inventing it remains subtly in the background of the poem, each an extreme to which the speaker himself and the poem as a whole refuse to succumb. The pull between the mimetic and the solipsistic forces—and the dangers of each—are in the foreground of Fernandez's essay "Of Philosophic Criticism." The essay is collected, along with others by him on Balzac, Conrad, Newman, Freud, Stendhal, Maritain, Meredith, Pater, and Eliot, in a book called *Messages* published in 1926 and later translated into English by Montgomery Belgion. Lionel Abel once called this collection "the most important book of criticism since Eliot's 'Sacred Wood'" (Fernandez, "Open Letter" 271).

"Of Philosophic Criticism" begins with a warning about the hazards of perceiving the world purely scientifically, what Fernandez calls in one place "rational analysis" (*Messages* 11) and in another "descriptive thought." The latter "tells us of the object" and "shows it through the description" (17). Though such description may be necessary as the foundation of the artistic act, it cannot be its end because such an act of impersonal mimesis omits the role of our own psychic responses: "For that is a mediocre art which demands from us an effort of *reflection* in order that we may be in a position to apprehend its images" (8). (He means "reflection" here in the sense of a mirroring.) A "masterpiece," he insists, "is not in the least the copy of a thing" (19).

As previously noted, in Stevens's poem the initial response of the observer to the song of the woman is to note imitation: the cry of "mimic motion" and the song as "what she heard"; in her "phrases stirred / The grinding water and the gasping wind." As readers of Stevens know, the poet was powerfully driven throughout his career to possess the real as *ding an sich*, as "[p]art of the res itself and not about it" (404). "The accuracy of accurate letters is an accuracy with respect to the structure of reality" (686). However, in this poem, as we have noted, the observer is equally eager in the first thirty lines to *dissociate* the song of the singer from the sound of the sea ("But it was she and not the sea we heard"), as if this *imitation* by the singer must be allowed—if it is allowed at all—tentatively, momentarily, and as a begrudging concession.

If the artist's inclination toward merely copying nature is his first major temptation, the other extreme for Fernandez is equally dangerous and far more insidious. This is the form of art, and, indeed, of perception itself, that is "embalmed in sensibility alone." To illustrate this danger, Fernandez points to the example of Marcel Proust. While admitting that Proust "has established a close reciprocity between intelligence and sensation from which the latter has benefited," nonetheless such "title to glory . . . must not be allowed to mask his inadequacies" (*Messages* 45).

The work of Proust, like that of other writers referred to in *Messages,* is described by Fernandez in general terms, with few references to individual novels, scenes, or characters. As a result, his reservations are founded upon summaries and general applications. Proust, he tells us, "instead of seeking to render an account of the object . . . succeeds in *defining* the affective states corresponding to it" (*Messages* 44–45). For him, "there is no direct effect of spiritual activity on life, but only one of the memory of life embalmed in sensibility alone. . . . Even as in the philosophy of fact, in the Proustian psychology intelligence, by relation to life, is allowed only a *retrospective* function" (48–49). Elsewhere in the essay, here with no direct reference to Proust, Fernandez states, "I hold that in isolating intelligence from reality, in making of it a sort of receiving-post indifferent to what it registers, intelligence and reality are both out of gear. . . . Now, what it [such an intelligence] does is to cut up reality into facts and thought into laws, that is to say that it is pretended on principle that it *discovers* what it *conceives*" (30–31). In another essay, Fernandez finds that Walter Pater, too, in his preference for "*life as beauty*" and as "*picture*," failed "*to allow the mind to escape from itself to gain a booty really conquered*" (*Messages* 295).

Fernandez's point, so emphatically reiterated, is an important one and seems to have a conspicuous relevance to Stevens's poem. If the speaker in the poem moves beyond the mimetic mode in the nature of the woman's song, he seems to arrive at a different mode, one that is given great apparent significance in the poem, the song of solipsism:

> She was the single artificer of the world
> In which she sang. And when she sang, the sea,
> Whatever self it had, became the self
> That was her song, for she was the maker.

As many commentaries on the poem have observed, such a powerful making seems, on the one hand, to call attention to the Aristotelian notion of *poiein*, "to make, to craft, to construct"—the artist-poet as the journeyman of the world.[4] However, unlike the speaker, we have not heard this song, nor do we know the intent of the singer whose words, we are told, create for her the sea. Vendler has identified the nature of this problem for the poem: "The endangering sentimentality of *The Idea of Order* lies in the girl's becoming entirely the maker of the world she sings" (70–71). Fernandez, too, would be immediately suspicious of such a conclusion, and so is Stevens.

Stevens struggled with his own leanings toward solipsism. In a poem like "Tea at the Palaz of Hoon" he seems to indulge them: "I was myself the compass of that sea: // I was the world in which I walked, and what I saw / Or heard or felt came not but from myself" (51). But in "The Pediment of Appearance" he mocks just such "young men" like Hoon who "go crying / The world is myself, life is myself" (314), and in "Notes toward a Supreme Fiction" he insists that one must "[n]ever suppose an inventing mind as source" of the "idea" of the sun (329).

The speaker in "The Idea of Order at Key West" is not interpreting or making his world at this point in the poem but reporting the putative nature of the singer's own separate and personal world: *she* was the single artificer of a world in which *she* sang, and there never was a world *for her* except in her song. Once again, in the words of Fernandez she "pretend[s] on principle that [she] *discovers* what [she] *conceives*" (*Messages* 31). Her lyric interlude seems to be of the kind described by Donald Davie in his *Czeslaw Milosz and the Insufficiency of Lyric:* "The pristine and definitive form of lyric is the song; and the singer of a song is not on oath. The sentiment and opinion expressed in song . . . are to be understood as true only for as long as the singing lasts. They are true only to that occasion and that mood" (42).

In his book *Molière: The Man Seen through the Plays,* Fernandez restates the same danger of excessive imaginings separated from the real as it is worked out in Molière's play *Les précieuses ridicules.* Such is the object of the dramatist's satire: "At another moment the trick is to give the *Précieuses* [those who deny instinctual life] speeches in which they recoil from laying a finger on whatever object they are mentioning, even on things no more repulsive than a chair or a mirror. Again, the light will be focused on 'imaginings'—on the fancy of making life over and daydreaming it according to the convention of fiction" (56).

The speaker in "The Idea of Order at Key West," as he lays out the processes of associating and then disassociating the unity between "she" and "sea" in the poem's opening lines, seems intent on preserving the autonomy of both even as they move toward unity in song. In the light of Fernandez's admonitions on the dangers of "subjectivism," the speaker in the poem never himself succumbs to them. The song of the singing woman, however, does become the song of solipsism—at least in the speaker's interpretation. It is important to note that there is no counterpart to Ramon Fernandez to whom the woman directs her words. Of course, one might argue that the singing woman does have a listener, the speaker himself. However, she seems unaware of his presence or at least never gives any evidence that she is aware of him. In fact, she seems totally enveloped in her own "striding there alone" in lyric absorption with the world around her. She does not sing to him or for him, intent as she is on making *her* world.

Fernandez returns again and again to the idea that all utterances require an independent ear in order to skirt the danger of just such subjectivism. To avoid confounding "genuine intuition with the phantoms of the imagination" it is necessary to possess "a public, an *elite* capable of understanding, and especially of feeling" (*Messages* 18). Every complete personal experience must "set going the experience of others, and this through the medium of a dramatic intuition, consequently a synthetic intuition" (37). And again, "Now, can a personal experience be held valid if it does not enlighten us about others at the same time as ourselves, not in the manner of a dictionary or inventory, that is to say, abstractly, but by an intuition analogous to that which we have or our own being? At least an artistic work which does not rest on this intuition seems destined to a more or less complete failure." Such a "philosophy of life" forces us into "as much repugnance for the solipsism as for the strict methods of science" (35). Stevens's poem proposes *the* idea of order at Key West, not *an* idea of order, not mine in isolation nor hers in isolation. Orders are privately perceived, he implies, but socially validated.

As if he were giving a summary of Stevens's poem, and the song of the woman who sings "word by word," Heidegger exalts the poet as one who "speaks the essential word, the existent is by this naming nominated as what it is. So it becomes known *as* existent. Poetry is the establishment of being by means of the word" (762). But Heidegger also goes on, as Stevens's poem does, to affirm the power of the poet not in isolation but in the society of conversation: "The being of men is founded in language. But this only becomes actual in *conversation.* . . . The ability to speak and the ability to hear are equally fundamental. We are a conversation—and that means: we can hear from one another" (760–61). The language of a poet creates a world, but a world in discourse.

In one other important way, the conclusions of Ramon Fernandez come close to serving as a précis for Stevens's poem. If literalism and solipsism are the twin sirens whose isolated seductions must be resisted, how then can one create a synthetic union between these extremes? In the last lines of the poem the speaker turns to Fernandez in his own dramatic and synthetic intuition. He moves away from the "solitude" that was "measured to the hour" by the singer and turns "Toward the town," moving from isolation into community. His "tell me, if you know, / Why . . . ," addressed to Fernandez, draws the latter into a dialogic relation with the speaker's own act of creation:

> . . . tell why the glassy lights
>
> .   .   .   .
>
> Mastered the night and portioned out the sea,
> Fixing emblazoned zones and fiery poles,
> Arranging, deepening, enchanting night.

He creates his own enchanted world, one of color, order, and mastery. In his essay on Jacques Maritain, Fernandez describes such moments of the "luminous spot" for which we all yearn but rarely attain: "We are advancing step by step in a narrow circle of light which is not always displaced to suit us, between the chiaroscuro of the past and the night of the future . . . ; but the little luminous spot, which moves, which advances when one of us succeeds—after how much effort!—in making flash a clarity, such is intelligence, and our joy" (*Messages* 273).

The speaker in Stevens's poem has discovered his "luminous spot" wherein there is "making flash" a clarity, intelligence, and joy in "emblazoned zones and fiery poles." But, unlike the woman of the song, he has not made his discovery in isolation. If one might say that "there never was a world for him except the one he saw, and, seeing, made," it is not one seen and made "for him" alone.

The basis of his intuition of the world is the world itself, what Fernandez would call "common-sense reality": harbor, sea surface, fishing boats, lights, reflections. The identity of Key West in the title situates us in a real place on the map of the world. "The real is only the base. But it is the base" (917), insists Stevens. Fernandez would say that such perceptions of the base, however, are then remade, now in balance instead of distorting either side: "In spite of our worst extravagances we are moving towards unity: I mean that in us the unity of the dislocated and scattered object is remade, *this time in a purely sentimental form*. . . . Thus are formed in us *psychic equivalents* of things containing within themselves the principle of their elucidation" (*Messages* 43). A similar conclusion results from the fiction of George Meredith, whom Fernandez prefers over that of Proust. In Meredith's characters, "the mind escapes from the tyranny of the object, but meets the object in itself and re-creates its essential reality" (162). Earlier, in "Of Philosophic Criticism," Fernandez declares that the "artistic object" can never be swept aside by fancy. Such an object is an "independent complex of which the organic unity and cohesion result from a synthesis ensuring to it a life of its own. . . . In it [the work of art] the mind seizes itself as having accomplished itself in an object" (12). Again, Meredith is the artist's model: "he creates, if one may say so, what he understands, in such a way that his creation incessantly modifies reality without betraying it" (50).

In another essay, "A Note on Intelligence and Intuition," one that was translated by Eliot and appeared in his *Criterion,* Fernandez implies yet another part in the process: "The poet offers us the concrete side of fact, vision, rhythm, affective emanation, etc., but as we discern through it the abstract side, the *idea* of this reality [emphasis added] attaches itself to the prehension of this reality" (337). That which is concrete, including both "fact" and "affective emanation," leads to the vision of the abstract, or "idea." This observation seems to me to illustrate the lines of the final stanza of Stevens's poem: "Oh! Blessed rage for order, pale Ramon, / The maker's rage to order words of the sea." From "affective emanation," in this case "rage," one arrives at "the idea of this reality," or, in the words of the poem, ordering words of the sea in order to discover the "idea of order."

Ramon Fernandez as critic points to and, I believe, elucidates many of the issues of Stevens's poem, whether Stevens's choice of the name was accidental or not. But his presence in the poem by name and vocative address, I am arguing, is crucial because he establishes the third part of the triangulation that constitutes any work of art: the artist, the object(s), and the audience. Here Ramon Fernandez as critic and Ramon Fernandez as dramatis persona converge. We do not need his reply to the "tell me . . . / Why" command because, in the very process of being given that command, he authenticates the speaker as his own maker-in-community, his own utterer of "words . . . of ourselves." For this artist, there can never be a world for *him* in isolation. For *us*, for the speaker, for Fernandez, and for you and me who hear the poem, there never was a world for *us* except the one he sees and sings and, seeing and singing, makes—even as we will go on to make our own worlds by making and singing them in social intercourse. It is only one step further removed to note that Wallace Stevens also speaks to us as his audience through his speaker and through a performative poem called "The Idea of Order at Key West."

NOTES

1. Unless otherwise indicated, all quotations from the works of Stevens are taken from *Wallace Stevens: Collected Poetry and Prose*. "The Idea of Order at Key West" appears on 105–6, and quotations from that poem will not otherwise be indicated by page number.

2. In stanza xix from "Like Decorations in a Nigger Cemetery," Stevens uses the word "portals" with the same theatrical association: "An opening of portals when night ends, / A running forward, arms stretched out as drilled. / Act I, Scene I, at a German Staats-Oper" (123).

3. For references to Fernandez's collaboration with the Germans during World War II, see Lottman.

4. In his essay "Three Academic Pieces," Stevens differentiates between seeing the world and begetting or making it through "resemblance"—such as song resembling sea: "What the eye beholds may be the text of life. It is, nevertheless, a text that we do not write. The eye does not beget in resemblance. It sees. But the mind begets in resemblance as the painter begets in representation; *that is to say, as the painter makes his world within a world*" (*Necessary Angel* 689; emphasis added).

WORKS CITED

"Contributors." *Partisan Review* 1 (Sept.–Oct. 1934): 2.

Davie, Donald. "Milosz and the Dithyramb." *Czeslaw Milosz and the Insufficiency of Lyric.* Knoxville: U of Tennessee P, 1986.

Eliot, T. S. "Books of the Quarter." *Criterion* 4 (October 1926): 751–57.

Fernandez, Ramon. *Messages: Literary Essays.* Trans. Montgomery Belgion. Port Washington, NY: Kennikat, 1964.

———. *Molière: The Man Seen through the Plays.* Trans. Wilson Follett. New York: Hill and Wang, 1958.

———. "A Note on Intelligence and Intuition." Trans. T. S. Eliot. *Criterion* 6 (October 1927): 332–39.

———. "An Open Letter to Andre Gide." Trans. Lionel Abel. *Modern Monthly* 8 (June 1934): 271–74.

Heidegger, Martin. "Hölderlin and the Essence of Poetry." *Critical Theory since 1965.* Ed. Hazard Adams and Leroy Searle. Tallahassee: Florida State UP, 1986. 758–65.

Litz, A. Walton. *Introspective Voyager: The Poetic Development of Wallace Stevens.* New York: Oxford UP, 1972.

Lottman, Herbert R. *The Left Bank: Writers, Artists, and Politics from the Popular Front to the Cold War.* Boston: Houghton Mifflin, 1982.

Stevens, Wallace. *Letters of Wallace Stevens.* Ed. Holly Stevens. New York: Alfred A. Knopf, 1966.

———. *The Necessary Angel: Essays on Reality and the Imagination.* New York: Vintage, 1951.

———. *Wallace Stevens: Collected Poetry and Prose.* Selected by Frank Kermode and Joan Richardson. New York: Library of America, 1997.

Vendler, Helen. *Wallace Stevens: Words Chosen Out of Desire.* Knoxville: U of Tennessee P, 1984.

Restlessness and Deformation

Sylvia Plath's Feet

DESALES HARRISON

Bare or in shoes, in boots, as toes, as heels, as hooves, crutches, or stilts, in motion, in stasis, fleet, halt, lamed, dragging—feet appear and reappear throughout Sylvia Plath's poems. Why should this be? And where are we when we note this: in the kingdom of obsession? in the uncanny realm of dream symbolization? in a region of privately nourished fixed ideas? Asking this is a way of asking what interpretive posture these recurrences invite us to assume. What can we say about a poetic oeuvre when a motif (aesthetic and ordered) blurs into, and indeed describes itself as, an obsession (psychological and disordered)? What problem are we trying to solve when we parse out such distinctions? Is it enough to say—and indeed, is it interesting at all to say—that Plath, like so many other poets, is endeavoring to get the physical body into the poem, at least as much as possible, or even in spite of the impossibility of doing so? Should we retreat behind a grim joke that her work is, after all, a poetry of extremities?

In response to these uncertainties, the temptation is strong to pledge allegiance to one of two contrasting beliefs. The first claims that such an insistent motif is in fact a mark of pathology (a compelled repetition, however brilliantly varied) and therefore in its essence a symptom of psychic conflict. The second is that for all the rhetoric of intense psychological presence that the poems manifest, they are no less structured or ordered than any other body of strong poetic work; the foot motif like any other motif, takes its meaning not from a hidden psychic conflict but from a set of linguistic, conceptual, and aesthetic tensions that spread out across the surface of these and other texts. And of course, to make either of these assertions is to engage in an ongoing political debate; the border separating psychological diagnosis from violation or colonization is no more distinct than the border between literary analysis and the suppression or effacement of historical contingency and moral obligation. What I will argue here, however, is that her deepest preoccupation is not with intrapsychic conflict, or with aesthetic and linguistic tensions, or even, ulti-mately, with the social, intersubjective relations that constitute political reality. Rather, her central concern is with a tension importantly different from all these: that between inner, embodied, opaque mortal experience on the one hand, and the demands, indeed the costs, of representation on the other. For Plath, this means of representation is the constrained, mea-sured, and terminated medium of lyric speech, which is to say, speech in lines, or rather (in a manner for her both abstract and disturbingly con-crete) speech in feet. For her, the foot, as a part of the body and a part of the poem, requires her readers to rethink the troubled relations between mind, body, and text. Unseemly, pallid, often vestigial or deformed, dis-rupting our sense of the difference between speaker and speech, the rest-less, insistent foot of Plath's poetry ultimately suggests a new account of the poetic medium itself as a medium of disruption and deformation.

The foot appears most visibly in Plath's poetry as the vestige or print of absolute fact, specifically the fact of a bodily reality essentially and intran-sigently resistant to idealization. In "Edge," the last, or next-to-last, poem that Plath wrote, the feet of the woman testify mutely to the completion or abruption of a journey. In this poem a life, lived in the present, mired in flaws and imperfection, is now, after the moment of death, rendered per-fect, a closed form, an "accomplished" fact, a fait accompli:

> The woman is perfected.
> Her dead
>
> Body wears the smile of accomplishment,
> The illusion of a Greek necessity
>
> Flows in the scrolls of her toga,
> Her bare
>
> Feet seem to be saying:
> We have come so far, it is over.
>
> (272)

Any movement here is the movement of fate itself, flowing in the (writ-ten, determined and determining) scrolls of the toga, where flowing is nothing more than mimetic illusion of flowing, but also nothing less than the perfect mimetic illusion of flowing. The woman herself is stopped, perfected. The feet "come / To show how cold she is, and dumb," to quote from Stevens's "The Emperor of Ice-Cream," a poem that "Edge" recalls and rewrites. The foot, like Stevens's "horny feet," protrudes, thrusting itself into the world from beneath the artistic surface, which Stevens characterizes as "that sheet / On which she embroidered fantails once." The foot protrudes as a form of mortal being that makes an end to all seeming: Where Stevens delivers his imperative to "Let be be finale of seem," Plath states, flatly, declaratively, "it is over." But where Stevens could formulate a stark opposition between being and seeming, between feet and fantails, for Plath the relation is more fraughtly blurred. The Greek necessity is the "illusion of a Greek necessity." The feet only "seem" to say "it is over." The conflict between the imaginary or aesthetic and the plainly propounded, between the mythic and the factual, is a dispute that no part of Plath's work attempts to settle; indeed, the work seems to agitate within that dispute as an agent provocateur. In "Edge," the Hellenic, stony perfection of the woman is virtually indistinguishable from that of utter ruin, a landscape of stones (however perfectly shaped) without human vitality.

Such a scene of ruin, for instance, is the setting of Plath's first mature poem, "The Colossus." The ruin in this early poem is a vast marmoreal dismemberment, the fragments of an immense god-hero-father, not so much strewn across a landscape as constituting the very landscape itself. In "The Colossus," the father's body is a monstrous wreckage of divinity, or rather, the body is divinity monstrously wrecked; unliftable, unpurgable, it vies with the very Atlantic Ocean itself for permanence. The trouble this poem introduces is a condition where the mythic is, for Plath, precisely the site of the unredeemable corporeality. The work of "The Colossus" is to force the conjunction of the two:

> I shall never get you put together entirely,
> Pieced, glued, and properly joined.
> Mule-bray, pig-grunt and bawdy cackles
> Proceed from your great lips.
> It's worse than a barnyard.
>
> Perhaps you consider yourself an oracle,
> Mouthpiece of the dead, or of some god or another.
> Thirty years now I have labored
> To dredge the silt from your throat.
> I am none the wiser.
>
> (129)

Whatever is oracular about this shattered father is also bestial and profane. What silts the throat is divinity pulverized, a sedimentation of mythic meanings compacted to mere meaninglessness, in which speech itself is a plug of unutterables. The divine love between gods and mortals, and the forbidden love between fathers and daughters, are both attenuated here to a blank futility, in a vestal self-sacrifice to an endless labor of reconstruction. In her self-sacrifice, the daughter is reduced to an endless, Sisyphean traverse: "Your fluted bones and acanthine hair are littered // In their old anarchy to the horizon-line. [...] My hours are married to shadow" (129). The "perfection" of "Edge" includes, by dint of the close, antiquarian, and perhaps even incestuous affinity between these two poems, an allusion to speech that is perfectly unintelligible, and to a task of reconstruction or redemption that is perfectly impossible.[1]

"The Colossus," when compared with Plath's other ruin poems, father poems, and poems of endless, fruitless activity, is notable insofar as feet are entirely absent. Taken by itself, this is of no consequence. The poem merely assumes its position in the long list of other poems in which feet do not appear, and feet themselves take their place in the even longer list of things that this poem is not about. But it is this absence of the foot—and more importantly, the absence of those troubled concepts and dynamics that the foot brings into play—that Plath seeks to fill, three years later, when she reframes "The Colossus" as the infamous "Daddy." In "The Colossus," the opposition between temple and barnyard is too schematic, a facile transvaluation from high to low, from divine to animal, delighting in its gleeful detour away from the realm of the human. The father in "The Colossus" was never what Nietzsche calls the mere, actual "walking man." The animal expletives and eructations insist not on the father's humanity but on his subhumanity. On the other hand, we are left to guess how he achieved his gigantic and gigantically dismantled status. In "Daddy," the mortality of the "walking man" surges into the forefront. It is precisely the "foot" of this "walking man" that consumes the attention of the speaker. This foot, however, is also the sign of the father's Satanic, demonic power, so it is precisely in the foot of "Daddy" that the mortal and the divine converge:

You do not do, you do not do
Any more, black shoe
In which I have lived like a foot
For thirty years, poor and white,
Barely daring to breathe or Achoo.

Daddy, I have had to kill you.
You died before I had time—
Marble-heavy, a bag full of God,
Ghastly statue with one gray toe
Big as a Frisco seal

And a head in the freakish Atlantic
Were it pours bean green over blue
In the waters off beautiful Nauset.
I used to pray to recover you.
Ach, du.

(222)

Like the god fragments in "The Colossus," the father's body makes a land-scape of ruin, stretching from Frisco to Nauset, but here, the ruin is felt also as a physical encumbrance, an unliftable burden: "Marble-heavy, a bag full of God."[2] This encumbrance is not that of obsession or resigna-tion, but of unshakable physical impediment. The weight is registered as a downward pull on the speaker's own body.

It is this element of factuality and rootedness which discussions of the more notoriously sensuous masochism of a later stanza leave out:[3]

Every woman adores a Fascist,
The boot in the face, the brute
Brute heart of a brute like you.

This boot, as Jacqueline Rose has argued (205–38), makes a claim for the amorality of fantasy, the mind's prerogative to alloy its loves and hatreds, for its capacity to experience in loathing (of self as well as of others) a sense of sexual satisfaction. Isolated in this way, the boot becomes the accoutre-ment of pure power, power in which brute implies mere brutality, and the boot is what decorporealizes the body, turns the leg into a peg, and the foot into a bludgeon, and cudgel. In the larger context of the poem, how-ever, the brutal boot is also a brutish boot, an embodiment not merely of pure power, but of animal corporeality, a foot not of leather or steel but of clay, blooded with the brute blood of the earth, to paraphrase Yeats.[4] The foot is the shared extremity with reference to which the speaker describes both herself ("like a foot / [. . .] poor and white") and her father ("one gray toe"). To view this paternal foot, then, only as a weapon of domination is to ignore the suggestion, less assimilable to a narrative of emancipation, that the speaker longs less for domination or submission than she does for rootedness, for a knowledge of origins prior to the devastations of "wars, wars, wars."

> In the German tongue, in the Polish town
> Scraped flat by the roller
> Of wars, wars, wars.
> But the name of the town is common.
> My Polack friend
>
> Says there are a dozen or two.
> So I never could tell where you
> Put your foot, your root,
> I never could talk to you.
> The tongue stuck in my jaw.
>
> (222)

The foot as root embodies an origin prior to the step-parenthood of fatherland and mother tongue, an origin in the earth itself, a sort of preverbal Roethkean interpretation of the Yeatsian desideratum "to live like some green laurel / Rooted in one dear perpetual place" ("A Prayer for My Daughter"). The German father, however, is no more rooted in a national identity than is his daughter. Often ignored in discussions of this poem is the fact that the German father is a Pole of German extraction, where the disparagement of "Polacks" establishes a middle term between the father's Fascism and the speaker's downtrodden Jewishness.[5] Her desire to get "back, back, back" to you is the desire to find their shared rootedness in a middle ground, to join with the father in a subterranean, historically buried, and politically ambivalent point of convergence. From this perspective the father's Fascism inheres, for the speaker, in his refusal to acknowledge—in the fraught no-man's-land between ethnicity and eros—a shared root.

This rooted and rooting foot is for Plath a foot barely human; it is not animal or subhuman so much as it is protohuman, pseudopodial, an instrument less of will than of mere impulse. "Mushrooms" imagines this lowly life as one of meekly unstoppable "nudging and shoving":

> Our toes, our noses
> Take hold on the loam,
> Acquire the air. [...]

Soft fists insist on
Heaving the needles,
The leafy bedding,

Even the paving.
Our hammers, our rams,
Earless and eyeless,

Perfectly voiceless,
Widen the crannies,
Shoulder through holes. [...]

We shall by morning
Inherit the earth.
Our foot's in the door.

(139)

The section of "Poem for a Birthday" entitled "Dark House" explores the depths of similarly lowly and Roethkean humility:

Pebble smells, turnipy chambers.
Small nostrils are breathing.
Little humble loves!
Footlings, boneless as noses,
It is warm and tolerable
In the bowel of the root.
Here's a cuddly mother.

(131)

It is a strong temptation to extrapolate from these experiments an idealization of a cuddly, earthly mother-region, in whose safe tummy-cupboard one might hide from bad booted daddy and his squadrons of goat-choking German nouns. This opposition, however, strips the poems of much of their interior complexity. Just as "Daddy" entails a fantasy (however hidden) of rootedness, "Mushrooms" and "Poem for a Birthday" entail a fantasy of power—the power chiefly of insatiable hunger—a power wielded relentlessly by the eyeless and larval creatures of the shadowy netherworld.

If this opposition between cuddly mother and booted daddy is in fact an oversimplification, then the foot's complexity as a central figure in

Plath's work derives from other tensions, from discords other than those between the political and the personal, between the collective and the individual, or—to frame the issue in terms more consistent with those of the specific poems I have discussed—between oedipal and preoedipal desires. To break free from these axes of interpretation I propose here to consider other accounts of the foot's privilege and uncertainty in the realm of bodily representations. Heidegger's work, specifically his essay "The Origin of the Work of Art," has enjoyed a mistrustful renown similar to that of Plath's "Daddy." I want to suggest that such a troublous and fraught reputation has something more than exactly nothing to do with feet, or rather, with the fact that Heidegger's essay, like Plath's poem, pivots around an account of the foot, specifically the pair of peasant shoes depicted in a painting by Van Gogh. In this essay, as in the poem, the problem of how the foot might embody (or complicate) a state of rootedness comes to the fore. Heidegger sees the artwork as a revealing of being; in the painting what is revealed is the "equipmental being" of the shoes, their fitness for a certain kind of work, and the world that such equipment and such work implies:

> As long as we only imagine a pair of shoes in general, or simply look at the empty, unused shoes as they merely stand there in the picture, we shall never discover what the equipmental being of the equipment in truth is. From Van Gogh's painting we cannot even tell where these shoes stand. There is nothing surrounding this pair of peasant shoes in or to which they might belong—only an undefined space. There are not even clods of soil from the field or the field-path sticking to them, which would at least hint at their use. A pair of peasant shoes and nothing more. And yet—
>
> From the dark opening of the worn insides of the shoes the toilsome tread of the worker stares forth. In the stiffly rugged heaviness of the shoes there is the accumulated tenacity of her slow trudge through the far-spreading and ever-uniform furrows of the field swept by a raw wind. On the leather lie the dampness and richness of the soil. Under the soles slides the loneliness of the field-path as evening falls. In the shoes vibrates the silent call of the earth, its quiet gift of the ripening grain and its unexplained self-refusal in the fallow desolation of the wintry field. This equipment is pervaded by uncomplaining anxiety as to the certainty of bread, the wordless joy of having once more withstood want, the trembling before the impending childbed and shivering at the surrounding menace of death. This

equipment belongs to the *earth,* and it is protected in the *world* of the peasant woman. From out of this protected belonging the equipment itself rises to its resting-within-itself. (33–34)

The shoes fulfill their equipmental being exactly to the extent that they disclose—or, to use the Heideggerian term, unconceal—from a dark or withheld interior a vision of the work in which they assist, and of the world in which they partake. The work is not just any work but the work of a peasant woman, a worker in fields, a solitary walker of desolate rural paths. The path described traverses not only fields but states of mind and body: anxiety, pain of want, childbirth, and mortality. It is through this rural groundedness that the shoes, as equipment, belong to the earth, the earth that underpins the world of the peasant woman. Heidegger later says that it is the act of the artwork, this depiction of equipment, which "lets the earth be an earth"—and not just any earth, but the tilled, planted, and plowed earth of the farm, where the woman's labor, Heidegger imagines, draws all its vitality from the soil itself.

In the painting, however, the foot is present as an emptiness, the scene of a departure. The shoes are "empty, unused." Without this emptiness, there would be no "dark opening" from which the "toilsome tread" would "stare forth" in whatever weird way a tread can stare. (I will say more about this blurring or deforming of the implied body shortly.) It is this absenting of the body part itself that emphasizes the "equipmental being" of the shoe and not the corporeal being of the foot itself, without which the woman could not walk, without which there would be neither path nor furrow.

Nevertheless, because the emphasis here is on the equipment, the equipmental being of the shoes points not only outward toward the work and world that the peasant woman inhabits but inward to the body for which the shoes are fit. This body is on the one hand starkly displaced, but on the other hand it asserts itself through its very absence. The foot is absent, but its absence creates the aperture from which the "toilsome tread of the worker stares forth." It is "in" the shoes that the silent call of the earth "calls." As the aperture for a call, the shoes resemble a mouth. As the manifestation of a staring, the shoes have the qualities of eyes, a gaze. Together, as mouth and gaze, they make up a visage, a form of equipmental countenance, a manifestation that is, while not a human face, a face nevertheless, replete with expression, memory, and care. Its expressiveness is constituted precisely in and through the absenting or displacement of the human body part itself.

George Bataille, in a manifestly different but profoundly related passage, contemplates not only the abject and displaceable attributes of the foot, but its insistent qualities as well. For Bataille, the part of the earth that is excluded from such an artwork and from such a philosophical work is the part of earth that is the foot itself. The foot asserts what Bataille calls its baseness. Any coherence of intent, labor, or self-presence is what the foot startles into disarray. Useful action, for Bataille, is essentially foreign to the foot. It is this idea that he explores in detail in his quasi-psychotic reverie "The Big Toe":

> The play of fantasies and fears, of human necessities and aberrations, is in fact such that fingers have come to signify useful action and firm character, the toes stupor and base idiocy. The vicissitudes of organs, the profusion of stomachs, larynxes, and brains traversing innumer- able animal species and individuals, carries the imagination along in an ebb and flow it does not willingly follow, due to a hatred of the still painfully perceptible frenzy of the bloody palpitations of the body. Man willingly imagines himself to be like the god Neptune, stilling his own waves, with majesty: nevertheless, the bellowing waves of the viscera, in more or less incessant inflation and upheaval, brusquely put an end to his dignity. Blind, but tranquil and strangely despis- ing his obscure baseness, a given person, ready to call to mind the grandeurs of human history, as when his glance ascends a monument testifying to the grandeur of his nation, is stopped in mid-flight by an atrocious pain in his big toe because, though the most noble of ani- mals, he nevertheless has corns on his feet; in other words, he has feet, and these feet independently lead an ignoble life. (22)

Bataille suggests the possibility of a completely different kind of ground- ing, a grounding in "*obscure* baseness." It is a quality of this baseness that it fascinates and arouses us. We must not allow ourselves to be ener- vated and tranquilized by what he later terms "a poetic haze" but instead must acknowledge how baseness itself exerts "an extreme seductiveness." Heidegger's passage would appear to Bataille, one feels certain, as a dream distilled from such a poetic haze, if only to the extent that the obscurely base foot is elided from Heidegger's account of the painting.

This opposition, however, between Heidegger's Apollonian reserve and Bataille's Dionysian, or rather, Rabelaisian viscerality is, as I hope I have already suggested, merely superficial; the passages display an uncanny tropism toward each other. For Bataille, the body makes itself known in "palpitation," in "ebb and flow" in "waves," in "inflation and upheaval." In other words, the "violent discord of the organs" asserts itself as an unending oscillation between differing forms of unrest. As humans, however, we are driven to suppress this knowledge, and to view our foot, the foundation or pediment for our upright posture, as the base or basis of our superior natures:

> The big toe is the most human part of the human body, in the sense that no other element of this body is as differentiated from the corresponding element of the anthropoid ape (chimpanzee, gorilla, orangutan, or gibbon). This is due to the fact that the ape is tree dwelling, whereas man moves on the earth without clinging to branches, having himself become a tree, and all the more beautiful for the correctness of his erection. In addition, the function of the human foot consists in giving a firm foundation to the erection of which man is so proud (the big toe, ceasing to grasp branches, is applied to the ground on the same plane as the other toes). (22)

In viewing the foot as a base, Bataille goes on to say, we not only deny but also perversely affirm its insistent baseness. The foundation of the "human" foot is what the "incessant upheaval" of the body undermines. It is not, then, what is rooted or muddy about the foot that constitutes its baseness for Bataille, but this condition of discord and upheaval, its signification of incessant palpitation. Similarly, for Heidegger, "In the shoes *vibrates* the silent call of the earth," the cyclical alternation of harvest and want, "the *trembling* before impending childbed and *shivering* at the surrounding menace of death" (33; emphasis added). Sustaining all this, as though the concrete and visible imprint of these oscillations, are "the far-spreading and ever-uniform *furrows*" (emphasis added) of the worked field. The groundedness of Heidegger's shoes does not inhere in their partial immersion in the damp soil. In fact, he takes pains to say "there are not even clods of soil from the field or the field-path sticking to them." Instead, the ground of their being is an oscillating ground, defined not by fixity but by period and interval, states of excitement and tension, an oscillation of alternating charge and stasis. In both Bataille and Heidegger, then, there is a tension—largely unresolved and disavowed—between on the one hand groundedness and rootedness and on the other the oscillations and disruptions of bodily need and desire. For Heidegger it is not the steady grounding rhythm of the seasons and of night and day but a different oscillation, between the ongoingness of the nonhuman earth and the corporeality and mortality of the woman. Heidegger suggests that these cycles are compatible, harmonically attuned to one another, but in the context of Bataille's assertions, they reveal a troubling lack of attunement, a disarticulation and an unease.

It is not only because a name like Martin Heidegger too infrequently shares a sentence with a name like Sydney Joseph Perelman that I turn now to S. J. Perelman's story "Is There an Osteosychrondroitrician in the House?" Perelman's story, while rendering even the gravest preoccupations incapable of being taken seriously, exploits the same tensions between cartoonish distortion and dire surmise as do Plath and Bataille, and like Plath, Bataille, and Heidegger, he describes a foot that is the sign both of death's claim (because Perelman's foot is a skeletal foot) and of a deathless vitality (because his skeletal foot is, like Plath's, automated and indefatigably animated). The story narrates the predicament of a writer consumed with dread of and loathing for the motorized display of human foot bones he passes each day in a shoe-store window:

> I was hurrying homeward that holiday afternoon pretty much in
> the groove, humming an aria from "Till Tom Special" and wishing I
> could play the clarinet like a man named Goodman. Just as it oc-
> curred to me that I might drug this individual and torture his secret
> out of him, I came abreast the window of the shoestore containing the
> bones of the human foot. My mouth suddenly developed that curious
> dry feeling when I saw that they were *vibrating*, as usual, from north
> to south, every little metatarsal *working* with the blandest contempt
> for all I hold dear. I pressed my ear against the window and heard the
> faint *clicking* of the motor housed in the box beneath. A little scratch
> here and there on the *shellac* surface showed where one of the more
> enterprising toes had tried to do a *solo* but had quickly rejoined the
> band. Not only was the entire arch rolling forward and backward in
> an oily fashion, but it had evolved an obscene side sway at the same
> time, a good deal like the *danse à ventre.* Maybe the foot had belonged
> to an Ouled-Naïl girl, but I felt I didn't care to find out. I was aware
> immediately of an active desire to rush home and lie down attended
> by my loved ones. The only trouble was that when I started to leave
> that place, I could feel my arches acting according to all the proper or-
> thopedic laws, and I swear people turned to look at me as if they heard
> a clicking sound. (762; emphasis added, except for *danse à ventre*)

The dreadful, mindless automatism of the foot is not only terrifying to Perelman but, in his fancy, contagious. The "active desire to rush home and lie down" is overrun by the awareness of the same mechanical impersonality at work in the movement of his own arches. It is this awareness that dislodges him, like a record needle knocked from its furrow, from the "groove" of his humming reverie concerning "a man named Goodman."[6] In his acknowledgment of this automatism, Perelman feels the shiver of doom, a doom explicitly linked to that of the serpent in Eden, condemned to slither on its belly and bruise the heel of man. (In fact, it is the unholy and satanic *snakiness* of the foot's movement that unhinges Perelman most irreparably.) For Perelman, however, the bitterest aspect of the serpent's punishment is not consignment to a life spent on the belly, the *ventre*, but the *danse* part, the "obscene side sway" that brings to mind the image of an Ouled-Naïl girl, dancing somewhere far away, though perhaps now (he can't bear to think) without the participation of one of her feet. The groundedness of Perelman's foot, like that of Heidegger's and Bataille's, is in its oscillation, vibration, and dreadful, fateful sway. It is also in its state of dismemberment, of alienation, and isolation from its proper body, a body not accidentally imagined as that of a dancer. The foot is established in an exile of permanent dance.[7]

One reflects, staring into the window with Perelman, that Heidegger's essay itself had flirted with and then repudiated something of the same possibility:

> Everyone knows what shoes consist of. If there are not wooden or bast
> shoes, there will be leather soles and uppers, joined together by thread
> and nails. Such gear serves to clothe the feet. Depending on the use
> to which the shoes are to be put, whether for work in the field or for
> dancing, matter and form will differ. (32)

Not only matter and form, one suspects, but the entire account of work elaborated in Heidegger's essay will differ. With respect to the "equipmental being" of the shoes, it cannot be a matter of indifferent concern whether they are for "work in the field" or "for dancing." Manifestly, of course, the choice is constrained by the painting itself. The description of *this* work of art requires an account of *these* shoes, and the work for which they are fashioned. For that reason alone, Heidegger's account could not be about dancing shoes. The irony, of course, is that Heidegger's description of the shoes, as well as Bataille's and Perelman's description of the foot, gives both shoe and foot over to the rhythmic interval of dance. The footness of the foot, these passages suggest, inheres not in their relation to the earth beneath them but in dance itself—for Heidegger the polyrhythmic, epi-cyclic vibration of trudging, slogging, sliding, trembling, and shivering; for Perelman, the *danse à ventre;* and for Bataille, and indeed for Plath herself, the *danse macabre.*

It is at this place, the place of the foot animated in a *danse macabre,* that I would like to return to Plath's work. For Plath, the foot signifies that aspect of the body available to influences and agencies that are separate, distinct, and wholly independent of the speaker. Among those agencies that can take over or supplant consciously willed human agency is the agency of the lyric medium itself. In this light, it is something more than a coincidence that the lyric is that mode of discourse articulated in metrical feet. However, it is a matter of growing and dreadful certainty for Plath, as she approaches the end of her life, that the feet of the poem and the feet of the poet cannot fall in step with one another. For Plath the agency of the poem is precisely that agency that defeats and surpasses human will. It is not, then, merely a mythological commonplace that the power of the medium is a power both nonhuman and subjugated, a power for which the iconic figure is specifically the horse: great-thewed, hooved, bridled, bitted, and shod. "Words" is her great, late poem of the divide between poem and writer, here expressed, in a near homonym, as the separation between horse and rider:

> Axes
> After whose stroke the wood rings,
> And the echoes!
> Echoes traveling
> Off from the center like horses.
>
> The sap
> Wells like tears, like the
> Water striving
> To re-establish its mirror
> Over the rock
>
> That drops and turns,
> A white skull,
> Eaten by weedy greens.
> Years later I
> Encounter them on the road—

Words dry and riderless,
The indefatigable hoof-taps.
While
From the bottom of the pool, fixed stars
Govern a life.

(270)

I discuss this poem, and the topic of automatization in Plath's medium, at greater length elsewhere;[8] what I would like to emphasize here, however, is the fact that the separation between horse and rider is in fact a deathly one. We may surmise, of course, that the horse is riderless merely because the rider has dismounted by dispatching her poem-horse-echoes into the world and now perceives them in retrospect. But the ambience of the poem is more menacing. There is of course the iconographic tradition in which the riderless horse stands as a metonymy for the departed warrior or statesman, as in presidential funeral processions, for instance, or in Stevens's great death poem "Farewell without a Guitar," "in which the horse rides home without a rider,/head down." The separation described here between horse and rider is the result of a killing blow. What descends from the masterful poise of the seated rider falls at first like a stone, one that passes through the still, mimetic, representational surface of the pool and into its depths. It is in this pool that the stone suffers a change and becomes a skull, "eaten by weedy greens." The record of the life is not a representation (reproducible, safely distinct from the body or life it represents) but a relic, a skeletal fragment, not an image of the face, the mortal countenance, but the skull, the image of mortality itself, subject to a vegetative version of Shakespeare's "devouring time" (Sonnet 19). The head is cast forth from the body, not as a copy but as a body part, that part without which the body cannot live. The horse, then, is riderless, but more horridly, the erstwhile rider is also headless. The act of utterance, which could have preserved the living countenance, here converges upon an act of killing and eating, an act that destroys the countenance, turns it into a leering, socketed visage of terror. The echo-horses are constituted, or rather, dispatched, by the blow of an ax, the report of whose blow carries with it the rumor of a violent death. The words themselves are made known only through this process of division. What survives survives in an endless, inexhaustible afterlife, the report of the hoof-taps "dry," unblooded, "indefatigable," no longer subject to mortal limit.

This disseveration is not unique in Plath to "Words." In "Morning Song," it is the dislocation of the speaker into an image of her vanishing:

I'm no more your mother
Than the cloud that distills a mirror to reflect its own slow
Effacement at the wind's hand.

$$(156)$$

In "Daddy" the striking of utterer into utterance is a mechanized, relent-lessly efficient deportation:

I thought every German was you.
And the language obscene

An engine, an engine
Chuffing me off like a Jew.
A Jew to Dachau, Auschwitz, Belsen.

$$(222)$$

Hooves and engine join together in the poem "Years," in which hoof and piston derive their power from the life they take, the soul they consume:

What I love is
The piston in motion—
My soul dies before it.
And the hooves of the horses,
Their merciless churn.

$$(255)$$

What these examples dramatize is a fundamental break or rift between speakers and their speech. The action of detached, riderless speech is not only separate from the original speaker (if ultimately such a person exists in Plath's world) but fatal to her as well.

This sharp, lethal distinction between speakers and the medium of speech itself, between human will and mechanical automatism, is a fundamental element of Plath's world. If, however, they were the only element, or the deepest element, then Plath's poems would fit more easily into familiar poststructuralist or psychoanalytic frameworks than they do, or than they have been made to. On the one hand, to assert the poststructuralist claim that such a poem as "Words" merely emphasizes the irreparable break between utterance and utterer, or more radically, the violent displacements of reference that discourse necessarily enacts, is to ignore the implication in "Words" of a fateful and vulnerable fusion between speaker and spoken. (Likewise in "Ariel," poet-rider and horse-medium merge into one integrated force: "how one we grow,/pivot of heels and knees! [239].) On the other hand, if for instance the injuries threatened and sustained in "Daddy" were closer than they in fact are to castration in any psychoanalytically legible sense, then Plath would be a more famil-iarly Freudian poet. Similarly, while she seems elsewhere to be exploring the lyric potential of certain other psychoanalytic concepts—repetition compulsion, the uncanny, the totemic father, and the death instinct—application of these schema reveals how unfit they are to account for the least programmatic and most disturbing elements of her art.

What I am trying to argue, by emphasizing the foot-root-boot-shoe se-ries as I have done, is that an element of Plath's work remains impervious to psychoanalytic and poststructuralist assimilation, to the extent that these discourses conceive of themselves as discourses of differentiation—the discourse of the trauma of difference and its subsequent disavowal. Whether the difference in question is that between the body of the mother and that of the child, or between men and women, or between the body and the signifying chain, or most profoundly, between one mind and an-other, psychoanalysis, to the extent that it remains a technique of analysis at all, is a strategy for addressing itself to the problem of fundamental, essential differentiation.[9] Similarly, if the dancingness of the foot or hoof, its eternal unrestingness and indefatigable agitation, is an expression of this difference, or *différance,* as Derrida has suggested in his long es-say on Heidegger and Van Gogh, *The Truth in Painting,* then we content ourselves with seeing in Plath the drama of a poet yielding herself (or acknowledging herself as already yielded) to the differential medium of speech. What I would like to suggest, however, is that such an account leaves out a crucial condition of the speaker in the poems, a condition expressed—frequently, repetitively, insuppressibly—as a condition of the foot itself. This condition proliferates in a new series, one that does not run parallel to the continuum between, on the one hand, the rooted and grounded and, on the other, the rootless and eternally wandering or danc-ing. This new series characterizes the body, and specifically the foot, in nonbinary terms, in terms other than the differentials of male and female, castrated and whole, dead and alive, autonomous and automatous, self and other, hegemony and revolution, signifier and signified. It is the series that comprises instead lameness, woundedness, deformation, malforma-tion, and injury. The deepest and most disruptive threats Plath's speakers encounter—and this is what I most want to emphasize about her work—are not threats of obliteration, castration, fragmentation, or engulfment.

The threat of injury that results not in death or division but in lameness, disfiguration, and malformation is, Plath's poetry suggests, fundamentally distinct from those that threaten a speaker's autonomous being.[10]

An early poem, "The Disquieting Muses" (74), suggests something of Plath's complex relation to the concept of injury, sickness, and disfiguration. In the poem, Plath constructs a family romance, imagining not an idealized set of parents but a group of terrible and obscure relatives, "three ladies / Nodding by night around my bed, / Mouthless, eyeless, with stitched bald head." Plath inquires of her mother:

> Mother, mother, what illbred aunt
> Or what disfigured and unsightly
> Cousin did you so unwisely keep
> Unasked to my christening, that she
> Sent these ladies in her stead
> With heads like darning-eggs to nod
> And nod and nod at foot and head
> And at the left side of my crib?

When Plath says that they are "illbred," she suggests not only a violation of propriety but a different, deeper condition, that of being born into and native to a world of illness and disfiguration. In many of her more familiar poems, Plath acknowledges but turns away from acknowledgment of this condition. We recall that Plath's father, Otto Plath, lost a leg to gangrene and diabetes, and that it was from complications of this amputation that he suddenly died. In "Daddy," by turning herself and finally her father into a victim of uncaring power, by turning the foot (poor, white, abject) into a boot, by turning the father with one gray toe into a "man in black" with a stake in his heart, the speaker turns a sick man first into a murderer and then into a dead man, and thereby changes the substance of her father into a compounding of power and obliteration. Passive illness is supplanted by active cruelty or sadism. The injured, sick "gray toe" is sheathed in the black boot of totalitarian power. Injury is a pathology and pathos the poem sets aside. The sheer bravura and éclat of the performance strenuously denies the weakness and disgust at the base, or the root, of this later, altogether crueler, family romance. Such a pathos, such an organic pathology, however, is the topic of an early, experimental poem, "Electra on Azalea Path," a fascinating failure that anticipates by only a few months the first fully realized poems, while illuminating briefly a road not taken in Plath's poetry. Before arriving at "blue sky out of the Oresteia" in "The Colossus," she conjures, with a conspicuous and *literal* stiltedness, the illusion of a Greek tragic scene in which her father both is and is not Agamemnon.

> *The day your slack sail drank my sister's breath*
> *The flat sea purpled like that evil cloth*
> *My mother unrolled at your last homecoming.*

How menacing, how talented, how strange. But what is most striking about this mythologizing is the instantaneous rebuke it receives from the speaker's scrutinizing conscience:

> I borrow the stilts of an old tragedy.
> . . . .
> The stony actors poise and pause for breath.
> I brought my love to bear, and then you died.
> It was the gangrene ate you to the bone
> My mother said; you died like any man.
> How shall I age into that state of mind?
> I am the ghost of an infamous suicide,
> My own blue razor rusting in my throat.
> O pardon the one who knocks for pardon at
> Your gate, father—your hound-bitch, daughter, friend.
> It was my love that did us both to death.
>
> (116)

The pathos here is of a speaker seized by an awareness of illness as distinct from the divine and fated determinations of tragedy; such an illness, intimately connected to love itself, is what "Daddy" later and more forcefully will disavow. This awareness (however vague), this understanding (however occult) that illness and love might have something to do with each other, is one the poet realizes she is incapable of "aging into"; she is, at the moment of the poem's composition, only three years from becoming, all too literally, that "ghost of an infamous suicide" she remains for us today. But in the brief moment of relenting that the poem affords, the speaker entertains the possibility that love itself, manifested as an illness, does them both to death. "I brought my love to bear, and then you died. / *It was the gangrene ate you to the bone*."

How it is that love and sickness might really resemble each other, how one could be confused with the other, and most importantly, how they could act as *disfiguring forces,* is a notion that remains clouded in the poem, as indeed it does in Plath's entire oeuvre. It is precisely this notion, however, that Plath's poetry invites us to consider. The suggestion Plath's work makes is that the lyric itself, as footed speech, what Keats calls "the naked foot of poesy," is uniquely suited to convey a specific human countenance, a countenance registered as a contour of deformations. These deformations are those caused by love-as-illness, which is one way of translating Eros, at least in Freud's most unflinching conceptions of it. Love is what distorts, deforms, renders pathetic or abject.[11] This countenance is the hidden face of the subject as she is constituted in desire and mortality. To say that poetry is the medium for such a representation is to say that its fitness derives from those deformations imposed upon speech by the form of the line, its vitality as poetry animated by the back pressure of the terminal caesura and reticulated by the metrical intrusions upon spoken language (whether such intrusions are regular, as in accentual syllabic verse, or merely the vestigial tremors of a metrical tradition). Such deformations, such naked feet, are those described in Plath's poetry and elucidated, uncannily, in the passages from Heidegger, Bataille, and Perelman I have quoted. Such a countenance is one that requires, it would seem, both an infinite tenderness and an infinitely steely nerve to contemplate, because it is this countenance in ourselves, and in others, that solicits most irresistibly our cruelty and revulsion.

In the end, Plath's only response to this face is violence and flight, but a poem such as "Thalidomide" remains capable, if only briefly, of glimpsing such a face in all its terrible vulnerability:

THALIDOMIDE

O half moon—

Half-brain, luminosity—
Negro, masked like a white,

Your dark
Amputations crawl and appall—

Spidery, unsafe.
What glove

What leatheriness
Has protected

Me from that shadow—
The indelible buds,

Knuckles at the shoulder-blades, the
Faces that

Shove into being, dragging
The lopped

Blood-caul of absences.
All night I carpenter

A space for the thing I am given,
A love

Of two wet eyes and a screech.
White spit

Of indifference!
The dark fruits revolve and fall.

The glass cracks across,
The image

Flees and aborts like dropped mercury.
(252)

"Thalidomide," like "Words," is a mirror poem, but whereas in "Words" the mirror of representation had managed to "re-establish itself," here the mirror is broken, the image permanently aborted. The "White spit // Of indifference" is not merely heartlessness or the absence of sympathy, but rather too dreadful an acknowledgment that the image is not in fact *different*, is in fact a faithful manifestation of the deformed countenance. The extremities here are like the footlings, toes, and noses earlier noted in "Mushrooms" and elsewhere; they are the "indelible buds" nurtured in "the blood-caul of absences." The body so nurtured is the disordered body, a body constituted in injury and deformation, neither rooted nor dancing, but crawling and dragging. Plath, through the dutiful labors of her art, attempts, hammering all night, to construct a space for this countenance, "the thing I am given," the poem's dreadful, monstrous *donnée*. Most striking, most astonishing, is the fact that this given is neither fate, nor doom, nor vengeance, but love itself, that which in "Electra on Azalea Path" Plath had distinguished so clearly, if so briefly, from tragedy. This love draws her toward this face, this vague coalescence of "two wet eyes and a screech." Ultimately the experience of such a love is intolerable, and the reflective medium, the mirror or mercuric mind, must expel it. "The glass cracks across, / The image // Flees and aborts like dropped mercury." But before it vanishes, we get a glimpse of a new possibility—the possibility that a medium could be found to sustain such terrible moments of recognition. How the lyric itself might nourish among its potentials the potential to be such a medium, Plath's work calls us to reflect. Whereas Eliot said that "verse, whatever else it may or may not be, is itself a system of *punctuation*," what Plath's poetry suggests is that verse is also a system of deformation. The deformations it imposes (as it accommodates itself to interval and line, to stress and foot) forms a surface toward which love's deformed countenance might incline, in search of what it—what each of us—lacks: an image fit to bear witness to human passion and anguish.

NOTES

Excerpts from poems by Sylvia Plath: "Thalidomide" from *Winter Trees*, © 1963 by Ted Hughes. "Edge," "Daddy," "Words," and "Years" from *Ariel*, © 1961, 1962, 1963, 1964, 1965, 1966 by Ted Hughes. "Poem for a Birthday" and "Electra on Azalea Path" from *The Collected Poems of Sylvia Plath*, © 1960, 1965, 1971, 1981 by the Estate of Sylvia Plath. Reprinted by permission of Faber and Faber, Ltd., and HarperCollins Publishers.

1. My discussion of "Edge," as well as my consideration of "Words," to say nothing of my analysis of all the Plath poems I discuss here, to say nothing of my entire career as a student and critic, owes an immense debt of gratitude to Helen Vendler. For the purposes of this essay, see particularly her chapter on Plath in *Coming of Age*.

Unless otherwise stated, all quotations of Plath's poems are from *The Collected Poems*.

2. Helen Vendler, in a private communication (ca. 1995), noted the significance, both thematic and metrical, of Plath's preference for "bag full" over "bagful." The spondee disrupts the dactylic lilt of the line enough to call attention to the emphasized "full"; abjection and plenitude combine more perfectly in the line than they might have had Plath chosen "bagful" instead.

3. See esp. Wieseltier, Oates, Heaney, Howe, and Perloff. Jacqueline Rose offers the most searching and trenchant engagement with Plath's history of reception in *The Haunting of Sylvia Plath,* particularly in the chapter "Daddy."

4. For a close analysis of Plath's affinities with Yeats, see Gilbert. Like "Leda and the Swan," "The Colossus" experiments with the possibility of refracting the human into a ration of the animality and divinity.

5. See also Tim Kendall's excellent discussion of Plath's portrayals of Jewishness in her poems, as well as in her drafts and letters (112–13). Rose also discusses the various signifiers of abjection in Plath, including Jewishness. Both writers, together with Julia Kristeva (whom Rose discusses at length) suggest but do not pursue the possibility that in employing such patently scandalous terms as "Jewy" and "Nigger," the poet is doing something more than either disparaging groups (Jews, African Americans) or identifying with disparaged groups. The third possibility, and the subject of a different essay, is that Plath might be situating the voice of her speakers in such a way that they destroy the proper boundaries between subject and abject, as Kristeva defines them in *Powers of Horror.* Such an effect might ultimately annihilate in the reader (solicited as s/he is to feel both complacency and revulsion) any capacity for rational, ethical, or aesthetic judgment. If, as Bataille suggests later, the foot is what we cannot but respond to with both loathing and desire, loathing and desire emerge as forms of interpersonal connection wholly distinct from the more Apollonian, Heideggerian values of thought and care. See below.

6. More perhaps could be said here about the uncanny presence or shadow of a phonograph record in this description, which "shellac" and "groove" particularly suggest. A wholly less panicky but equally hilarious metaphysical meditation on the phonograph-as-map-of-the-abyss is James Merrill's "The Victor Dog" (353). In the passage I have italicized the word "work" as well, not merely on account of Merrill's and Perelman's association of the uncanny phonograph with the Yeatsian notion of the artist as partially demented martyr, the perfection of the work always in some sense *destroying* the perfection of the life (the phonograph is in some way the Yeatsian eternal and artificial "golden bird" from "Sailing to Byzantium" as well as a kind of concrete gyre, a winding stair); I emphasize it also to suggest a link, however indirect and indeed perhaps demented, between Heidegger's reference to a furrowed field and the French term for furrowed field, which is *labour,* a coincidence which in turn might have suggested to Bataille an uncanny resonance between *l'oeuvre, labour,* and the furrowed, vibrating path of the needle on a phonograph record.

7. This discussion of the dancer owes a debt to Helen Vendler's extensive and illuminating discussion of Yeats's "Among School Children" in *Poets Thinking.*

8. See the chapter "The Star's Dark Address," in *End of the Mind.*

9. For a longer treatment of this issue in the world of clinical theory, see Bass.

10. There is not space to consider in detail the ways in which psychoanalysis—for all its investment in trauma, danger, anxiety, and threat—is not in fact a the-

ory of injury. It will have to stand as an emblem of this position that Freud at no point in his writings on Oedipus makes an account of Oedipus's wounded or lame foot. This persistent woundedness is exiled from Freud's considerations in such a way that it comes to resemble instead the foot of Philoctetes, snakebitten, suppurating, rank, unspeakable, radically offstage, but also, in the *Iliad* and the eponymous play by Sophocles, required for the resolution of apparently indissoluble conflicts.

11. See also Bass and Kristeva on this topic.

BIBLIOGRAPHY

Alexander, Paul, ed. *Ariel Ascending: Writings about Sylvia Plath.* New York: Harper and Row, 1985.

Annas, Pamela J. *A Disturbance in Mirrors.* New York: Greenwood, 1988.

Axelrod, Steven. *Sylvia Plath: The Wound and the Cure of Words.* Baltimore: Johns Hopkins UP, 1990.

Bass, Alan. *Difference and Disavowal: The Trauma of Eros.* Stanford: Stanford UP, 2000.

Bataille, George. "The Big Toe." *Visions of Excess: Selected Writings, 1927–1939.* Ed. and trans. Allan Stoekl. Minneapolis: U of Minnesota P, 1985. 20–23.

Bronfen, Elisabeth. *Sylvia Plath.* Plymouth: Northcote House, 1998.

Butscher, Edward, ed. *Sylvia Plath: The Woman and the Work.* New York: Dodd, Mead, 1977.

Derrida, Jacques. *The Truth in Painting.* Trans. Geoffrey Bennington and Ian McLeod. Chicago: U of Chicago P, 1987.

Easthope, Anthony. "Reading the Poetry of Sylvia Plath." *English* 43.177 (Autumn 1994): 223–35.

Eliot, T. S. *On Poetry and Poets: Essays.* London: Faber and Faber, 1985.

Gilbert, Sandra. "In Yeats' House: The Death and Resurrection of Sylvia Plath." *Critical Essays on Sylvia Plath*, ed. Linda W. Wagner. Boston: G. K. Hall, 1985. 204–22.

Grossman, Allen, and Mark Halliday. *The Sighted Singer: Two Works on Poetry for Readers and Writers.* Baltimore: Johns Hopkins UP, 1991.

Halpern, Nick. *Everyday and Prophetic: The Poetry of Lowell, Ammons, Merrill, and Rich.* Madison: U of Wisconsin P, 2003.

Harrison, DeSales. *The End of the Mind: The Edge of the Intelligible in Hardy, Stevens, Larkin, Plath, and Glück.* New York: Routledge, 2005.

Heaney, Seamus. "The Indefatigable Hoof-Taps." *Times Literary Supplement* 5–11 Feb. 1988: 134–44.

Heidegger, Martin. "The Origin of the Work of Art." *Poetry, Language, Thought.* Trans. Albert Hofstadter. New York: Harper & Row, 1971. 15–86.

Homer. *The Iliad.* Trans. Robert Fagels. New York: Penguin, 1998.

Howe, Irving. "The Plath Celebration: A Partial Dissent." In Butscher 224–35.

Hughes, Ted. "Notes on the Chronological Order of Sylvia Plath's Poems." *Tri-Quarterly* 7 (Fall 1966): 81–88.

Keats, John. *The Poems of John Keats.* Ed. Jack Stillinger. Cambridge, MA: Belknap, 1978.

Kendall, Tim. *Sylvia Plath: A Critical Study.* London: Faber and Faber, 2001.

Kristeva, Julia. *Powers of Horror: An Essay on Abjection.* New York: Columbia UP, 1982.

Kroll, Judith. *Chapters in a Mythology: The Poetry of Sylvia Plath.* New York: Harper and Row, 1976.

Lane, Gary, ed. *Sylvia Plath: New Views on the Poetry.* Baltimore: Johns Hopkins UP, 1979.

Lowell, Robert. "Foreword." *Ariel.* By Sylvia Plath. New York: Harper and Row, 1966. xiii–xvi.

Merrill, James. *The Collected Poems.* New York: Knopf, 2001.

Nietzsche, Friedrich. *Beyond Good and Evil: Prelude to a Philosophy of the Future.* Trans. Marion Faber. Oxford: Oxford UP, 1999.

Oates, Joyce Carol. "The Death Throes of Romanticism." In Alexander.

Perelman, S. J. "Is There an Osteosynchrondroitrician in the House?" *Reading I've Liked.* Ed. Clifton Fadiman. New York: Simon and Schuster, 1941. 761–63.

Perloff, Marjorie. "The Two Ariels: The (Re)making of the Sylvia Plath Canon." *American Poetry Review* 13.6 (Nov.–Dec. 1984): 10–18.

Plath, Sylvia. *The Collected Poems.* New York: Harper & Row, 1981.

———. *Johnny Panic and the Bible of Dreams and Other Prose Writings.* Introduction by Ted Hughes. London: Faber and Faber, 1979.

———. *The Journals of Sylvia Plath.* Ed. Frances McCullough; consulting ed. Ted Hughes. New York: Random House, 1982.

Rose, Jacqueline. *The Haunting of Sylvia Plath.* Cambridge, MA: Harvard UP, 1991.

Sophocles. *Philoctetes.* Ed. David R. Slavitt and Palmer Bovie. Trans. Armand Schwerner. Philadelphia: U of Pennsylvania P, 1998.

Stevens, Wallace. *The Collected Poetry and Prose.* New York: Library of America, 1997.

Stevenson, Anne. *Bitter Fame: A Life of Sylvia Plath.* New York: Houghton Mifflin, 1998.

Vendler, Helen. *The Art of Shakespeare's Sonnets.* Cambridge, MA: Belknap, 1997.

———. *Coming of Age as a Poet: Milton, Keats, Eliot, Plath.* Cambridge, MA: Harvard UP, 2004.

———. "An Intractable Metal." In Alexander 1–12.

———. *The Music of What Happens: Poems, Poets, Critics.* Cambridge, MA: Harvard UP, 1988.

———. *Poets Thinking: Pope, Whitman, Dickinson, Yeats.* Cambridge, MA: Harvard UP, 2006.

Wagner, Linda W., ed. *Critical Essays on Sylvia Plath*. Boston: G. K. Hall, 1985.

Wieseltier, Leon. "In a Universe of Ghosts." *New York Review of Books* 25 Nov. 1976: 20–23.

Yeats, W. B. *The Poems*. Ed. Richard J. Finneran. London: Palgrave McMillan, 1991.

Vendler's Ammons

The Snow Poems *and After*

ROGER GILBERT

A. R. Ammons was blessed to count among his many admirers the two most influential poetry critics of his generation, Harold Bloom and Helen Vendler. Their eloquent advocacy was crucial in establishing him as a major figure in the 1970s and '80s. More importantly, their praise (and occasional complaints) had a significant impact on Ammons's own evolving sense of his work. Like many poets, Ammons professed a general indifference to criticism, but in fact he was acutely interested in the responses of those few readers whom he believed to possess real discrimination. Bloom and Vendler were the two readers whose opinions mattered most to him in his later years, not simply because both commanded wide respect, but because both were deeply learned in the whole tradition of Anglo-American poetry and could measure his work against its highest achievements. It seems fair to say that Ammons wrote much of his later poetry with these two critics in mind—not with the aim of winning their unqualified approval, but with an awareness that their keen intelligences and acute sensibilities would be brought to bear on virtually everything he published.

Bloom and Vendler are often lumped together as magisterial upholders of aesthetic standards, yet their tastes and temperaments are actually quite distinct. This has not prevented their judgments from converging frequently, of course, as they do in the case of Ammons and a number of other poets. Yet even where their enthusiasms overlap, they tend to offer sharply divergent accounts of the author or work in question. Indeed at times they seem to be in open competition over the right to define a particular poet's achievement. The clearest instance may be Wallace Stevens, about whom both Bloom and Vendler have written extensively. Vendler's Stevens is the severe phenomenologist of "The Snow Man," committed to a wintry lucidity; Bloom's Stevens is a Romantic seer in the line of Emerson and Whitman. Equally telling are their preferences in Romantic poetry. Where Bloom tends to reserve his highest praise for the visionaries Blake and Shelley (about whom he wrote his first two books), Vendler is drawn more to the naturalism of Wordsworth and, especially, Keats.[1] It's in the area of contemporary poetry, though, that their differences are most clearly in evidence. While they share a high regard for a number of figures, including Bishop, Merrill, Ashbery, and Ammons, they disagree about many others—most notably Robert Lowell, whom Vendler reveres and Bloom deplores.

Taken together, these particular judgments point to a much deeper difference in sensibility. If Bloom's aesthetic bias is expressivist, Vendler's is mimetic; put in the terms famously elaborated by M. H. Abrams, Vendler tends to favor the mirror, Bloom the lamp. For Bloom the measure of great poetry is the power with which it articulates a unique selfhood or personality, typically one that imposes itself with a kind of fierce aggressivity upon both the outer world and literary tradition. For Vendler, by contrast, poetry is fundamentally representational: as she puts it in her textbook *Poems, Poets, Poetry,* "The accurate representation of reality is, for the artist, the highest morality" (297).[2] The two critics' vocabulary of superlatives is accordingly quite different as well. Bloom's favorite terms of approbation include "original," "intense," "exuberant," and most famously, "strong"; Vendler is more likely to use words like "accurate," "reticent," "transparent," and "truthful." At the level of content, Bloom manifests a strong appetite for poems that address matters traditionally placed under the rubric of the sublime—transcendence, epiphany, vision, quest, prophecy, apocalypse—while Vendler is more receptive to poems that deal with domestic and quotidian realities: family, memory, place, love, desire, work, play, weather. Finally, Bloom is notoriously indifferent to questions of poetic form, whereas Vendler is a scrupulous and exacting formalist.

Given these differences, it might seem unlikely that Bloom and Vendler would ever be drawn to the same poets; yet modern American poetry abounds in figures who blend sublime and quotidian matters in equal measure, beginning with its great progenitors Whitman and Dickinson. The poetry of A. R. Ammons falls squarely in this tradition. As Nick Halpern has recently shown, Ammons's work moves between prophetic and everyday registers with enormous ease and assurance; its insistent collocation of high and low realms of language and experience may in fact be its most distinctive trait. It would be a gross oversimplification to suggest that Bloom takes up only the high or sublime strain in Ammons, or that Vendler focuses exclusively on the low or quotidian strain; each critic acknowledges the centrality of this dialectic to his work. But their responses to Ammons's poetry clearly reflect their different sensibilities. For Bloom, Ammons is a perpetually thwarted quester, an Emersonian seer who has resigned himself to the failure of vision but who nevertheless blazes his own eccentric path to the sublime. Bloom's account of Ammons's work, as set forth in a series of essays published in the early 1970s, is at once forceful and selective. What Bloom regards as the "authentic" Ammons, a strain he traces from the Blakean parables of *Ommateum* to the Whitmanian affirmations of "The City Limits" and *Sphere,* is for him only slightly tinged by other elements he dismisses as inessential or distracting. These include the poet's experimental impulse, which issues in works like *Tape for the Turn of the Year* (a work Bloom calls "a heroic failure"); his penchant for colloquialisms and earthy humor; his occasional forays into childhood memory; his fascination with scientific language and thought; and his flirtation with Eastern mysticism, especially the Taoism of Lao-Tzu. Bloom identifies as Ammons's "largest flaw" his Thoreauvian interest in natural particulars, which he characterizes as a destructive "literalness" (*Ringers* 270). This is a surprising judgment, given the prominence of such particulars in Ammons's work, but one very much in keeping with Bloom's general preference for visionary over empirical modes of seeing. As we'll see, many of the elements bracketed or disparaged by Bloom are precisely those seized upon by Helen Vendler in her appreciations of Ammons's poetry.

Before considering Vendler's response to Ammons in detail, let me briefly sketch in the biographical dimension of the two critics' connection to the poet, again with an eye toward contrast. While both Bloom and Vendler enjoyed warm personal relations with Ammons, the nature of those relations was quite different. Bloom met Ammons in 1968, while spending a year at Cornell's Society for the Humanities. The two men quickly took a liking to each other, and their friendship deepened steadily in the course of what proved to be a tumultuous year for the university, continuing long after Bloom's return to Yale. Both men spoke of their bond in the language of love, and their intense dialogue over the next five years does indeed exhibit the contours of a passionate affair—one that, perhaps inevitably, waned with time. The many letters they exchanged between 1969 and 1974 show two very different minds meeting on the common ground of poetry.[3] Ammons in particular used their correspondence to articulate his belief in the consonance between mental and natural processes, in sharp contention with Bloom's Gnostic dualism. Bloom's essays on Ammons and the several poems Ammons dedicated to Bloom constituted reciprocal offerings in a kind of literary potlatch that culminated in

Ammons's long poem *Sphere,* a work Bloom had a major hand in shaping. In 1973 Bloom made a serious effort to lure Ammons to Yale; while evidently tempted, Ammons ultimately chose to remain at Cornell, safely distant from the literary metropolises.

From a critical point of view, the interest of this episode lies not just in the strong personal attachment between the two men, but also in Bloom's quite open efforts to guide Ammons toward a fuller solicitation of the sublime.[4] To a remarkable extent Bloom's writings on Ammons are not merely descriptive but prescriptive. His forthright diagnoses of flaws or weaknesses in Ammons's poetry can be understood as cautions for his future work, even as his praise marks out the path he wants the poet to pursue with renewed vigor. Ammons welcomed this scrupulous attention while ultimately resisting the substance of Bloom's exhortations. If *Sphere* represents their moment of greatest confluence—the poem is, as each acknowledged, a virtual dialogue between them—Ammons's next major work, *The Snow Poems,* marks the point at which he definitively casts off Bloom's influence and strikes out in a different direction. Where *Sphere* is a full-throated engagement with Whitmanian and Emersonian themes, *The Snow Poems* revives the low-key, quotidian mode of *Tape for the Turn of the Year.* By turns confessional and raunchy, playful and perverse, the book seems intent on frustrating the expectations of *Sphere*'s readers, not least its dedicatee. And indeed Bloom was not happy with it, privately voicing his disappointment to Ammons while withholding his usual blurb. Perhaps significantly, he wrote nothing of substance on Ammons after this point, though he did provide effusive blurbs for later works like *Garbage* and *Glare.*[5]

Enter Helen Vendler. Her association with Ammons began when she served on the committee that gave him the National Book Award in 1972 for his *Collected Poems, 1951–1971.* (Thanks to the poet's diffidence about appearing in public, Vendler literally spoke for him at the awards ceremony, reading a short speech he had composed.) Though she published brief reviews of his work over the next few years, the two didn't actually meet until 1981, when Vendler traveled to Ithaca to interview the poet in connection with the PBS series *Voices and Visions,* for which she served as an adviser. They met several more times over the next two decades—usually in Ithaca when Vendler came to lecture, but once also at Wake Forest University when she gave the keynote address at a symposium in Ammons's honor. (Though she made numerous attempts, Vendler never succeeded in luring Ammons to Harvard to read the annual Phi Beta Kappa poem at commencement.) But their friendship was primarily epistolary,

and while always warm it lacked the simultaneously amorous and ago-
nistic intensity of Ammons's relationship with Bloom. Bloom's fearsome
erudition and impossible demands pushed Ammons toward a deeper ex-
ploration of his ties to earlier traditions, while sharpening his sense of
where he departed from those traditions. Vendler made no demands, but
her praise ratified Ammons's sense of what he could already do and where
he wanted to go next.

Some of the difference in their responses arises from the fact that Bloom
and Vendler take up distinct phases of Ammons's poetry. Ammons's career can be roughly divided into two halves, the first dating from his debut
volume *Ommateum* (published in 1956, but begun in 1951) to *Sphere* (1974),
the second extending from *Diversifications* (1975) through his final poems, written in 1998. Bloom's published commentary on Ammons deals
exclusively with works from the first half of his career, while Vendler's
writing focuses mainly on the second half, only occasionally looking back
at earlier works. This bifurcation of the Ammonsian corpus is more than
chronological, however, for Ammons's later poetry obeys very different
impulses from his earlier work. Ammons himself repeatedly dramatized
this shift in ambition and sensibility, as in a short poem from his 1980 volume *A Coast of Trees* called "Breaking Out":

I have let all my balloons aloose
what will become of them now
pricked they will show some weight
or caught under a cloud lack
ebullience to feel through

but they are all let loose
yellow, red, blue, thin-skinned, tough
and let go they have put me down
I was an earth thing all along
my feet are catching in the brush

(32)

It's hard not to associate these balloons with both the transcendental motions and orbicular imagery of *Sphere*. Where Bloom had extolled the
high ambition and conceptual density of the work leading up to and including *Sphere*, Vendler applauded the close engagement with the earth
and with ordinary life that came increasingly to be the focus of Ammons's
later work. In the remainder of this essay I want to trace Vendler's recep-

tion of that work, from her first brief notice of it in 1972 to the valedictory pieces she wrote after Ammons's death in 2001. Though Vendler is better known for her writings on Jorie Graham, Robert Lowell, Seamus Heaney, and others, her ongoing chronicle of the second half of Ammons's career constitutes a remarkable instance of critical generosity and devotion. Few poets of any period have received such sustained attention from a single critic during their lifetimes. Not surprisingly, the portrait of Ammons that emerges from these pieces is very different from the one Bloom paints in his essays on the poet. In part that difference simply reflects the changed nature of Ammons's later poetry, but of course it also reflects Vendler's own critical sensibility, which seems at times perfectly attuned to the poet's imagination.

That attunement did not occur all at once. Compared to her later pieces, Vendler's first discussion of Ammons's poetry is decidedly lukewarm. In an omnibus review published in 1973, Vendler considers Ammons's *Collected Poems, 1951–1971*, issued when the poet was only forty-six. Sandwiched between E. E. Cummings and John Berryman, both already dead, Ammons comes off as something of a prolific crackpot. After some initial grumbling about the book's eccentric organization, Vendler gives a measured account of the poet's style, noting the dearth of human beings and the dominance of "objective" adjectives. Throughout this discussion her tone wavers between bemusement and admiration, as she acknowledges the originality of Ammons's procedures while questioning their aesthetic force. Characteristically, her emphasis falls on the mimetic dimension of Ammons's work, which she tells us attempts "an imitative recreation, no less, of the whole variety of the natural world, if not, regrettably, of what Stevens called its 'affluence'" (*Part of Nature* 330–31). The "regrettably" gently registers Vendler's misgivings about the "ascetic unattributiveness" of Ammons's poetry, its refusal to let emotion, pleasure, and desire color its renderings of natural phenomena. This severe "discipline of perfect notation" leads to a poetry that submits itself with a kind of monastic piety to the impingements of daily perception. Vendler commends the ambition of the project but notes that "it risks being merely fussy" in its insistence on absorbing trivial data, like the minutiae of weather or the details of an auto-repair invoice. She goes so far as to impute some of her own doubt to the poet, who in her words "tries to reassure himself on the value of his poetics by comparing it to the geological and organic motions of the universe." But in the wittiest and most telling sentence of the review, she concedes that Ammons does not seem overly concerned with his readers' capacities: "Never has there been a poetry so sublimely above the possible appetite of its potential readers."

Vendler's tone becomes more positive as she considers his short poems, noting that many chart "the climb up to perspective and the slide down to particularity," while singling out for special praise "another group, not making points at all, just seeing how things are." She closes with a guarded assessment that emphasizes the unfinished character of Ammons's work:

> It is a severe poetry, attempting the particularity of Hopkins with none of what Hopkins' schoolmates called his "gush," trying for the abstraction of Stevens without Stevens' inhuman remove from the world of fact, aiming at Williams' affectionateness toward the quotidian without Williams' romantic drift. Since Ammons is still in mid-career, we can watch the experiment, we hope, for a good while yet: if he can succeed (even granting the absurdity of some of the niches and odd corners of his enterprise), he will have written the first twentieth-century poetry wholly purged of the romantic. (335)

Even here, before her own appetite for Ammons's poetry has fully developed, Vendler expresses an interest in its future unfolding that will be amplified over the next thirty years in many more pages of prose.[6] In the process her initial sense of its essential severity will be considerably complicated. While this review identifies a number of key elements in Ammons's verse, its portrait of the poet as an austere, cold-eyed realist overlooks the powerful undercurrent of feeling that becomes more pronounced in his later work. Perhaps Vendler's most startling assertion is that Ammons's poetry, when fully realized, will be "wholly purged of the romantic." This claim stands in stark contrast to Bloom's emphatic placement of Ammons within the Romantic tradition (and may have been formulated in conscious opposition to it). Vendler's subsequent accounts of Ammons's work give considerably more scope to its expressive tendencies, while continuing to insist on its strongly mimetic orientation.

If Vendler wrote her first review as a newcomer to Ammons's poetry, at once fascinated and skeptical, by the time she revisited his work in print she seemed to have undergone something like a full conversion. The occasion was not the 1974 *Sphere*—a book almost universally admired, yet one about which Vendler has had surprisingly little to say—but rather the 1977 volume *The Snow Poems,* which provoked much scorn and little praise. The improvised, quirkily playful style of that book was anticipated by an earlier poem, "Pray without Ceasing," written in 1967 but not published until 1973 in the *Hudson Review,* then included in Ammons's 1975 collection *Diversifications.* Though she never commented on it in print, Vendler expressed her admiration for the poem in a postcard to Ammons dated 7 January 1974:

> I just felt impelled to tell you that "Pray without Ceasing" was like a blood transfusion, only of nectar from the "banks where amaranths grow"; I felt myself being fed, almost literally, by it as I haven't been by a new poem in a very long time—it's a wonderful thing. (Ammons Papers)

(Many years later Vendler came upon a sampler embroidered with the words "Pray without Ceasing" in an antique store and sent it to Ammons, who promptly hung it in his office.) With its formal variability, its doodles and word games, its wild veering between raunchy humor and deep pathos, its refusal of any organizing theme or symbol, "Pray without Ceasing" has a great deal in common with *The Snow Poems,* and Vendler's delighted response to it may well have helped inspire Ammons to pursue that mode even further.[7]

It's tempting to read *The Snow Poems* as a palinode to *Sphere,* a conscious repudiation of the earlier poem's high ambition, totalizing vision, and formal consistency—qualities that had earned it wide acclaim, including the 1975 Bollingen Prize. The work's visual formatting alone signals its departure from its immediate predecessors. As Michael McFee points out in a spirited defense of the book, *The Snow Poems* breaks entirely from the strophic forms that had dominated Ammons's recent work, culminating in the numbered, four-tercet stanzas of *Sphere* (Kirschten 59–65).[8] The spatial uniformity and neatness of those poems (which call to mind the "blocks and boxes of thought" Ammons had famously sought to escape in "Corsons Inlet") give way in *The Snow Poems* to a visual surface bristling with anomalies: irregular indentations and spaces, wildly variable line lengths, typewriter doodles, and, most strikingly, numerous passages arranged in double and occasionally even triple columns. Like Ammons's first long poem, *The Snow Poems* was composed on adding-machine tape; but unlike *Tape for the Turn of the Year,* the tapes varied in width and were torn off as each segment was completed, another index of the work's resistance to formal unity.

Several passages in the book suggest that Ammons is consciously rejecting the poetic and thematic impulses that underlay *Sphere.* At one point he casually reports, "I cut the quince down the other day" (*Snow Poems* 9); in doing so he dismantles one of the earlier poem's key tropes, his backyard quince bush, which in *Sphere* had embodied a kind of expansive ambition, a "green rage to possess, / make and take room" (*Sphere* 56). The most explicit instance of self-revision comes in a passage in which Ammons turns against the image of the sphere itself, substituting for it that of a spiral:

> the
> spiral drills a more
> majestic form, centralizing
>
> spheres, binaries, clumps,
> arms and windings into
> vast discs turning but more
> open to variety on the
>
> edge than spheres, a malleability
> outward to diversity:
> moving to sweet heaps as of
> rocks or garbage in spill:
>   (*Snow Poems* 98)

A poem that models itself on a spiral galaxy will clearly obey very different aesthetic principles from one modeled on a planetary sphere. It will be more chaotic, more "open to variety," more sinuously winding in its motions ("winding" is a recurrent word in the poem), more centrifugal than centripetal. It will appear more like an aggregate of separate bodies than a single homogenous solid; hence the plural title *The Snow Poems*, which belies Ammons's conception of the work as one long poem. It will unfold more like a diaristic scattering of notations, reflections, whimsies, and confidences than a gathering meditation on a philosophical theme. Ammons's insistence that the spiral is in fact "a more / majestic form" than the sphere suggests a loss of faith in the vision of sublime unity that the earlier work had propounded. A more ragged, multifarious, random order now seems to him to offer greater scope and grandeur than the sphere's geometric perfection.[9]

In repudiating *Sphere,* Ammons was of course also distancing himself from that poem's most ardent champion, who happened to be its dedicatee as well. One detects a streak of defiance in the book, at least some of it directed against Ammons's great critical patron, Harold Bloom. In the mid-length poem "A Summer Place," written after *Sphere* and before *The Snow Poems,* Ammons had confessed that

> my last fallacy of imitative form, my book on
> roundness, disappointed me some (oh, yes, it did), I meant
> to write one unreadable, but a lot of people have
>
> bought it, reading it or not: I wanted something
> standing recalcitrant in its own nasty massiveness,
> bowing to no one, nonpatronizing and ungrateful:
>
> (Brink Road 185)

and goes on to fantasize about writing

> a big gritty poem that would just stand
> there and spit, accommodating itself to nothing and
>
> too disfigured to be approached, no one
> able to imagine what line to take: and not necessarily
> being interesting enough to invite anybody to read it:
>
> (186–87)

"A Summer Place" is still written in the discursive tercets of *Sphere,* even as it gestures toward a less inviting form. *The Snow Poems* fulfills this vision of "nasty massiveness" in every respect, including in its resistance to critical exegesis. It's hard not to suspect that by the time he wrote *The Snow Poems* Ammons was feeling serious qualms about the close association that had developed between his work and Bloom's critical writing (an association he himself had underscored with the dedication of *Sphere*). With *The Snow Poems* he would forgo all acts of accommodation, obeisance, and gratitude, spitting in the face of reader and critic alike. Not surprisingly, Bloom was unhappy with the poem, and accurately caught the note of hostility behind it, telling Ammons in a letter that parts of it seemed to be "so many turnips thrust at the reader."[10] Bloom was not the only critic who found *The Snow Poems* to be a major disappointment. Negative reviewers included Hayden Carruth ("a dull, dull book"), Peter Stitt ("a monumental failure"), and, surprisingly, Marjorie Perloff, a critic known for her championing of avant-garde poetry, but who seems not to have been at all taken with Ammons's formal experiments.[11] (One reviewer who admired the book was William Harmon, a close friend of Ammons's who shared his predilection for lexical and typographical hijinks.)

Against this background of general displeasure, Vendler's enthusiastic response to *The Snow Poems* bears striking witness to her evaluative self-reliance. To proclaim one's liking for a book that seems determined not to be liked (and for the most part succeeds) requires a faith in one's aesthetic compass that few critics possess. Once again Vendler reviewed the book as part of an omnibus, this one covering ten titles, and so she could only give it two paragraphs. They are extremely rich paragraphs, however. The first moves from an initial shock of recognition—"Perhaps only someone who has lived through the full interminableness of winters in upstate New York can feel, as I did, the weight of A. R. Ammons's *Snow Poems*"—to a detailed inventory of the book's topical and stylistic repertoire: "Open the book anywhere and there is a ripple of thought, a weather report, a lament, a curious observation of the out-of-doors, and a hard inquiry" (*Part of Nature* 368–69). As though acknowledging the book's cool reception and its own recalcitrance, Vendler offers practical advice for penetrating its thorny surface: "The book needs to be lived in for days, reread after the first reading has sorted out its preoccupations and methods, and used as a *livre de chevêt* if its leisurely paths are to be followed in their waywardness." She concludes the paragraph by noting both the book's formal departure from the long lines of *Sphere* and its affinity with the earlier *Tape for the Turn of the Year*. The review's most charming moment occurs in the second paragraph, when Vendler literally talks back to the poem to call attention to its conversational intimacy:

> you have to feel pretty
> good to have a good time:
> the aspirant spiral: you remember
> the aspirant spiral
>
> Uh huh, we remember the aspirant spiral; we felt pretty good; we had a good time. And so we talk back to Ammons' mumble over the one-way telephone of verse. (370–71)

Vendler's dialogic engagement with the poem here becomes comically literalized, but her point is serious: Ammons addresses us in a way that presumes a common well of experience, not a hieratic wisdom.

What allowed Vendler to respond with such deep appreciation and pleasure to a work that left so many other readers cold? I've already noted her fundamentally mimetic orientation, and this is doubtless part of what made her the ideal reader for *The Snow Poems.* Ammons himself spoke of the book in essentially mimetic terms, calling it his favorite among his long poems because in it he "had a more ready availability to the names of things and to images of them than in any of the other long poems" (*Set in Motion* 101). Vendler praises the book's meticulous representation of external realities—"all Ithacans and ex-Ithacans will recognize that Ammons has delineated that landscape and that climate for good and all"— while lauding its more introspective effort "to write down life as it is at fifty, during a long winter, in a solitary epoch." (The idiom "to write down life" is a favorite of Vendler's, a pseudo-naive characterization of the transcriptive function she values so highly in poetry.)[12] Many years later she revisited *The Snow Poems,* in an essay comparing the book to the recently published *Garbage* ("*The Snow Poems* and *Garbage*"). Looking back on her first encounter with the book, Vendler once again pays homage to its evocative power, this time in a more personal register:

> If I hadn't lived in Ithaca between 1960 and 1963, I might not have so joyously recognized the components of *The Snow Poems,* but the volume so completely transferred not only the weather and the scenery but the "handcrafted gifts" of that (then rural) town to the page that I was a hypnotized reader, ready to forgive (and at first I felt the need to forgive) any disturbances to my sense of the aesthetic from a poet so marvelously gifted at summoning up a known environment. (29)

Vendler seems retrospectively both bemused and pleased by her readiness to embrace a work whose transgressive mien had put off so many others. As she suggests, *The Snow Poems* is an unusually candid work for Ammons, full of personal musings on age, his childhood, family, and particularly his father, whose death haunts him throughout the book, though it occurred ten years earlier. In its transparency to physical reality, quotidian experience, and emotional history, *The Snow Poems* moves beyond the representational severity that Vendler had ascribed to *Collected Poems,* achieving a richer, more inclusive picture of both inner and outer life.

It might be complained that Vendler's emphasis on the book's mimetic range comes at the expense of its formal inventiveness, which she notes only passingly in her review. In the later essay she has room to explore the book's formal dimension in depth, and here too she proves to be its ideal reader. One of Vendler's critical trademarks has always been her penchant for rearranging verse passages on the page in order to highlight hidden patterns of meaning and syntax. With its use of columns and other spatial designs to array and juxtapose contrasting strains of language, one could say *The Snow Poems* is pre-Vendlerized. This does not prevent her from applying her signature technique, however; she simply proceeds in reverse, first showing us the more conventional version of a passage—

march one and
in the clear
thicket highchoired
grackles grate squeak,
dissonant as
a music school

then its exploded form—

march	one and
in the	clear
thicket	highchoired
grackles	grate squeak,
dissonant	as
a music	school

and finally the doubled version that actually appears in the book:

march one and	march	one and
in the clear	in the	clear
thicket highchoired	thicket	highchoired
grackles grate squeak,	grackles	grate squeak,
dissonant as	dissonant	as
a music school	a music	school

Through this incremental presentation Vendler makes us feel both the strangeness of Ammons's methods and their curious logic: "it is a mark of the 'reveal-all' workshop-poetics of *The Snow Poems* that the mind says 'I am divided *and* I choose both, so here they are, both kept in print, exhibiting a right-left stand-off'" (37). The centerpiece of Vendler's discussion of *The Snow Poems* is an extended analysis of a section entitled "Poetry Is the Smallest," which makes elaborate and varied use of the two-column format (interestingly, John Ashbery was also experimenting with this form in his exactly contemporary long poem "Litany"). Vendler persuasively shows how this section, like much of the book, anatomizes what she calls the "bicameral mind," playing various aspects of consciousness against each other: lyric and philosophical, empirical and reflective, male and female, and so on. Ultimately, then, she understands the book's formal ploys to be working in the service of a broadly mimetic project, enabling Ammons to represent the divided nature of experience with diagrammatic clarity.

Vendler's next important encounter with Ammons's work centered on his poem "Easter Morning," which she first read in *Poetry* magazine, a year before its appearance in his 1980 collection *A Coast of Trees*. She immediately recognized it as a masterpiece, and some months later wrote to Ammons: "I remember saying to a friend who dropped by last year on the morning *Poetry* came in the mail with your 'Easter Morning' in it (which I had just, in tears, finished reading the moment the doorbell rang), that the only comparable piece of mail I could think of coming in the door, was when George Keats, in Kentucky, opened his mail and read 'To Autumn.'" From this point on, "Easter Morning" becomes a recurrent touchstone for Vendler's writing on Ammons, her central instance of his poetic gifts at their fullest height. The poem is a compound elegy that mourns many losses: the poet's younger brother Elbert, who died at eighteen months, his parents and other kinfolk buried in the same small churchyard, the rural world they inhabited, and the "life that did not become"—perhaps the life Ammons might have lived had he stayed in North Carolina. The poem was written the day Ammons learned of the death of his beloved father-in-law, another loss that is never mentioned in the poem but stands behind it. Voicing grief with a directness and intensity unprecedented in Ammons's work, "Easter Morning" climaxes in a wrenching outburst:

> I stand on the stump
> of a child, whether myself
> or my little brother who died, and
> yell as far as I can, I cannot leave this place, for
> for me it is the dearest and the worst,
> it is life nearest to life which is
> life lost: it is my place where
> I must stand and fail,
> calling attention with tears
> to the branches not lofting
> boughs into space, to the barren
> air that holds the world that was my world
>
>   (*Coast of Trees* 21)

These lines exchange Ammons's customary elegance of phrasing for a rawness of feeling that verges on sentimentality. Part of the poem's power comes from this sense of a newly direct access to emotion, unmediated by concept or design. From here the poem shifts into Ammons's more familiar descriptive mode, evoking the flight of two great eagles whose weaving trajectories suggest a larger patterning that implicitly answers the despair of the poem's first half.

Vendler opens her review of *A Coast of Trees* in the *New Republic* by hailing the arrival of "Easter Morning": "A classic poem, when it appears, comes not as a surprise but as a confirmation" (*Music* 327). After quoting its opening passage, she praises the poem in language couched in universalism yet suggesting a deeply personal response:

> Ammons's lines rivet us where we stand and we find ourselves uttering them as though our own life had suddenly found outlet-speech: "I have a life that did not become . . . the grave will not heal." Ammons's arrow strikes straight to the heart, and to the unhealed grave in it. "How did you know," we ask Ammons, "when we didn't know ourselves, till you told us?" This is a poetry of eerie power, dependent not so much on the particular circumstances of Ammons's life as on his unsettling skill as an allegorist. Anything he tells us about his life ("I have a life that did not become") turns out to be true of everyone: he is a poet of the universal human condition, not of particular idiosyncrasy. This great poem, "Easter Morning," turns out to be about the damage which every child undergoes as members of his family—a sibling, an aunt, a grandparent—die. It is an elegy in a family churchyard. (328)

While one might quibble with Vendler's characterization of Ammons as an allegorist, it's hard to imagine a more eloquent tribute to the poem's power of transference. Her confident judgment of "Easter Morning" as a "new treasure in American poetry" has been upheld over the past twenty-five years by anthologists, scholars, and common readers alike. Vendler returned to the poem a number of times in her subsequent writing on Ammons. In her 1986 essay "A. R. Ammons: Dwelling in the Flow of Shapes," she again quotes the poem's opening passage and declares: "These lines, I am certain, will be as familiar in a hundred years as Wordsworth's 'There was a time when meadow, grove, and stream, / The earth, and every common sight, / To me did seem / Apparelled in celestial light / The glory and the freshness of a dream'" (*Music* 312). And in a final tribute to the poem and its author, she reprints "Easter Morning" in its entirety at the end of her valedictory essay "The Titles: A. R. Ammons, 1926–2001," originally delivered at a memorial service in Winston-Salem.

The Snow Poems and "Easter Morning" are the two Ammons works that seem to have moved Vendler most deeply. Given their obvious differences, one might well wonder how the same reader could embrace them both with equal passion. Where "Easter Morning" is profoundly serious in tone, The Snow Poems is predominantly whimsical; where "Easter Morning" displays a tragic unity, The Snow Poems is ostentatiously disjointed. In fact, though, the two poems are more closely related than might at first appear. The poem that became "Easter Morning" was originally composed in 1977 as part of a long sequence under the collective title "Improvisations." Perhaps fearing it would meet a similar reception to The Snow Poems, Ammons apparently rethought his original plan of publishing it as a separate work and instead included only a few of the constituent poems in later collections.[13] Many of these continue the playful, disjunctive style of The Snow Poems, as the term "improvisation" might suggest. Ammons showed the sequence to his close friend Jerald Bullis, who picked out a section entitled "Improvisation for the Other Way Around" and suggested that it be drastically cut, retitled, and published separately; the result was "Easter Morning." In its original form, the poem continued for another two and a half pages, thus occluding the classic movement from lament to consolation that the final poem so majestically performs. One might say that Bullis did for Ammons what Pound did for Eliot, chipping away the excess marble to reveal a latent form of great power and beauty.

This genetic narrative suggests that "Easter Morning" grew out of the same compositional milieu as The Snow Poems, an origin visible both in its formal looseness and its intimacy of tone. (Ammons himself later expressed misgivings about "Easter Morning," claiming that its conception as part of a long poem kept it from assuming the shapeliness and density he generally sought for his shorter poems.)[14] While the poem's somber cast may seem far removed from the comic brio of the earlier work, it should be noted that The Snow Poems also contains several elegiac passages that directly prefigure "Easter Morning," among them a poignant lyric entitled "One Must Remember as One Mourns the Dead" that Vendler quotes at the end of her later discussion of the book. What sets both works apart from most of Ammons's earlier poetry is an emotional directness that verges on the confessional. Vendler glosses the opening of "Easter Morning" with a line by Robert Lowell ("Always inside me is the child who died"), and while Ammons professed to despise Lowell, the conjunction is not entirely farfetched. If Bloom's Ammons is the impersonal rhapsode of *Sphere* and "The City Limits," blending Stevensian abstraction and Whitmanian loft, Vendler's Ammons is the intimate self-chronicler of *The Snow Poems* and "Easter Morning," rendering both outer and inner worlds with unflinching candor.

While "Easter Morning" and *The Snow Poems* can together be said to occupy the center of Vendler's personal canon of Ammons's work, many other poems have received her praise as well. Two lectures on Ammons that she delivered in the 1980s offer wide-ranging accounts of his poetry. The first was given at Harvard in the summer of 1981 and never published (though Vendler sent a copy to Ammons); the second was the keynote address at a Wake Forest symposium in 1986 in celebration of Ammons's sixtieth birthday, and was subsequently published under the title "A. R. Ammons: Dwelling in the Flow of Shapes." Again it's instructive to compare Vendler's choice of exemplary poems to those of Bloom, whose essays had defined Ammons's corpus for many readers. In her first lecture she considers a number of shorter poems, most of them not ones discussed by Bloom ("Lion:Mouse," "Clarity," "The Eternal City," "Body Politic," "Bonus," "Weather-bound," "Lonesome Valley"), singling out for special praise "Grace Abounding," which she describes as "a poem of thanksgiving for the fact that something [Ammons] sees always clarifies his inchoate moods" (7). Not surprisingly, the lecture also includes a discussion of *The Snow Poems* and a brief glance at "Easter Morning." The one poem extolled by Bloom that Vendler quotes is "The City Limits," which she treats as an instance of Ammons's affinity with Whitman, while also stressing their differences: Ammons's "music is not the full-throated ease of Whitman's operatic soprano but the plectrum, as he says, of the eave-drops' clink" (13).

In her second lecture, "Dwelling in the Flow of Shapes," Vendler highlights an area of Ammons's earlier poetry that Bloom more or less ignores: poems that deal with his North Carolina childhood. (Vendler's emphasis on this facet of Ammons's work reflects the occasion for which the lecture was prepared, a symposium entitled "The Home Country of A. R. Ammons.") Unabashedly local poems like "Hardweed Path Going," the two "Carolina Said Songs," and "Nelly Myers" (the last a poignant elegy for a retarded woman who lived with the Ammonses) forgo the universalizing gestures prized by Bloom, instead offering a richly mimetic picture of a remembered environment and the emotional atmosphere that suffused it. They are, in Vendler's words, "obstinate commemorations of reality, tributes determined in their obligation of exactness to hog-killing, sore-leg and hardship. Whitman gives them some of their courage, but they are homelier and more domestic than Whitman's work tends to be. They embody, in fact, a new style declaring itself. They are written perhaps in revolt against the more allegorical pieces that Ammons had been writing in his twenties, and to which he would return" (*Music* 313–14). (In fact a number of these poems were written at the behest of Ammons's friend John Logan, who had urged him to explore autobiographical subjects after the stark parables of *Ommateum*.)

After praising these poems for their fidelity both to people and events and to the language of home, Vendler notes that they "are largely mimetic efforts—a transcription of what is in some sense already 'there.' But in every poet's life there comes a moment in which the poet must forsake mimesis, must decide to impose inner motions on outer material" (317). Vendler locates this moment in Ammons's 1964 poem "Four Motions for the Pea Vines," which mingles the particulars of farming with the meditative rhythms that characterize his mature work. It's perhaps worth noting that the imposition of inner motions upon outer material is precisely what Vendler had lamented the absence of in her review of *Collected Poems;* there she saw only a severely mimetic art that gave no scope to the poet's imaginative constructions. By the time she writes "Dwelling in the Flow of Shapes," she has come to recognize the subtle ways in which Ammons blends mimetic and expressive energies. Tellingly, however, she closes her lecture by applying to Ammons's work a phrase from Elizabeth Bishop: "a mirror in which to dwell." For Vendler, the abiding value of Ammons's poetry remains mimetic, its luster that of the mirror rather than the lamp.

I've been suggesting that Vendler's repeated praise of Ammons's mimetic powers constitutes an implicit critique of Bloom's account of Ammons as a primarily visionary or sublime poet. That critique remains implicit in large part because, virtually alone among critics of Ammons, Vendler never mentions Bloom, though the two men's names have become inextricably linked. There is, however, a moment in "Dwelling in the Flow of Shapes" that can only be read as a thinly disguised rebuke to Bloom. In his second major essay on Ammons, "A. R. Ammons: The Breaking of the Vessels" (which was itself delivered as a lecture at Wake Forest in 1974, twelve years before Vendler delivered "Dwelling in the Flow of Shapes" there), Bloom had in a rare moment of pique complained of "such wasted postures of the spirit as section 38 of *Sphere,* where the hard-pressed writers of New York City (who have troubles enough) are urged out into the woods to watch the redwing" (*Figures* 220). This dig is part of Bloom's larger argument that Ammons is not truly a nature poet but, like all Bloom's favorite authors, a Gnostic visionary permanently alienated from nature. Speaking in the same place and to many of the same listeners, Vendler goes out of her way to cite section 38 of *Sphere* with considerably more sympathy than Bloom. Rather than mere sentimentalizing of nature, she sees in Ammons's exhortation an attack on compartmentalized thought:

> most of our writers live in New York City
> densely: there in the abstractions of squares and glassy
> floors they cut up and parcel out the nothingness they
>
> think America is: I wish they would venture the rural and
> see that the woods are undisturbed by their bothering
> reputations and that the brooks have taken to flowing
>
> the way they always have and that the redwing pauses
> to consider his perch before he lights in a cedar:

> Ammons does not say explicitly what he expects New York poets to learn from the flowing of the brooks and the pauses of the redwing, but we deduce that it has something to do with a poetry that would not be cut up and parceled out. The unpredictability of natural movement, which is always "uncapturable and vanishing" like a brook, is the rural and organic intuition, brought from home, that governs the motion of Ammons's lines. (316)

One suspects that it was precisely Bloom's brusque dismissal of this passage that compelled Vendler to offer a serious commentary on it. Bloom may be right to question Ammons's motives in urging his urban brethren to the woods—poetic rivalry was always a powerful motivation for him, as Bloom no doubt knew firsthand—but Vendler sees beyond the facetious gesture to the underlying affirmation because she honors Ammons's engagement with natural processes as Bloom does not.

I will pass over the many responses to particular Ammons books that Vendler published in the 1980s and '90s, including her reviews of the collections *A Coast of Trees, Worldly Hopes,* and *Sumerian Vistas,* and her essays on the long poems *Garbage* and *Glare,* in order to focus on her two most recent Ammons pieces, both written after the poet's death in February of 2001. The first, "The Titles: A. R. Ammons, 1926–2001," was delivered at a memorial service in Winston-Salem and then published in *Poetry* magazine. Here Vendler offers a final overview of Ammons's career, synecdochically represented by the titles of his published volumes. This conceit allows her to touch on many strands of his work, beginning with the conjunction of science and religion announced by his first title, *Ommateum, with Doxology.* She goes on to note the recurrent obeisance to the spirit of place conveyed by titles like *Corsons Inlet, Northfield Poems, Highgate Road,* and *Uplands,* as well as the immersion in time and season suggested by *Tape for the Turn of the Year* and *The Snow Poems.* In the title *Sphere* she remarks "the Platonic side of Ammons's mind," an impulse toward abstraction and wholeness that appeals less to Vendler than the countervailing impulse toward dispersal and diversification—the latter term furnishing the title of Ammons's next book, *Diversifications.* Vendler's most extended commentaries are reserved for titles that carry a complex array of connotations: *A Coast of Trees,* which evokes "nature as habitable but as yet uncivilized"; *Worldly Hopes,* which highlights the dialectic between secularism and religious language central to Ammons's work; *Sumerian Vistas,* which recalls the poet's earlier "invocations of ancientness" in his Ezra poems and reiterates his "claim to be part of a prophetic and inscriptive genealogy stretching back, in its vistas, as far as the historical eye can see"; *Brink Road,* which tells both of human incursions into nature and of the imminence of death. Her glosses on the one-word titles of Ammons's final long poems, *Garbage* and *Glare,* constitute pithy accounts of each work as a whole, the first a "sustained tragic and comic meditation on the Heraclitean conversion of matter into energy," the second a more personal meditation on "the rock-bottom glare of extinction." The essay culminates in a virtuoso passage that weaves Ammons's titles together into a single sentence:

> As we evoke his titles, Ammons's spirit becomes present to us, as it walks over uplands and by Corsons Inlet, through lake-effect country and on Brink Road; as it looks back to Sumer while taping the turn of the current year; as it scrutinizes—with and without irony—worldly hopes; as it makes small briefings and large gestural spherings; as it notes with its ommateum the infinite forms of snow through an Ithaca winter; and as, in the last two of its book-length diversifications, it describes the glare of the harshest reality, the endless recycling of human bodies into elemental fire and ash. ("Titles" 228)

She concludes her tribute with "Easter Morning," the poem she says "I always come back to as I remember Ammons, our astonishing, touching, and much-missed great poet."

Vendler's attempt to encompass the full range of Ammons's poetry, as represented by all his book titles, is an exemplary act of critical appreciation, uncompromised by the impulse to sort, rank, and exclude. What she could not have known when she wrote "The Titles" is that another book of poems would soon be added to the Ammons canon. That book, *Bosh and Flapdoodle,* was assembled and titled by Ammons himself in late 1996. After taking some initial steps toward publishing it, he apparently changed his mind and withdrew the manuscript. In 2005, four years after his death, the book was published by Norton to largely enthusiastic reviews. The previous year I edited a special issue of the Cornell literary magazine *Epoch* devoted to Ammons's life and work in which I included seventeen poems from the *Bosh and Flapdoodle* manuscript, along with thirteen other late poems. For each poem I solicited a short comment from a friend or admirer of Ammons. Knowing her love of "Easter Morning," I sent Vendler a poem called "In View of the Fact," which mines a similar vein of sorrow and nostalgia. A proleptic elegy for Ammons's own generation, the poem begins "The people of my time are passing away," and proceeds to catalog the mounting afflictions and losses that beset his friends and peers. The poem ends with a fragile paradisal vision:

> ... we

> think the sun may shine someday when we'll
> drink wine together and think of what used to

> be: until we die we will remember every
> single thing, recall every word, love every

> loss: then we will, as we must, leave it to
> others to love, love that can grow brighter

> and deeper till the very end, gaining strength
> and getting more precious all the way. . . .
>   (*Bosh* 30)

Vendler's comment is a superb close reading that mixes expert analysis with the sensitivity to tonal nuance that has always been a hallmark of her criticism: "The poem skirts sentimentality, but is saved by its modals: the sun 'may' shine, we will 'as we must' bequeath the past to others, and love 'can' (but it may not necessarily) grow. Hope and necessity and possibility, in the stoic candor of those about to die, replace the former self-solacing illusions of prophecy and will. In this moving lament for the lost, ego and effacement meet in the anteroom of death" ("On 'In View'"). Characteristically, Vendler calls attention both to the poem's emotional candor and to its subtle artistry. As of this writing these are her last published sentences on Ammons; one hopes there will be many more.

While Ammons never dedicated either a book or a poem to Helen Vendler as he did to Harold Bloom, he was always deeply grateful for her attention and her praise. Vendler's recognition of the mimetic power of his work, along with its formal inventiveness, its psychological honesty, and its autobiographical resonance, must have been enormously helpful to Ammons as he struggled to break out of the compelling yet ultimately limiting construction Bloom had placed upon his poetry. Indeed Vendler was perhaps the only literary critic with enough authority to counter Bloom's sublime exhortations. It would no doubt be overstating the case to attribute the more earthbound, emotionally forthright character of Ammons's later poetry solely to Vendler's criticism, but her enthusiastic response to these emerging qualities surely helped to confirm the rightness of his choices. His feelings for her may be gauged from a poem discovered after his death, written on the back of an envelope from Vendler dated 28 November 1981, soon after their second meeting in Ithaca:[15]

EVERYTHING

You came one day and
as usual in such matters
significance filled everything—
your eyes, the things you
knew, the way you turned,
leaned, stood, or sat,
this way or that: when
you left, the area around here rose
a tilted tide, and everything that
offers desolation drained away.

As these lines attest, Vendler's words and her presence made a tidal difference to Ammons, filling his environment with significance while draining away the desolation and doubt that chronically plagued him. If this sounds a little like a poet's address to his muse, in the end Vendler was something even more precious to Ammons: a devoted reader who saw his work with clarity and wrote of it with love.

NOTES

"Breaking Out," from *A Coast of Trees* by A. R. Ammons, copyright © 1981 by A. R. Ammons. Used by permission of W. W. Norton & Company, Inc. "Everything" by A. R. Ammons used by permission of John Ammons. Excerpts from correspondence from Helen Vendler to A. R. Ammons reprinted by permission of Helen Vendler.

1. In a review of Bloom's 1976 book *Poetry and Repression,* reprinted in *The Music of What Happens,* Vendler comments on Bloom's uneven affinities: "The line of stern public prophetic poets from Milton through Blake to Shelley and Yeats is more congenial to Bloom than the more flexible, inward-looking and sinuous line of poets from Spenser through Keats and Tennyson to Stevens and Eliot. Wordsworth, while aspiring to belong to the first line, was temperamentally of the second, and therefore also eludes, to some degree, Bloom's grasp" (55). Vendler's own preference for this second line shows itself in the adjectives she applies to each group. (Her placement of Stevens in the second group represents another subtle sally in their ongoing dispute over that poet.) While Vendler has not been as centrally concerned with Romanticism as Bloom has, her book on Keats's odes and her important essay on Wordsworth's Intimations Ode reflect her affinity for the more pastoral strain in Romantic poetry.

2. In a review essay reprinted in *The Music of What Happens,* Vendler speaks against a mimetic approach to poetry: "No matter how apparently mimetic it may look, a poem is an analogous not a mimetic imitation, algebraic and not photographic, allegorical and not historical. What it represents, ultimately, is its author's sensibility and temperament, rather than the 'outside world'" (39). Like most important critics, Vendler invokes different criteria on different occasions; here she seems to be challenging a naively mimetic view that does not allow for the shaping presence of authorial sensibility. I think it fair to say, however, that as a practical critic her bearings remain deeply mimetic.

3. A selection of Ammons's letters to Bloom, as edited by Kevin McGuirk, can be found in Gilbert 625–52.

4. In a journal entry recording "A Visit to the Mighty Blooms" in August of 1973, Ammons confides: "Harold wants me to be intense, mad, consistently high. I want to be ordinary, casual, a man of *this* world" (Gilbert 649). The tension between Ammons's impulse toward ordinariness and Bloom's urgings toward the sublime informs much of the poet's work in the 1970s, especially *Sphere* and *The Snow Poems.*

5. In fairness, Bloom stopped writing about contemporary poetry almost entirely in the 1980s, turning his attention instead to the Bible, Shakespeare, and

other canonical monuments. Nevertheless, it's clear from correspondence and other sources that Ammons felt neglected by his friend and champion.

6. Vendler's published commentary on Ammons amounts to over 110 pages.

7. For an excellent discussion of the poem's postmodern or experimental cast, see Cushman.

8. Ammons's use of tercets, which predominate in the poems written between 1969 and 1974, seems clearly indebted to Stevens, whom Bloom was urging on him as a model during this period. Ammons later expressed strong reservations about Stevens; see *Glare* 25.

9. Ammons includes a similar passage in *Glare,* in which he explicitly contrasts his previous long poem, *Garbage,* whose central trope is a majestic mountain of refuse, with the more scattered and miscellaneous organization of the present poem, which he likens to litter: "the central / image of this poem is that it has no / mound gather stuff up but strews / itself across a random plain randomly" (54).

10. In the same letter, dated 17 May 1976, Bloom writes, "The poem is *very great* and on purpose wildly uneven" (Ammons Papers), but he could not disguise his consternation. In another letter dated 16 July 1977, after the poem's publication, he writes: "I want you—not to write less—but to go back to Emerson, to worrying again why and when you/everyone can or can't transcend. You are (in *Snow Poems*) as good as Frost, but potentially you could be better than Stevens" (Ammons Papers). In an omnibus review for the *New Republic,* Bloom tempered his disappointment with the poem, calling it a "mixed achievement," while complaining that the "energy of response demanded from the reader is bewildering and finally perhaps transcends possibility" (25).

11. Robert Kirschten ably summarizes the critical response to *The Snow Poems* in his introduction to *Critical Essays* (14–16).

12. In a review of James Merrill's *Braving the Elements,* Vendler speaks of knowing "that someone out there is writing down your century, your generation, your language, your life"; in a review of Adrienne Rich's *Diving into the Wreck,* she recalls her wonder on reading Rich's first book: "someone my age was writing down my life" (*Part of Nature* 205, 237).

13. Ammons included two improvisations in *A Coast of Trees* ("An Improvisation for the Stately Dwelling" and "An Improvisation for Jerald Bullis"), and two in *Brink Road* ("An Improvisation for Soot and Suet" and "An Improvisation for the Killers of Meat"), all of them written in 1977. Another poem from the sequence, "An Improvisation for Angular Momentum," appeared in *Poetry* magazine in 1994.

14. In *"Easter Morning": A. R. Ammons and His Poem,* a short film by Joanna Hudson, Ammons voices some dissatisfaction with the poem's rhythm, which he attributes to its origin as part of a long sequence.

15. A revised version of this poem appears in *The Really Short Poems,* under the title "That Day."

WORKS CITED

Ammons, A. R. Archie Ammons Papers. Cornell University Library, Ithaca, NY. (Cited as Ammons Papers.)

——. *Bosh and Flapdoodle.* New York: Norton, 2005.

——. *Brink Road.* New York: Norton, 1997.

——. *A Coast of Trees.* New York: Norton, 1981.

——. *Collected Poems, 1951–1971.* New York: Norton, 1972.

——. *Diversifications.* New York: Norton, 1975.

——. "Everything." *Paris Review* 165 (Spring 2003): 33.

——. *Garbage.* New York: Norton, 1993.

——. *Glare.* New York: Norton, 1997.

——. *Lake Effect Country.* New York: Norton, 1983.

——. *The Really Short Poems.* New York: Norton, 1990.

——. *The Selected Poems, 1951–1977.* New York: Norton, 1977; exp. ed., 1987.

——. *Set in Motion: Essays and Interviews.* Ann Arbor: U of Michigan P, 1996.

——. *The Snow Poems.* New York: Norton, 1977.

——. *Sphere: The Form of a Motion.* New York: Norton, 1974.

——. *Sumerian Vistas.* New York: Norton, 1987.

——. *Worldly Hopes.* New York: Norton, 1982.

Bloom, Harold. *Figures of Capable Imagination.* New York: Seabury, 1971.

——. "Harold Bloom on Poetry." *New Republic* 26 Nov. 1977: 24–26.

——. Letter to A. R. Ammons. 17 May 1976. Ammons Papers.

——. Letter to A. R. Ammons. 16 July 1977. Ammons Papers.

——. *The Ringers in the Tower: Studies in Romantic Tradition.* Chicago: U of Chicago P, 1971.

Burak, David, and Roger Gilbert, eds. *Considering the Radiance: Essays on the Poetry of A. R. Ammons.* New York: Norton, 2005.

Cushman, Stephen. "'Pray without Ceasing' and the Postmodern Canon." In Schneider 261–78.

Gilbert, Roger, ed. *This Is Just a Place: The Life and Work of A. R. Ammons.* Special issue of *Epoch* 52.3 (2004): 257–736.

Halpern, Nick. *Everyday and Prophetic: The Poetry of Lowell, Ammons, Merrill, and Rich.* Madison: U of Wisconsin P, 2003.

Hudson, Joanna, dir. *"Easter Morning": A. R. Ammons and His Poem.* Film, 11 minutes. 1995.

Kirschten, Robert, ed. *Critical Essays on A. R. Ammons.* New York: G. K. Hall, 1997.

Schneider, Steven, ed. *Complexities of Motion: New Essays on A. R. Ammons's Long Poems.* Madison, NJ: Fairleigh Dickinson UP, 1999.

Vendler, Helen. Letter to A. R. Ammons. 7 Jan. 1974. Ammons Papers.

——. Letter to A. R. Ammons. 1980 (exact date unclear). Ammons Papers.

——. *The Music of What Happens: Poems, Poets, Critics.* Cambridge, MA: Harvard UP, 1988.

———. "On 'In View of the Fact.'" In Gilbert 347–48.

———. *Part of Nature, Part of Us: Modern American Poets.* Cambridge, MA: Harvard UP, 1980.

———. *Poems, Poets, Poetry: An Introduction and Anthology.* Boston: Bedford, 1997.

———. "Poetry in Review" [on *Glare*]. *Yale Review* 90.1 (Jan. 2002): 157–75.

———. "The Poetry of A. R. Ammons." Unpublished lecture, 1981. Ammons Papers.

———. "*The Snow Poems* and *Garbage:* Episodes in an Evolving Poetics." In Schneider 23–50.

———. *Soul Says: On Recent Poetry.* Cambridge, MA: Harvard UP, 1995.

———. "The Titles: A. R. Ammons, 1926–2001." *Poetry* 179:1 (2001): 31–46. Rpt. in Burak and Gilbert 213–32.

Ashbery the Neoplatonist

LAURA QUINNEY

In the 1980s Helen Vendler began an essay with the salvo, "It seems time to write about John Ashbery's subject matter" (224). Her essay goes on to demonstrate the continuity of Ashbery's topics with those of the "Western lyric tradition" (231). In the twenty years since, as Ashbery's audience has assimilated his work, that continuity has come to be generally recognized. And yet, it still seems time to write about Ashbery's subject matter—it is always time—because it is always appropriate to be reminded of what a moving writer he is. The emotional power of a poet, though never divorced from rhetoric, turns on theme.

Love stands out as a subject, especially in Ashbery's recent poetry. Some critics claim that Ashbery has a "closeted sensibility," and they fault him for neglecting to treat his homosexuality in his poems (qtd. in Herd 195). This is an odd complaint to make of a poet who says almost nothing about his life in his poems—nothing, that is, of a factual nature. There seem to be oblique references to his childhood, and occasionally a stray detail from his adult life emerges (he saw Parmigianino's *Self-Portrait in a Convex Mirror* "with Pierre in the summer of 1959"). But generally Ashbery's poems—intimate, personal, affecting—adduce the experiences of the inner life by any other means than by describing their empirical occasion. He eschews autobiographical detail, and so does not have much that is explicit to say about being gay. But certainly he writes about love, as Charles Altieri demonstrated in an article provocatively entitled "Ashbery as Love Poet."[1]

Your Name Here (2000) offers a concentration of love poems, not only poems reflecting on love but poems addressed to a beloved (love poetry in the more conventional sense). I shall concentrate on this single volume of Ashbery's, in part because it seems to me to have an especial integrity among Ashbery's lyric collections—a notable density of focus—and in part because, although the standard critical practice (for good reason) is to range among Ashbery's volumes, I would like to preserve the "lonesomeness of [his] words," marooned between the covers of this particular book (qtd. in Costello 496). Ashbery's ruminative technique makes all his poems seem to belong to one continuous epic of thinking, but the contrary tendency ought sometimes to be honored—the tendency for each poem, and each volume, to seem isolated and adrift, as each represents the orphan murmur of solitary thought. Some of the poems in *Your Name Here* may be elegies, in fact, since the book is dedicated to Ashbery's friend Pierre Martory, who died in 1998. (He is presumably the Pierre with whom Ashbery was traveling in the summer of 1959.) The opening work, "This Room," is likely to be a poem of mourning:

> The room I entered was a dream of this room.
> Surely all those feet on the sofa were mine.
> The oval portrait
> of a dog was me at an early age.
> Something shimmers, something is hushed up.
>
> We had macaroni for lunch every day
> except Sunday, when a small quail was induced
> to be served to us. Why do I tell you these things?
> You are not even here.

Ashbery has his characteristic light touch—the surreal oneiric details, the comedy of the mundane—and this lightness serves to vindicate the plain, sad ending. "Weekend" strikes the same plangent note, with the same naked banality of phrase:

> Something might come out in group therapy:
> Your velvet soul as I just realized it.
> Please come back. I liked you so much.
>
> (25)

This "you" is most easily read as another person, rather than the "you" who is Ashbery himself. But do we know that the "you" is Pierre Martory? We do not. Without the context of the book's dedication, the poem might be taken to address a "you" separated from the speaker merely by distance. It might be the reader herself. These interpretations are perfectly possible, and would seem to change the feeling of the lines. Yet I do not think they make a drastic change. The addressee is still "gone," in whatever sense.

Bonnie Costello argues that the ubiquitous "you" of Ashbery's poems refers to the reader (even when it also refers to an unnamed addressee, or to Ashbery himself), and that in this way Ashbery takes up the theme of the frustrated relation of reader to writer, and vice versa, in "the bond of art" (497). Ashbery inclines to the reader, and the reader inclines to Ashbery, but there can be no union. "Ashbery's general cries of desire seem to reach directly to the reader as he vies against the belatedness of reading. 'Why can't you spend the night, here in my bed, with my arms wrapped tightly around you.' . . . Writing is always in a sense unrequited since no voice responds out of the written page" (499). Costello renders Ashbery's treatment of the "bond of art" in terms of thwarted Eros. As in "This Room," the beloved "you" is invoked in the context of loss and disappointment. Ashbery's poems are often elegiac, rather literally or not: they reveal the loss or absence of the other, and how it hollows out an aporia in the self.

Ashbery is a love poet, then, "of a kind." He is a love poet of the kind who writes about the failure of love. "Not You Again" begins with an homage to Eros, in which humor and pathos converge:

> You came at me and that was something.
> I was more than a match for you, you
> were a match for me, we undid the clasps
> in our shirtings, it was a semblance of all right.
>
> > (7)

Ashbery handles the conventionality of the theme by comically mixing slang, cliché, and weird anachronisms from the collective unconscious ("clasps" and "shirtings" sound vaguely Edwardian—are we to think of barbershop quartets?). But the emotion is still legible: it was a semblance of all right. (Again, it's not necessary to take this passage as empirical reference. A good rule of thumb with Ashbery: the happenings aren't real but the affects are.) This is an adducement of erotic satisfaction. But soon it gives way.

> Then you took me and held me like I was a child
> or a prize. For a moment there I thought I knew you,
> but you back away, wiping your specs, "Oh,
> excuse . . ." It's okay,
> will come another time.

Love falls short, as in a novel by Henry James. The poem ends in defeat—"Now it's too late, the books are closed, the salmon/no longer spewing." But its last words resume the idle gesture of communication—"Just so you know."

The next poem, "Terminal," picks up the theme of aborted contact. It begins, "Didn't you get my card?" then wanders off into a fragment of narrative about expression that is internally diverted:

> When it came time for my speech
> I could think of nothing, of course.
> I gave a little talk about the onion—how its flavor
> inspires us, its shape informs our architecture.
> There were so many other things I wanted to say, too,
> but, dandified, I couldn't strut,
> couldn't sit down for all the spit and polish.
> Now it's your turn to say something about the wall
> in the garden. It can be anything.
>
> (9)

Maybe the last lines contain a hint of urgency; maybe not. Maybe the "you" is the reader rather than a third person, and the theme is metapoetic. The possibilities coalesce in significance rather than diverging—because in any case, the approach of one person to another, or others, fails.

Ashbery treats this desire for, and repulsion from, erotic contact (as distinguished from sexual contact) with some ambivalence. One poem calls interpersonal communication an "invasive procedure," drawing the term from its mordant epigraph by Robert Walser: "I flee from those who are gifted with understanding, fearing that all their great and illuminating invasions of my being still won't satisfy me." Here the motive for shunning people is the fear of disappointment, or perhaps it is really the pleasure of self-enclosure masquerading as the fear of disappointment. Ashbery makes fun of his misanthropy—"But how can I be in this bar and also be a recluse?" ("Your Name Here" [126])—just as much as he mocks his convivial longings: "Today a stoat came to tea/and that was so nice it almost made me cry" ("Merrily We Live" [11]). He sums up the absurdity of the dialectic by telling himself, like a hopeful student, "I know I shall once day come to the reason/for manners and intercourse with persons" ("Paperwork" [30]). Even an apparently companionable routine leads to desperation:

Now I can sample your shorts.
So much is there for us now—
runnels that threaten to drown the indifferent one
who sticks his toe in them.
Much, much more light.

To whose office shall we go tomorrow?
I'd like to hear the new recording of clavier
variations. Oh, help us someone!
                    ("Strange Occupations" [36])

Mundanity is suffocating, and one longs to be rescued from it. The dialectic of self and other can never reach a happy equilibrium.

In a much earlier poem, "Wet Casements" (*Houseboat Days*), Ashbery addressed what might be termed the limitation of subjectivity, or the impossibility of achieving transparency between self and other. Frustration and sadness led him to "anger," and he had concluded in despair, "I shall keep to myself. / I shall not repeat others' comments about me" (225). Longanimity rather than resistance is the keynote of *Your Name Here*. Trials have been made, truth clarified, limits revealed. "And still the feeling comes on" ("Frogs and Gospels"). Feeling persists though it is known to be unanswerable. This is notably the case of Eros, the desire for the fulfillment of the erotic ideal. In "Life Is a Dream," Ashbery divulges this desire under the sign of negation—that is, he expresses the desire at the same time that he acknowledges its futility:

I know I'll have a chance to learn more
later on. Waiting is what's called for, meanwhile.
It's true that life can be anything, but certain things
definitely aren't it. This gloved hand,
for instance, that glides
so securely into mine, as though it intends to stay.
                                (59)

Life can "be anything," they tell us (playing on the platitude: you can be anything you want when you grow up). But Ashbery swats the cliché aside: there are some things life will never bring us, as for example: heart's peace. Odd that the hand is gloved—the detail is thrown in to bend the pathos of the moment slightly—but the last line resonates with hopeless longing, crossing maternal and erotic imagery in a dream of union. In particular, it is a fantasy because it promises "security," and in the last phrase the promise is canceled out—"*as though* it intends to stay." The dream knows it is only a dream.

The skeptical reader may raise an objection to this rendering: how can we know that the satisfaction imaged here is specifically erotic? Why not see the erotic disappointment as a type of the larger existential disappointment—the reluctant acknowledgment that the soul's desires shall go unmet—that is so prominent a theme in Ashbery's poems over-all? To this objection the proper reply is: Exactly. We cannot distinguish in Ashbery between erotic and existential disappointment. That is what makes him a Platonist, or better, a neoplatonist: someone who turns Platonic ideas to his or her own uses.[2] In *The Symposium*, Diotima teaches Socrates that Eros is the desire for the Beautiful, which is to say, for the transcendent, a perfection not to be found in our world. Eros can take many forms, including a sexual one, but it is essentially desire for that which one lacks and must always lack in this life. It is a gauge of the distance between the mundane and the intelligible world. Eros as unfulfill-able desire provides us with an intuition of this gulf, and the intimations that follow, as Wordsworth put it, give proof of the immortality of the soul.[3] Through disappointment the soul recognizes that it is in exile here. Ashbery does not share Wordsworth's version of Platonic religion; that is, he does without reference to the soul's immortality and the existence of a higher world. But he shares the psychology: though eros must re-main unsatisfied, its presence and power teach him to quarrel with the terms of his existence. Our longings seem to have been crafted for a different life.

Throughout his career, Ashbery has written poems about the tantaliz-ing approach of the promise ("At North Farm") and also its evaporation or retreat. The themes recur in *Your Name Here*. "Honored Guest" evokes potential—it speaks of "wanting to show you this tremendous thing,/ boxed in forever, always getting closer" (91)—whereas "Lost Profile" records the undoing, "It seems we were so happy once, just for a min-ute./Then the sky got clouded, no one was happy or unhappy/forever, and the dream of the oppressor had come true" (83). Lost possibilities—gaps and mistimings—are often invoked:

I was going to say I kissed you once
when you were asleep, and that you took no notice.

Since that day I have been as a traveler
who scurries to and fro among nettles
                ("Humble Pie" [85])

And all the time I thought I was being a pest
someone was desperately in love with me.
The person sickened and apparently died
in a hospital far away. Now I have no one,
no friends to gripe with or call coaxing names to.
I was definitely born at the wrong time
or in the wrong city.
                ("Pot Luck" [103–4])

These are humorous versions of the conclusion reached by the Fifth and
Sixth Spirits in Shelley's *Prometheus Unbound*: "Ruin" is now Love's
shadow, its consequence. As the Sixth Spirit says:

Desolation is a delicate thing:
It walks not on the Earth, it floats not on the air,
But treads with silent footstep, and fans with silent wing
The tender hopes which in their hearts the best and gentlest bear,
Who, soothed to false repose by the fanning plumes above
And the music-stirring motion of its soft and busy feet,
Dream visions of aerial joy, and call the monster, Love,
And wake, and find the shadow Pain.
                                        (233)

By "Love," Shelley means Platonic Eros: idealistic aspiration of any
form, which must come to grief. When the Sixth Spirit calls Desolation "a
delicate thing," he is altering a phrase from Agathon's speech, which Shelley rendered this way in his translation of *The Symposium*: "For Homer
says, that the goddess Calamity is delicate, and that her feet are tender.
'Her feet are soft,' he says, 'for she treads not upon the ground, but makes
her path upon the heads of men.' He gives as an evidence of her tenderness, that she walks not upon that which is hard, but that which is soft.
The same evidence is sufficient to make manifest the tenderness of Love"
(196). Love and Desolation are interchangeably "tender" because they act
on what is susceptible in us; Eros is a sensitive register for both expectation
and bafflement. It is because erotic dreams can be formed—apparently

without much encouragement from real life—that they can be promptly dispelled. And still the feeling comes on. A curious intuition refuses to subside. It survives not to be realized but to create uneasiness. I call this uneasiness "transcendental remorse," or the sense of having failed, or been caused to fail, at the impossible task of surmounting mundanity. Ashbery is a poet of this desolation and its delicacy. We are compelled, but the goal is elusive, unclear; we know and have long known that we cannot reach it.

> It has been a life of qualification and delay.
> Yet we knew we were on the right track: something surged in us,
> telling us otherwise, that we'd arrive too early at the airport
> or something about the drips on the taxi in the dusk.
> We doctored it all up,
> and I think I have an explanation for the manna
> that falls softly as pollen, and tastes like coconut or some other
> unaccountable sherbet. It seems clothes never do fit.
>
> Yes, I could have told you that some time ago.
>
> ("A Suit" [75])

Once the invisible promptings and their futility have been recognized, what is one to do? Ashbery finds himself in the predicament of Wordsworth at the end of the Intimations Ode: he must learn how patiently to occupy a devalued reality. Sometimes in fact he is impatient—"Accept these nice things we have no use for" ("Honored Guests")—and sometimes he struggles to be reconciled:

> The ship is already far from here, like a ghost ship.
> The core of the sermon is always distance, landscape
> waiting to be considered, maybe loved a little
> eventually. And I do, I do.
>
> ("Nobody Is Going Anywhere" [98])

He protests his willingness to accept reality, as Wordsworth too claims: "We will grieve not, rather find / Strength in what remains behind." Ashbery shows us that he knows who he sounds like when he parodies Wordsworth's conversation with the infirm leech gatherer in "Resolution and Independence." The parody appears at the end of a poem pointedly called "Pale Siblings":

So I wandered fleecy as a cloud and one day an old shepherd crossed
my path, looking very wise with his crook. How much use do you get
out of that thing, I asked him. Depends, he replied. Sometimes one
of 'em doesn't go astray for months on end. Other times I've got my
hands full with them running around in all directions, laughing at
me. *At me!* Well, I never would have taken on this job, this added responsibility, rather, if being thanked was all I'd had on my mind. Yes,
I said, but how do you avoid it when someone's really grateful, and
graceful, and you're fading away like you're doing now, your rain-
bow cap a cigar-store Indian's wooden feather headdress, and all your
daughters frantic with glee or misapprehension as you slide by, close
to them though they can't see you? Oh, I've learned to cope shall we
say, and leave it at that. Yes, I said, by all means, let's. (97)

Self-conscious as ever, Ashbery mocks the naif in himself who still wants
to learn, even if it means only "learning to cope." Other passages, despite
undermining surreal twists, preserve the sense that there is an emergency
at hand:

Father, I can go no farther, the lamp blinds me
and the man behind me keeps whispering things in my ear
I'd prefer not to be able to understand . . .
Yet you must, my child, for the sake of the cousins
and the rabbit who awaits us in the dooryard.
("They Don't Just Go Away, Either" [65])

Once one concludes that Eros is unfulfillable, and that desire is lodged
in us senselessly, then it becomes a pressing question what to do with the
feelings that still come on. Plato and Wordsworth, each in his own idiom, propose constructive uses for residual Eros. But these turn on the
dualist assumption that the soul has a transcendental origin and destiny. Ashbery is a Platonic "monist" (I say half in jest): the soul is in exile here, but there is no other world to which it more properly belongs.
He is more severe in this respect than Shelley, who remained agnostic
on the question of whether there is an afterlife. If reality and value have
no other world into which they may migrate, then it becomes all the
more urgent to discover a place for them here. Ashbery is not a senti-
mentalist, but he is in no position to repudiate all sentiment. That is why
erotic feeling reenters, no matter how hedged it may be, no matter how
ridiculous.

If there is more to remember, I gift you with it
because of the eternal person you were sometimes, and the loveliness
of your being, shaken clear of you like duck feathers.

("Vintage Masquerade" [110])

Stevens sublimates the erotic object in its transcendence: his paramour is interior. But in Ashbery it is the other to whom he still appeals. The passion for the object maintains its integrity, and lingers on in an urgent if compromised Platonic idiom. This is the note on which the volume concludes, as Ashbery gives a parting amorous salute, self-mocking in its bathos and yet undisavowed.

But I was totally taken with you, always have been.
Light a candle in my wreath, I'll be yours forever and will kiss you.

("Your Name Here" [127])

NOTES

1. Altieri describes the paradoxical character of love in the poetry. It awakens desire for transcendence that it cannot satisfy: "Whatever makes love possible also makes it problematic by offering a domain that in fact the lovers cannot inhabit except in a fantasy of an alternative present distinguished by a full transparency" (31). But somehow desire does not die. "Even one's most solipsistic moments become haunted by addresses to a beloved, addresses that keep alive the hope there is something that the isolated consciousness can share, something that Ashbery calls elsewhere 'the permanent tug of a home'" (32). I rejoice in the implicit Platonism of this sentence.

2. A "new Platonist," as distinguished from the philosophical school of Neoplatonism, founded by Plotinus in the third century C.E.

3. John Koethe underscores Ashbery's involvement in "the fundamental impulses of romanticism, which I would characterize as subjectivity's contestation of its objective setting in a world which has no place for it, and which threatens to reduce it to nonexistence" (87). This theme can be characterized, in specific terms, as a legacy of Romantic Platonism.

WORKS CITED

Altieri, Charles. "Ashbery as Love Poet." *The Tribe of John: Ashbery and Contemporary Poetry.* Ed. Susan M. Schultz. Tuscaloosa: U of Alabama P, 1995. 26–37.

Ashbery, John. *Houseboat Days.* New York: Penguin, 1975.

———. *Your Name Here.* New York: Farrar, Straus and Giroux, 2000.

Costello, Bonnie. "John Ashbery and the Idea of the Reader." *Contemporary Literature* 23.4 (1982): 493–514.

Herd, David. *John Ashbery and American Poetry*. New York: Palgrave, 2000.

Koethe, John. "The Absence of a Noble Presence." *The Tribe of John: Ashbery and Contemporary Poetry*. Ed. Susan M. Schultz. Tuscaloosa: U of Alabama P, 1995. 83–90.

Shelley, Percy Bysshe. *Shelley's Poetry and Prose: Authoritative Texts, Criticism*. Ed. Donald H. Reiman and Neil Fraistat. New York: Norton, 2002.

———. *The Works of Percy Bysshe Shelley*. Ed. Harry Buxton Forman. London: Reeve and Turner, 1880.

Vendler, Helen. "John Ashbery, Louise Glück." *The Music of What Happens: Poems, Poets, Critics*. Cambridge, MA: Harvard UP, 1988. 224–61.

Called to Poetry
Hardy, Heaney, Hennessy

ELAINE SCARRY

None of the handbooks on poetry seem to contain an entry for the word "call." Yet we know that for some persons there comes a moment—a specifiable, concrete moment—when life stops and starts again. On one side of this heartbeat there is no obligation to poetry; on the other side, the full weight of the obligation is somehow securely in place. Or to put it another way, on one side of the heartbeat there is no sense that certain sounds are missing from the world; on the other side comes not only the knowledge that certain sounds are missing but the knowledge that you yourself will have to supply them.

Remarkably, it appears that this event sometimes happens in childhood, long before the child's own language has completely formed. Let us say (to begin with an unlikely picture) that the call should arrive while the child is still trailing Wordsworth's clouds of glory at, say, the age of two—the age when the child (according to recent counts) is learning six new words every hour. The age of two—unlikely for poets, more likely for musicians—is mentioned simply as a reminder of how open language still is at the age of four (the age when Thomas Hardy's father handed him a miniature concertina; or Rainer Maria Rilke stood listening to his dolls) or at the ages of six or eight or eleven (the amorphous period of young boyhood when Walt Whitman heard the mockingbird calling to his mate and realized it was he who would have to answer; or when Seamus Heaney, disguised as a bush to lure birds, crouched down to the ground and realized this was what he was supposed to become).

Like spring, with its unfinished green, the call to poetry in childhood arrives when the person's own language is far from finished: one book on sound making designates the age of thirty-one as the youngest age at which the ability to speak is ever complete. The child's sense that certain sounds are missing from the world—far from being based on having surveyed the language and noticing phrases missing, or having heard all

302

the poems in the language and perceiving the repertoire incomplete—has come when the small person, each day all day practicing the formation of words and sentences, has just recently waded into the river of already existing sound whose full flow will only become audible many years later.

Now it may be the case that the call to poetry which arrives in childhood—rather than being *oddly* poised against the child's half-knowledge of already existing language—is instead appropriately poised there because it is here, at the place in the mind that is receiving the instruction to form new words, that a confusion arises, that the instruction to form *new-to-me* words gets confused with an instruction to form *new-to-the-world* words; and more important, the part of the brain that is profoundly (but routinely) engaged in the act of making *new-to-me* words now gets conscripted into this other act and—this is key—now remains accessible to the poet all life long in a way that is simply not the case for those of us who understood that we were only being asked to create *new-to-me* words and stopped conversing with this part of our minds once that task was complete. When at the age of six John Milton is given his first Latin word to decline—*Musa, Musae*—does he understand that he is being asked to use the word-forging powers of his mind to make already-existing but new-to-him Latin? Or does he believe it is Latin that is new-to-the-world that he has just been called upon to create?

This phenomenon of incurring, at a very young age, *an obligation to a language one does not oneself know* can be glimpsed not only in those who are called upon to make poems and to make themselves poets but also in those who are called to serve poems and to make themselves ready to serve poets. Helen Hennessy, listening with rapt attention to poems at the age of three and writing them herself by the age of six, could not have intuited the scale and duration of the obligation to which she had been summoned, any more than Whitman knew the utterance of the mockingbird or Milton comprehended the full expanse of Latin pressed into the brief compass of *Musa, Musae.*

Thomas Hardy, at eighty-eight, said he could still feel in his hand the bird he and his father found newly dead in a field when he was a child. Hardy's father placed the featherlight bird in his hand not long after he placed the miniature concertina there, two memories that Hardy recites to his wife, Florence Emily Hardy, at the end of his life—along with a third vivid childhood memory about getting down on the ground in a field of sheep.

It is inside this third memory—a young child getting down on the ground in a field of sheep—that Seamus Heaney discovers Thomas Hardy's call to poetry.

Once, as a child, out in a field of sheep,
Thomas Hardy pretended to be dead
And lay down flat among their dainty shins.

In that sniffed-at, bleated-into, grassy space
He experimented with infinity.
His small cool brow was like an anvil waiting

For sky to make it sing the perfect pitch
Of his dumb being, and that stir he caused
In the fleece-hustle was the original

Of a ripple that would travel eighty years
Outward from there, to be the same ripple
Inside him at its last circumference.

The poem speaks aloud a truth about creation: each poem a poet writes reenacts the first call; the call is "the original // Of a ripple that would travel . . . / Outward from there, to be the same ripple / Inside him at its last circumference" ("Lightenings vi").

Is this true? We can see its straightforward truth in Seamus Heaney's own poems. Forever heading down beneath grass, dirt, or stone, they reenact the moment of his childhood call when, disguised as a bush, he crouched down into the ground; or earlier, the moment at age two when he took the slats out of his cot and lowered his feet onto the cool stone floor. We can see its truth, too, in Whitman's poems. The singing of a mateless mockingbird is audible not only in "Out of the Cradle Endlessly Rocking" but, as Helen Vendler shows, in Whitman's many poems that yearn to confer material substance on "invisible listeners" in the present and in the future. We can see it, too, in Milton where conjugation (marital, celestial, linguistic) and declension (political, theological, linguistic) reappear everywhere in lineation and large structure.

Since this is the case—since the call reappears in the subsequent work of poetic creation—it means that we can, by glimpsing the partially exposed mental event at the interior of the call, perhaps also glimpse the hidden mental event at the interior of the ongoing work of poetic creation. And since Heaney's account of Hardy's call already lies open in front of us, let us look there to see what it is we learn.

What kind of mental event takes place in the poem? Whatever it is, it is brief. Now it is often the case that a manifest act of thinking—what we often refer to as "brilliant thinking," by which we mean an act of thinking that is at once recognizable as an act of thinking—tends to be associated with condensed verbal forms: the maxim, the remark, the retort, the aperçu, and (up through the seventeenth century, when it still retained its power) the pun. The twentieth- and twenty-first-century "soundbite" joins these others. It is, like them, a highly compressed verbal form in which the quality of voiced thought, for better or for worse, stands nakedly exposed: if the thinking is weak or nonexistent, that is audible; if instead a powerful act of thinking has taken place, we hear that too. In this poem, two forms of sound are referred to but are themselves unsounded: a soundbite is literalized, then gives way to the even more condensed single stroke of a hammer blow.

In the poem, the child drops to the ground, then lets himself become the ground on which things standing over him—the sheep, the sky—press down on him. "Anything can happen," Seamus Heaney writes in another poem, and "anything can happen" here during the boy's experiment with infinity. The child has suppressed his own aliveness ("pretended to be dead") and made himself available to the aliveness of other beings. The aliveness of the sheep is registered in the most elementary way aliveness can be registered: they are breathing. They breathe in ("sniffed-at") and they breathe out ("bleated-into") as they lean their faces down to his. They query, test, and may even bite him. The lines are deft, quick, unmelodramatic: we are simply expected to know that when you are surrounded by nonhuman beings, anything can happen.

When in "Ministry of Fear" Heaney wants to describe the fear of being suddenly surrounded by police, here is what he says—

> ... policemen
> Swung their crimson flashlamps, crowding round
> The car like black cattle, snuffing and pointing
> The muzzle of a sten-gun in my eye:
> 'What's your name, driver?'
> 'Seamus ...'

Six lines are required to convey the psychic disarray of being surrounded at night by police; no lines are required to convey the psychic disarray of being suddenly surrounded by "black cattle, snuffing." Instead, the big cows are counted on to assist, instantly, our comprehension of the human source of terror. Unlike Seamus in "Ministry of Fear," Thomas in "Lightenings vi" is not upright with a metal car between himself and his interrogators; he is lying face up on the ground, his eyes level with the interrogators' "dainty shins."

He has made himself available, even assailable. He has made himself eligible to be acted on by their nervy nervousness. And it is their shrill aliveness (inaudible because its notes are too high to be heard) rather than their teeth that get etched into his own nervous system. The soft bleats and sniffing, the low murmuring sounds of the lines, have the overtone of high aliveness in the EE's and I's—chIld, fEEld, shEEp, HardEE, prEEtended, bEE, daintEE, blEEted, infinitEE, hEE, lIke, skI, flEEce, eightEE, bEE—in flight along the crest of the poem's other sounds.

Few poems or stories place the face—let alone the face of an eight-year-old—in such a vulnerable location. Perhaps only the beautiful boy Hyacinth—beloved by Apollo, whose discus (hurled in play) struck Hyacinth in the face—prepares us for the way the child in "Lightenings vi" makes himself available to receive the blow of the sky: "His small cool brow was like an anvil waiting // For sky to make it sing the perfect pitch / Of his dumb being. . . ." The sky is wide; his forehead is small. It is as though sky and boy have become the hammer and anvil of a single ear. The boy's willfully chosen angle of bodily inclination—his downward pitch—waits to be translated by the sky into its sonic equivalent: the perfect pitch of his dumb being. Ground yields to sky, the kinesthetic to the auditory, willed posture to unwilled music.

The fulcrum from bodily pitch to musical pitch, from active to passive, resides in that "stir he caused"—

> and that stir he caused
> In the fleece-hustle was the original
>
> Of a ripple that would travel eighty years
> Outward from there, to be the same ripple
> Inside him at its last circumference.

The word "stir" refers both to a motion and to the sound made by the motion. Like pitch, which may be either high or low and varies between 8 and 30,000 vibrations a second, stir may be either a barely perceptible kinesthetic and sonic event ("to move, especially in a slight way," says Webster) or an emphatic one ("to move briskly," "to affect strongly"). Pitch is a sound, but sound is itself an iterated series of motions or waves; pitch, in other words, is an instigating event but is also itself its own ongoing iterations.

When raindrops or pebbles hit the surface of a pond, each strike produces a smooth series of rings in rapid sequence—one)two)three)—with no temporal interruption. That is the way we hear the three even stresses of "small cool brow," "his dumb being," "make it sing," "stir he caused." Each three-stress phrase records not the strike of the sky on the anvil or the soundbite of the sheep on the nerves but the three-tiered ripple of consequence that follows the silent instigating event. In his Nobel Prize acceptance speech, Heaney compares his own childhood "impressionability" to "the drinking water that stood in a bucket in our scullery: every time a passing train made the earth shake, the surface of that water used to ripple delicately, concentrically, and in utter silence." The bucket of unheard sound, like an urn full of unheard melody, reminds us that the call comes before language is available to answer or even comprehend it. For Hardy, the connection between a languageless aspiration to language-making and the setting of a ewe-leaze seems to have reappeared in young manhood, for an early chapter in Florence Emily Hardy's biography mentions that he taught himself the Greek of the New Testament during repeated visits to a ewe-leaze.[1]

The rippling at the close of "Lightenings vi" at once gives rise to another poem, "Lightenings vii," whose entire twelve lines are enclosed within a parenthesis. The sign of the parenthesis—the fragment of an arc—visually echoes the concentric rippling already underway, as Heaney, having gone back to read the Florence Emily biography, now adjusts and rewrites his first account:

(I misremembered. He went down on all fours,
Florence Emily says, crossing a ewe-leaze.
Hardy sought the creatures face to face,

Their witless eyes and liability
To panic made him feel less alone,
Made proleptic sorrow stand a moment

Over him, perfectly known and sure.
And then the flock's dismay went swimming on
Into the blinks and murmurs and deflections

He'd know at parties in renowned old age
When sometimes he imagined himself a ghost
And circulated with that new perspective.)

Does this poem alter, or instead magnify, the account of poetic consciousness in "Lightenings vi"?

Helen Vendler's book *Poets Thinking: Pope, Whitman, Dickinson, Yeats* describes "reprise" and "repetition" as one of four fundamental forms of poetic thinking, a form in which the "retinal innocence" of a first description comes to have more thought folded into it the second time it is described. Especially relevant to "Lightenings vi and vii" is the fact that two of Vendler's examples—Whitman's "Sparkles from the Wheel" and "A Noiseless Patient Spider"—are, like Heaney's accounts of Hardy, about the nature of poetic creation. Even more striking is the fact that Vendler's book *Seamus Heaney* identifies "second thoughts" as the key feature of Heaney's own poetic consciousness: the book describes in turn each volume of his poetry, each time pausing, before proceeding to the next chapter, with a section entitled "Second Thoughts" where Vendler describes how what Heaney has just made in *North,* or *Field Work,* or *Seeing Things* he also partially unmakes, like Keats's "innumerable compositions and decompositions" upon the snailhorn of beauty.

"Lightenings vi and vii" enact the structure of second thoughts more directly than almost any other Heaney poem. Not only does the second poem qualify the first but the thesis of both—that poetic creation reenacts the initial call—is itself a "second thought" structure: it is as though one must turn and let oneself be hit in the forehead by the first ripple of consequence, so that another will then occur, which in turn must be faced in the same way for there to be a third. Although the word "ripple" is said by most etymologists to be of obscure origin, most agree that it is a "frequentive": a frequentive is a word, often involving an "le" or "er" suffix, that entails ongoing repetition of whatever the (in this case, mysterious) central root word is. And, despite the missing suffix, we can perhaps say that poetic creation is the frequentive of being called.

Now the word "parenthesis" refers both to the ripple marks, ( ), and to the matter enclosed within those marks; if we accordingly see "Lightenings vii" as identical with its own terminal markings, we see how literally the poem becomes one more wave of what has come before. A parenthesis, according to its dictionary definition, interrupts and qualifies what is outside the parenthesis without affecting that outer material, even when it stands in opposition to it.

If "Lightenings vii" corrects "Lightenings vi," far from thinning out the claims of the earlier poem, as we often think of corrections as doing, it instead thickens them. "Pitch" can mean a musical event or the incline of the ground; but "pitch" is also a verb meaning to fall forward, and this third meaning is added to the other two in "Lightenings vii": "I misre-membered. He went down on all fours." Further, by restoring the boy to his upright position and having him willfully go down again, Heaney re-connects us to the instigating volitional element in an event that centrally requires capacious receptivity, the willed suspension of the volitional. Heaney has also doubled Thomas Hardy's contact with the ground: the first poem placed the back of his head, torso, and legs on the earth; now Heaney turns him over, placing the front of his body on the ground. Ven-dler speaks of the way a reprise can act as a palimpsest overlaying the lines it recites or revises; in "Lightenings vi and vii," the palimpsest of front and back confers on the child his full-frail-bodiedness.

Even the ripple thickens across the two poems. The rippling in "Light-enings vi," with its circles and circumference, takes place in clear water, a meaning of the word ("a light ruffling of the surface of water") that arises in the eighteenth century, according to C. T. Onions; Robert Barn-hart specifies that "the meaning of a very small wave" first appeared in Coleridge's 1798 "Rime of the Ancient Mariner." But in "Lightenings vii," the liquidity of rippling is transferred to the tremulous, panicky, fleecy bodies of the sheep and to Hardy himself—

And then the flock's dismay went swimming on
Into the blinks and murmurs and deflections

He'd know at parties in renowned old age

—in a way that returns the word to its pre-eighteenth-century roots. While etymologists see the elusive root word *rip* as probably meaning "crease," "fold," "tear" (and, in the case of Barnhart, "touch" or "move"), Ernest Klein speculates that its meaning entailed placing the hands in the material stuff of life, for he says that it meant "to cleanse flax or hemp by removing the seeds," that it is connected to Old English *repan, ripan,* "to reap," and that its noun equivalent is the word "flax comb" (German, *riffle*).

It is as though this second poem lifts into visibility the active verbs embedded in the grassy enclosure of the noun "fleece-hustle" in "Lighten-ings vi." "Hustle" is (like "ripple") a frequentative, in this case referring to the repeated act of shaking. "Fleece," a noun (used by Chaucer in his 1380 translation of Boethius), was once also the verb "to fleece," to shear the sheep of its wool. The poem is about a kind of shakedown in the ewe-leaze, for there is a slight dusting of thievery throughout. To fleece someone, to hustle someone, and to rip (or rip off) someone (*rip* is connected to *rep*, in *rep*robate) all convey the idea of appropriation. The boy in the poem is there to get something from the sheep—that's what poets do, Helen Vendler reminds us, "they incorporate"—though it is not the creatures' fleece but their sheer aliveness, their "liability to panic," that he will carry away inside him until the end of his life.

Across the two poems, the perfect pitch of the boy's bodily incline becomes more audible. This ground has its own sound: it is not the "infantile labile music" that Heaney hears, through Mandelstam, in Dante's Italian, or the "Scottish speech" Heaney heard as a child in Ballymena and later in the poems of Burns, or the "clear ring" of Northern Ireland. It is the *purling* sound that Hardy himself identified as Dorset's central syllable in describing Tess Durbeyfield: "The dialect was on her tongue to some extent, despite the village school: the characteristic intonation of that dialect for this district being the voicing approximately rendered by the syllable UR, probably as rich an utterance as any to be found in human speech." The repeated sound across "Lightenings vi and vii"—what Vendler quoting Heaney calls "the binding secret," and what Heaney quoting Nadezhda Mandelstam calls the "nugget of harmony" or, in his own words, "this phonetic jewel, to hit upon and hold one's true note"—is the syllable UR which occurs in "stUR," "pURfect," "cURcumfURence," "misremembURed," "pURfectly," "sURe," "mURmURs," "cURculated," "pURspective." The same sound thrown deeper into the throat recurs in the ULL sound of "anvULL," "hustULL," "originULL," "rippULL," "travULL," "rippULL," "yULLeaze." It is as though the frequentive "er" and "le" suffixes in standard English have here become the richer UR and ULL sounds so that, despite the absence of frequentive verbs in modern English, the two poems carry the sonic signature of the frequentive in their description of a childhood call that recurs across eighty years of poetic creation.

Heaney's conception of sky and boy as the hammer and anvil of a single ear in "Lightenings vi" reminds us how central Rilke's phrase "the temple inside our hearing" has long been to Heaney. He invokes it at least three times: in his essay "On W. B. Yeats and Thoor Ballylee," in his description of Hardy in his introduction to *The Redress of Poetry*, and in his Nobel acceptance speech. But it is harder to say with precision with what degree of literalness we are to understand the claim that acoustical pitch is preceded by, and requires, kinesthetic pitch. The temple in the ear requires a prone foundation. Must one be lying down, must one maximize one's contact with the ground, in order to become the willing instrument of poetic creation? Heaney seems to mean it more literally than we might suppose.

One can locate the question in two places that are distinct, and possibly should be decoupled, from one another: in the space of transfer from the poet of one century to the next; and then, in any one poet's relation with himself or herself. Hardy believed that there was no new poetry, just a new poet continuing what had come before. To come into contact with the physical ground of an earlier poet was something that shook him. As a child he and his mother had stayed in—actually lain down in—the third floor of an inn where Shelley and Mary Godwin had (several decades earlier) sometimes stayed. Hardy was thrilled by the possibility that they may have inhabited the very same room. Four other times he felt he "impinged on the penumbra of the poet he loved": when he stood in St. Pancras churchyard (where Percy and Mary first made love), by Shelley's grave in Rome, by Mary Shelley's grave in Dorset, and when he spoke with Shelley's son.

Heaney has similarly impinged on Hardy's penumbra. Of Heaney's frequent visits to Hardy's Brockhampton, the first is described in the poem "The Birthplace." The poem is so rich in its account of Heaney's thoughts about Hardy that one may forget that section ii chronicles the way being there incites Marie and Seamus Heaney to lie down on the ground: " . . . driven / into the damp-floored wood // where we made an episode / of ourselves . . . only yards from the house." Hardy's physical importance to Heaney, were any evidence needed, can be grasped in his periodic return to Hardy's grave, one year in the company of both Marie Heaney and Helen Vendler. There is a fleeting snapshot of Vendler and Heaney, taken by Marie Heaney, that registers the shared impulse to maximize their bodily contact with Hardy. Their hands and knees make contact with the grave as though in secret, as though neither we nor they themselves need notice what they do. Thomas Hardy himself, Florence Emily tells us, made repeated visits to his birth cottage in Brockhampton, to nearby Egdon Heath to see the rhododendrons and the purple heather in bloom, and to Stinsford graveyard (trowel in hand to clear away the moss from the stone tablets).

The urge of living poets to visit the live ground of no longer alive poets is in part a corollary to the wish of living poets to meet living poets, even when they do not know, and have no abiding friendship with, the other. What can be gotten in such a meeting is not one another's fleece or meter or voice—all of which can be gleaned from the poems—but the panicky fact of actual aliveness. Thus on Hardy's eighty-first birthday, Virginia Woolf, James Joyce, Siegfried Sassoon, and Robert Graves came to Hardy's house in Dorset and gave to him a first edition of Keats's poems. Keats and Coleridge, in their turn strangers, met by accident one evening and walked a short distance together along a road, Keats afterward recording with great excitement that Coleridge had spoken about a dazzling!!!! array!!!! of subjects,[2] and Coleridge remembering only that he had briefly held Keats's hand in his own, and perceived in the temperature of his hand that he would not be in the world much longer. A hundred years from now, others will read the archives of papers in Houghton Library at Harvard and will come upon the record of fleeting meetings between poets of our own time, often arranged by Helen Vendler, such as the coming together of Elizabeth Bishop and Seamus Heaney. Sent by Helen Vendler a copy of *North* ("Dear Elizabeth, Herewith, *North*"), two pages of annotations ("Brandywell is a football pitch"), and an invitation to her house following Seamus Heaney's poetry reading, Elizabeth Bishop several years later writes to Ashley Brown, "Seamus Heaney is at Harvard this term—perhaps you know him. I'd met him here before & I like his poetry a lot. . . . He's reading at Harvard next week. . . . I avoid readings whenever I can, but I did like Heaney's reading—the one I heard two years ago."[3]

The wish to be in contact with the ground inhabited by another poet can be generalized as a wish to stay in contact with the deep foundations of one's own living language, as Heaney says in "Something to Write Home About," as well as to stay in contact with the aliveness of those who have helped create that living language. Heaney, like the child Thomas Hardy in "Lightenings vi," is almost as open to the sky as to the ground. From "The Rain Stick" to "The Mud Vision" to "Postscript" to "Anything Can Happen" to "Midnight Anvil," he is in part a sky poet. But a poet's attention to the sky puzzles us less than a commitment to the ground; and therefore it will be helpful to take one last look at the connection between the call to poetry and the volitional act of dropping to the ground. Three different veins of thought may coax us into grasping how literal that relation may be.

The first is the record of composition from the first to the thirteenth century A.D. Mary Carruthers in *The Craft of Thought* shows that in *The Consolation of Philosophy,* Boethius is lying prone in the act of composing poetry, a bodily posture also adopted by Anselm (according to his biographer, the monk Eadmer) in his composition of *Proslogion* in the eleventh century. The posture is again adopted in the monastic practice of Bernard of Clairvaux in the twelfth century, and again by Thomas Aquinas (according to Bernardo Gui) in the thirteenth century. Carruthers shows the same posture in earlier writers. Augustine assigns himself multiple compositional postures in the *Confessions,* but he "resolves his crisis in thinking" by throwing himself into "a prone posture" under a fig tree. In the first century A.D., Quintilian assumes that composition may require going to bed. In the first century B.C., Cicero's Lucius Crassus adopts the same posture in "On Oratory." Horizontal composition occurs much earlier and much later than the many-centuries-long period Carruthers reviews: Dimitrios Yatromanolakis shows that participants in fifth-century Greek symposia are pictured reclining on couches in Greek vase paintings (as are certain male poets); and Proust, by his own account, only rarely got out of bed.

A second, wholly distinct tradition that presses us to take Heaney at his word is the account of mental deliberation by philosophers such as Thomas Hobbes, John Locke, and John Dewey, each of whom emphasizes the felt materiality or groundedness of the mental act. Locke in *The Conduct of the Understanding* complains that our speech outpaces our thinking, and our thinking outpaces evidence. He argues that we only actually carry out the act of thinking when we fold material encumbrance into the act, a process that he calls "bottoming." He juxtaposes three persons: one who races across the landscape, one who walks slowly enough to see the plants, the third who stops and digs in the ground. Only the third bottoms. John Dewey in *How We Think* says that deliberation begins when there is a felt obstruction in the mind that causes us to interrupt our forward motion, stop and range around, searching for a solution; only once the solution is found are we released from the "painful" process of deliberation and can the mind resume its free and forward motion. Thomas Hobbes registers the same idea of material obstruction when he says in *Leviathan,* that's why it's called de-liberation; because it is a state in which one has ceased to be at liberty: "And it is called *Deliberation;* because it is a putting an end to the *Liberty* we had of doing, or omitting, according to our own Appetite, or Aversion."

Now it could be argued that while the Quintilian, Ciceronian, Augustinian, Boethian, Anselmian, Aquinian tradition of horizontal composition has clear associations with Heaney's vision, the account of the felt materiality of mental deliberation provided by Hobbes, Locke, and Dewey stands to the side of poetic practice. But Helen Vendler in *Poets Thinking* tells us that poetic composition is an act of thinking; and the "second thoughts" structure she identifies in Heaney's poetry is a structure of deliberation. Seamus Heaney in his small book on Gerard Manley Hopkins, *The Fire i' the Flint,* explicitly identifies in poetry "a conscious push of the deliberating intelligence." A passage Heaney quotes from T. S. Eliot's "The Three Voices of Poetry" almost exactly reproduces, in its account of poetic composition, Dewey's account of the act of deliberation: "[The poet] is going to all that trouble, not in order to communicate with anyone, but to gain relief from acute discomfort. And when the words are finally arranged in the right way . . . he may experience a moment of exhaustion, of appeasement, of absolution, and of something very near annihilation which is itself indescribable."

The connection of poetic composition to deliberation—even to the "pro" and "con" of debate—is present in the very first description we have of the Muses singing, the one Homer gives at the close of the first book of the *Iliad*. Here is how someone acutely interested in deliberation, Thomas Hobbes—in his 1676 translation of the *Iliad*—gives the lines, beginning with the feasting of the gods:

> And all the day from morning unto night
> Ambrosia they eat, and nectar drink.
> Apollo played, and alternately
> The Muses to him sung.

The alternating voices of the Muses are audible in Alexander Pope's later translation ("Apollo tun'd the Lyre; the Muses round / With Voice alternate aid the silver Sound"), as in John Ogilby's earlier one ("Apollo playd, the Muses heavenly Quire / Alternate parts sung to his Golden Lyre"). In the preface to his translation, Hobbes says that he will give no commentary because it would be impossible to improve on the extraordinary commentary of John Ogilby.[4] Ogilby's annotation to the lines just quoted states: "The Muses sung in course answering one the other [ἀμοιβαδόν] Anthemwise; [λόγος ἀμοιβαῖος] being such Orations as were made *pro* and *con* upon the same Argument"; and he then invokes Virgil's *Eclogue*, "The Muses always lov'd alternate Verse," and Hesiod's *Theogony*, "Muses begin, and Muses end the Song." Though later translators do not use the explicit phrase "alternate verse," the argumentative or "second thought" structure is almost always present, as in Samuel Butler's translation, "Apollo struck his lyre, and the Muses lifted up their sweet voices, calling and answering to one another," or Richmond Lattimore's "antiphonal sweet sound of the Muses singing," or Robert Fagles's "Muses singing / voice to voice in choirs."[5] Homer's conception of the deliberative "pro" and "con" structure of the Muses' song, echoed in Virgil and Hesiod, continues to ripple across the centuries, as in Eliot's "I have heard the mermaids singing, each to each."

A third source of persuasion about the relation between poetic creation and heading toward the ground comes from research in cognitive psychology on the "hypnagogic" state, the mental state between waking and sleeping that occurs as one begins to fall asleep or as one begins to wake. Only a small number of poems are self-announcing transcriptions of the hypnagogic state—Frost's "After Apple Picking," Coleridge's "Kubla Khan"—but the general connection between hypnagogia and creation is widely recognized. Though this mental state may sound remote from the deliberative act described a moment ago, some research has shown that the brain waves occurring during hypnagogia more closely resemble those that occur when solving a difficult math problem than those which occur when solving an easy math problem. (Thomas Hardy heard poetry in the procedure for finding cube roots.)

Directly relevant to Heaney's conception of the call to poetry are not the visual facets of hypnagogia, which, rather than narrative images, usually entail pyrotechnically colored geometries, swaying fractals, and skeins of pulsing threads. (These visual geometries, sometimes referred to by researchers as "hieroglyphs," are certainly not irrelevant to Heaney, who, in his small book on Hopkins, says the poem survives as "a hieroglyph of a numinous nativity.") Most immediately relevant to Heaney's conception of the call, and its anchoring in a downward motion, are instead the acoustical and kinesthetic facets of hypnagogia. The most often reported kinesthetic event—an event described not only by adults but by children as young as four—is the sensation while falling asleep of falling, or dropping beneath the floor.[6] The most common acoustical event is that of hearing one's own name called.

Three different veins of mental life, then, press us to see how *literally* the call to poetry pitches the poet back toward the ground: the reclining posture of composers from ancient Greece to Proust; the felt experience of material encumbrance required by the mental act of deliberation; and the simultaneous sensations of falling and of hearing one's name called as one enters the state of hypnagogia. Perhaps there is no need to insist on the literal. But for all the poet's commitment to metaphor and invention, the call to poetry does—it sometimes seems—originate in taking things more literally than they are ordinarily taken; and I have tried to suggest here how Hardy, Heaney, and Hennessy may have acquired their ardent obligation to poetry by carrying out with utmost and inexhaustible strictness the early instruction to make and protect new language—not metaphorically new, not locally new, not new-to-me, but literally new, new-to-the-world. Framed by this gravity toward the literal, their writings always have about them an aura of earliness. This is not to compromise their exalted adulthood, but only to say that when the fork in the language road came—the point where most people stop dedicating the whole day to trying out new words and sentences and move on to a new path of using the by-now-well-practiced ones—they instead continued to walk along the original path, the one everyone else had crossed away from.

Helen Vendler has remarked on the oddity of the fact that poets are often pictured on book jackets and formal portraits in exalted adulthood—what Heaney in "Lightenings vii" calls "renowned old age"—rather than in their turbulent youth when they first wrote poems (and certainly not in their childhood when they first heard their names called or received their language instructions). The snapshot mentioned above shows Hardy, Heaney, and Vendler in the period of renown rather than the period of early childhood. And yet, visible there as in their writings is the "Once as a child . . ." state of things, the belief in the not-yet-opened words still in their radiant envelope, traveling through but not yet in the stream of common language.

Earliness is not always credited, and is often scolded. When Wordsworth addresses the "six year's darling" as "O best philosopher!" Coleridge has a two-age-long scolding fit: "In what sense is a child of that age a philosopher? . . . Children at this age give us no such information of themselves. . . . In what sense can the magnificent attributes . . . be appropriated to a child, which would not make them equally suitable to a *bee,* or a *dog,* or *a field of corn;* . . . or to the wind . . . ?" And Shakespeare's beautiful line "This lapwing runs away with the shell on his head"—so perfectly suited to describe the ongoing "new to the world" prematurity of the poet—is instead thrown away on Horatio's reprimand to Osric as he leaps prematurely into a duel. Poets, some poets anyway, do seem to travel through the world with pieces of shell still on their heads, pieces of the encircling ring inside them. And if Shakespeare throws away his lapwing line, he picks it up again in the dazzling last second of his last play where Ariel—receiving Prospero's final instruction—is addressed as though he were, even at this late hour, a hatchling still: "My Ariel, chick, That is thy charge. Then to the elements be free, and fare thou well!"

NOTES

Excerpt from "The Ministry of Fear" from *Opened Ground: Selected Poems, 1966–1996* by Seamus Heaney. © 1998 by Seamus Heaney. "vi" and "vii" from "Lightenings" from *Seeing Things* by Seamus Heaney. © 1991 by Seamus Heaney. Reprinted by permission of Faber and Faber, Ltd., and Farrar, Straus and Giroux.

Poems seem to travel through the world, passing from one person to another, hand to hand. This is concretely the case in the poems at the center of this essay, "Lightenings vi and vii." The two poems were first placed in my hands by Helen Vendler. Later, Seamus Heaney handwrote them for me. I can, in each case, remember where I was standing when I looked down and found them in my hands.

During the months when I was writing this essay, Matthew Spellberg was my often surprising, always brilliant and kind, research assistant.

1. In his *Essay on the Origin of Language,* Johann Gottfried Herder three times pictures the birth of speech coming at the moment when a human being stands in the presence of bleating sheep. (My thanks to the linguist Paul Kiparsky for sending me back to Herder.)

2. "In those two Miles he broached a thousand things—let me see if I can give you a list—Nightingales, Poetry—on Poetical Sensation—Metaphysics—Different genera and species of Dreams—Nightmare—a dream accompanied by a sense of touch—single and double touch—A dream related—First and second consciousness—the difference explained between will and Volition—so m(an)y metaphysicians from a want of smoking the second consciousness—Monsters—the Kraken—Mermaids—Southey believes in them—Southey's belief too much diluted—A Ghost story—Good morning—I heard his voice as he came towards me—I heard it as he moved away—I had heard it all the interval—if it may be called so"

3. The 21 Mar. 1977 letter from Helen Hennessy Vendler to Elizabeth Bishop, and the 1 Mar. 1979 letter from Elizabeth Bishop to Ashley Brown were found in Houghton Library by my former student Jamie Jones during her 1999–2000 senior thesis research on Bishop and Heaney.

4. I am grateful not only to Hobbes but to Matthew Spellberg for bringing me into contact with the rich annotations of John Ogilby.

5. See also the translations of Robert Fitzgerald and A. T. Murray. In four hundred years of translations, only Chapman seems to omit the idea from his Homer.

6. The widely reported sensation of dropping to the ground while falling asleep is in some articles described in some detail, as in the following three passages.

A sensation of falling down the axis of the body interior from the head to the feet. When the movement hit the bottom I came to, with no obvious jerk. As if some undefined space within simply fell to the ground. (Nielsen)

As the eyes closed a sudden and dramatic falling sensation occurred. It was as if inside the body I dropped about 3 or 4 inches in space down and to the right and then stopped suddenly. The location started around the neck area and slightly to the right of midline. It had a smooth though rapid flowing sense to it. There was a sense of feeling very heavy during the drop as if the part falling weighed a lot. (Nielsen)

Mama, do you see pictures, when you shut your eyes when it's dark? . . .
Sometimes, when I shut my eyes, I seem to go right down through the floor.
(Chamberlain and Chamberlain)

BIBLIOGRAPHY

Barnhart, Robert K., ed. *The Barnhart Dictionary of Etymology.* New York: H. W.
Wilson, 1988. S.vv. "fleece," "hustle," "-le," "ripple," "rip," "stir."

Bishop, Elizabeth. Letter to Ashley Brown, 1 Mar. 1979. Bishop Papers. Houghton
Library, Harvard University, Cambridge, MA.

Carruthers, Mary. *The Craft of Thought: Meditation, Rhetoric, and the Making of
Images, 400–1200.* Cambridge: Cambridge UP, 1998. 173–78.

Chamberlain, Alexander F., and Isabel C. Chamberlain. "Hypnagogic Images
and Bi-Vision in Early Childhood: A Note." *American Journal of Psychology*
17.2 (Apr. 1906): 272–73.

Coleridge, S. T. "Kubla Khan," *Biographia Literaria* (1817), chap. 22, and *Table
Talk* (1835), 2:89–90 (14 Aug. 1832). *Coleridge's Poetry and Prose,* selected and
ed. Nicholas Halmi, Paul Magnusen, and Raimonda Modiano. New York:
W. W. Norton, 2004. 182–83, 534, 594.

Costello, Robert B., ed. *Webster's College Dictionary.* New York: Random House,
1991. S.vv. "pitch," "parenthesis," "stir."

Dewey, John. *How We Think and Selected Essays, 1910–1911.* Vol. 6 of *The Middle Works of John Dewey, 1899–1924.* Ed. Jo Ann Boydston, introduction
by H. S. Thayer and V. T. Thayer. Carbondale: Southern Illinois UP, 1985.
188–91.

Frost, Robert. "After Apple-Picking." *Selected Poems of Robert Frost.* Introduction by Robert Graves. New York: Holt, Rinehart and Winston, 1963. 52.

Freedman, Ralph. *Life of a Poet: Rainer Maria Rilke.* New York: Farrar, Straus and
Giroux, 1996. 10.

Gregory, E. R. *Milton and the Muses.* Tuscaloosa: U of Alabama P, 1989. 22.

Hardy, Florence Emily. *The Life of Thomas Hardy, 1840–1928: Compiled Largely
from Contemporary Notes, Letters, Diaries, and Biographical Memoranda, as
well as from Oral Information in Conversations Extending over Many Years.*
London: Macmillan, 1962. 17, 21, 24, 31, 131, 300, 425, 433, 442, 444.

Hardy, Thomas. *Tess of the D'Urbervilles.* 1891. London: Penguin, 1985. 51–52.

Heaney, Seamus. "Anything Can Happen." *Anything Can Happen: A Poem and
Essay by Seamus Heaney with Translations in Support of Art for Amnesty.*
Dublin: TownHouse, 2004. 11.

———. "The Birthplace" and "The King of the Ditchbacks." *Station Island.* New
York: Farrar, Straus and Giroux, 1985. 34, 56.

———. "Crediting Poetry: The Nobel Lecture." 1995. *Opened Ground: Selected Poems, 1966–1996.* New York: Farrar, Straus and Giroux, 1999. 415, 429.

———. *The Fire i' the Flint: Reflections on the Poetry of Gerard Manley Hopkins.* London: Oxford UP for the British Academy, 1975. 6, 9.

———. "Introduction," and "John Clare's Prog." *The Redress of Poetry.* New York: Farrar, Straus and Giroux, 1995. xvii–xviii; 73–77.

———. "Lightenings vi and vii." *Seeing Things.* New York: Farrar Straus and Giroux, 1991. 60, 61.

———. "The Ministry of Fear." *North.* London: Faber and Faber, 1975. 64.

———. "The Mud Vision." *The Haw Lantern.* New York: Farrar, Straus and Giroux, 1987. 48.

———. "Something to Write Home About," "Dante and the Modern Poet," "On W. B. Yeats and Thoor Ballylee," and "Burns's Art Speech." *Finders Keepers: Selected Prose, 1971–2001.* New York: Farrar, Straus and Giroux, 2002. 54–55, 191–94, 258, 379, 382.

Herder, Johann Gottfried. *Essay on the Origin of Language.* In *On the Origin of Language: Two Essays by Jean-Jacques Rousseau and Johann Gottfried Herder.* Trans. John H. Moran and Alexander Gode. New York: Frederick Ungar, 1966. 116–17, 129, 132.

Hobbes, Thomas. *Leviathan.* Ed. and with an introduction by C. B. MacPherson. New York: Penguin, 1985. Book 1, chap. 6, 127.

Homer. *Iliad.*

Translated, Adorn'd with Sculpture, and Illustrated with Annotations, by John Ogilby. London: Thomas Roycroft, 1660. Book 1, p. 30.

Trans. Thomas Hobbes of Malmsbury. London: William Crook, 1676. Book 1, lines 563–66.

Trans. Alexander Pope. Ed. and with an introduction by Reuben Brower and W. H. Bond. New York: Macmillan, 1965. Book 1, lines 774–75.

Trans. Samuel Butler. London: Jonathan Cape, 1925. Book 1, lines 601–4.

Trans. and with an introduction by Richmond Lattimore. Chicago: U of Chicago P, 1951. Book 1, line 604.

Trans. Robert Fagles. Introduction and notes by Bernard Knox. New York: Viking Penguin, 1990. Book 1, 726–27.

Keats, John. "Letter to Benjamin Robert Haydon," 8 Apr. 1818, and "Letter to George and Georgiana Keats," 14 Feb.–3 May 1819. *Letters of John Keats,* selected and introduced by Hugh L'Anson Fausset. Edinburgh: Thomas Nelson and Sons, n.d. 129, 277.

Klein, Ernest. *A Comprehensive Etymological Dictionary of the English Language.* Amsterdam: Elsevier, 1971. S.vv. "fleece" "plume," "ripple," "rip," "reap."

Locke, John. *Of the Conduct of the Understanding.* Ed. Francis W. Garforth. New York: Teachers' College P, Columbia U, 1966. 74, 75, 100, 104, 105, 123.

Marckwardt, Albert H. "The Verbal Suffix-ettan in Old English." *Language* 18.4 (Oct.–Dec. 1942): 275–81, esp. 275.

Nielsen, Tore A. "Describing and Modeling Hypnagogic Imagery Using a Systematic Self-Observation Procedure." *Dreaming* 5.2 (June 1995): 75–94, esp. 81.

Onions, C. T., ed. *The Oxford Dictionary of English Etymology.* Oxford: Clarendon, 1995. S.vv. "ripple," "rip."

Partridge, Eric. *Origins: A Short Etymological Dictionary of Modern English.* New York: Macmillan, 1966. S.vv. "fleece," "plume," "hustle," "riffle," "ripple," "rip," "stir," "storm."

Pinion, F. B. "Keats." *Oxford Reader's Companion to Hardy.* Ed. Norman Page. Oxford: Oxford UP, 2000. 224.

Preminger, Alex, ed. *Princeton Encyclopedia of Poetry and Poetics.* Princeton: Princeton UP, 1974. S.vv. "pitch" (by Paul Fussell), "pun" (by Stephen F. Fogle).

Schacter, Daniel L. "EEG Theta Waves and Psychological Phenomena: A Review and Analysis." *Biological Psychology* 5 (1977): 47–82, esp. 49, 55, 57, 61.

———. "The Hypnagogic State: A Critical Review of the Literature." *Psychological Bulletin* 83.3 (1976): 452–81, esp. 460, 461, 462.

Schacter, Daniel L., and Herbert F. Crovitz. "'Falling' While Falling Asleep: Sex Differences." *Perceptual and Motor Skills* 44 (1977): 656.

Shakespeare, William. *Riverside Shakespeare.* Ed. Blakemore Evans. 2nd ed. Boston: Houghton Mifflin, 1997. *Hamlet* 5.2.186; *The Tempest* 5.1.317–20.

Vendler, Helen. *Invisible Listeners: Lyric Intimacy in Herbert, Whitman, and Ashbery.* Princeton: Princeton UP, 2005. 31–56.

———. Letter to Elizabeth Bishop. 21 Mar. 1977. Bishop Papers. Houghton Library, Harvard University, Cambridge, MA.

———. *Poets Thinking: Pope, Whitman, Dickinson, Yeats.* Cambridge, MA: Harvard UP, 2004. Chap. 2, "Walt Whitman Thinking: Transcription, Reprise, and Temptations Resisted," 37–63.

———. *Seamus Heaney.* Cambridge, MA: Harvard UP, 1998.

Whitman, Walt. "Out of the Cradle Endlessly Rocking." 1859. *The Portable Walt Whitman.* Ed. Mark Van Doren. New York: Viking, 1945. 220–28.

Yatromanolakis, Dimitrios. *Sappho in the Making: The Early Reception.* Cambridge, MA: Harvard UP, 2008. Esp. chap. 2, "Ethnographic Archives of Vraisemblance in Attic Ceramics."

———. "Visualizing Poetry: An Early Representation of Sappho." *Classical Philology* 96 (2001): 159–68.

Contributors

JOHN ASHBERY has published more than twenty collections of poetry, including, most recently, *A Worldly Country: New Poems* and *Notes from the Air: Selected Later Poems*. His *Selected Prose* was published in 2004. Since 1990 he has been the Charles P. Stevenson Jr. Professor of Languages and Literature at Bard College in Annandale-on-Hudson, New York.

FRANK BIDART is the author of several works of poetry, including *In the Western Night: Collected Poems, 1965–90, Desire,* and *Music Like Dirt.* He coedited *The Collected Poems of Robert Lowell.* His latest book of poetry is *Star Dust.* He has won the Lila Acheson Wallace/Reader's Digest Fund Writer's Award; the Morton Dauwen Zabel Award, given by the American Academy of Arts and Letters; the Shelley Award, of the Poetry Society of America; and the Lannan Literary Award. In 2007 he won the Bollingen Prize in American Poetry. He teaches at Wellesley.

LUCIE BROCK-BROIDO is Director of Poetry in the Writing Division of the School of the Arts at Columbia University. She is the author of three collections of poetry, *A Hunger, The Master Letters,* and *Trouble in Mind.*

STEPHEN BURT's writings on poetry appear in the *Times Literary Supplement,* the *Believer,* the *London Review of Books,* the *Yale Review,* and elsewhere. His books include *The Forms of Youth: 20th-Century Poetry and Adolescence* and *Parallel Play,* a collection of poems, and a book of essays on contemporary poetry, *Close Calls with Nonsense.* He teaches at Harvard.

ELEANOR COOK is Professor Emerita of English, University of Toronto. Her books include studies of Robert Browning and Wallace Stevens, and, most recently, *Against Coercion: Games Poets Play, Enigmas and Riddles in Literature,* and *A Reader's Guide to Wallace Stevens.* She has served as president of the Association of Literary Scholars and Critics and is a Guggenheim Fellow, a Senior Killam Research Fellow, and a Fellow of the Royal Society of Canada.

BONNIE COSTELLO is Professor of English and American Literature at Boston University. She is the author of numerous articles and several books on modern poetry, including *Shifting Ground: Reinventing Landscape in Modern American Poetry*. Her latest book is *Planets on Tables: Poetry, Still Life and the Turning World*.

RITA DOVE is the author most recently of *American Smooth*. Earlier books of poetry include *Thomas and Beulah, Mother Love*, and *On the Bus with Rosa Parks*. She served as Poet Laureate of the United States and Consultant to the Library of Congress from 1993 to 1995. She has received the Pulitzer Prize, the Heinz Award in the Arts and Humanities, the National Humanities Medal, and the Common Wealth Award of Distinguished Service.

HEATHER DUBROW, Tighe-Evans Professor and John Bascom Professor at the University of Wisconsin–Madison, is the author of five single-authored books, most recently *The Challenges of Orpheus: Lyric Poetry and Early Modern England*. Her other publications include numerous articles on early modern literature and pedagogy and two chapbooks of poetry.

WILLIAM FLESCH is the author of *Generosity and the Limits of Authority: Shakespeare, Herbert, Milton* and *Comeuppance: Costly Signaling, Altruistic Punishment, and Other Biological Components of Fiction*. He teaches at Brandeis.

DEBORAH FORBES is the author of *Sincerity's Shadow: Self-Consciousness in British Romantic and Mid-Twentieth-Century American Poetry*. She lived in Lusaka, Zambia, from 2003 to 2006. She currently resides in Fairfax, Virginia, where she is working on a novel about expatriates in Africa.

MARK FORD has published two collections of poetry, *Landlocked* and *Soft Silt*. He is also the author of the critical biography *Raymond Roussel and the Republic of Dreams* and a collection of his reviews and essays, *A Driftwood Altar*. He is a professor in the English Department at University College London.

ROGER GILBERT is Professor of English at Cornell University. He is the author of *Walks in the World: Representation and Experience in Modern American Poetry*. He recently edited a special issue of *Epoch* devoted to the life and work of A. R. Ammons, and coedited *Considering the Radiance: Essays on the Poetry of A. R. Ammons*. He is currently working on a critical biography of Ammons, for which he was awarded fellowships from the Guggenheim Foundation and the National Humanities Center.

ALBERT GOLDBARTH has published more than twenty-five collections of poetry, including *The Kitchen Sink: New and Selected Poems, 1972–2007*, and *Saving Lives* and *Heaven and Earth: A Cosmology*, both of which won the National Book Critics Circle award for poetry. He has been a Guggenheim Fellow and won the National Book Critics Circle award in 1991 and 2001. He is Distinguished Professor of the Humanities in the Department of English at Wichita State University.

JORIE GRAHAM is the author of numerous collections of poetry, including *Overlord, Never, Swarm, The Errancy,* and *The Dream of the Unified Field: Selected Poems, 1974–1994,* which won the 1996 Pulitzer Prize for Poetry. She has edited two anthologies, *Earth Took of Earth: 100 Great Poems of the English Language* and *The Best American Poetry 1990.* Her honors include a John D. and Catherine T. MacArthur Fellowship and the Morton Dauwen Zabel Award from the American Academy and Institute of Arts and Letters. She is the Boylston Professor of Rhetoric and Oratory at Harvard University.

NICK HALPERN is an associate professor in the English Department at North Carolina State University. He is the author of *Everyday and Prophetic: The Poetry of Lowell, Ammons, Merrill, and Rich.* He is coeditor of *In the Frame: Ekphrastic Poetry from Marianne Moore to Susan Wheeler.* He is working on a book about the figure of the embarrassing father in early twentieth-century literature.

DESALES HARRISON is an assistant professor of English at Oberlin College. He is the author of *The End of the Mind: The Edge of the Unintelligible in Hardy, Stevens, Larkin, Plath, and Glück.* He was assistant editor for *The Collected Poems of Robert Lowell.* His next book concerns the figure of Eros in modernist and contemporary poetry.

SEAMUS HEANEY's latest book is *District and Circle.* His essays were collected in *Finders Keepers: Selected Prose, 1971–2001,* and he has published a verse translation of *Beowulf.* Earlier volumes of poetry include *Electric Light* and *The Spirit Level.* He was awarded the Nobel Prize in Literature in 1995.

AUGUST KLEINZAHLER's most recent collection of poetry is *Sleeping It Off in Rapid City: Poems, New and Selected.* His books include *The Strange Hours Travelers Keep, Green Sees Things in Waves, Red Sauce, Whiskey and Snow,* and the essay collection *Cutty, One Rock.* He has been awarded a Guggenheim Fellowship, an Academy Award in Literature from the American Academy of Arts and Letters, and the Griffin Poetry Prize.

GEORGE S. LENSING is Mann Family Distinguished Professor of English and Comparative Literature at the University of North Carolina at Chapel Hill. He is the author of *Wallace Stevens: A Poet's Growth* and *Wallace Stevens and the Seasons.*

CHRISTOPHER R. MILLER is associate professor of English at Yale University. He is author of *The Invention of Evening: Perception and Time in Romantic Poetry.* He has recently completed a new book project entitled "The Elements of Surprise: Fictions of the Unexpected in the Long Eighteenth Century."

CARL PHILLIPS is the author of nine books of poetry, most recently *Quiver of Arrows: Selected Poems, 1986–2006*. He teaches at Washington University in St. Louis.

D. A. POWELL teaches in the Department of English at the University of San Francisco. His books include *Tea, Lunch,* and *Cocktails.* The latter was a finalist for the PEN West, Lambda, and National Book Critics Circle awards. His fourth collection will be published in 2009.

LAURA QUINNEY has published reviews of contemporary poetry in the *London Review of Books.* An associate professor at Brandeis University, she is the author of *Literary Power: The Criteria of Truth* and *The Poetics of Disappointment: Wordsworth to Ashbery.* Her book *Blake on Self and Soul* is forthcoming.

JAHAN RAMAZANI is the Edgar F. Shannon Professor of English at the University of Virginia. He is the author of *Yeats and the Poetry of Death: Elegy, Self-Elegy, and the Sublime; Poetry of Mourning: The Modern Elegy from Hardy to Heaney,* a finalist for the National Book Critics Circle Award; and *The Hybrid Muse: Postcolonial Poetry in English.* He coedited the third edition of *The Norton Anthology of Modern and Contemporary Poetry* and the eighth edition of "The Twentieth Century and After" in *The Norton Anthology of English Literature.* He is a recipient of a Guggenheim Fellowship, an NEH Fellowship, a Rhodes Scholarship, and the MLA's William Riley Parker Prize.

ELAINE SCARRY is Walter M. Cabot Professor of Aesthetics at Harvard University. Her many writings include *The Body in Pain: The Making and Unmaking of the World, Resisting Representation, Dreaming by the Book,* and *On Beauty and Being Just.* She is currently completing a book about war and the social contract entitled "The Matter of Consent."

DAVE SMITH is the Elliot Coleman Professor of Poetry and Chairman of the Writing Seminars Department at Johns Hopkins University. His most recent book is *Hunting Men: Reflections on a Life in American Poetry.* Recent books of poetry include *Little Boats, Unsalvaged,* and *The Wick of Memory: New and Selected Poems, 1970–2006.*

WILLARD SPIEGELMAN is the Hughes Professor of English at Southern Methodist University, and the editor-in-chief of the *Southwest Review.* He is the author of four critical works, most recently *How Poets See the World: The Art of Description in Contemporary Poetry,* and also the editor of *Love, Amy: The Selected Letters of Amy Clampitt.* Forthcoming books include *Imaginative Transcripts: Selected Literary Essays* and *Seven Pleasures: Essays on Ordinary Happiness.*

M. WYNN THOMAS is Professor of English and Director of CREW (Center for Research into the English Literature and Language of Wales), University of Wales Swansea. The author or editor of more than twenty books on the literatures of Wales and the United States, including *The Lunar Light of Whitman's Poetry,* he most recently published *Transatlantic Connections: Whitman US–Whitman UK.* Awarded an OBE for services to the literature of Wales in 2007, he is a fellow of the British Academy and of the English Association.

CHARLES WRIGHT is Souder Family Professor of English at the University of Virginia in Charlottesville. His most recent collection, *Scar Tissue,* was the international winner for the Griffin Poetry Prize. Recent books include *Buffalo Yoga; Negative Blue; Appalachia; Black Zodiac,* which won the Pulitzer Prize and the *Los Angeles Times* Book Prize; and *Chickamauga,* which won the 1996 Lenore Marshall Poetry Prize. He has won the American Academy of Arts and Letters Award of Merit Medal and the Ruth Lilly Poetry Prize.

Index

Abel, Lionel, 231
Abrams, M. H., 152, 266
abstraction, in poetry, 6, 7, 197, 204
Addison, Joseph, "The Pleasures of the Imagination," 126, 144n10
"aesthetic criticism," 2, 6
Africa, 13, 105–22
Agee, James, 151
AIDS. *See* HIV/AIDS
Alexander, Elizabeth, 151
Altieri, Charles, "Ashbery as Love Poet," 291, 300n1
Ammons, A. R., 1, 7, 14, 265–90. Works: *Bosh and Flapdoodle,* 285; "Breaking Out," 269–70; *Brink Road,* 284, 288n13; "The City Limits," 267, 281; *A Coast of Trees,* 269, 278–80, 283, 288n13; *Collected Poems, 1951–71,* 268, 270–71, 276, 282; "Corsons Inlet," 272, 284; *Diversifications,* 269, 272, 284; "Easter Morning," 14, 278–81, 284–85, 288n14; "Everything," 286–87; "Four Motions for the Pea Vines," 282; *Garbage,* 268, 276, 284, 288n9; *Glare,* 268, 284, 288nn8–9; "Hardweed Path Going," 281; "An Improvisation for Angular Momentum," 288n13; "Improvisations," 280; "In View of the Fact," 285; "Nelly Myers," 281; *Ommateum,* 267, 269, 282, 284; "One Must Remember . . . ," 280; "Pray without Ceasing," 272; *The Snow Poems,* 14, 268–78, 284, 288nn10–11; *Sphere,* 14, 267–69, 271–75, 281, 282–83; *Sumerian Vistas,* 283, 284; "A Summer

Place," 274; *Tape for the Turn of the Year,* 267, 268, 272, 275; "That Day," 288n15; *Worldly Hopes,* 283, 284
aphorism, 4, 52
Aristotle, 222, 233
Arnold, Matthew, "Dover Beach," 55, 215, 225n15
ars poetica, 49
Ashbery, John, 19, 101, 291–301; and A. R. Ammons, 277; on Elizabeth Bishop, 218–19, 224n9; Helen Vendler on, 1, 5, 7, 14, 89, 266, 291. Works: "At North Farm," 296; "Frogs and Gospels," 295; "Honored Guests," 296, 298; "Life Is a Dream," 295; "Litany," 277; "Lost Profile," 296; "Merrily We Live," 294; "Nobody Is Going Anywhere," 298; "Not You Again," 293–94; "Pale Sibling," 298–99; "Paperwork," 294; "Paradoxes and Oxymorons," 193; "Pot Luck," 296–97; *Shadow Train,* 151; "A Suit," 297–98; "Terminal," 294; "They Don't Just Go . . . ," 299; "These Lacustrine Cities," 151; "This Room," 292–93; "Vintage Masquerade," 300; "Weekend," 292; "Wet Casements," 295; "Your Name Here," 294, 300; *Your Name Here,* 291–301
Attridge, Derek, 149
Auden, W. H., 150. Works of poetry: "In Memory of W. B. Yeats," 183; "Musée de Beaux Arts," 151; "September 1, 1939," 195; "Victor," 156. Works of prose: "The Poet and the City," 195–96

Augustine, St., 313–14
Austen, Jane, 89
Austin, J. L., *How to Do Things with Words*, 196, 204

Bailey, Benjamin, 120n4, 126–27, 130, 137, 139
ballad, 8, 153–55, 158. *See also* quatrain
Barbauld, Anna Letitia, "A Thought on Death," 157–58
Barnhart, Robert, 309
Bataille, Georges, 247–52, 258
Bate, Walter Jackson, 120n6, 145n19
Batty, William, 134, 146n22
beauty, 106–9, 115–20, 142. *See also* Keats, John, "Ode on a Grecian Urn"
Beckett, Samuel, 99
Belgion, Montgomery, 231
Belitt, Ben, 151
Bentham, Jeremy, 148
Berryman, John, 9, 190–91, 270
Bidart, Frank, 11, 20
Bishop, Elizabeth, 197–226, 266, 282, 312, 317n3; Helen Vendler on, 5, 13–14. Works of poetry: "Arrival at Santos," 201–2; "At the Fishhouses," 198; *A Cold Spring*, 198, 203; *Complete Poems* (1969), 207, 208; "Crusoe in England," 202; "The End of March," 186, 202; *Geography III*, 197–98, 202–4; "The Imaginary Iceberg," 198, 222; "In the Waiting Room," 197–98, 202; "The Map," 13–14, 199–200, 207–25; "A Miracle for Breakfast," 199; "The Monument," 221–22; "The Moose," 13, 202–4; "A Mother Made of Dress-Goods," 220; *North & South*, 198, 207, 222–23; "North Haven," 222; "Over 2,000 Illustrations . . . ," 200–201, 203; "Poem," 202, 222; *Questions of Travel*, 201–2; "Roosters," 200; "Sonnet," 218; "Swan-Boat Ride," 220; "12 O'Clock News," 202; "Varick Street," 198–99. Works of prose: "In the Village," 219
Blackmur, R. P., 188
Blake, William, 57, 152–54, 159, 189, 266, 267, 287n1. Works: "The Lamb," 124;

Songs of Experience, 153–54; *Songs of Innocence*, 152–53; "The Tyger," 147
Blau duPlessis, Rachel, 74–75
Bloom, Harold, 1, 14; and A. R. Ammons, 265–69, 271–72, 274, 282, 286, 287n1, 287nn3–5, 288n8, 288n10; "A. R. Ammons: The Breaking of the Vessels," 282–83; *Poetry and Repression*, 287n1
Boethius, 309
Bonaventure, St., 89
Boston, Mass., 202
Boston University, 8
Bowers, Grace, 208
Brawne, Fanny, 64
Brock-Broido, Lucie, 1, 11, 22–23
Bromwich, David, 146n24
Brooks, Gwendolyn, 51
Brown, Ashley, 312, 317n3
Bruccoli, Matthew, 90
Bucke, R. M., 168, 181n22
Buell, Laurence, 181n10
Bullis, Jerald, 280
Burns, Robert, 310
Butler, Samuel, 314
Byron, George Gordon, Lord, 152

California, 12
"calling" to poetry, 14, 302–16
Cambridge, Mass., 110. *See also* Harvard University
Campbell, Thomas, "Hohenlinden," 156–57
Campion, Thomas, "Lord Hay's Masque," 68
Canada, 14. *See also* Newfoundland and Labrador; Nova Scotia
Carey, John, 62
Carlyle, Thomas, 167, 169, 172, 181n23
Carruth, Hayden, 274
Carruthers, Mary, 313–14
Catholic Church, 8, 70
Catullus, Gaius Valerius, 2
Cavell, Stanley, 86
Celan, Paul, 60, 63, 79, 193
Chaucer, Geoffrey, 309
Christianity, 113–14, 121n8, 200–201. *See also* religion

Cicero, 312
Clampitt, Amy, 149
Clarke, Charles Cowden, 133
Coleridge, Samuel Taylor, 154, 158, 309, 311–12, 316; "Frost at Midnight," 152; "Kubla Khan," 315; "Rime of the Ancient Mariner," 309
Collins, Williams, "Ode on the Poetical Character," 136
Columbus, Christopher, 178–79, 212
compass, 207, 217–18
Cook, Eleanor, 13–14
Cornell University, 267–68, 285. See also Ithaca, N.Y.
Costello, Bonnie, 13, 293
couplet, 8
Crane, Hart, 151
Creeley, Robert, 151
Croft, Barbara, 185–86
Culler, Jonathan, 65
Cummings, E. E., 270
Cuttyhunk Island, 220

Dante Alighieri, 90–92, 189, 310; *Paradiso*, 90–91; *Vita nuova*, 69
Davenant, William, 150
Davie, Donald, 1, 8, 234
debate, in teaching poetry, 48–58
deconstruction, 72. See also poststructuralism
de Grazia, Margreta, 86, 101–2
deictics, 62, 63
de Man, Paul, 65, 66
Derrida, Jacques, 255
Dewey, John, 313
diagrams, in literary criticism, 4, 277
Dickinson, Emily, 9, 150, 266
disability studies, 14
distance. See immediacy
Donne, John, 60, 62, 148, 221; "The Canonization," 149; "The Indifferent," 60–62, 64, 78
Dove, Rita, 11, 24–25
Dryden, John, 150
Dubrow, Heather, 12
Dublin, Ireland, 194

Elgin Marbles. *See* Keats, John, "On Seeing the Elgin Marbles"
Eliot, T. S., 9, 10, 12, 107, 158, 224n13, 230, 236, 260, 280, 287n1, 314. Works of poetry: "The Dry Salvages," 225n16; *The Waste Land*, 52, 57. Works of prose: "Hamlet and His Problems," 213–14, 219, 224n13; *The Sacred Wood*, 224n13, 231; "The Three Voices of Poetry," 313; "Tradition and the Individual Talent," 198, 224n13
Ellis, Jonathan, 225n20
Emerson, Ralph Waldo, 167, 265, 267, 268, 288n10
Empson, William, 158
Englands Helicon, 69
ethics, 6–7, 13
eucharist, 70, 74

Fagles, Robert, 313
feet, 239–63. *See also* meter
Fernandez, Ramon, 195, 227–38. Works: *Messages*, 231–33; *MoliÈre*, 234; "A Note on Intelligence and Intuition," 237–38; "Of Philosophic Criticism," 231–32, 237; "Open Letter to Andre Gide," 230
Ferry, Anne, 74
FitzGerald, Edward, 173
Fitzgerald, Robert, 224n2, 314, 317n5
Flaubert, Gustave, 187
Flesch, William, 12
Forbes, Deborah, 13
Ford, Mark, 11, 26, 225n20
Forster, E. M., *A Passage to India*, 106
Foster, Roy, 189
France, 9
Freud, Sigmund, 90, 258, 261n10
Friedman, Albert, 150
Frost, Robert, 149, 288n10, 315; "After Apple-Picking," 315; "Mending Wall," 52; "The Road Not Taken," 48, 57
Fussell, Paul, 149, 150, 159

Gilbert, Roger, 14
Ginsberg, Allen, 9
Glück, Louise, 1, 2

Goldbarth, Albert, 8, 11, 27–28
Goldberg, Jonathan, 86, 101–2
Gonne, Maud, 189
Graff, Gerald, 54–55
Graham, Jorie, 1, 6, 11–12, 29–30, 270
Graves, Robert, 311
Gray, Thomas, "Elegy Written in a Country Churchyard," 150, 158
Greger, Deborah, 151
Gregory, Lady Augusta, 189, 190
grief, 5, 52, 116–18, 292–300
Grossman, Allen, 185

Haft, Adele, 213, 217, 224n5
Halpern, Nick, 13, 266
Hardy, Florence Emily, 302, 307, 311
Hardy, Thomas, 83–84, 302–3, 307, 310, 311, 315; Tess of the D'Urbervilles, 310
Harmon, William, 275
Harrison, DeSales, 14
Hartford, Conn., 227
Hartman, Geoffrey, 1
Harvard University, 7, 8, 12, 202, 268, 281, 312
Hayden, Robert, 151
Haydon, Benjamin, 126, 133, 134
Hazlitt, William, 142
headnotes, 64, 68–69, 78
Heaney, Marie, 311
Heaney, Seamus, 31–37, 270, 302–11, 313, 315, 316, 317n4; and Thomas Hardy, 302–16; Helen Vendler on, 1, 2, 5, 6, 12. Works of poetry: "Anything Can Happen," 305, 312; "The Birthplace," 311; Field Work, 308; "Lightenings," 303–10, 312, 314; "Midnight Anvil," 312; "Ministry of Fear," 305; "The Mud Vision," 312; North, 312; "Post-script," 312; "Punishment," 55, 57; "The Rain Stick," 312; Seeing Things, 308. Works of prose: The Fire i' the Flint, 313; Nobel Prize acceptance speech, 307, 312; "On W. B. Yeats and Thoor Ballylee," 310; The Redress of Poetry, 310; "Something to Write Home About," 312
Heidegger, Martin, 235, 246–52, 255, 258, 261n6; "The Origin of the Work of Art," 246–50
Hemans, Felicia, 151; "Casabianca," 151; "The Image in Lava," 155
Hennessy, Helen. See Vendler, Helen
Heraclitus, 284
Herbert, George, 1, 3, 4, 6, 9, 10, 165; "Antiphon," 4; "The Collar," 3; "Prayer," 1, 6
Herder, Johann Gottfried, 317n1
Hesiod, 314
HIV/AIDS, 106, 110, 111, 114
Hobbes, Thomas, 313, 314
Hollander, John, 147–48, 149–50
Homer, 132, 133, 136, 296, 315, 317n5
Hopkins, Gerard Manley, 13, 270, 313, 315
Horace, 72
horizontal composition, 314
Housman, A. E., 150
Hudson, Joanna, "Easter Morning: A. R. Ammons and His Poem," 288n14
Hughes, Langston, "The Weary Blues," 52, 57
Hughes, Ted, 151
Hunt, Leigh, 133, 134–38, 145n19, 146n20, 146n22
Hutchinson, Robert, 207, 223n1

immediacy, 59–79
Ireland, 194
Ithaca, N.Y., 268, 286. See also Cornell University

Jacobsen, Josephine, 151
James, Henry, 101, 179, 294
James, William, 99
Jarrell, Randall, 1, 10, 150, 179; "A Girl in a Library," 186
Jews and Judaism, 8, 28
Johnson, Barbara, 121n10
Johnson, Samuel, 1, 85–86, 134, 154; preface to Dictionary, 86; "Preface to Shakespeare," 85
Johnson, W. R. (Ralph), 194, 196
Jones, Isabella, 127–28
Jonson, Ben, 84; "An Elegie," 150; "My Picture Left in Scotland," 163–64

Joseph, Gerhard, 182n25
Joyce, James, 92–93, 99, 310; *Ulysses,*
    92–93
Justice, Donald, 151

Kabitlogou, E. Douka, 121n6, 121n11
Kalstone, David, 219
Keats, John, 105–22, 123–46, 165, 308,
    311–12; and Milton, 136–38, 140–41;
    Helen Vendler on, 1, 2, 5, 7, 10, 13,
    123–24, 133, 287n1; and Wordsworth,
    138–40. Works: "La Belle Dame Sans
    Merci," 152; *Endymion,* 125, 131–32,
    134; "Isabella," 145n14; "I Stood Tip-
    toe," 128–29, 131; "Lamia," 125; "Lines
    on Seeing a Lock of Milton's Hair,"
    133, 134, 136–38, 145n19; "Meg Meril-
    lies," 152; "Ode on a Grecian Urn,"
    105–122, 130, 136, 137, 138, 145n16; "Ode
    on Indolence," 124; "Ode on Mel-
    ancholy," 123, 138, 140–42; "Ode to
    Apollo," 132; "Ode to a Nightingale,"
    122n12, 123, 138, 193; "Ode to Psyche,"
    124, 125, 128–31, 138; "On First Look-
    ing into Chapman's Homer," 132, 133,
    145n16; "On the Sea," 124–25; "On
    Seeing the Elgin Marbles," 105, 120n1,
    133, 145n16; "On Sitting Down to Read
    King Lear . . . ," 138, 145n16, 146n23;
    "On Visiting the Tomb of Burns,"
    145n15; "There was a naughty boy,"
    145n15; "This living hand," 63–64, 72;
    "To Autumn," 130, 278; "To Haydon
    with a Sonnet . . . ," 134; "Why Did I
    Laugh Tonight?" 138–40
Kendall, Tim, 261n5
Kennedy, William Sloane, 168
Key West, Fla., 227, 236–37. *See also*
    Stevens, Wallace, "The Idea of Order
    at Key West"
Khayyam, Omar. *See* FitzGerald,
    Edward
Kinzie, Mary, 150
Kleinzahler, August, 1, 12, 38
Koethe, John, 300n3
Kristeva, Julia, 261n5
Kuhn, Thomas, 9

Labrador. *See* Newfoundland and
    Labrador
Lao Tzu, 26
Larkin, Philip, "Church Going," 52–
    53, 57
Le Guin, Ursula K., 21
Lensing, George, 1
Lewalski, Barbara, 7
light verse, 83
Lipking, Lawrence, 64
Litz, A. Walton, 231
Locke, John, 313
Logan, John, 282
London, 127
Lowell, Robert, 10, 12, 270, 280; "For the
    Union Dead," 151; Helen Vendler on,
    10, 12, 266
Loy, Mina, "Anglo-Mongrels and the
    Rose," 51, 57
Lusaka. *See* Zambia
lyric (poetry), 2–3, 6, 7, 10, 11, 12, 50,
    60–79, 193–206, 234, 240, 260, 291

Mallarmé, Stephane, 187
Mandelstam, Nadezhda, 310
Mannin, Ethel, 185, 188
Marciano, Francesca, 10
Maritain, Jacques, 235
Marks, Herbert, 223
Marlowe, Christopher, *Dido, Queen
    of Carthage,* 100
marriage, 221
Martory, Pierre, 291–92
Marvell, Andrew, "Damon the
    Mower," 69
Masten, Jeffrey, 72
McFee, Michael, 272
Melville, Herman, 225n15
memorization, 48
Meredith, George, 23
Merrill, James, 1, 7, 10, 266. Works:
    Braving the Elements, 288n12; *The
    Changing Light at Sandover,* 185, 186;
    "The Thousand and Second Night,"
    148; "The Victor Dog," 261n6
meter, 14, 52, 148, 240, 252, 260
Miller, Christopher, 13

Miller, Margaret, 220–21
Milosz, Czeslaw, 9
Milton, John, 84, 124, 133, 135, 136, 146n22, 225n15, 287n1, 303, 304; "L'Allegro," 140–41; "Lycidas," 69; *Paradise Lost*, 84, 126, 135
Mitchell, W. J. T., 145n17
modernism, 2, 191, 197
Moore, Marianne, 151, 199, 224n3
Motion, Andrew, 145n19
mourning. *See* grief

New Criticism, 4, 49, 51
New England, 12, 14
Newfoundland and Labrador, 210–13, 216–18, 220, 221, 222, 224nn6–7, 224n10
New York City, 282–83
Nietzsche, Friedrich, 242
North Carolina, 278, 281
Norway, 211–12, 216, 218, 224n8
Nova Scotia, 202, 203, 210, 220

O'Donnell, Brendan, 154
Ogilby, John, 314, 317n4
O'Hara, Frank, 151
old age, 161–82
Oliver, Mary, 151
Onions, C. T., 309
Owen, Sue, 151

Parmigianino, "Self-Portrait in a Convex Mirror," 291
Pater, Walter, 2, 187, 233
pedagogy, 12, 47–58
Pelham, Lady Elizabeth, 190
Percy, Thomas, *Reliques of Ancient Poetry*, 15
Perelman, S. J., 250–52, 258
Perloff, Marjorie, 274
Petrarch, 69, 140, 149
Phillips, Carl, 12, 40
photography, 75–77
Pindar, 136
pitch, 306
Plath, Otto, 256
Plath, Sylvia, 239–63; Helen Vendler

on, 4–5, 14, 260n1. Works: "Ariel," 255; "The Colossus," 241–42, 243, 257, 260n4; "Daddy," 48, 51–52, 57, 242–45, 246, 254, 255, 257; "The Disquieting Muses," 256; "Edge," 240–41, 242; "Electra on Azalea Path," 256–57, 260, 260n1; "Morning Song," 253–54; "Mushrooms," 244–45, 259; "Poem for a Birthday," 245; "Thalidomide," 258–60; "Words," 252–55, 259, 260n1; "Years," 254
Plato, 14, 66, 83, 105, 296, 299–300; *Symposium*, 296–98
Plotinus, 300n2
Pope, Alexander, 7, 8, 9, 314
postcolonial writing, 48, 55–57
poststructuralism, 49, 64, 254–55
Pound, Ezra, 51, 158, 191
Powell, D. A., 12, 41
Price, Kenneth, 169
pronouns, 2, 13, 193–206, 293–94
prosopopoeia, 65
Protestants, 69
Prothero, G. W., 169
Proust, Marcel, 90, 91, 127, 232, 237, 313, 315
puns, 305
Puttenham, George, *Art of English Poesie*, 67

quatrain, 8, 13, 147–60
Quine, Willard van Orman, 85, 99, 101–2, 102n7
Quinney, Laura, 14
Quintilian, 67, 312–13
quotation, 84–85, 87–93. *See also* self-quotation

Rabelais, François, 248
Ramazani, Jahan, 12
"recipes" in literary criticism, 4
refrains, 69
religion, 8, 52–54, 68, 124, 295. *See also* Catholic Church; Christianity; Jews and Judaism; Protestants
repetition, 127–28, 143. *See also* self-quotation

Reynolds, John Hamilton, 126, 139, 143

Rich, Adrienne, 1, 6–7; "Diving into the Wreck," 196; *Diving into the Wreck*, 288n12

Richards, I. A., 4, 158

Ricks, Christopher, 134, 144n13, 145n18, 167, 181n11

Ricoeur, Paul, 49

Rilke, Rainer Maria, 72, 301, 310

Robson, Catherine, 150

Roethke, Theodore, 24

Rose, Jacqueline, 243, 260n3, 261n5

Ryan, Michael, 151

Saintsbury, George, 153

Sassoon, Siegfried, 311

Scarry, Elaine, 14

Scott, Grant, 145n17

Scott, Walter, 152, 155

Seaver, Robert, 225n21

second thoughts, 6, 307

self-quotation, 12–13, 93–102

Shakespeare, William, 21, 26, 85–87, 91, 93–102, 143, 214, 316; Helen Vendler on, 1, 2, 12, 316. Works: *Hamlet*, 96, 99, 104n15, 135, 213–14, 219, 315; *Henry IV*, 97, 100; *King Lear*, 86–87, 120n6; *Macbeth*, 98–99, 135; *The Merchant of Venice*, 95–96, 103n14; *The Rape of Lucrece*, 101; *Richard II*, 96–98; *Romeo and Juliet*, 93–95; sonnets, 1, 4, 5, 8–9, 10, 12, 65, 72, 84, 123, 144n5, 253; *The Tempest*, 315; *Twelfth Night*, 95

Sharp, Ronald, 120n3

Shelley, Mary, 310

Shelley, Percy Bysshe, 66, 152, 266, 287n1, 299; *Prometheus Unbound*, 297

shoes, 246–52, 255. *See also* feet

Sider, Michael, 122n13

Sidney, Sir Philip, 2, 66, 68; *Astrophel and Stella*, 68; "Defense of Poesy," 66

Sidney, Robert, 73

Simic, Charles, 151

sleep, 313–14

Smith, Dave, 12, 42

Snyder, Gary, 9

solipsism, 233

song, 11, 62, 112, 233–34

sonnets, 4, 11, 68–69, 135, 148–49, 211. *See also* Herbert, George; Keats, John; Shakespeare, William

Southwell, Robert, "The Burning Babe," 68

Sparrow, John, 89

Spender, Stephen, 5, 187

Spenser, Edmund, 68–69, 127, 287n1; *Amoretti*, 68–69; "Epithalamion," 68; "Prothalamion," 69

Spiegelman, Willard, 13

Stallybrass, Peter, 101–2

Steele, Timothy, 149

Stevens, Wallace, 13, 21, 151, 184, 186, 189, 227–38, 271, 281, 287n1, 288n8, 300; Helen Vendler on, 1, 5, 6, 7, 10, 11, 12, 88, 228, 233, 265. Works: "The Emperor of Ice-Cream," 55, 57, 241; "Farewell without a Guitar," 253; "The Idea of Order at Key West," 13, 195, 204, 225n15, 227–38; "Like Decorations in a Nigger Cemetery," 237; "Notes Toward a Supreme Fiction," 233; "The Pediment of Appearance," 233; "The Pure Good of Theory," 188; "The Snow Man," 265; "Tea at the Palaz of Hoon," 233

Stewart, Susan, 65

Stitt, Peter, 274

surprise, 124–43, 204

Swift, Jonathan, 134

Swinburne, Algernon Charles, 83–84

syllabus, construction of, 50–51

Taylor, Gary, 86–87, 101

Taylor, Jane, "Twinkle, twinkle, little star," 147

Taylor, John, 125

Tennyson, Alfred, Lord, 13, 91, 167–82; Helen Vendler on, 287n1. Works: "The Ancient Sage," 182n25; "Crossing the Bar," 155; "The Dead Prophet," 181n23; "Despair," 174; "Early Spring," 182n27; *In Memoriam A.H.H.*, 103n11, 150; "Locksley Hall," 170–71; "Locksley Hall Sixty Years After," 171–72; "Tire-

Tennyson, Alfred, Lord (*continued*)
sias," 172, 173, 181n22; "Ulysses," 169,
178, 182n25; "The Wreck," 172–73
Tennyson, Hallam, 168
Thackeray, William Makepeace, 89
Thomas, M. Wynn, 13
Thoreau, Henry David, 267
titles, 68–69, 74–75, 77
Traubel, Horace, 166–68, 169, 176, 177,
178, 180
Travisano, Thomas, 199
Trollope, Anthony, 89

Van Gogh, Vincent, 246, 255
Vassar College, 220, 224n4
Vendler, David, 8, 9
Vendler, Helen (Hennessy), 1–14, 63, 65,
70, 147–48, 193, 197, 204, 304, 308–313,
315, 316, 317n3; on Ammons, 266–88;
on Ashbery, 291; on Bishop, 5, 213,
223, 224n12; critical practice of, 1–11;
life of, 8–9; on Heaney, 5, 304, 306–13;
on Keats, 13, 123–24, 140, 144n3; and
pedagogy, 47, 50, 54, 55, 57–58; on
Plath, 4–5, 260n1, 260n2; on Stevens,
5, 7, 10–11, 83, 84, 88, 228, 233; on
Whitman, 6; on Yeats, 1, 4, 183, 184.
Works: "A. R. Ammons: Dwelling
in the Flow of Shapes," 279, 281–82;
The Art of Shakespeare's Sonnets,
84, 144n5; *The Breaking of Style*, 2;
Coming of Age as a Poet, 13, 260n1;
The Music of What Happens, 143n2,
287nn1–2; *The Odes of John Keats*, 13;
Our Secret Discipline, 4; *Poems, Poets,
Poetry*, 12, 47, 148, 266; *The Poetry of
George Herbert*, 4; *Poets Thinking*, 12,
261n7, 307; *Seamus Heaney*, 307; "The
Titles: A. R. Ammons, 1926–2001,"
280, 283–85; *Yeats's Vision and the
Later Plays*, 183, 184
Vendler, Zeno, 8
Virgil, 314

Wake Forest University, 268, 281, 282
Walcott, Derek, "A Far Cry from Africa," 48, 55–57

Walser, Robert, 294
Warren, Robert Penn, 151
Washington, D.C., 174
Waters, William, 60, 72
Weimann, Robert, 9
Wellfleet, Mass., 207
Whitman, Walt, 12, 13, 161–82, 303, 304,
308; and Ammons, 265, 266, 267, 268,
281, 282; and first-person pronouns,
194, 196, 205; and Tennyson, 161–82;
Helen Vendler on, 6, 304, 308. Works
of poetry: "After the Supper and
Talk," 161–62; "The Bravest Soldiers,"
174; *Calamus*, 178; "The Dismantled
Ship," 164; "Fancies at Navesink,"
164, 174; *Good-Bye My Fancy*, 172,
176, 177; "L. of G.'s Purport," 161; "A
Noiseless Patient Spider," 308; "Of
That Blithe Throat of Thine," 166;
"Old Age's Ship . . . ," 176; "Out of
the Cradle Endlessly Rocking," 304;
"Out of May's Shows Selected," 175;
"Prayer of Columbus," 169; "Sail
Out for Good . . . ," 176; *Sands at
Seventy*, 161, 170, 180; "Song of the
Exposition," 177; "Soon Shall the
Winter's Foil Be Here," 176; "Sounds
of Winter," 165; "Sparkles from the
Wheel," 308; "A Thought of Colum-
bus," 177–78; "To Get the Final Lilt
of Songs," 177; "To Those Who've
Failed," 174; "You Lingering Sparse
Leaves of Me," 164–65. Works of
prose: *A Backward Glance O'er Trav-
eled Roads*, 179; "A Death-Bouquet,"
176; *Specimen Days*, 175; "A Word
about Tennyson," 170–71
Whittier, John Greenleaf, 167
Williams, C. K., "Last Things," 75–78
Williams, William Carlos, 74–75, 151,
175, 271; "This Is Just to Say," 197; "To
a Young Housewife," 74–75
Winston-Salem, N.C., 284. *See also*
Wake Forest University
Winters, Yvor, 151
Wittgenstein, Ludwig, 86, 96, 99, 104n17,
183

Wodehouse, P. G., 189
Wolosky, Shira, 149
Woodhouse, Richard, 125
Woolf, Virginia, 310
Wordsworth, William, 66, 120n4, 121n8, 279, 287n1, 295, 298–99, 302, 316; and Keats, 138–40; and quatrains, 147, 150, 154, 158. Works: "The Force of Prayer," 154; "Lines Composed a Few Miles above Tintern Abbey," 152; *Lyrical Ballads,* 154; "Ode: Intimations of Immortality," 152, 298; "The Old Cumberland Beggar," 175; "Resolution and Independence," 298; "Surprised by Joy," 139–40; *The White Doe of Rylstone,* 154; "Yarrow Unvisited," 154–55; "Yarrow Visited," 154–55; "Yarrow Revisited," 154–55
Wright, Charles, 12, 43, 52
Wroth, Lady Mary, *Pamphilia to Amphilanthus,* 70–72, 73, 74

Yale University, 268
Yeats, John Butler, 190
Yeats, William Butler, 47, 164, 183–92, 194, 243, 260n4, 287n1; Seamus Heaney on, 310; Helen Vendler on, 1, 2, 3, 4, 6, 8, 10. Works of poetry: "All Souls Night," 187–88; "The Double Vision of Michael Robartes," 3; "Easter 1916," 48, 55, 57, 194; "Leda and the Swan," 260n4; "Meditations in Time of Civil War," 186; "Nineteen Hundred and Nineteen," 4; "A Prayer for My Daughter," 244; "Sailing to Byzantium," 3, 261n6; "The Second Coming," 188–89; "To a Friend Whose Work Has Come to Nothing," 4. Works of prose: "Per Amica Silentia Lunae," 187; "Reveries over Childhood and Youth," 191; *A Vision,* 13, 183–92

Zambia, 105–22